Birds in Watercolour

A BEGINNER'S GUIDE TO
DRAWING AND PAINTING BIRDS

SOFIA GAZARIAN

Quadrille

Contents

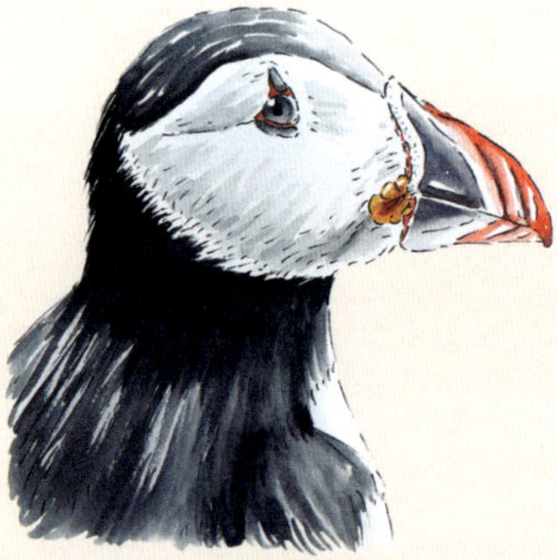

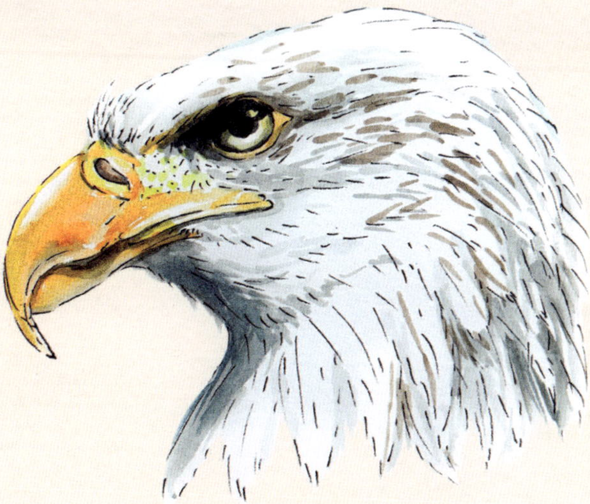

Introduction

Have you ever caught yourself feeling completely lost in chores and the mundane? As if the world has lost its colours and beauty and you're looking for something to grasp onto to bring you back to life. For me, birdwatching became a rescue – I started noticing magic around me again. It turned out there are so many amazing things to discover with all these wonderful wild creatures surrounding us, even in bustling cities. This connection to nature filled my days with joy and passion.

Art also helped me to escape routine. Whatever I was sketching, it immediately became more meaningful and interesting. I found that processing the world around me through art was muffling the noise in my head and filling my heart with happiness.

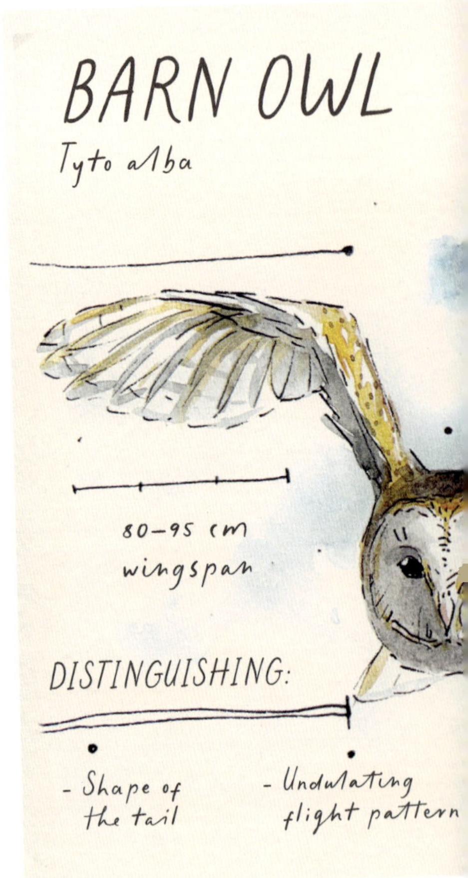

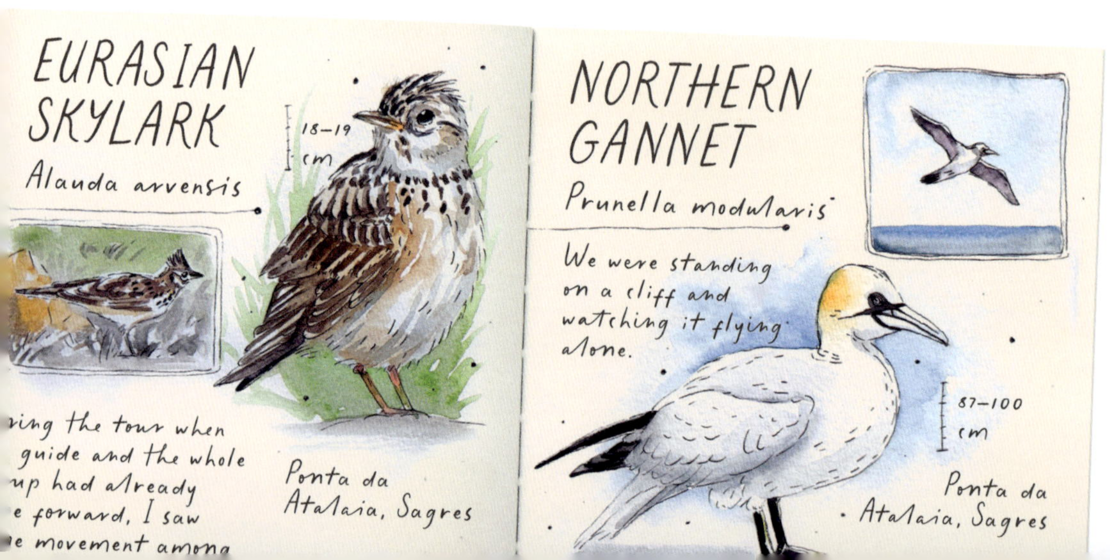

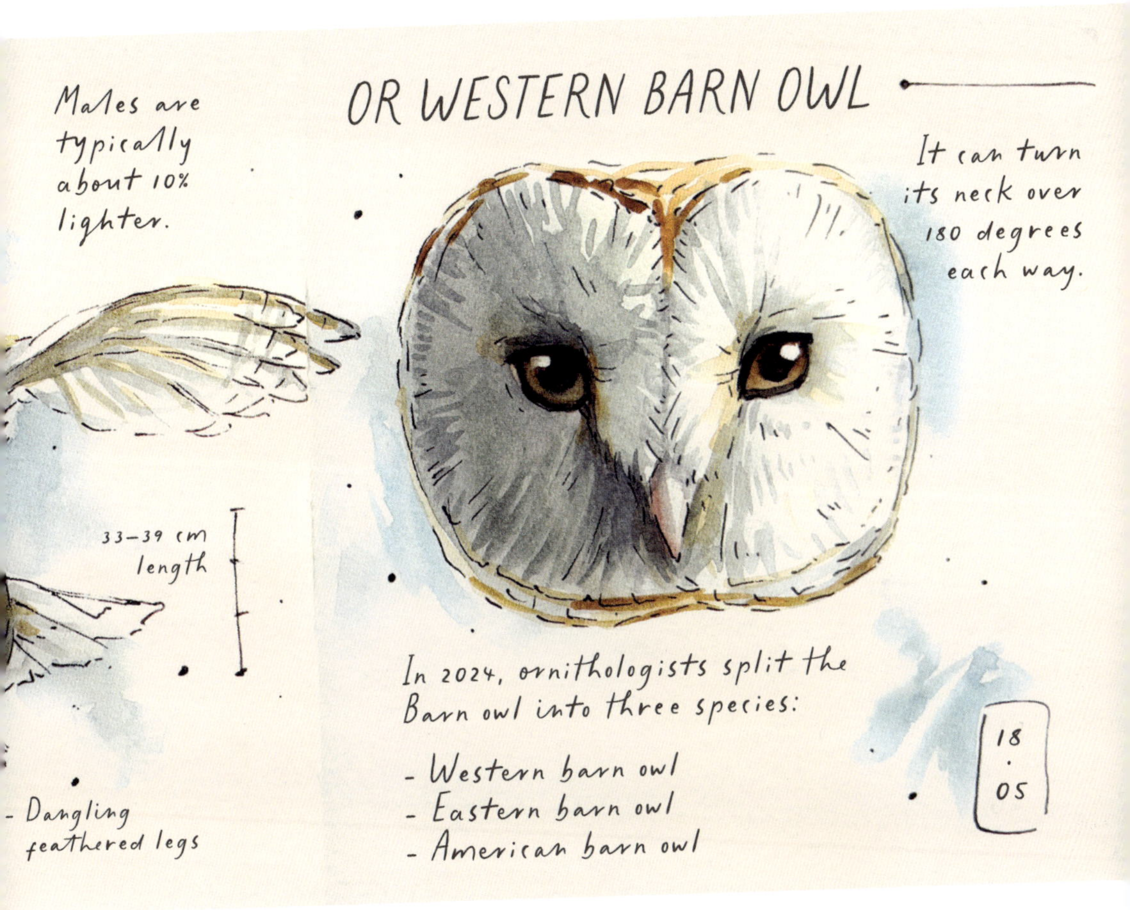

It's very hard to explain how it felt when I combined these two passions – birdwatching and art. Learning about birds through drawing, becoming lost in all the textures, colours and patterns that birds can offer... And all of this in the form of quick sketches that you can make anywhere and any time on a daily basis. Although I can't explain this feeling, I can help you to feel it yourself!

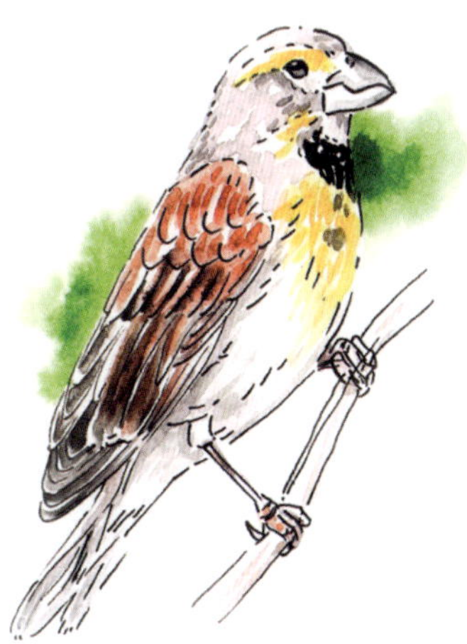

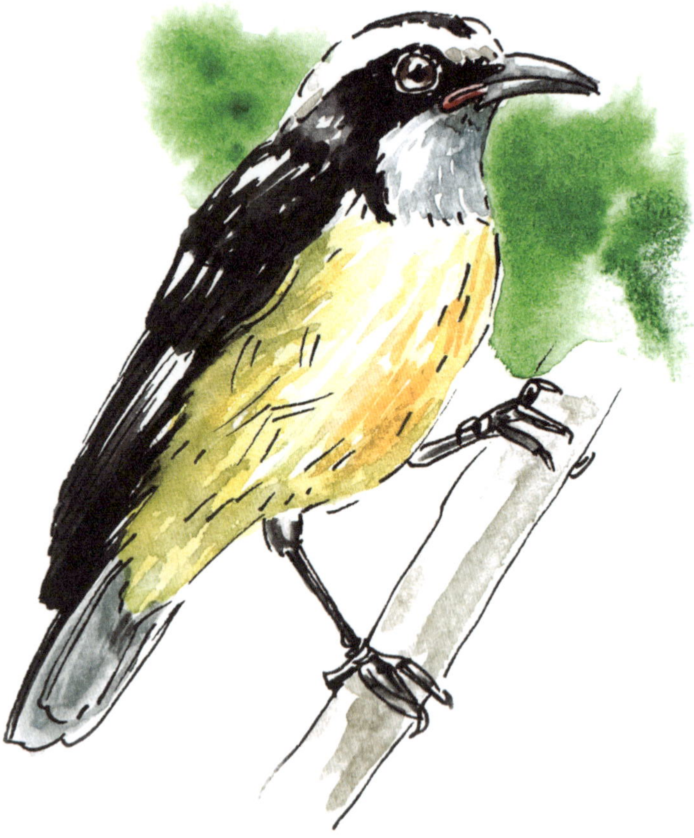

Chapter one

Spread your wings

Let's discuss the basics: materials, techniques, bird features and fun exercises to begin your journey into the world of art and birds.

Keeping a sketchbook

How to find time, courage and be consistent

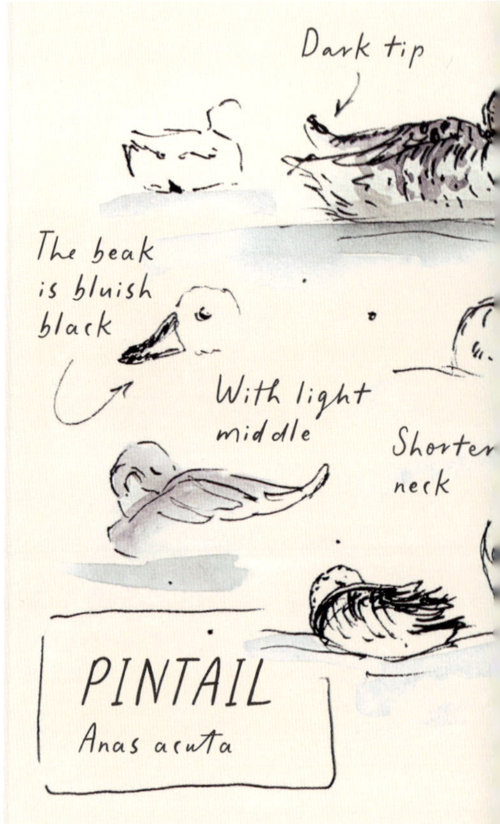

Step 1: Buy a sketchbook and a pen.

Step 2: Keep it with you everywhere.

Step 3: Draw something in it whenever you catch yourself scrolling on your phone.

If only it were that simple, you'll say! I totally agree – I know it's not, at least at first. But when you get into it, it will be as simple as that. If you are stuck on the first step, don't worry, I'll give you a hand with choosing the materials in just a second. But if you have a sketchbook, a pen and maybe even watercolours already, but still don't draw regularly, I have a few pieces of advice for you.

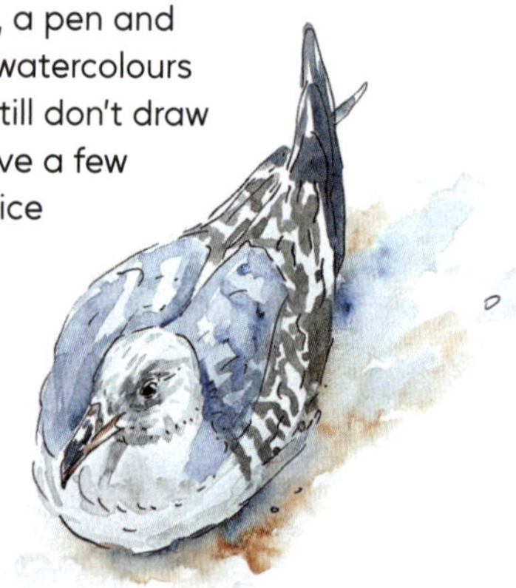

Forget about any rules

Everything that is considered essential for any artist to know, like composition, colour theory, perspective, and so on, is like the Pirate code – just guidance, not actual rules! Use it but don't be afraid to experiment. Art is all about creativity, which means any rules will be obstacles in your way. Forget about them.

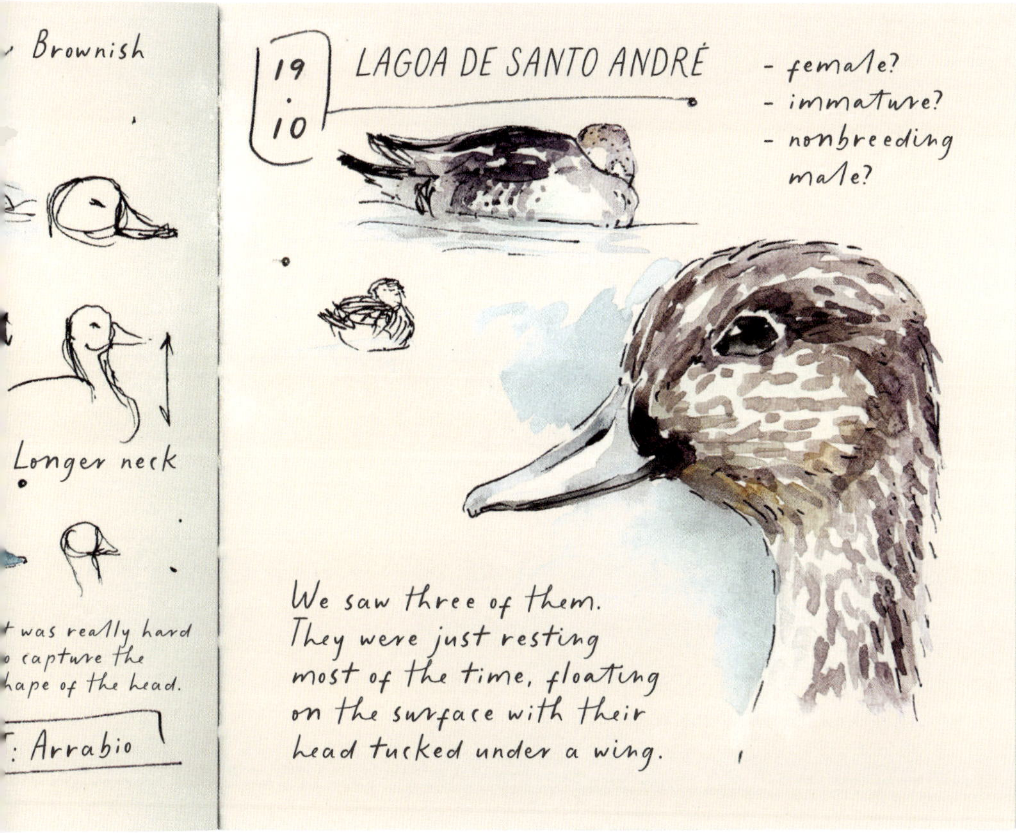

Better advice

Don't be harsh on yourself

You are learning, and it's okay if the results don't look as you might expect. That's art, not maths. Some of your "mistakes" can also lead to amazing discoveries, so embrace this artistic journey.

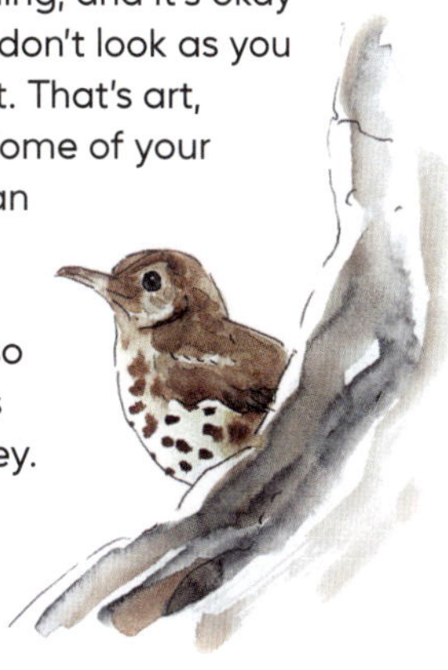

Let go of expectations

The best advice

Enjoy the process itself! I found inner peace when I stopped imagining the result before starting to draw. Focus on each stroke you make, relax into this wonderful feeling, and you will always love the result because it is a part of the joyful process.

Now grab your sketchbook and draw something. Still don't have a sketchbook? Then flip to the next page.

Materials

Let's check that you have everything you need

Sketchbook

You can use separate pieces of paper, but I think a sketchbook is much better:

- You can keep it everywhere with you.
- You can always close it so nobody will see your drawings.
- You don't tear paper out of a sketchbook, which means you have to live with your "mistakes" – trust me, that's a very valuable lesson.

I have some sketchbooks with non-watercolour paper, but they might be hard for a beginner to use. So pick one with watercolour paper to make your life easier. If you can choose between hot- and cold-pressed paper, go with the hot one – it has less texture and your pen lines will be cleaner. Bonus point if you can fit your sketchbook in a pocket!

Drawing pen

Your drawing pen has to be waterproof; if your pen bleeds when you are adding watercolour, this is the saddest thing that can happen. There are different sizes, but I think 0.5 is the perfect one to start with. When it comes to brands, Pigma Micron by Sakura is my personal choice.

Watercolour paints

Usually watercolour comes in tubes or pans. It also has different characteristics like covering or granulation, for example. If you are a beginner, you don't need to think too much about this. Some day you will buy very particular watercolours to your taste and create your perfect colour palette. But I truly believe that for a start you can purchase any set of watercolours that suits your budget instead of worrying about all the variations there are on the market.

Water brush

Most artists use regular brushes for watercolour. But to keep your drawing practice consistent, I recommend carrying your sketchbook with you and drawing whenever you have time. For this, it's better to have a water brush. This is a brush with a reservoir, which you fill with water and can carry around. Using a water brush seems challenging at first and I'll guide you on this when we discuss drawing techniques.

Paper towel

A paper towel is essential when you are working with watercolours, to remove extra water and paint from your drawing and from your water brush. Any napkin will do, but paper towels tend to stay alive a bit longer.

No pencils are needed for the technique I'll be teaching you. Fewer materials means an easier life!

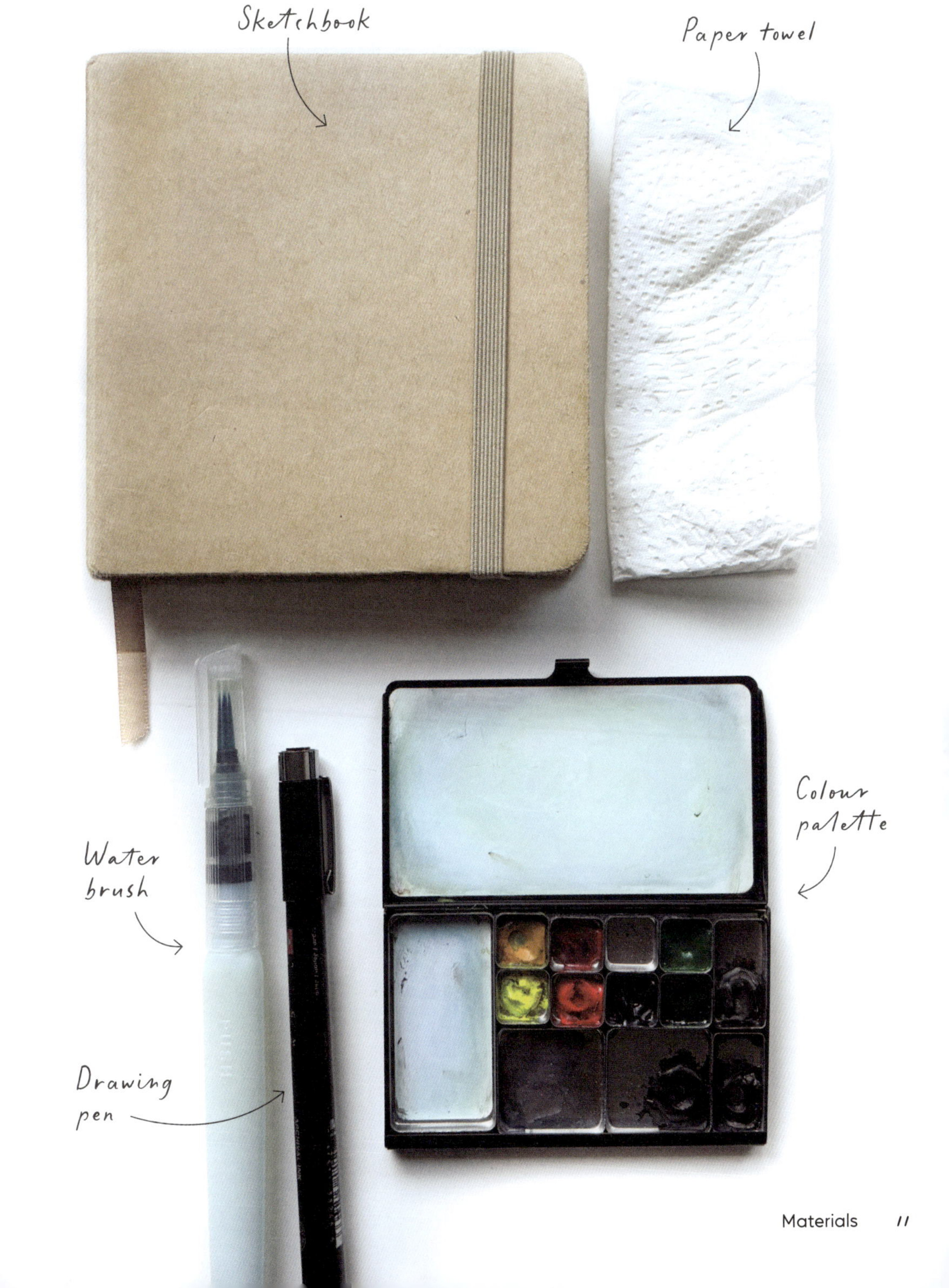
Sketchbook
Paper towel
Colour palette
Water brush
Drawing pen

Bird shapes

How to see the simple shapes of a bird's body

To build the body of a bird properly, you should take all its proportions into account. However, since we won't be making preliminary pencil sketches, we must simplify this complex structure as much as possible to be able to keep it in mind.

There are only two main shapes that you should clearly see in the bird's body before starting to draw: the head and the body. So to place your bird on the page and have some general structure in mind, just find and imagine on paper the oval of the head and the oval of the body. The rest you can recheck during the process and build on the go.

What you need to pay attention to:

- Shape – sometimes the ovals are more rounded, sometimes more elongated.
- Size of the ovals compared to each other – this is key for species identification.
- Position – is the head above, on the side of the body or underneath? Are the ovals touching each other, overlapping or maybe spaced apart to allow for a long neck?
- Extra space around. This will allow you to fit all the other parts of the bird. You don't need to plan the exact position of these parts – just the amount of space you'll need.

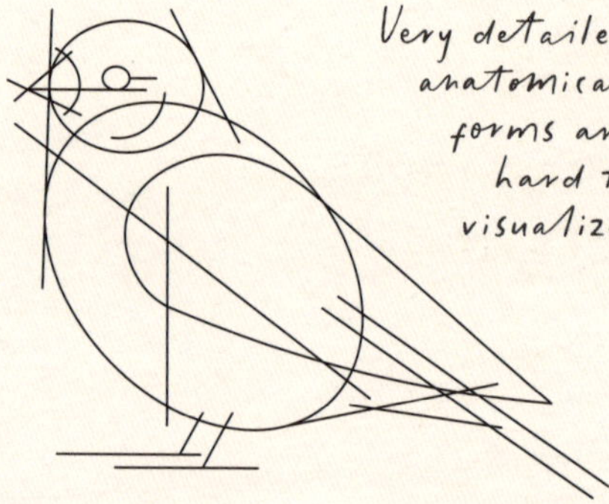

Very detailed anatomical forms are hard to visualize.

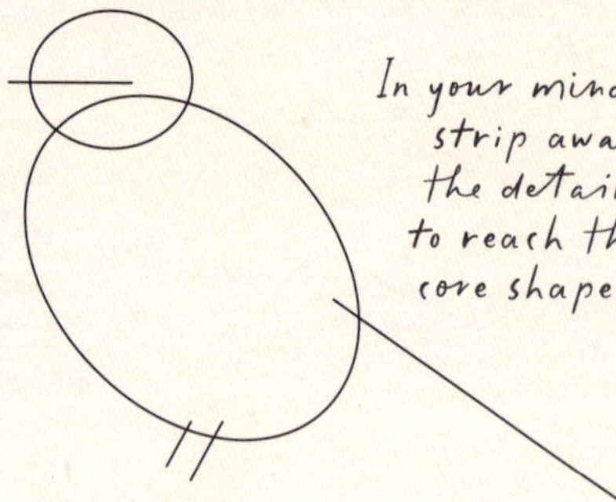

In your mind, strip away the details to reach the core shapes.

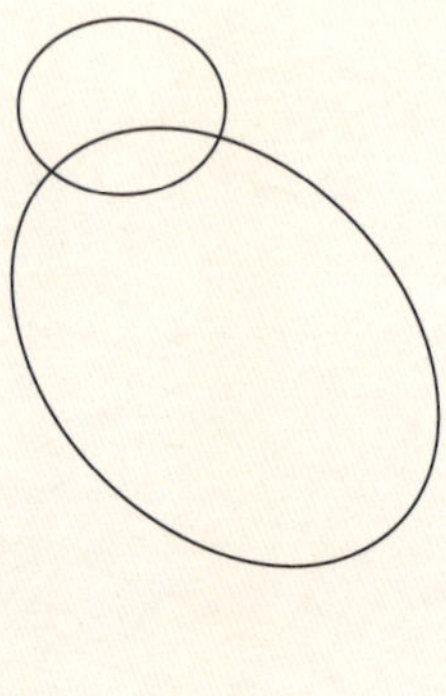

It's always better to leave more space than you think you need.

Take a look at these drawings and try to find the ovals. As you can see, no matter what pose the bird is in, the ovals are always there. You will practise finding all these shapes when we make step-by-step drawings. For now, whenever you see a bird, either in a drawing or in real life, just try to find these ovals – it's as simple as that.

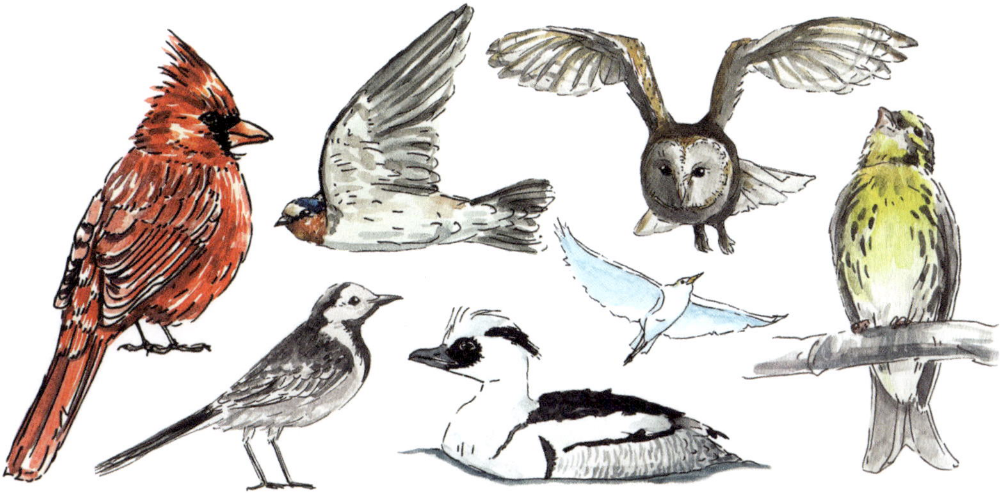

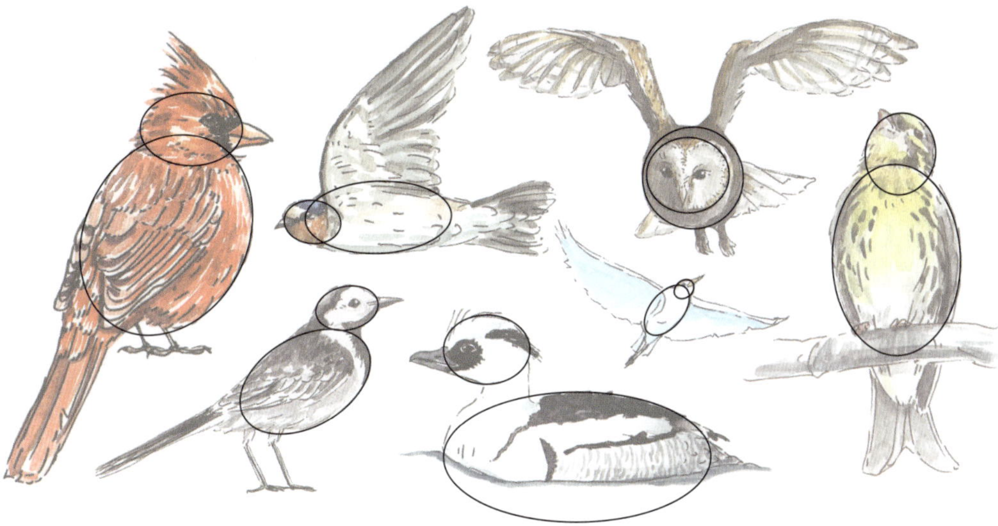

Bird features

Introduction to the key details

We found the ovals of the head and the body, but what about the rest? Bird anatomy is a very complicated subject. Instead of diving into the skeleton, the muscles and organs, the feather types and the markings birds can have, I want to simplify this for you as much as possible. So here are just a few features I think are the most important to pay attention to when sketching birds.

Eyes

Always leave a glimpse of white in the corner and fill the rest with a smooth gradient from dark to a lighter shade. Map out the eye-ring too, for extra detail.

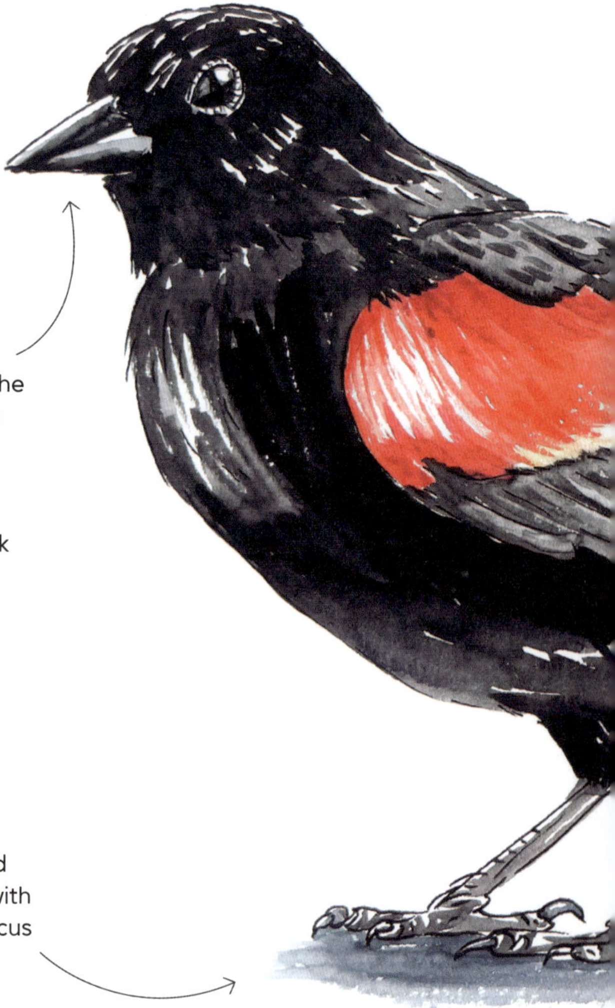

Beak

First of all, always make it clear that the beak has two parts, not just one. It's a minuscule but important detail, which will make your drawing more realistic. The shapes of beaks vary greatly but on most birds the top part of the beak is bigger than the bottom. Note how the beak is connected to the head and place it carefully.

Legs

These shouldn't draw too much attention, so don't over-detail them. Define their size, position, colour and texture (yes, they are not always just scaly). Be careful with the number and direction of toes. But show all of this with just a few strokes to keep the main focus on the head and body.

Wings

The wings are probably the most prominent feature of a bird. The structure is quite complicated; wings have different sections. But instead of remembering all of them and counting each feather, try to define these sections as a whole when you look at the bird, and show what you see. This will help you simplify the drawing while keeping it true to life. Study the exact bird you see while sketching, and the drawing process will become even more exciting and productive.

Don't be afraid to draw flying birds – simplify unfolded wings into sections and move from one to another.

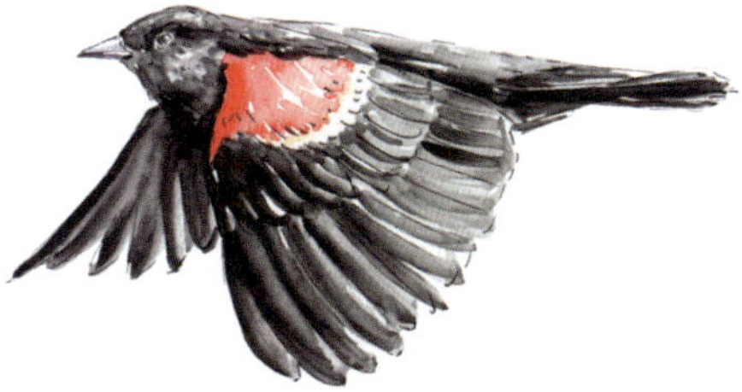

Tail

The tail has its own structure, but for a quick sketch you don't need to get too deep into it. Beside the size and colour, another thing to look at is how the feathers overlap each other, if this is visible. And of course pay attention to the angle between the tail and the body. However, since birds move their tails all the time, the tail direction can change depending on the posture.

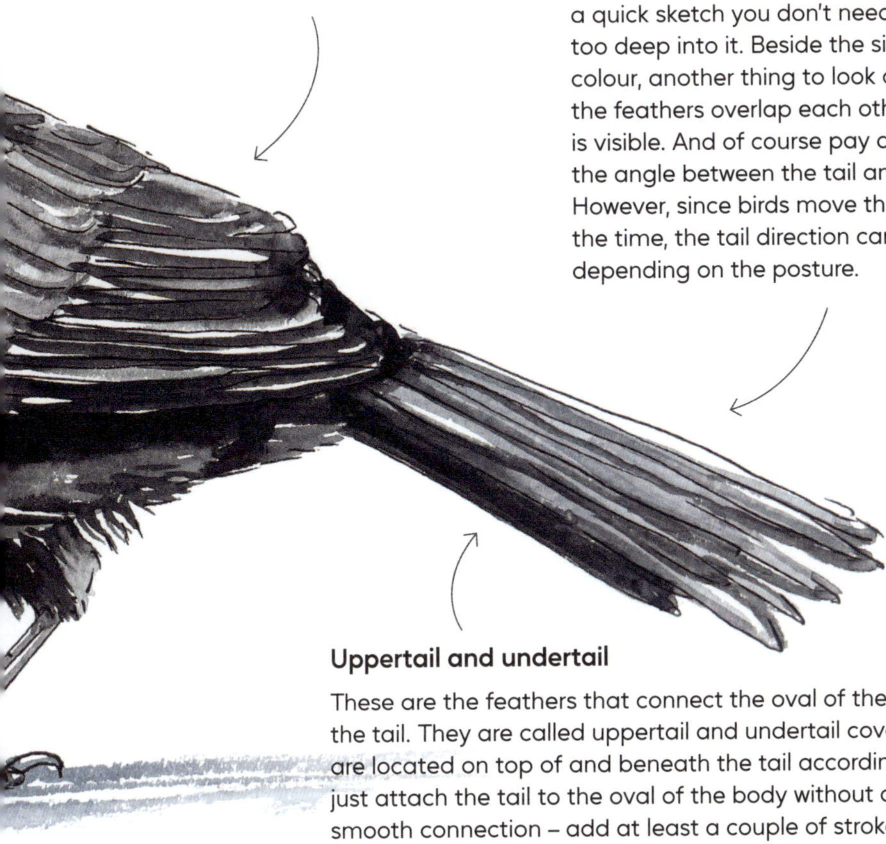

Uppertail and undertail

These are the feathers that connect the oval of the body with the tail. They are called uppertail and undertail coverts and are located on top of and beneath the tail accordingly. Don't just attach the tail to the oval of the body without creating this smooth connection – add at least a couple of strokes to show these connecting feathers.

Drawing pen techniques

The simplicity of bird line art

A drawing pen is a powerful tool! You can create really detailed drawings, showing volume and texture, adding depth and contrast. But I use mine just to map out the main shapes and textures, and for me this works very well when combined with watercolour.

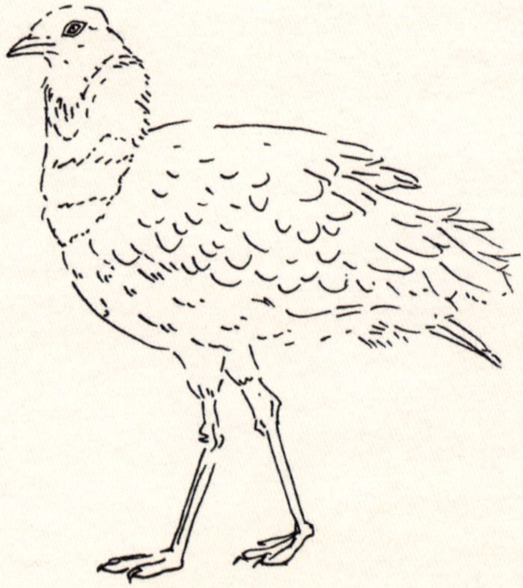

Using a drawing pen is very simple. If you know how to write, you're already great at using a drawing pen, because drawing is actually easier than writing! You don't need to know letters to make a drawing – you just need to know how to make lines.

Lines can be straight or curved. Sometimes they are so curved that they look like circles. Or they can be very short, so they look like dots. But they are still just lines of different lengths and curviness and I'm sure you are very good at drawing lines!

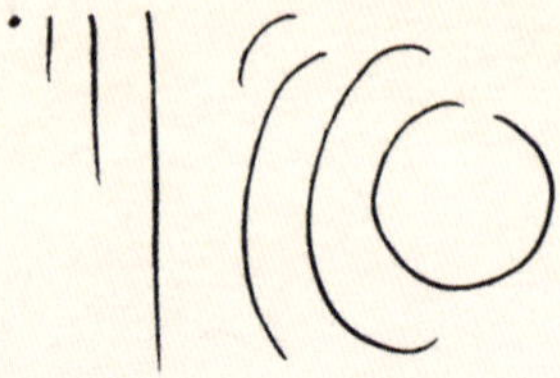

One of the things I like about drawing birds is that you don't need to draw long straight lines or perfect circles. You can use short strokes instead and they will look like the texture of the feathers. Do you agree that the head on the right looks more realistic?

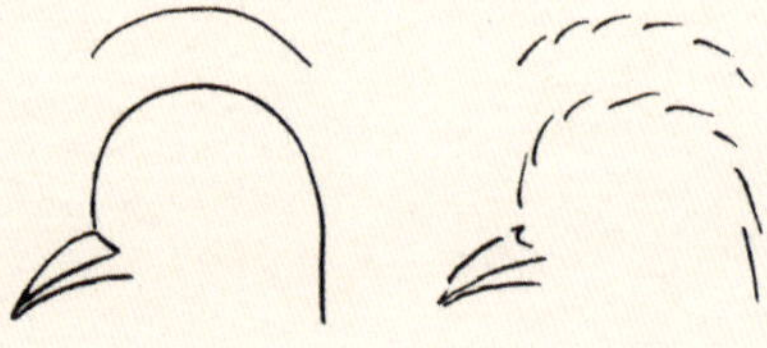

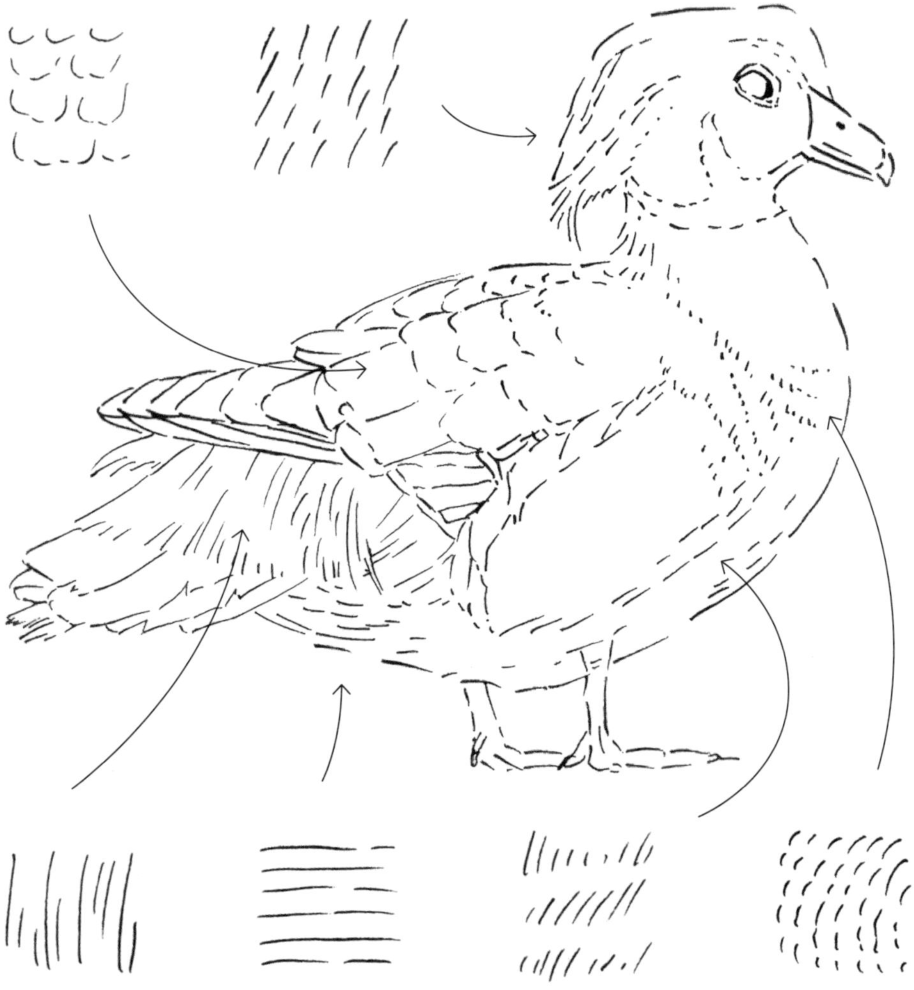

If this is your first time drawing ever, you might want to practise a little bit before drawing something as specific and complex as a bird. Look at the textures above and try making similar lines yourself. But don't get stuck in the exercises for too long – combine all of them to recreate this line-art sketch of a wood duck.

I told you – you are good at drawing lines! From now on, whenever you have a free 3 to 5 minutes, make a line art drawing of a bird. You can always add colour later or just enjoy the minimalism of the ink sketch.

And don't forget to practise drawing dots!

Watercolour techniques

Only essential knowledge

Now that you've found out you're great with a drawing pen, it's time to discover watercolour – a medium that might seem difficult at first. You can't predict everything that watercolour will do, and that can be hard to accept. But do you actually need to predict everything?

Watercolour can create interesting shapes and washes that other mediums can't. Use this! Let me show you some of the magic tricks that you can do with it. Make it your partner, not just a tool, and be surprised by the amazing things you can create together.

How to use a water brush

First, I'd like you to take a look at the water brush that I hope you already have. Here's my step-by-step guidance on how to use it:

1. Unscrew the barrel and fill it with clean water. Note that some water brushes screw in the opposite direction to what you might expect. This doesn't affect the quality of the brush – it's just something to keep in mind.

2. Gently squeeze the barrel until the tip is damp. Pick up some watercolour with it in the same way as you would with a regular brush.

3. Grip the brush close to the tip, so you're not squeezing the barrel constantly – let the water flow naturally. Squeeze it only for creating lighter colours. If there's too much water, remove it with a paper towel.

4. To clean the brush, wipe the tip on a paper towel while squeezing gently to flush out the paint. Do this to switch colours or at the end of the work.

Now you know how to use your water brush, let's find out what you can create with it. There are many different watercolour techniques, but I use only a few of them, so let's concentrate just on these.

Graduated wash

This is a very basic technique, which I'm constantly using. It means creating a gradient from a saturated colour to an almost transparent one. And it's very easy to do with a water brush: your wash becomes transparent by itself as you use up the paint and only have water on your brush. So you don't really need to learn how to do this – just practise a bit and you're good to go!

Top tip

Everything that has volume also has lighter and darker parts, which means you can apply this technique to any drawing instead of trying to create a perfect flat wash.

Colour transition

If you want to make a gradient from one colour to another, this is also not complicated to do. Just add another colour to the edge of the wet area and it will blend nicely with the first colour.

Layering

This means waiting for the first layer of colour to dry and then applying the same colour, or another one, right on top. The transparency of watercolour is an amazing feature – it is only with this medium that you can create such layers. We'll be using this technique to adjust colours, draw complicated patterns, add shadows and much more! The key here is to wait for the first layer to dry completely, otherwise you'll lose control over the marks you create. If you want one edge to be crisp and another to be soft, try blurring the edge by adding water.

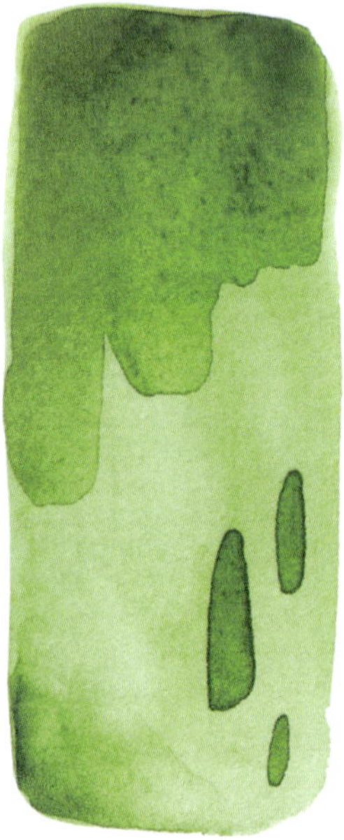

In this corner I also added a second layer, but blended it with the first one.

Wet-on-wet

The techniques I have described so far are all applied with a wet brush on dry paper. But there's another way to work with watercolour, called the wet-on-wet technique. This involves making a wash with water over the paper first and then adding colour, giving it an opportunity to create amazing shapes by itself.

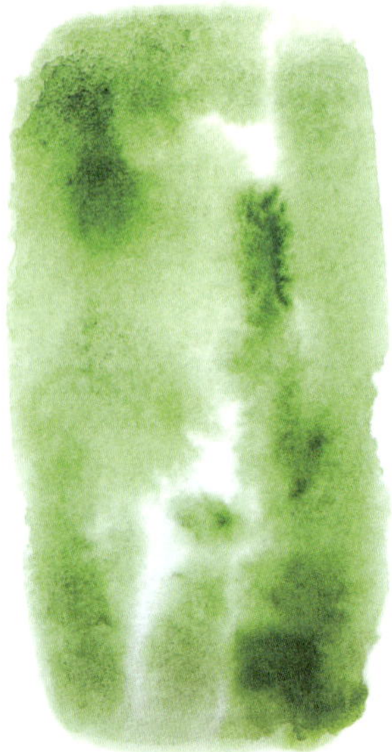

Top tip

Trying to paint crisp details with the wet-on-wet technique, or aiming for smooth abstract washes with wet-on-dry, can cause frustration. Learn the difference, and you'll save yourself the struggle.

Leaving white space

You don't have to cover the whole area with paint – use the white space of the paper as a part of your art. Keeping some areas unpainted creates natural highlights, brightness and contrast with no extra effort. Try leaving intentional white spaces in your next painting and see how it will transform your work.

Removing paint

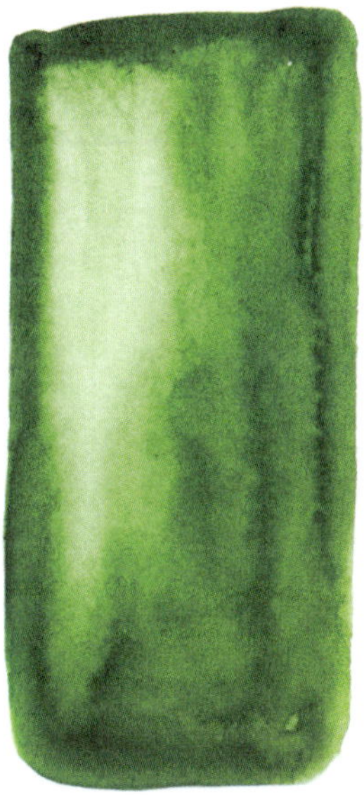

Another way to create difference between lighter and darker parts is to lift pigment from the wash you have already made. While the colour on the paper is still wet, remove paint from your brush, leaving just clean water on it, and apply it to the paper. The brush will pick up colour, making that spot lighter. You can also use this to remove unwanted marks. The ultimate way to remove paint is to use a paper towel! Try it yourself to see the results.

Dry brush

There is a technique that is great for showing the texture of the bird's feathers, called the dry brush method. Just pick up paint with a dry brush without using any water. For this you need a regular paint brush, because it's really hard to make your water brush that dry. So I don't use this technique that often, unfortunately, but I really wanted to share it with you. Feel free to try it and decide if you want to apply it more often.

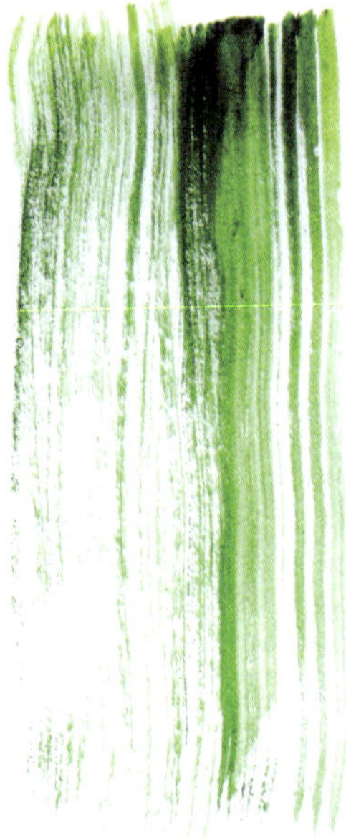

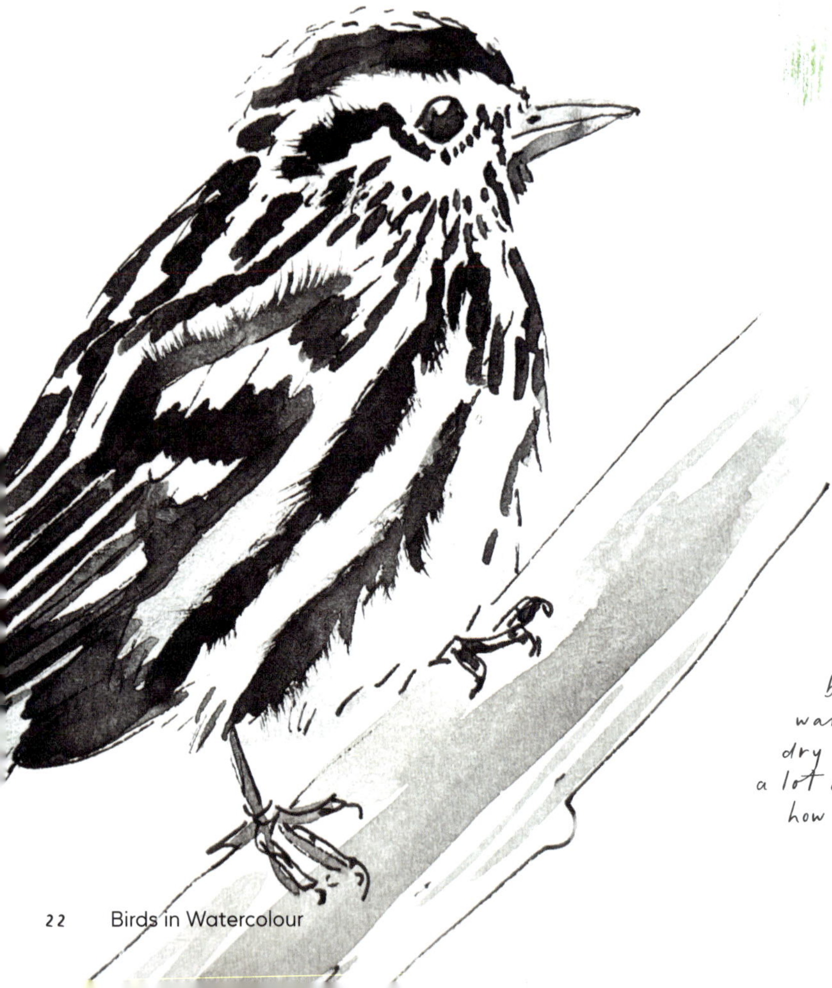

To draw this black-and-white warbler I used the dry brush technique a lot and you can see how fluffy the bird turned out.

Colour theory – express course!

I don't know about you but when I see those complicated schemes with colours, including a colour wheel, it makes me feel anxious. I don't want you to think about colour mixing as something that you need to learn or even to understand. Colour mixing is fun! It should be based on your experience, not on the theory. Here's the general idea for you to start from.

All paint colours come from red, yellow and blue. By mixing these in different proportions, you can get basically any colour you want. Try to get orange, purple and green for a start and feel like a true magician!

You can mix any colour, but to save yourself time it's better to make sure you have the colours you'll need most often. If you don't see these in your set, buy them in tubes and add them to your palette in the corner where you have empty space. You can start using them immediately, but give them time to dry before carrying the palette around.

Be sure to have these:

Any green will be useful.

Something brownish like burnt umber.

Indigo or dark violet for shadows.

Some black (yes, there are various shades).

Fun exercises

Time to draw!

You have your materials, you know how to use them, but you are still a bit scared of starting to draw – I've got you covered. Skip the first page of your sketchbook – you'll fill it some day – and start drawing on the next one. Here are several ideas for you to try and have some fun with.

Drawing from an abstract spot

Make some abstract watercolour shapes. When the paint dries, turn these shapes into objects by adding line art with a pen. You can choose a theme for these drawings, such as faces, vegetables or animals. Or you can just go ahead and see what each spot is telling you to turn it into. Beside being a very creative and fun thing to do, this also helps with understanding how to collaborate with watercolour when it doesn't act as you predict.

I saw fruits in some of these shapes, but they could be turned into anything.

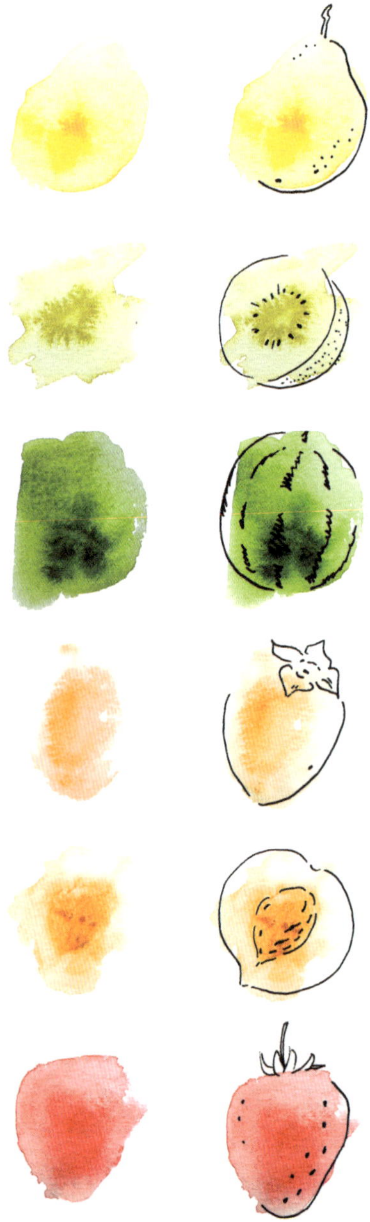

Blind contour drawing

The idea of this is to keep your eye on the object almost without looking at the paper. You need to keep your pen always touching the paper, so you can continue from the point where you finished your previous line. This is not only a quick way to sketch, but really brings you to another level of connection between observation and drawing.

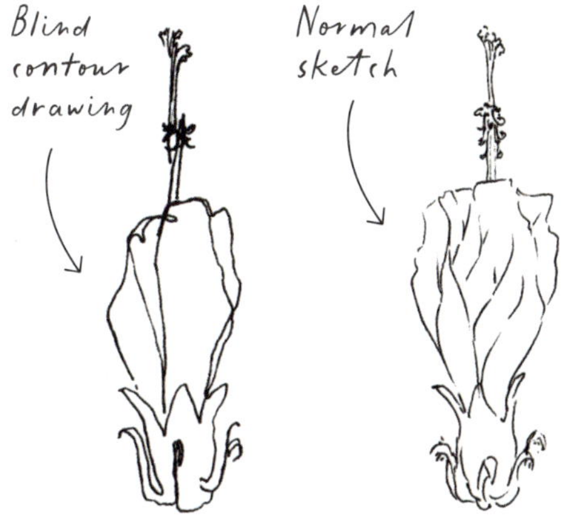

Time limits

Choose an object to draw and draw it several times but with different time limits. To keep it quick try 10 minutes, 5 minutes and 1 minute, for example. Keep the size of the sketches the same, though. This is the best exercise to learn how to simplify things and see only the essential parts.

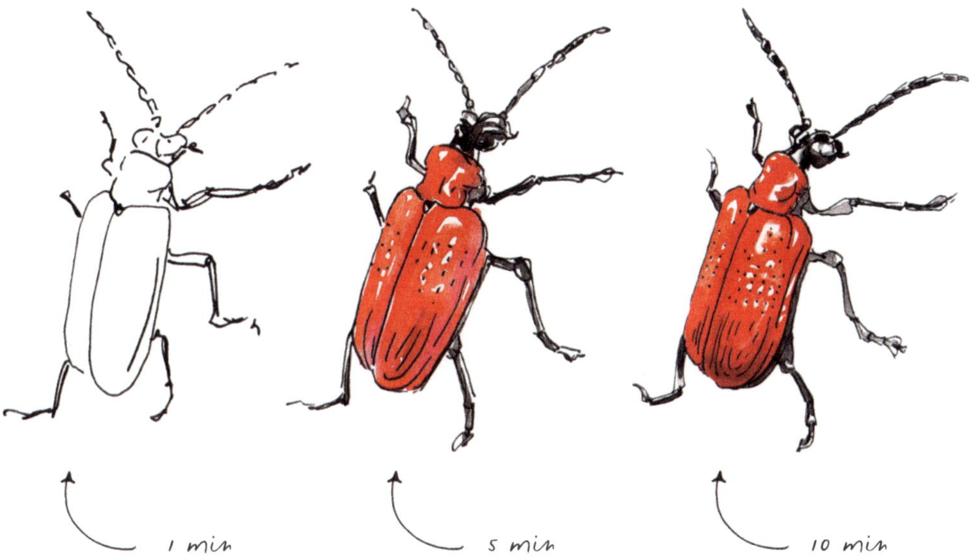

Drawing from memory

Set a timer for 1 minute, look at the object and try to remember it – the overall shape, all the details and how everything is connected. When the time is over, cover the object and draw it from your memory. When you finish, make a proper drawing next to it by looking at the reference as usual. What did you miss in the first sketch? This will practise your observational skills.

Drawing from different angles

Choose an object (not a photo but a physical object) and draw it from different angles. Try to understand the volume of this item and to show this in your drawing. By the time you make the last sketch, you'll know this object better than ever. In future, keep in mind all the other sides of the things you draw even if you make a sketch from one side – this way your drawings will never look flat.

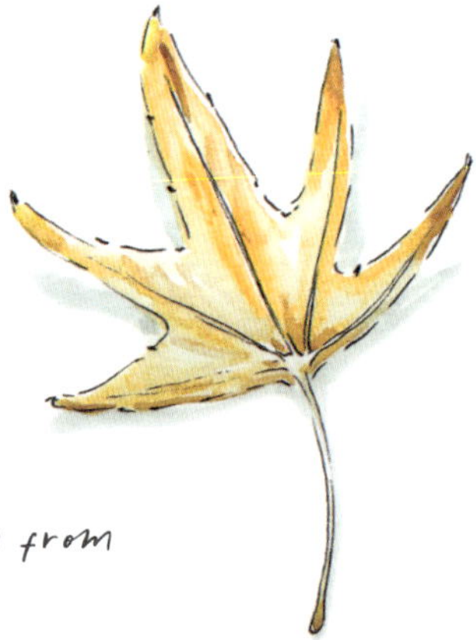

Drawing from memory

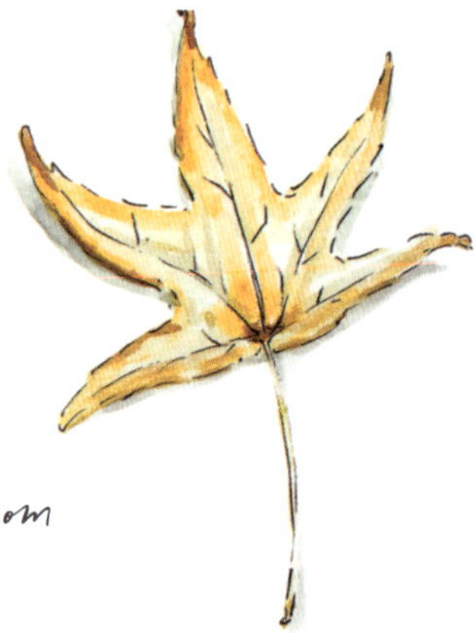

Drawing from reference

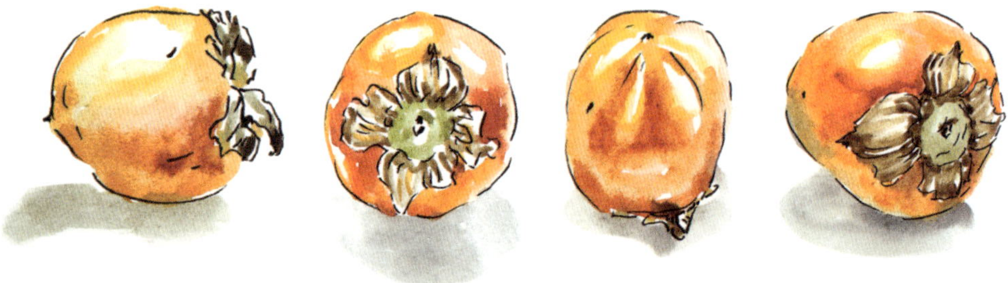

Imagine that you'll have only these sketches to build a 3D model of the object.

Different sizes

Depending on the size you choose, your drawing will be changing, too. See how different your drawings will be if you try to cover the whole page, cover half the page and cover just a quarter of the page. Understand the benefits of making drawings in each of the sizes.

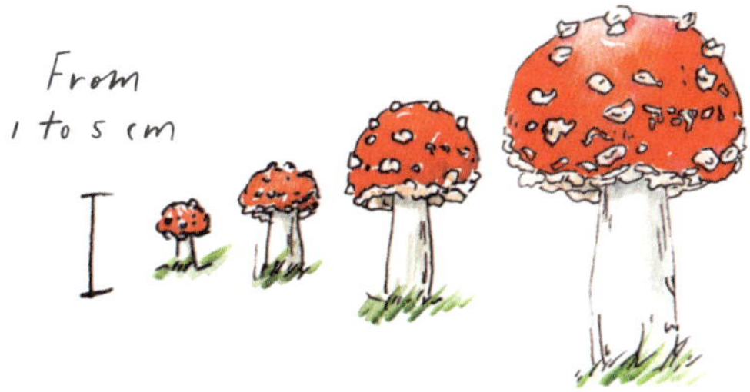

Drawing with non-dominant hand

If you still worry about the results of your sketches, this exercise will finally kill your inner perfectionist! I was laughing out loud when I made my left-handed drawing – those shaky lines were horrible. But the most surprising thing for me was that at the end I preferred the drawing I made with my left hand – it just felt more emotional and artistic. See if you can find something nice in the drawing you make with your non-dominant hand.

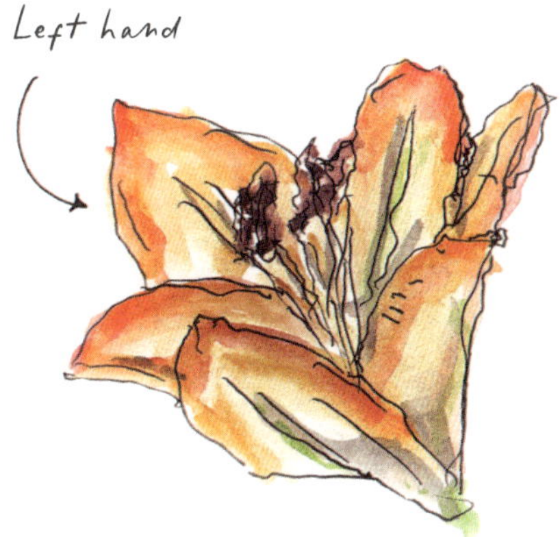

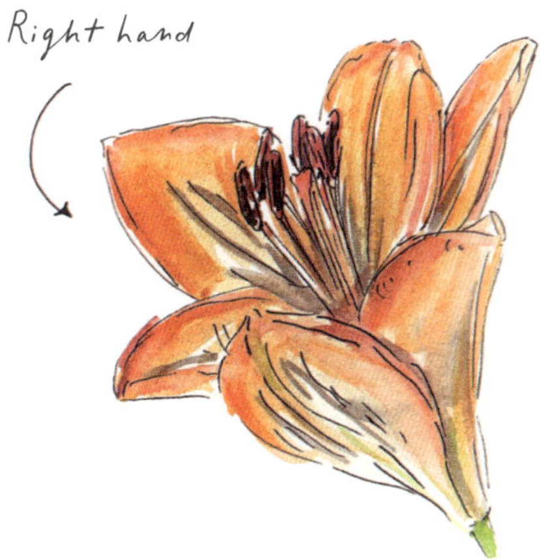

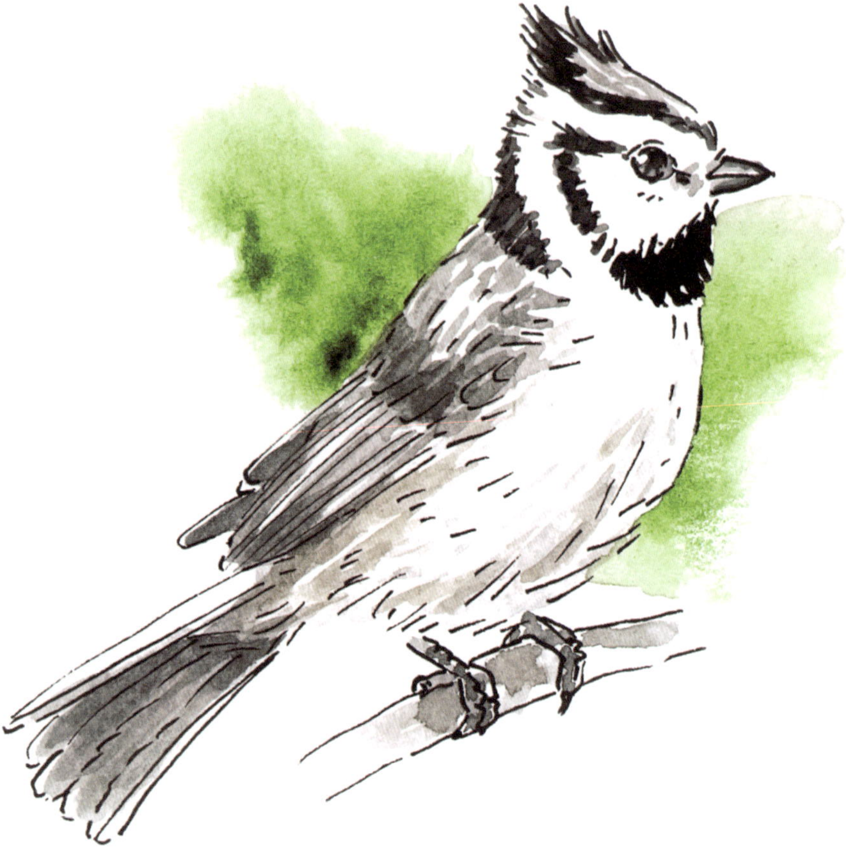

Chapter two

Diversity of birds

You're warmed up and ready to start sketching birds! Take a closer look at 20 different bird families and use step-by-step tutorials to make your own sketches.

These categories aren't scientifically based, but focus on the appearance and lifestyle of the birds. After drawing these 20 birds, you'll be ready to sketch any bird in the world.

Songbirds

Finches, thrushes, warblers, tits, orioles and many others

Songbirds, a suborder of Passeriformes, are known for their beautiful and complex songs. They live in almost every habitat around the world.

They are generally small to medium-sized and most of the small birds you see around are songbirds. They have three forward-pointing toes and one backward-pointing toe, which helps them grip branches firmly.

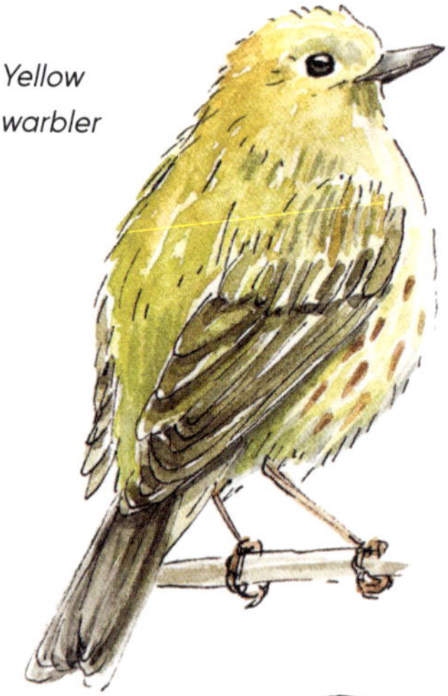

Yellow warbler

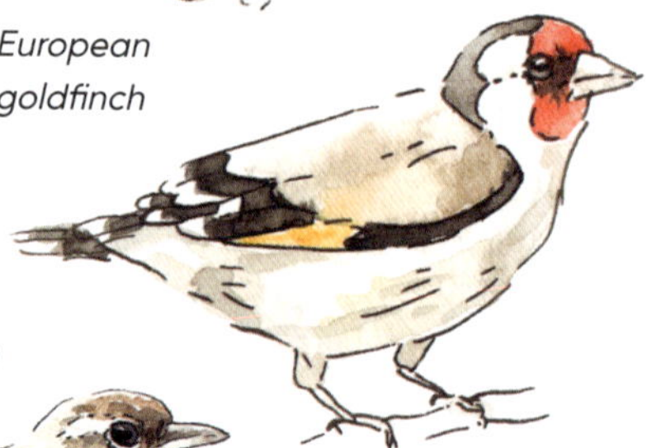

European goldfinch

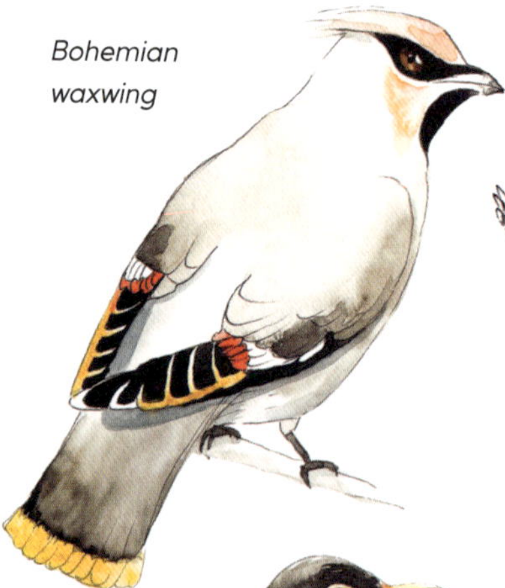

Bohemian waxwing

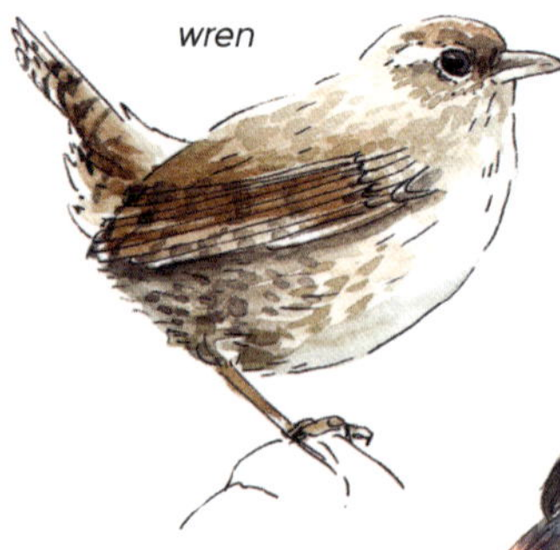

Eurasian wren

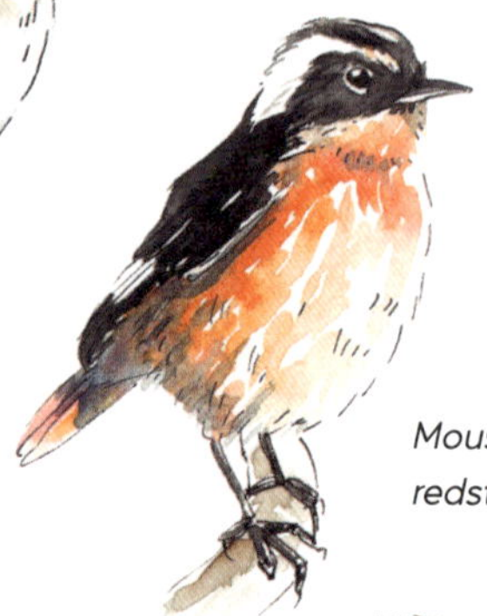

Moussier's redstart

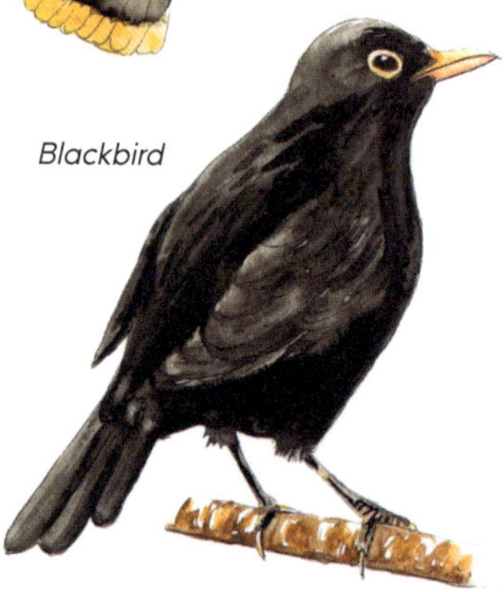

Blackbird

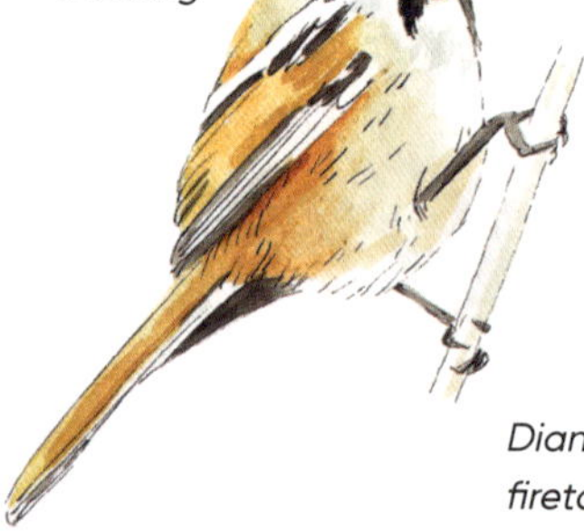

Bearded reedling

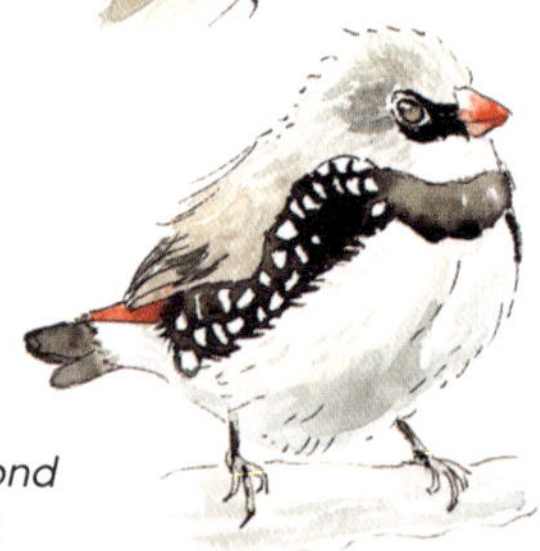

Diamond firetail

House sparrow

Passer domesticus

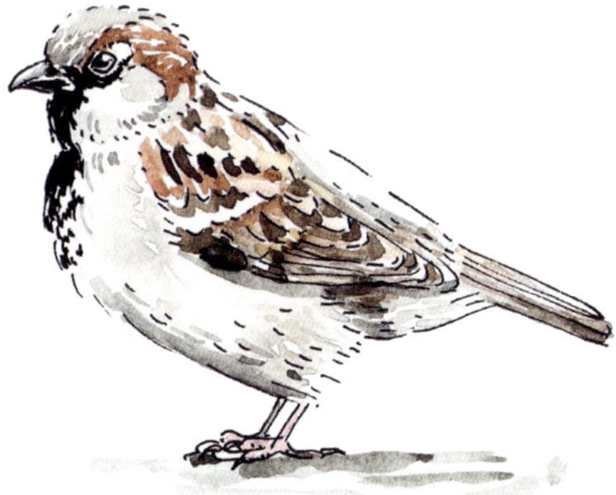

This small, cheerfully chirping bird is considered the most widespread bird in the world. It easily adapts to different environments and can live closely with humans.

The house sparrow has a plump body with short wings, and a small but strong bill. Male house sparrows are easily recognizable by their distinctive black throat patch, grey crown and chestnut nape. Females and young birds have more muted colours, with brown feathers streaked with lighter shades.

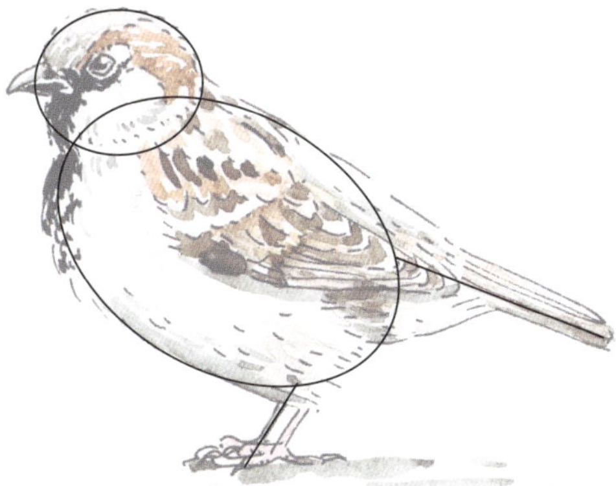

Key feature

We will be drawing the male as it has a more striking and distinctive pattern, and in the simplest pose for drawing a bird – the profile view.

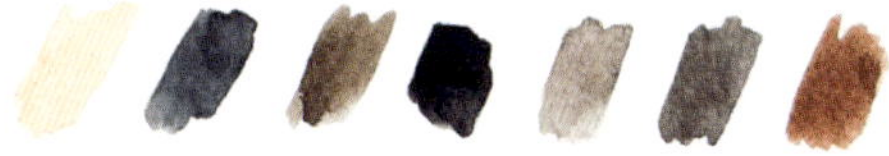

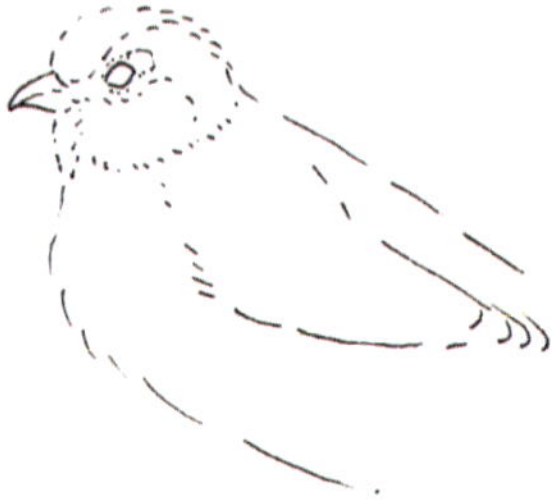

1. Start at the top left. Using short, confident strokes, draw the main features of the head and map out the top part of the body and the wing.

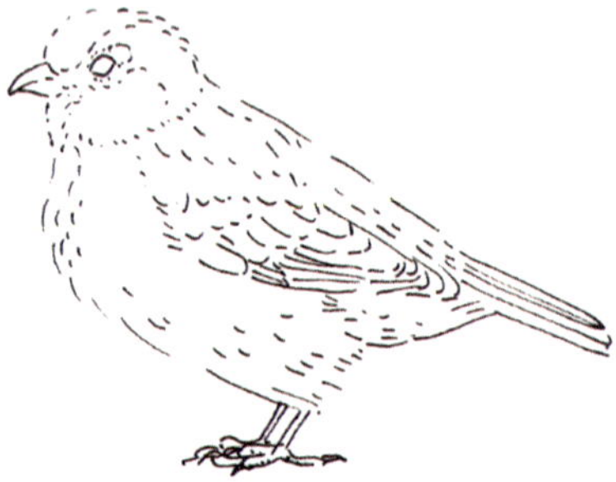

2. Continue shaping the bird's body by adding the texture of the feathers. Keep in mind the proportions of the ovals you defined before starting.

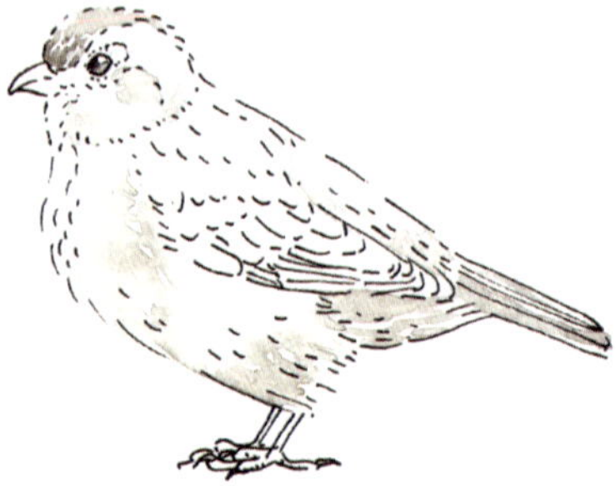

3. Time to add colour. Begin with the lightest shade – for a sparrow it's the grey colour on the nape, cheeks and body. When colouring the eye, leave a white highlight in the corner.

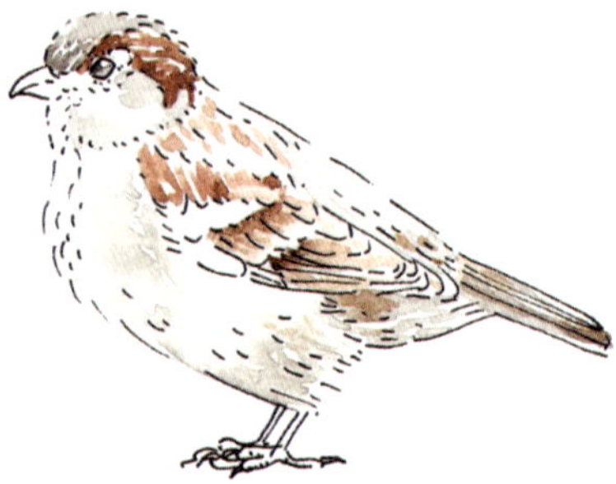

4. To create the chestnut colour, mix the reddish and brownish shades you have. Apply this colour with small strokes, leaving space between them to replicate the texture of the feathers.

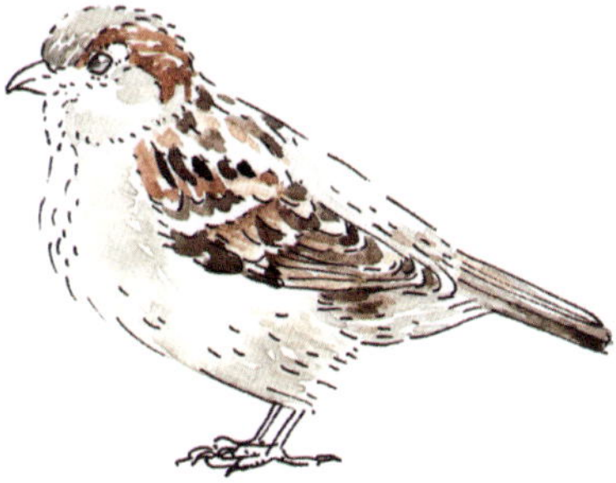

5. The male house sparrow has dark stripes on its back and wings. Mix a darker brown shade and apply it to the feathers loosely.

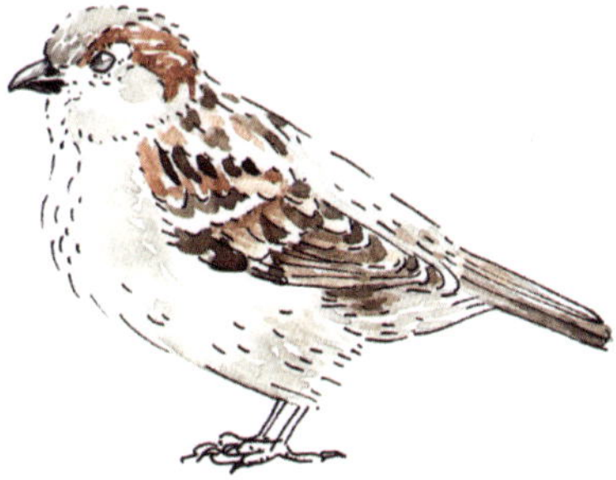

6. While colouring the beak, leave some white space at the top to create a glossy effect. Also, leave a small gap between the top and bottom parts of the beak.

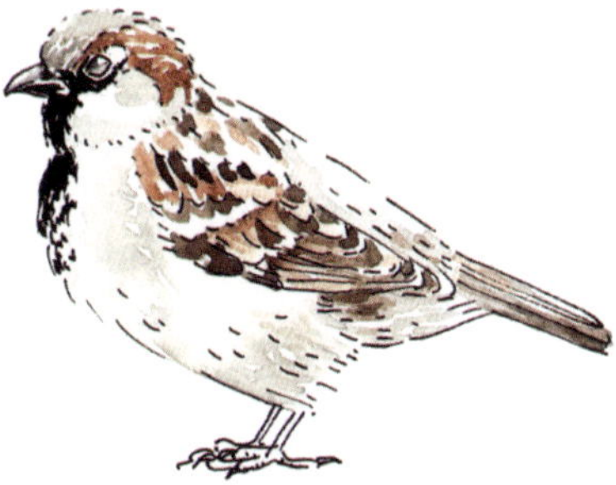

7. The last colour is the darkest. As with the beak, leave some space between the eye and the black feathers to differentiate them.

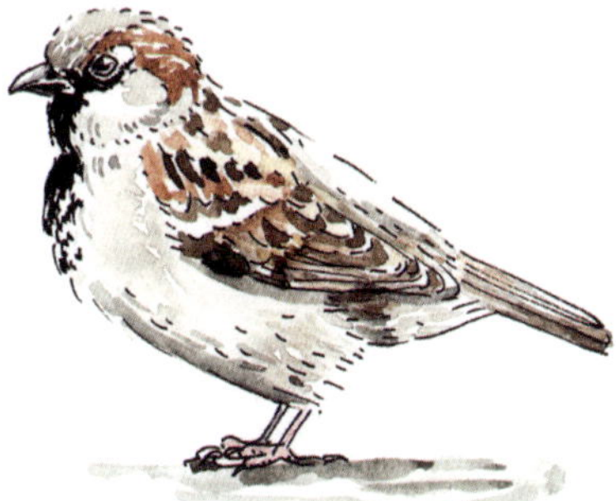

8. Shadows will make your drawing pop. Add some under the wing, on the belly and, of course, under the bird.

Pigeons

Doves, bleeding-hearts, bronzewings and similar species

The pigeon family Columbidae consists of more than 300 species that vary greatly in colour and shape. There's no scientific difference between pigeons and doves, and some species in the family even have curious names like bleeding-hearts and bronzewings, which are based on their appearance.

They have a primarily plant-based diet, high intelligence and excellent flight abilities. These birds are quite stocky, with comparatively small heads. They have short legs and a bill that usually has a fleshy part called a cere.

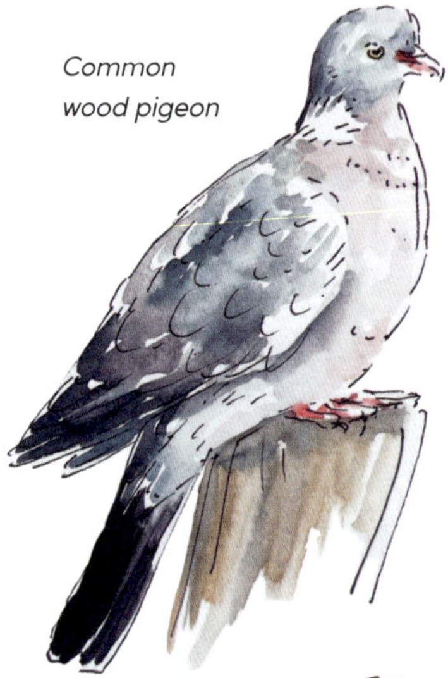

Common wood pigeon

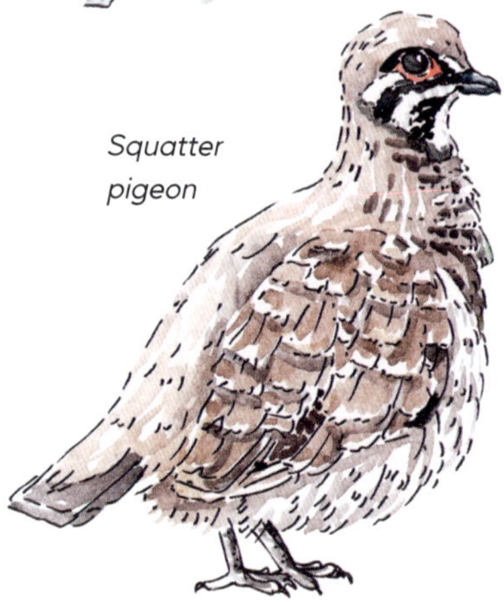

Squatter pigeon

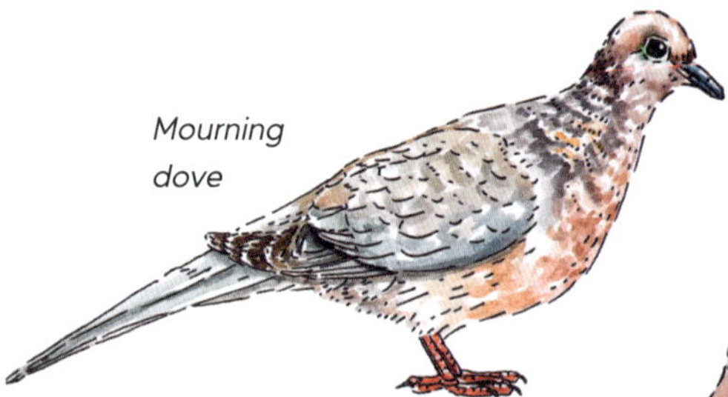

Mourning dove

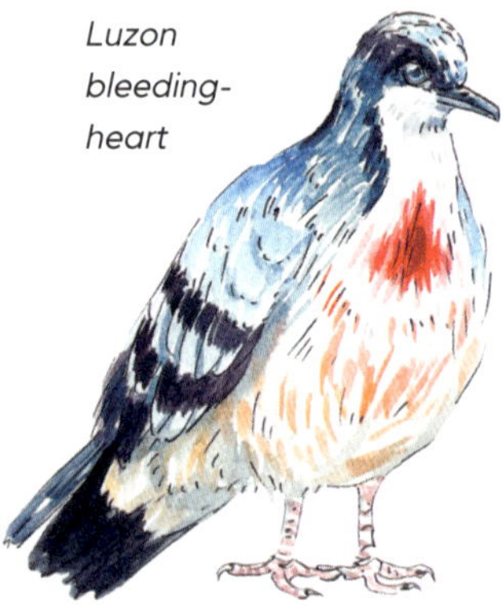

Luzon bleeding-heart

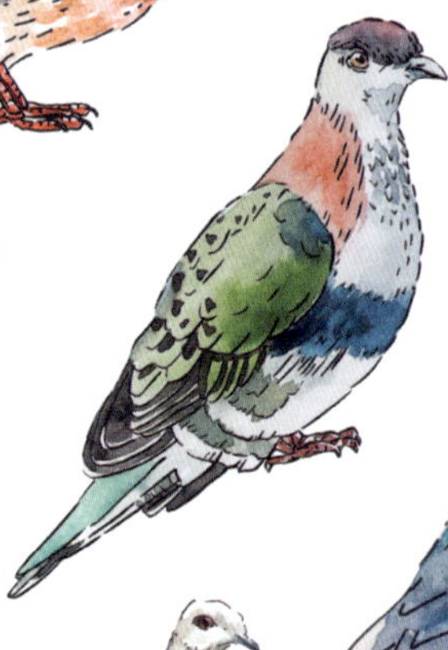

Superb fruit dove

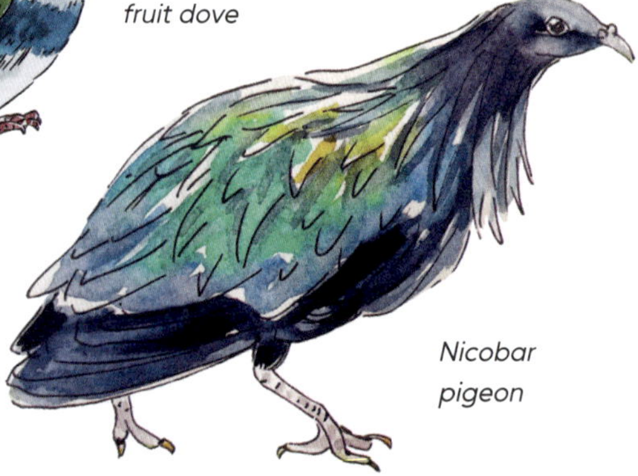

Nicobar pigeon

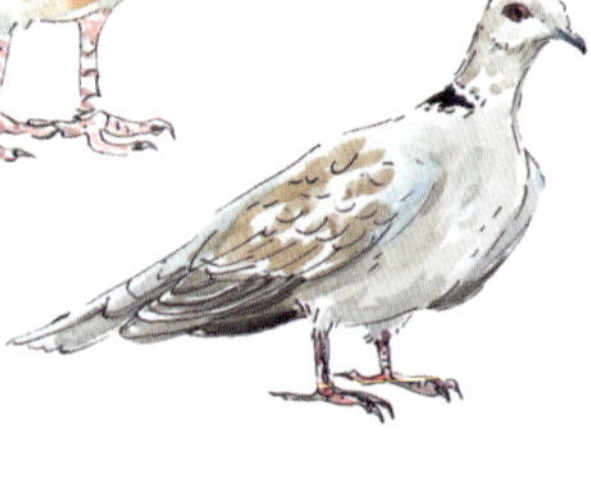

Eurasian collared dove

Feral pigeon

Columba livia

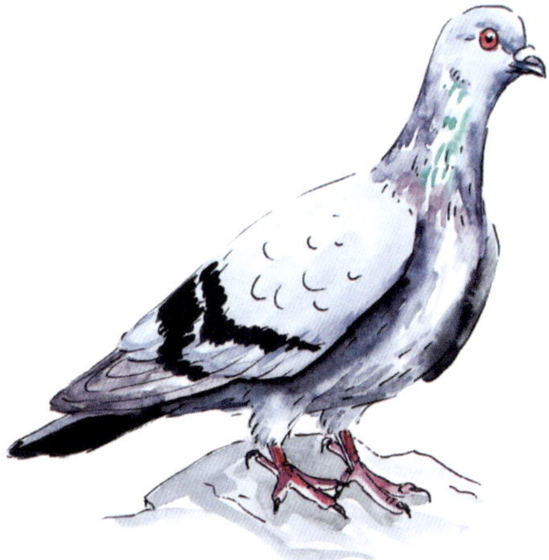

Despite the amazing variety of birds in the Columbidae family, when we think about pigeons, we usually imagine greyish, unhealthy-looking creatures rummaging through bins and trying to steal our crumbs.

These pigeons are descendants of the rock dove, which was domesticated by humans around 5,000 years ago. After returning to the wild, the species became known as the feral pigeon.

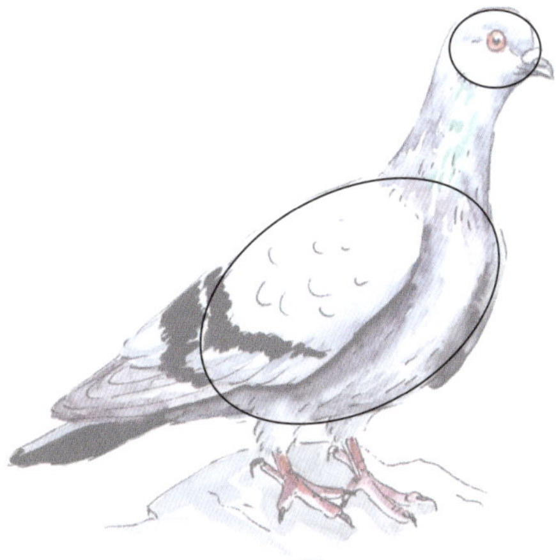

Key feature

We can still sometimes see birds that look very similar to rock doves – that is the plumage I would like us to capture today.

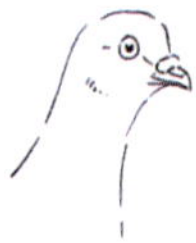

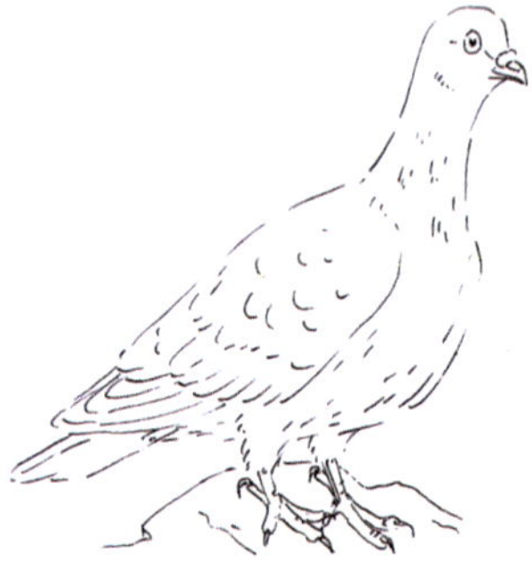

1. Since there's just empty space in the top left corner, let's start from the head again. Don't forget to outline the cere on the bill.

2. Keep going down by defining the main feather groups and textures. I also added the rock as a tribute to the ancestors of feral pigeons.

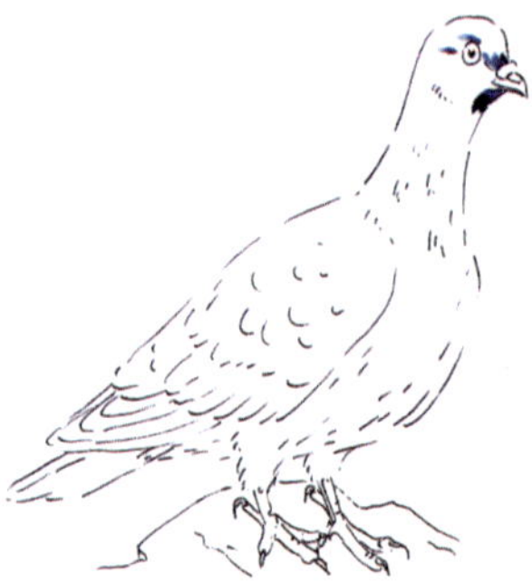

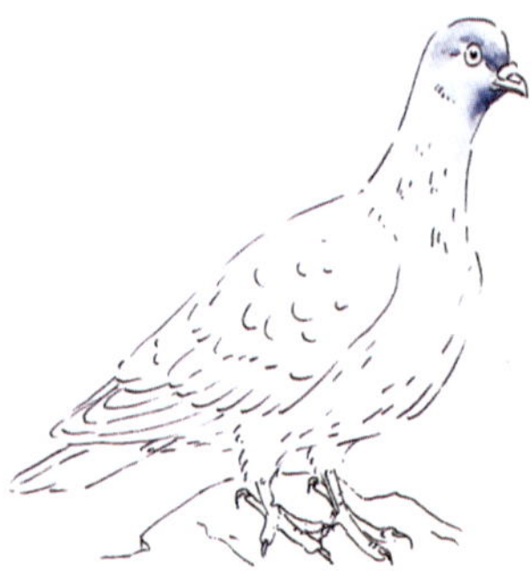

3. In this drawing I decided to start by applying a saturated colour to the darkest parts of the head. For this, I mixed indigo with a bit of ultramarine.

4. While the paint is still wet, smooth it with water, creating a velvety gradient; the feathers on a pigeon's head are usually not glossy.

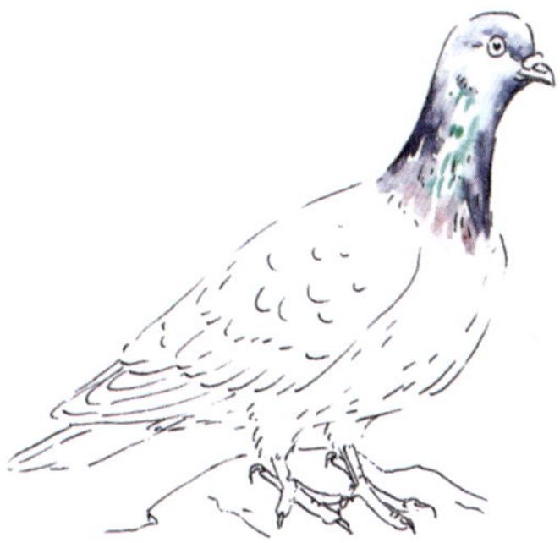

5. If you look at the neck, it's iridescent and shiny. You can see aqua and pink blending here, in short, sturdy feathers. Let's try to show this! For the darker parts, you can add more ultramarine.

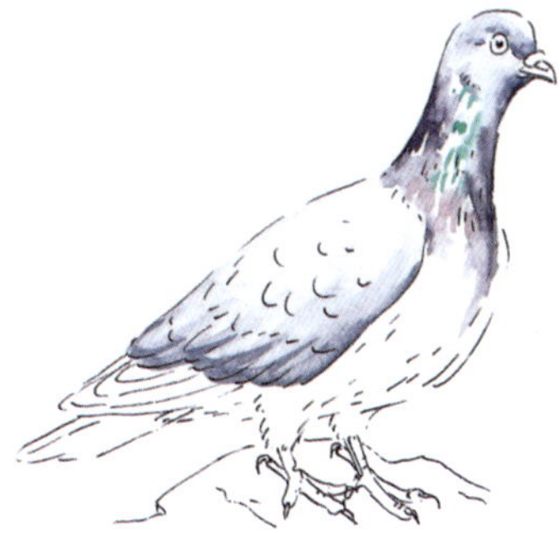

6. As with the head, after applying the colour to the darkest parts, create a graduated wash by adding water to the colour. You can make it a little darker on the left side, again to show volume.

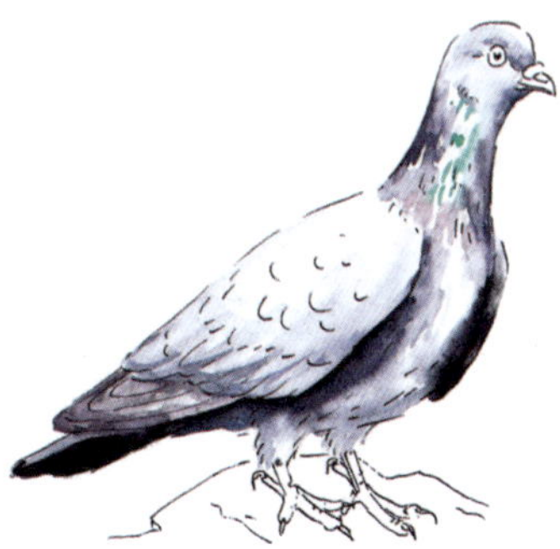

7. Colour the longest feathers of the wing and the tail. Make a shadow under the wing and quickly apply other colours, keeping the breast as the lightest part. Darken the second wing.

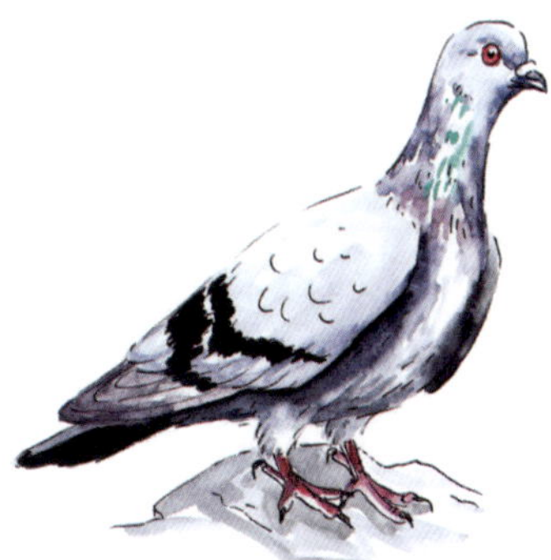

8. For the last touches, add colour to the eye, the beak and the legs. Note how the lower side of the legs is almost white. Colour the rock, or not – it is up to you!

Corvids

Crows, ravens, jays, jackdaws, rooks, nutcrackers and others

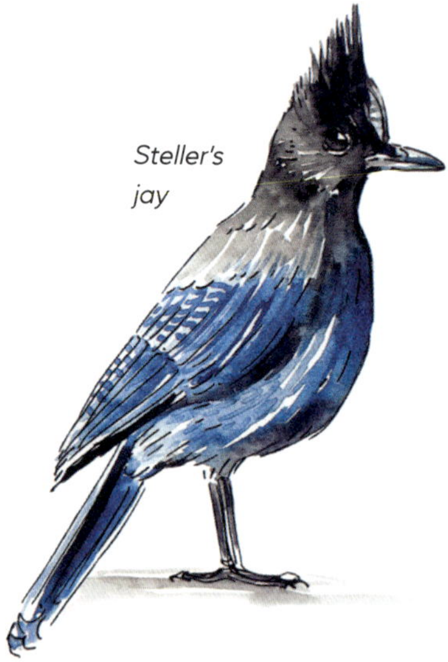

Steller's jay

Technically, these birds belong to the Passeriformes order, which means they are also songbirds, but for many people the sounds they make seem loud and unpleasant. These incredibly intelligent birds can also imitate other sounds, though, and you'll be amazed by how well they can mimic humans!

Their appearance is slightly different from other songbirds, too – they are usually bigger and have comparatively massive beaks and claws.

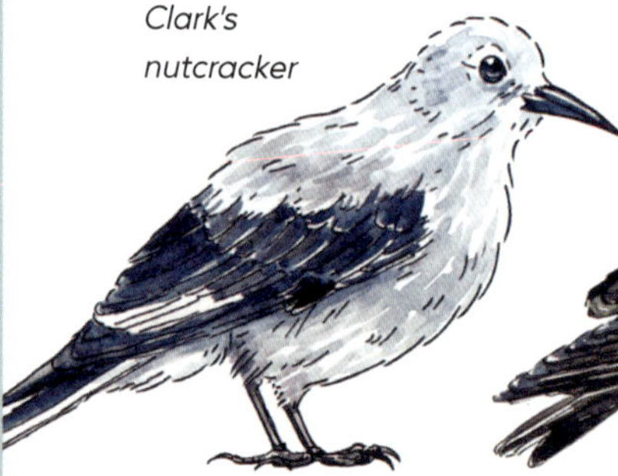

Clark's nutcracker

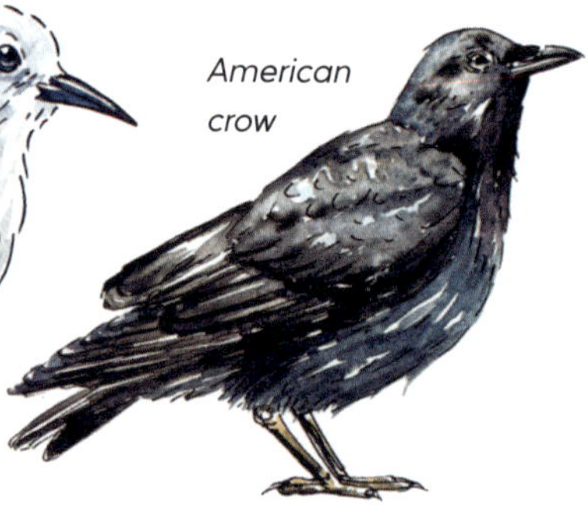

American crow

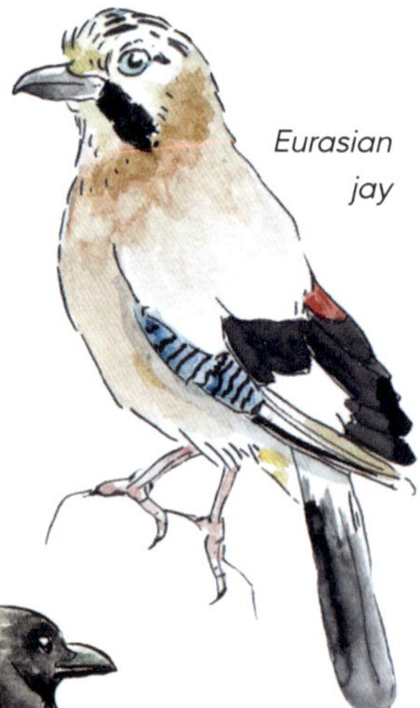

Eurasian jay

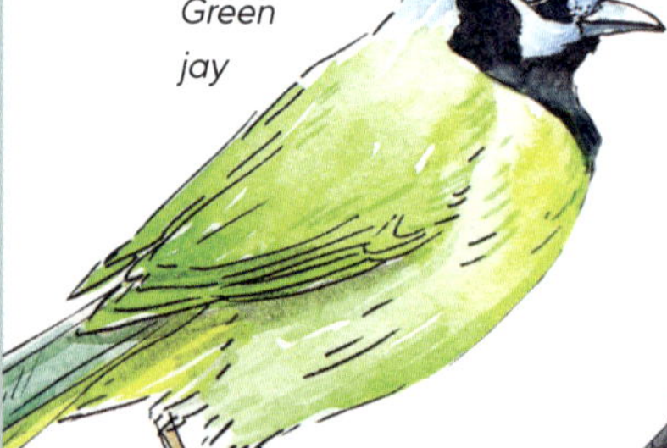

Green jay

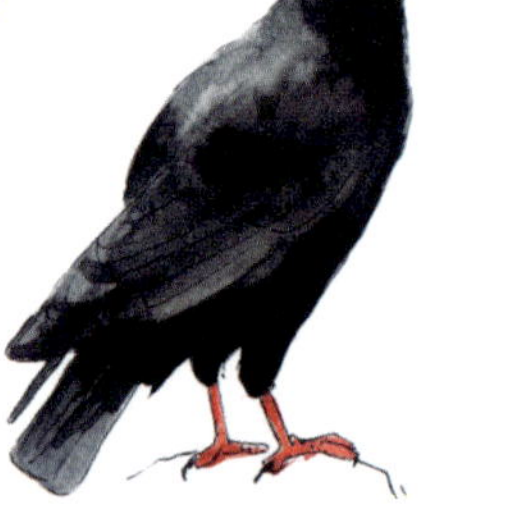

Red-billed chough

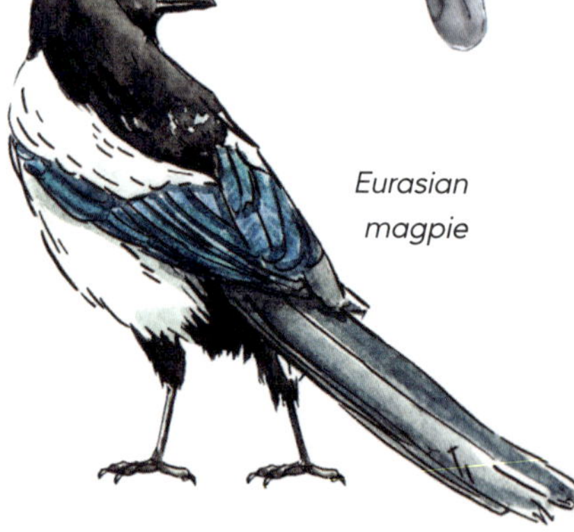

Eurasian magpie

Common raven

Corvus corax

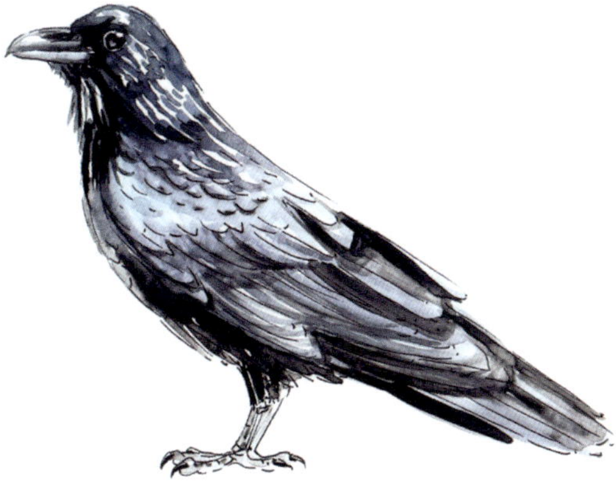

The common raven is the most widely distributed corvid and one of the largest and the heaviest of all passerine birds.

Ravens have lived alongside humans for centuries, thanks to their ability to feed on almost anything. Their size and dark appearance made them an important part of folklore and art. At the same time, you don't see these birds in cities too often, since they prefer more rural areas, which keeps them very mysterious – even nowadays.

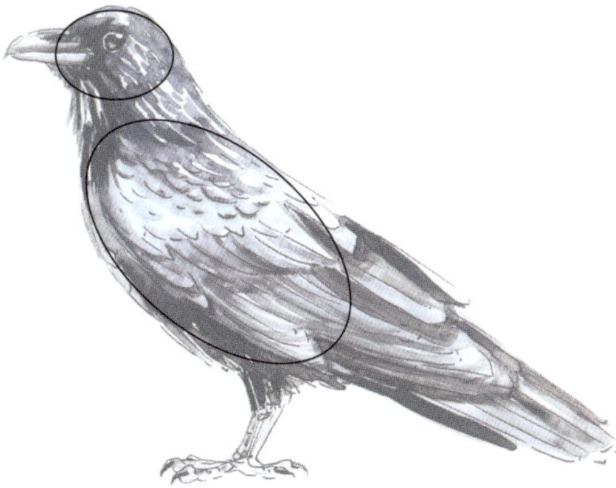

Key feature

Drawing birds with black plumage can be challenging, since dark paint covers all the details and tonal values. We'll learn how to make it more realistic, resembling the oily glossiness of a raven's feathers.

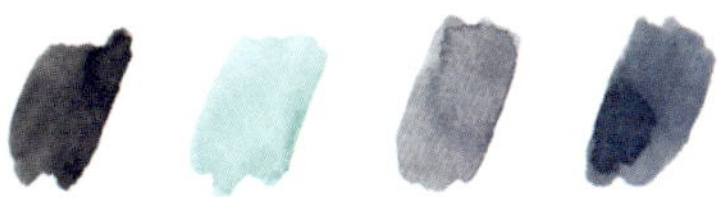

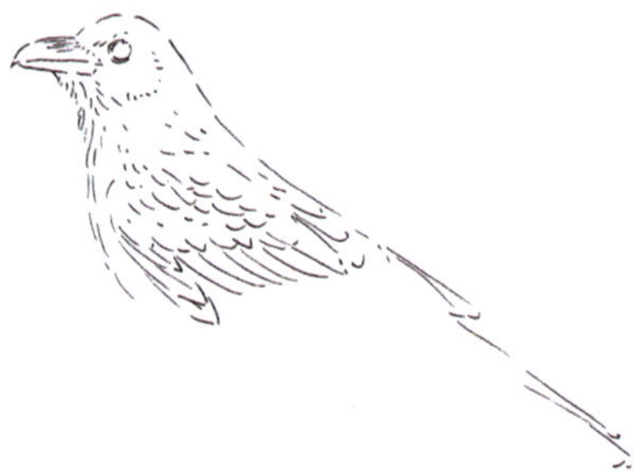

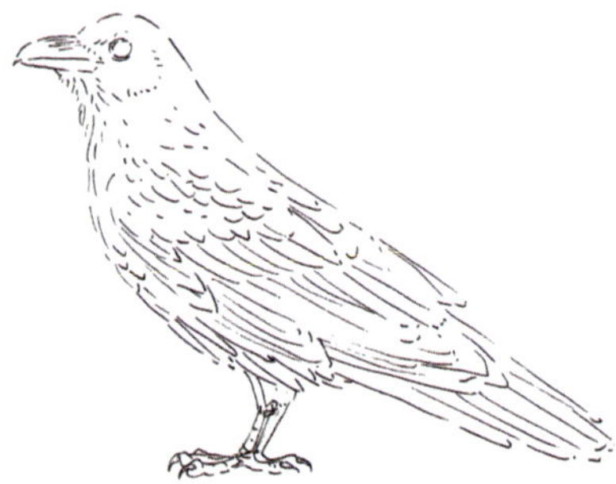

1. Begin with the head. Ravens have massive beaks – notice how thick, straight hair-like feathers cover the top of the beak. Outline the wing and add feather texture.

2. Finish the wing by adding other blocks of feathers, without going into too much detail. Here, the bird's tail appears as a continuation of the wing.

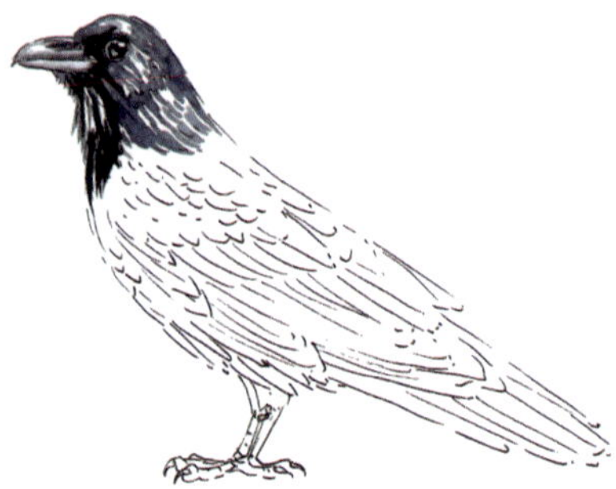

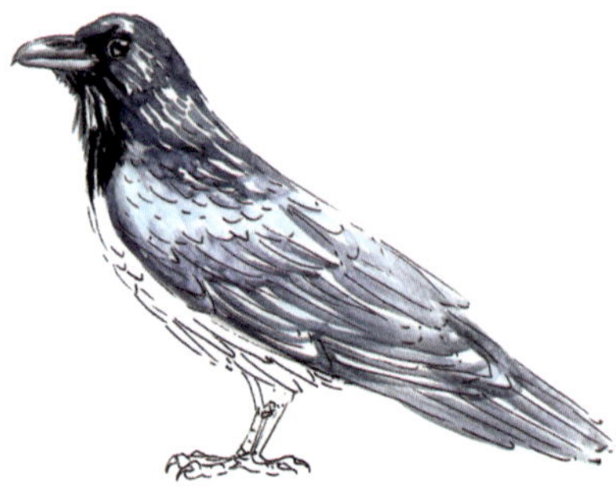

3. Mix some bluish hues into your black paint to make it more vivid. Apply this colour starting from darker parts and leaving a lot of white space.

4. To prevent the body from looking like a big black spot, let's add colour in layers. Start with a background wash – the underpainting. I added a bit of aqua blue to make it more interesting.

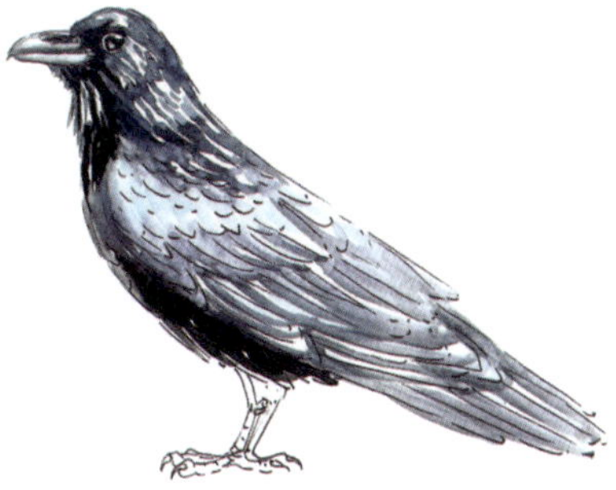

5. The belly under the wing is the darkest part here, so go straight in with black, smoothing it slightly as you move towards the neck.

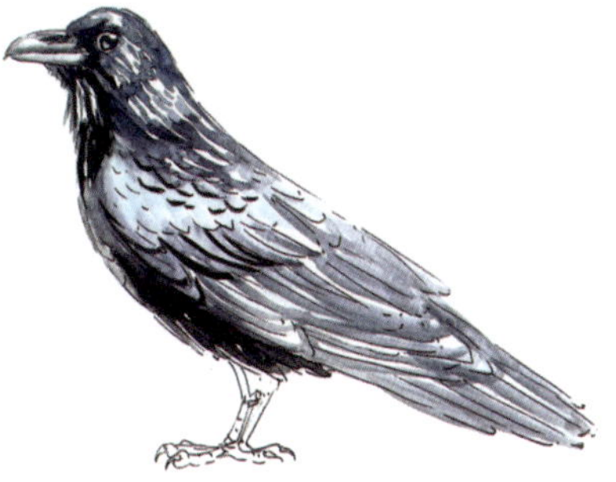

6. Now let's deepen the colours on the wing. Start by adding black strokes on the bottom parts of different feathers. Don't go too far – move to the next step before the paint dries.

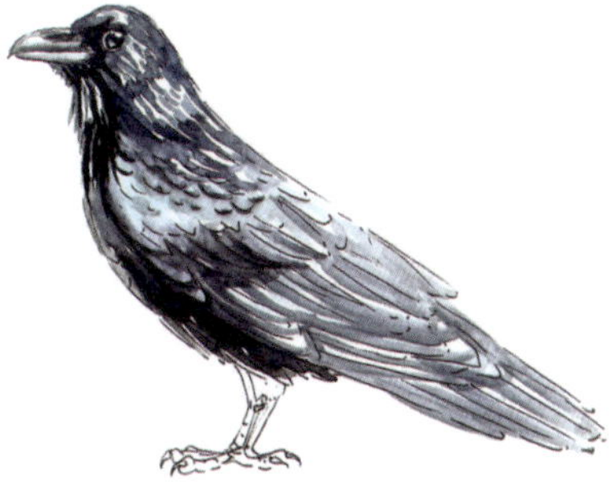

7. While it's still wet, slightly smooth the strokes to blend with the underpainting you created. The feathers become much darker, but don't look flat – great!

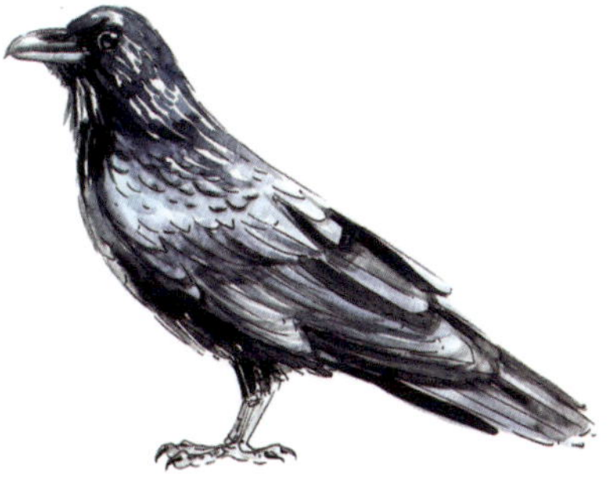

8. Continue in the same way to create value across the whole wing. Final touch: paint the feathers covering the legs and the legs themselves, which look lighter than the bird.

Woodpeckers

Along with flickers, sapsuckers, piculets and wrynecks

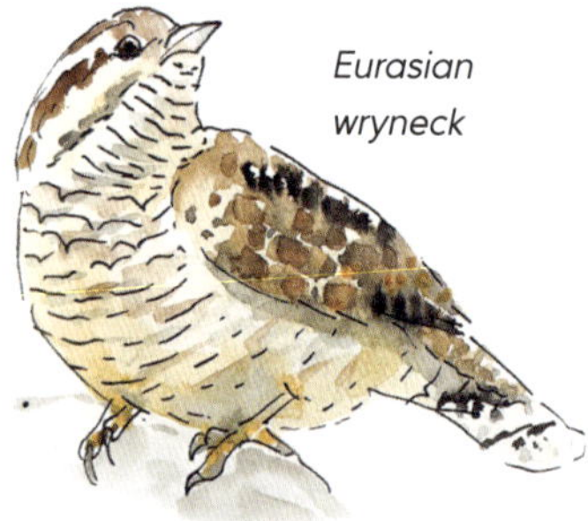

Eurasian wryneck

This amazing family of birds has many distinguishing characteristics but is best known for the drumming sounds they make to communicate. And of course, their habit of pecking wood gave the family its name. They do this to feed by picking out insects from trunks. For this, they use their very long tongues, which go far behind their eyes when folded.

Another anatomical peculiarity about these birds is their feet – unlike most birds, they have two toes pointing forward and two backward. This, along with the stiff feathers on the tail that some woodpeckers have, helps them grip firmly when they climb trees.

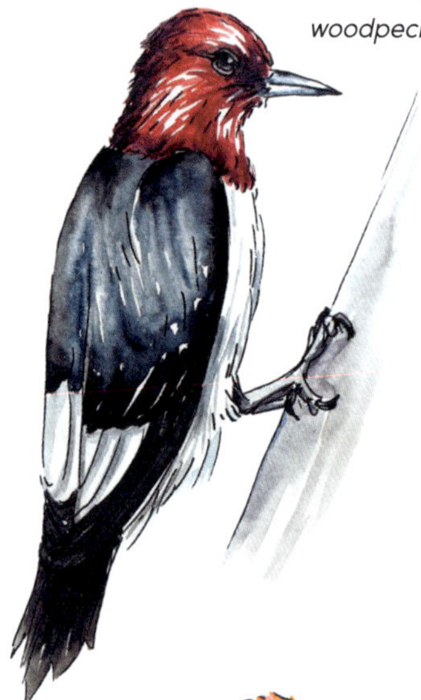

Red-headed woodpecker

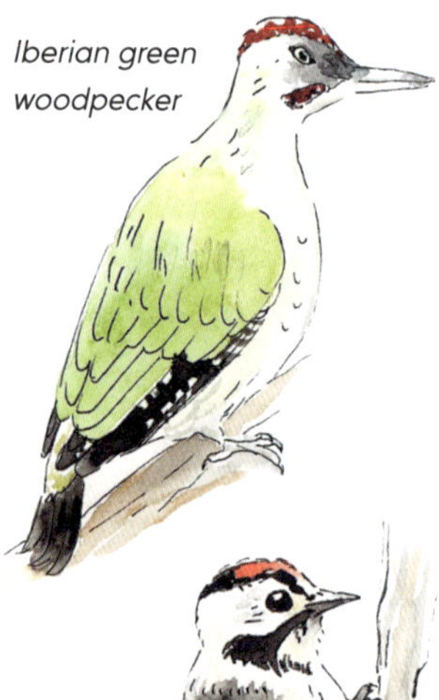

Iberian green woodpecker

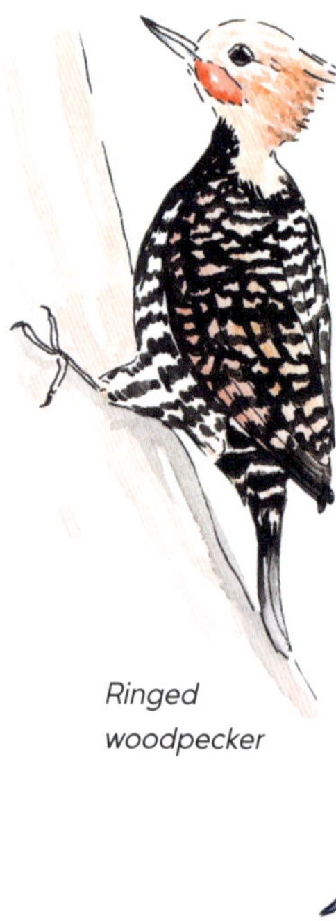

Ringed woodpecker

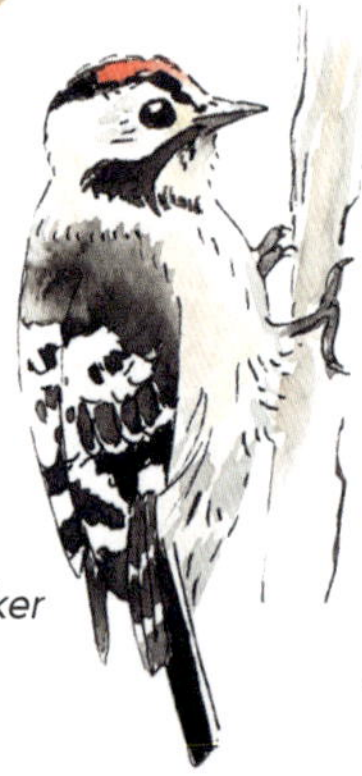

Lesser spotted woodpecker

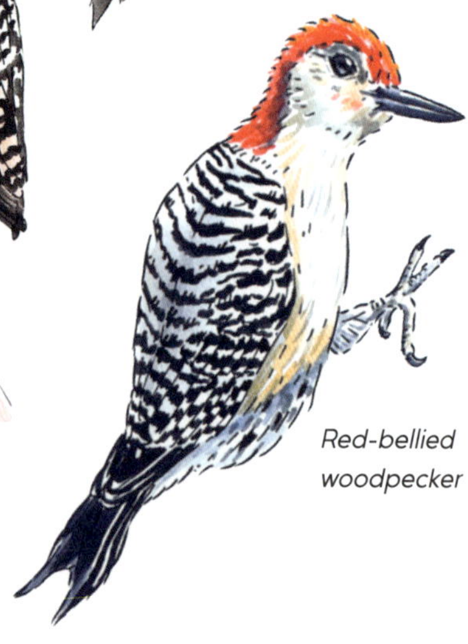

Red-bellied woodpecker

Great spotted woodpecker

Dendrocopos major

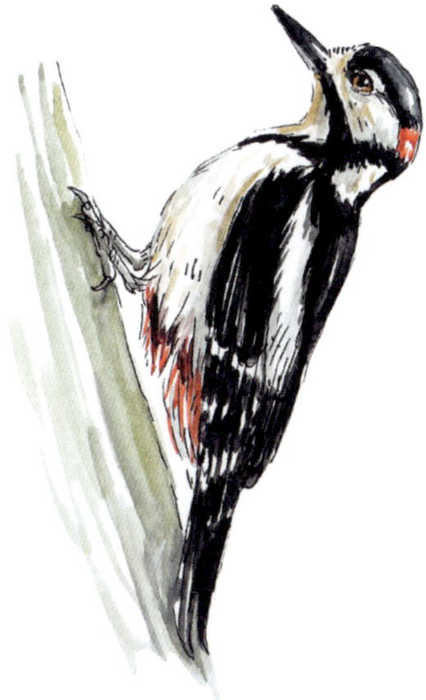

There are more than 200 species in the woodpecker family and the great spotted woodpecker is the most widespread among them, living across Europe, Asia and parts of North Africa.

Maybe it doesn't have a crest like some other woodpeckers and isn't brightly coloured, but it has this recognizable black-and-white colouration. Combined with a few red patches, this creates the classic, well-known look of woodpeckers.

Key feature

This is the typical pose of a woodpecker ready to peck wood: vertical profile with its claws clinging to the tree and the tail pressed against the trunk. Let's draw it!

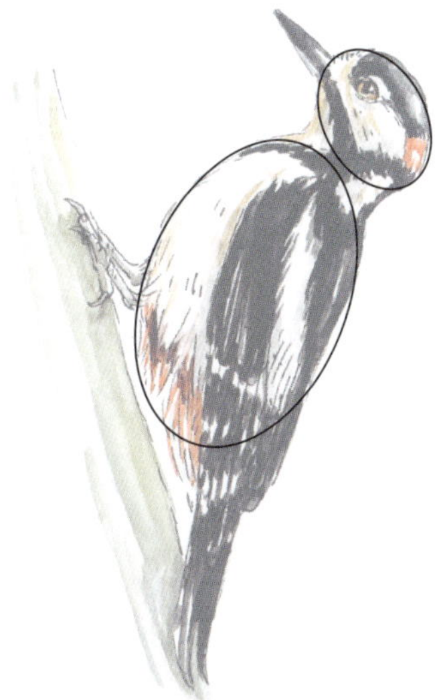

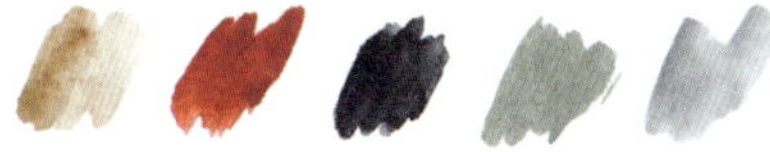

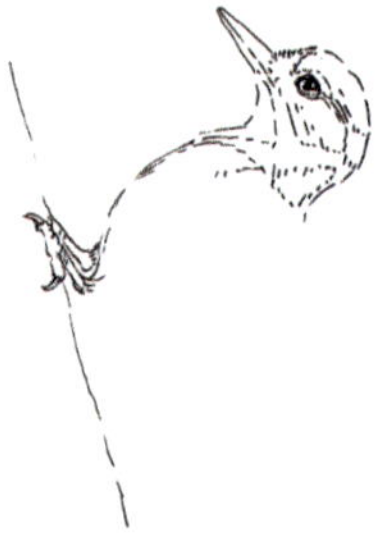

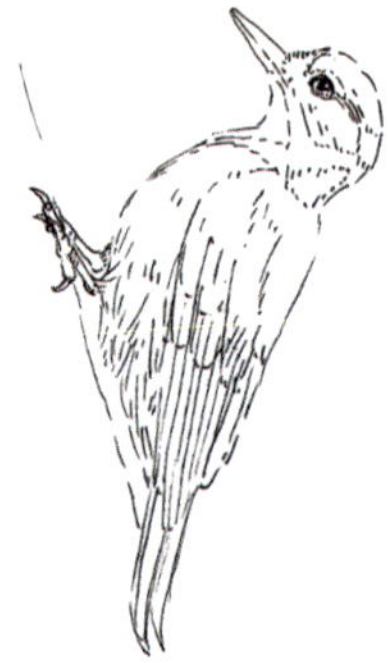

1. For this drawing, start by defining the surface the bird is clinging to. Then add the legs, breast and head along with the contours of the main colour patches.

2. We'll paint most of the wing with black, but it's still better to define the main parts with pen. Add messy feathers on the belly and undertail, and show how the tail is covering part of the trunk.

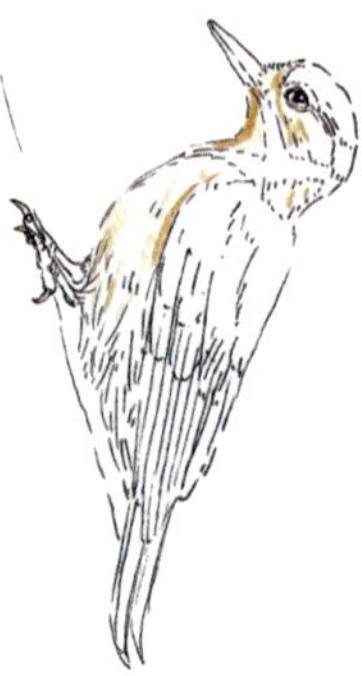

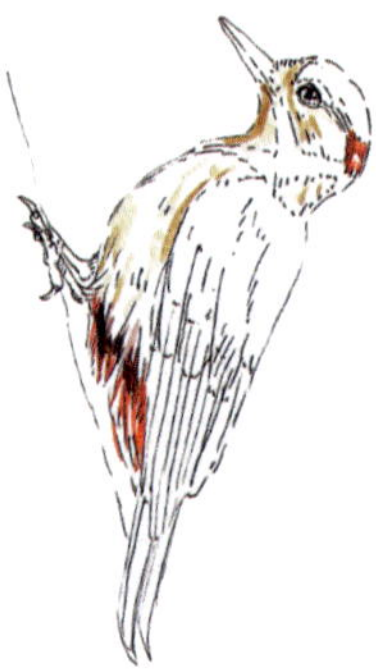

3. Start colouring from the lightest areas. These areas seem almost white, though they have a nice ochre shade in the darkest parts.

4. The next colour is red. Use it for a patch on the back of the head, the lower belly and undertail. Darken the bottom part a bit, since it's in shadow when a bird is in such a vertical pose.

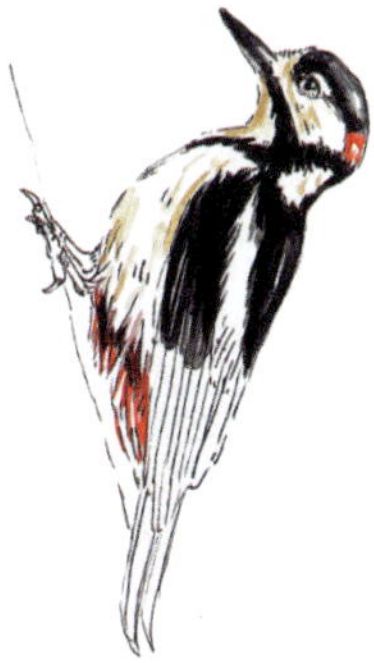

5. Be extra careful when adding the black – we need to repeat the shapes correctly. Leave a bit of white space here and there, and create a slight graduated wash to give a sense of volume.

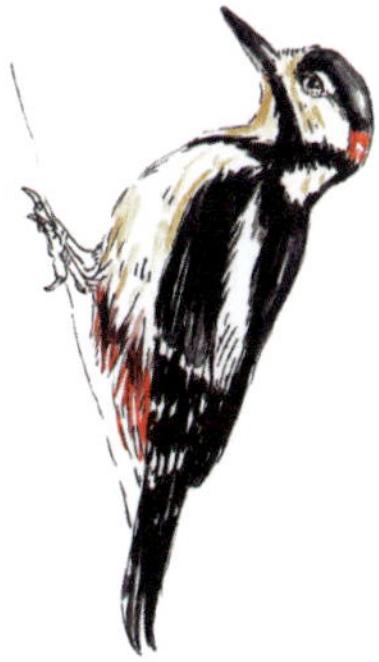

6. The white spots on the wing look like bars when it's folded – don't forget to show this. The side feathers of the tail are also striped, but we can barely see them from this angle.

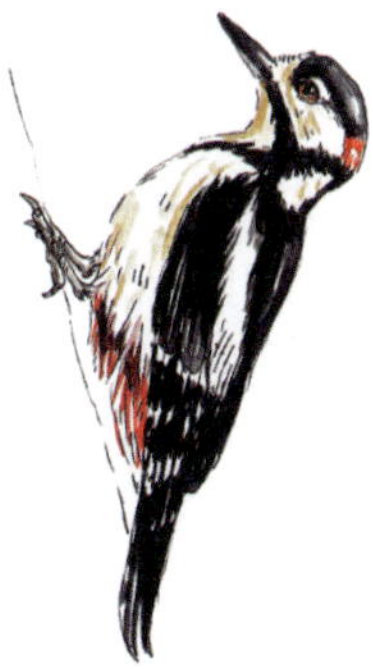

7. The eye is big enough in this sketch for us to see its dark reddish-brown colour. For the legs, use diluted black to create a grey shade.

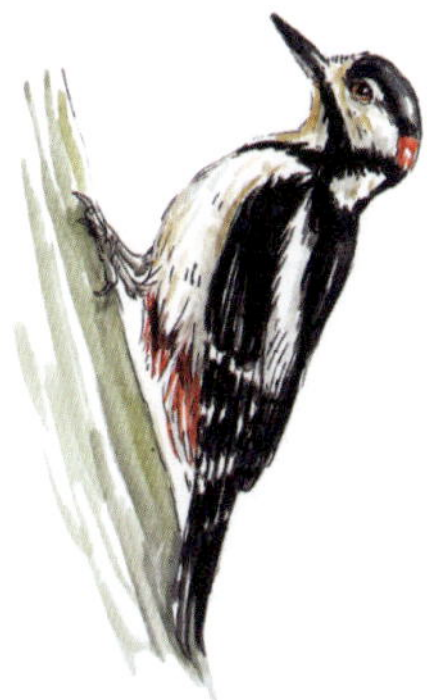

8. The shadows are not that dark along the wing here because of the pose, but we still have them on the neck and under the bird, of course. Paint the trunk if you have time.

Cuckoos

Coucals, couas, malkohas, roadrunners, anis and koels

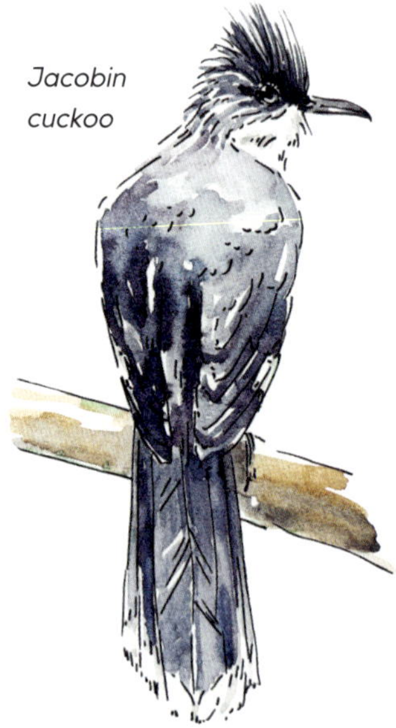

Jacobin cuckoo

Ranging across all continents except Antarctica, these usually solitary birds became famous as brood parasites – meaning they lay their eggs in other birds' nests. To be fair, only around a third of the species in the cuckoo family do so – most of them do build their own nests.

These birds are harder to see than to hear. The whole family was named after the call of the male common cuckoo. If you listen to the other species, you'll be surprised by the variety of sounds they produce.

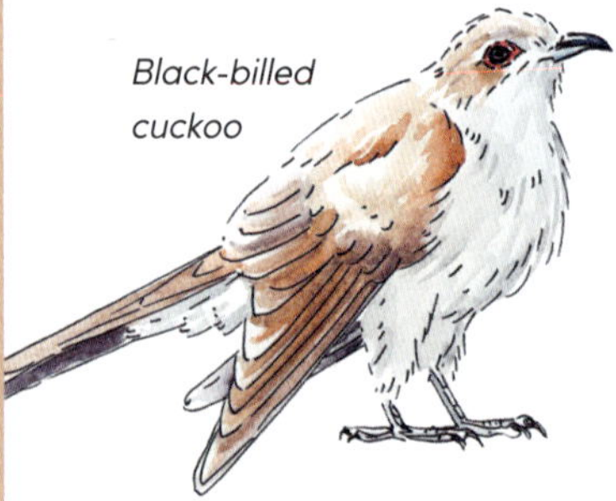

Black-billed cuckoo

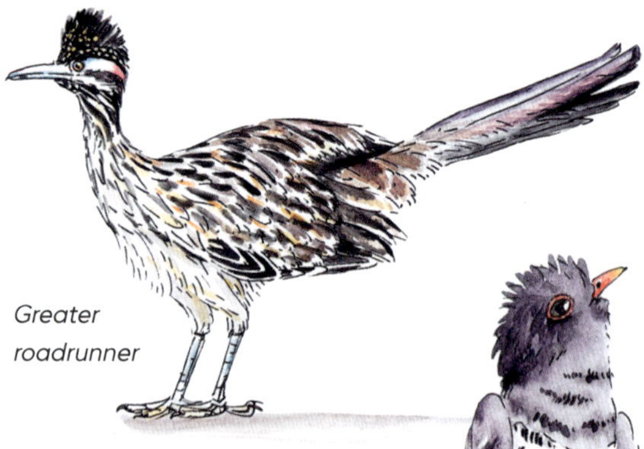

Greater roadrunner

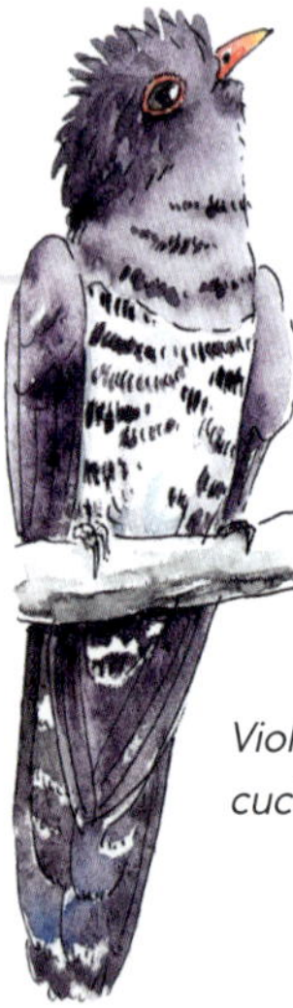

Violet cuckoo

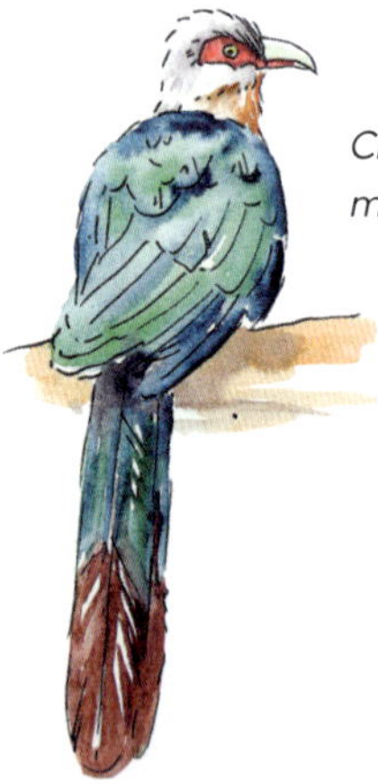

Chestnut-breasted malkoha

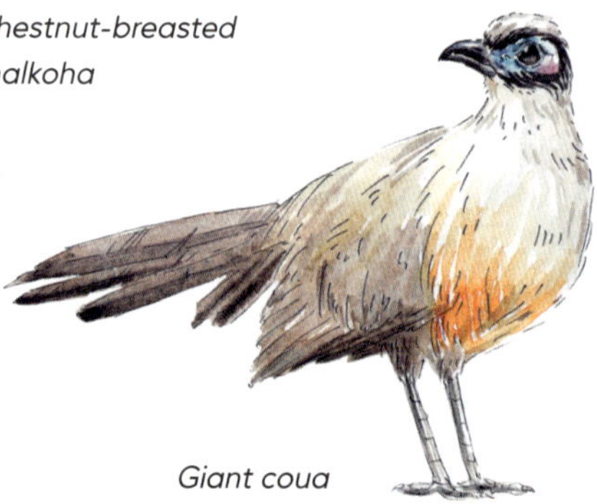

Giant coua

Common cuckoo

Cuculus canorus

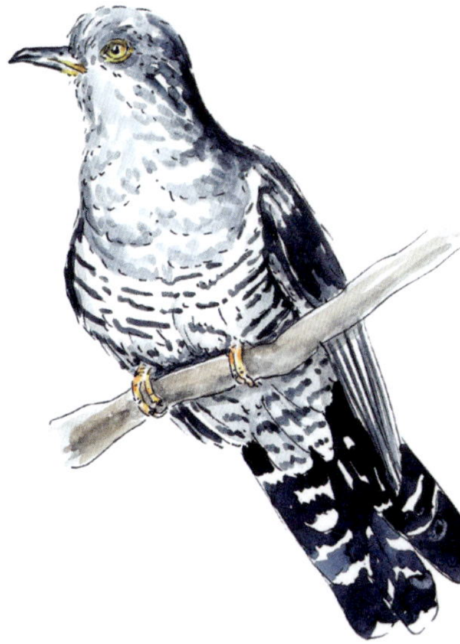

The common cuckoo doesn't just lay eggs that look like the eggs of the nest's hosts, but the adults themselves also imitate other birds! The stripes on the underparts of the bird resemble the plumage of some birds of prey, which the cuckoo uses to alarm the hosts of the nest and to lay its own egg there.

All cuckoos have slender bodies with a comparatively long tail. But we'll be drawing it with the tail slightly up, so it doesn't look that long and the overall drawing is more compact.

Key feature

We'll be drawing the bird with the body almost facing forward and the head in profile. In this pose you can see how feathers intersect each other in the middle of the belly.

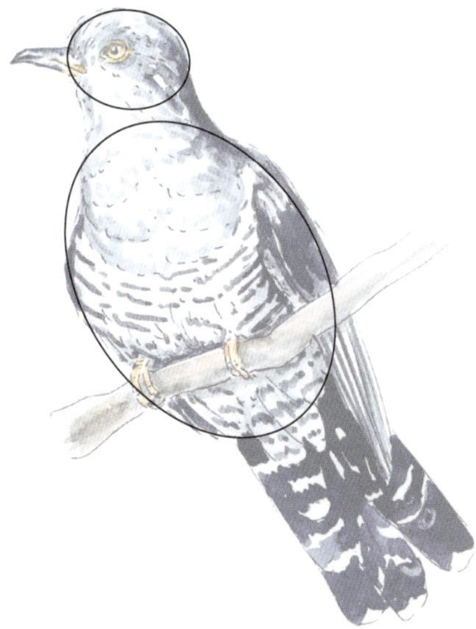

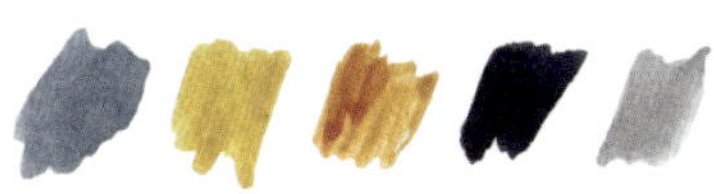

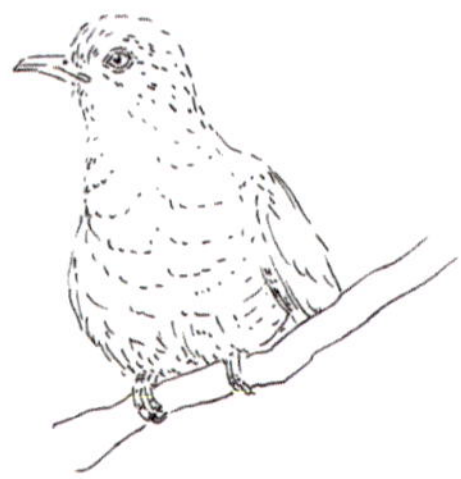

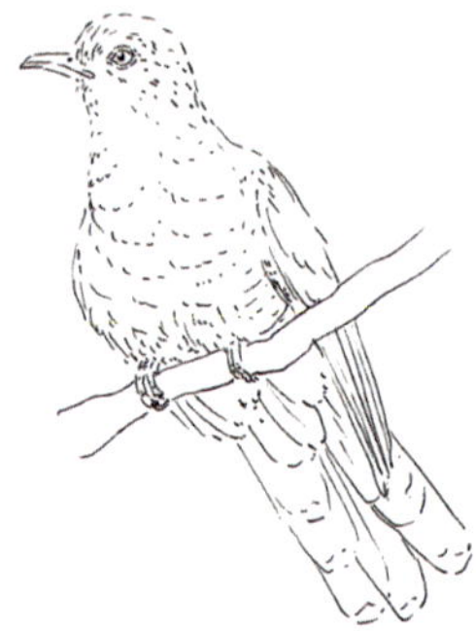

1. Important details are the eye-ring, the semicircled texture of the breast feathers and the structure of the feet – which is similar to the woodpecker's, so we see only two toes in front.

2. In this pose the branch is dividing the drawing into two parts. Add the bottom part of the belly, wing and the tail under the branch.

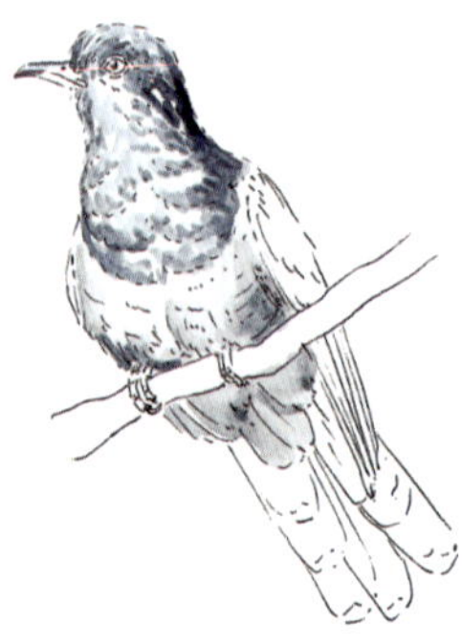

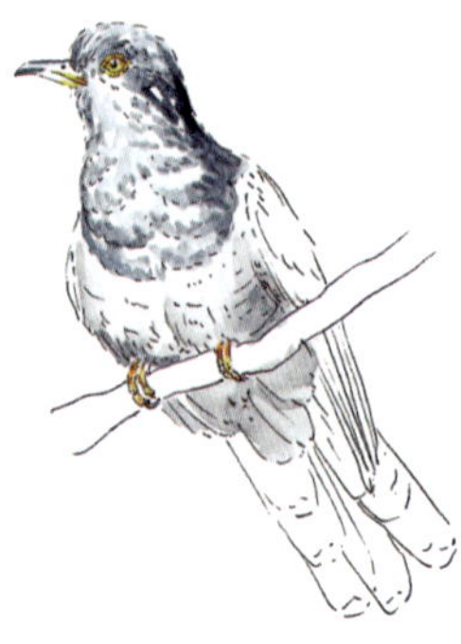

3. The bluish-grey plumage on the breast has visible layers. Use the same colour to create underpainting for the bottom part of the breast and belly. Create volume by darkening some parts.

4. While the wash is drying, colour the yellow parts: the base of the beak, the iris, the eye-ring and the legs. Don't make it flat – mix some brownish shades into your yellow to show depth.

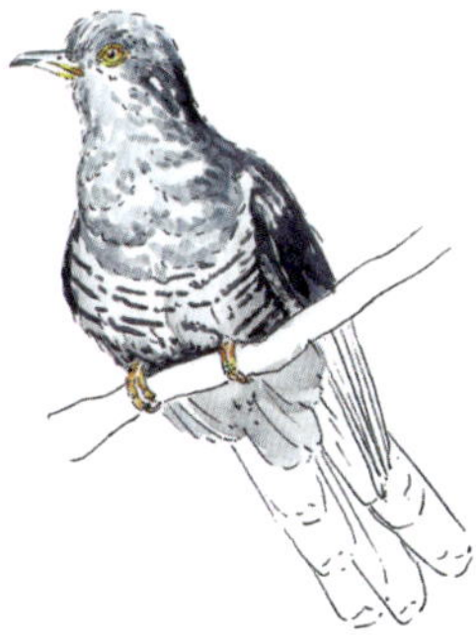

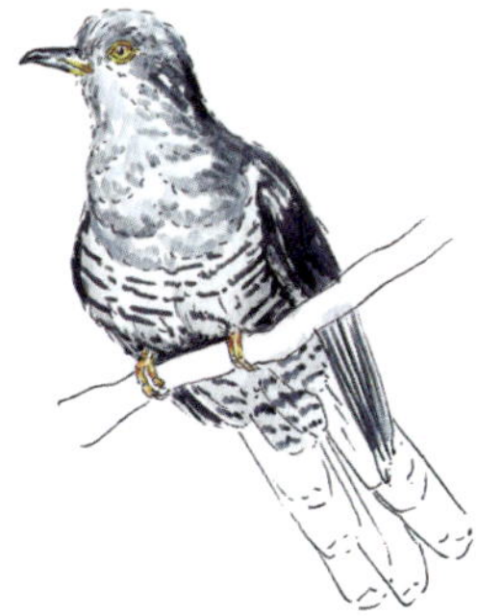

5. To paint the bars, be sure that your brush is dry enough to make thin clean lines. Darken the feathers that are behind the branch and paint the wing with the same colour.

6. Going below the branch, apply the same striped pattern on the bottom and add a few straight strokes to colour the wing feathers. Don't forget that we see the left wing, too!

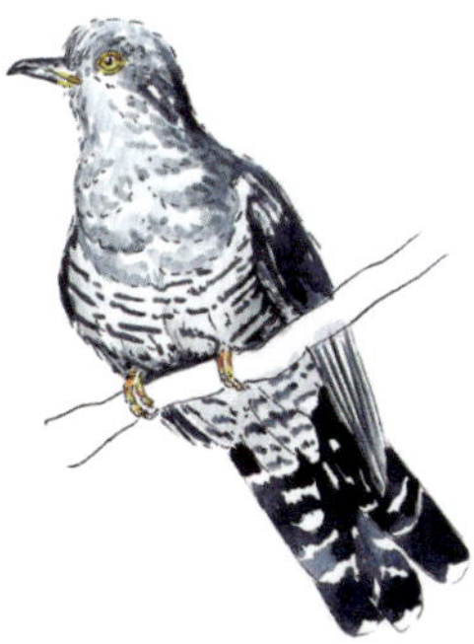

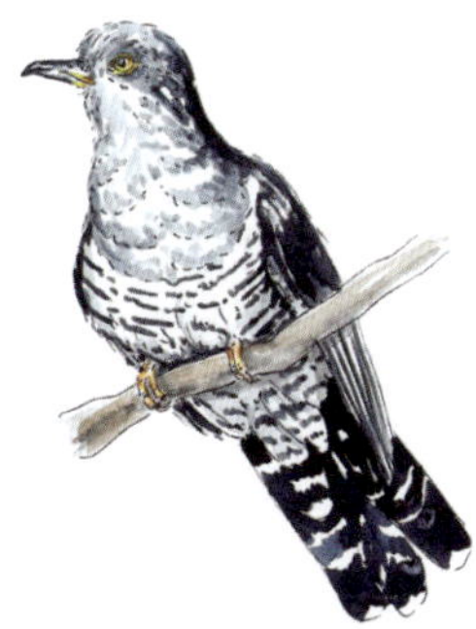

7. If the breast and belly looked like dark stripes on a white surface, the tail looks exactly opposite – cover it with dark colour, leaving white bars across and on the tips.

8. Colour the branch and add some shadows with a semi-transparent wash under the legs on the branch, and under the branch on the bird itself.

Penguins

From emperor to little blue

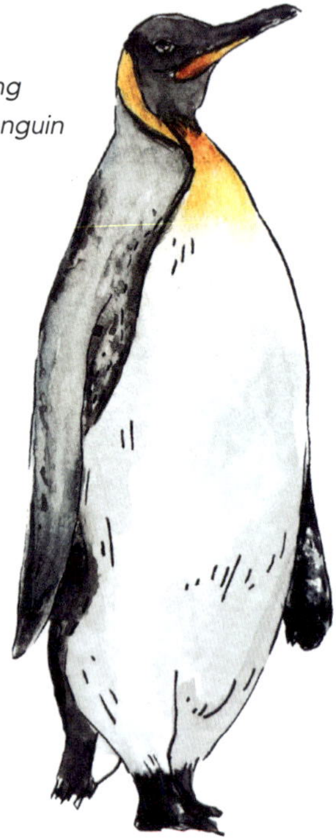

King penguin

Penguins are a group of birds that are loved by people around the world. These flightless birds live in colonies in different parts of the Southern Hemisphere. They eat fish and other sea creatures and are famous for their swimming skills. There are 18 recognized species and, although they are all different sizes, they share a similar body type with a thick layer of fat to keep them warm.

They usually have black and white plumage. Their wings have become flippers and the feathers are also quite different from those of other birds – they are short and thick, which also helps in swimming.

Fiordland penguin

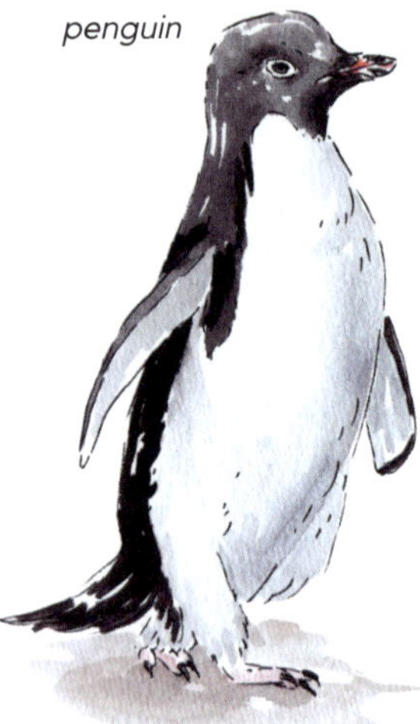

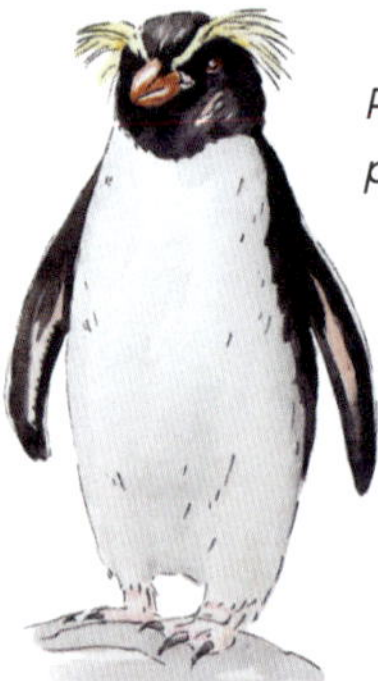

Rockhopper penguin

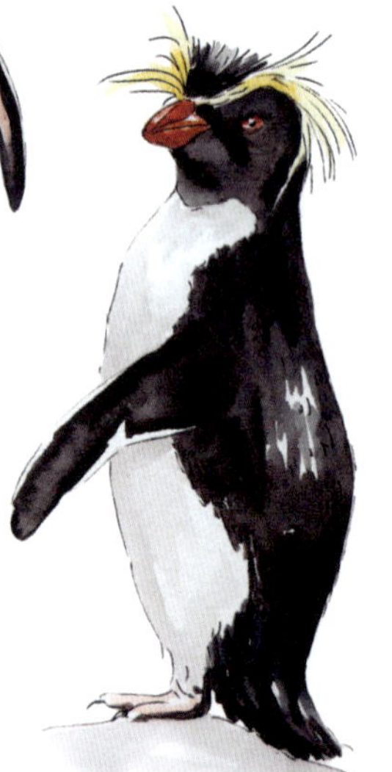

Little penguin

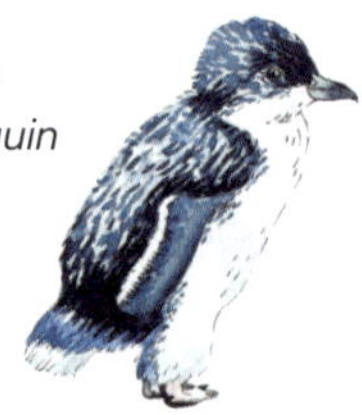

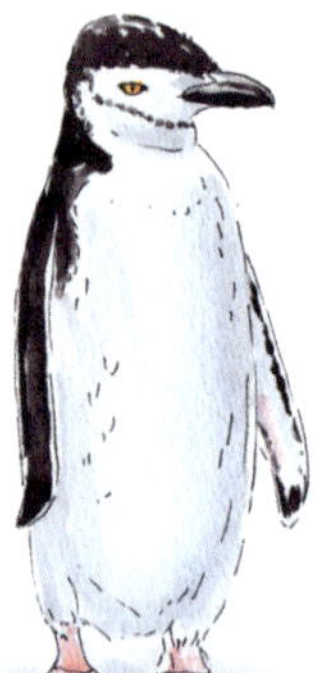

Chinstrap penguin

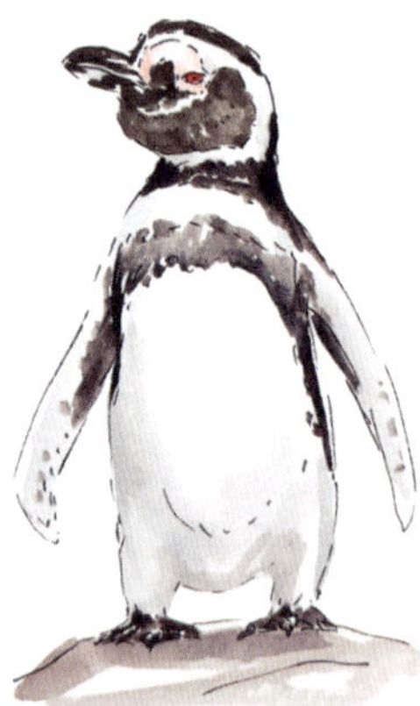

Magellanic penguin

Gentoo penguin

Pygoscelis papua

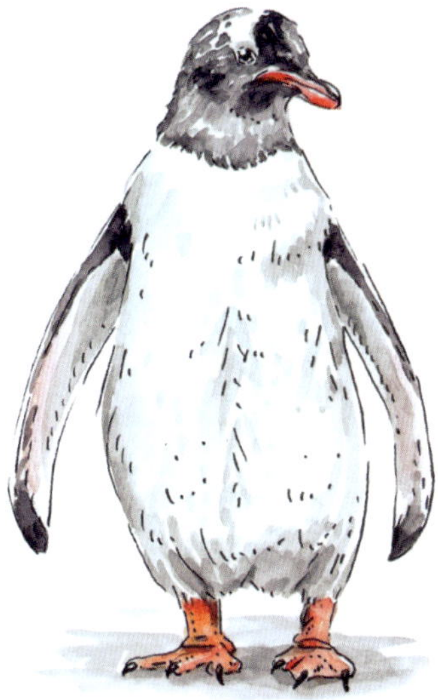

I personally find gentoo penguins one of the cutest among all the penguin species. These are the third-largest penguins and the fastest-swimming birds in the world!

They are easily recognized by the white patch going from one eye to the other across the top of the head. Apart from this patch and the bright beak, the rest of the body is typical for penguins.

Key feature

To show how most species of penguins look, we'll draw it standing with the body facing forward and the head slightly turned.

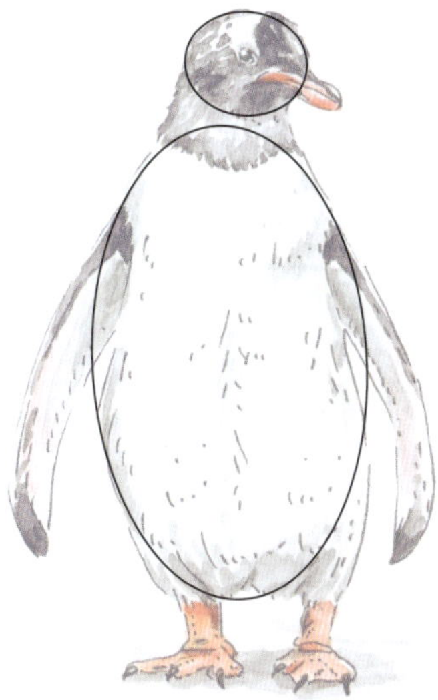

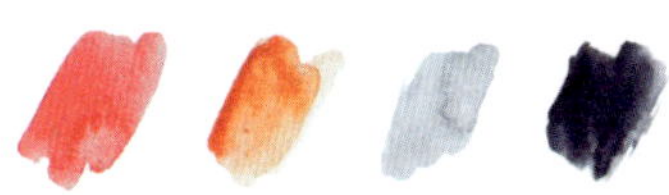

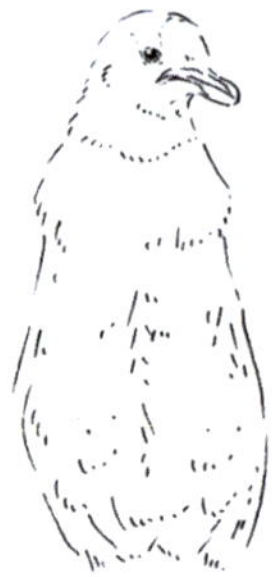

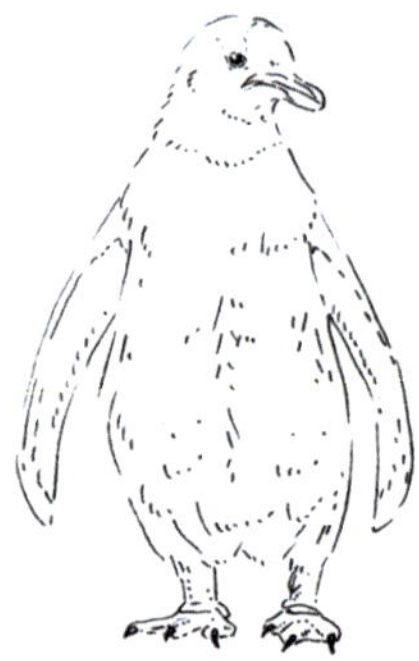

1. Move from top to bottom of the bird's body. Show the short feathers of the bird and the middle line going through the body.

2. Add the wings, which are really different from other birds' and have a much simpler shape. Draw the legs and the feet with the webbing between the toes.

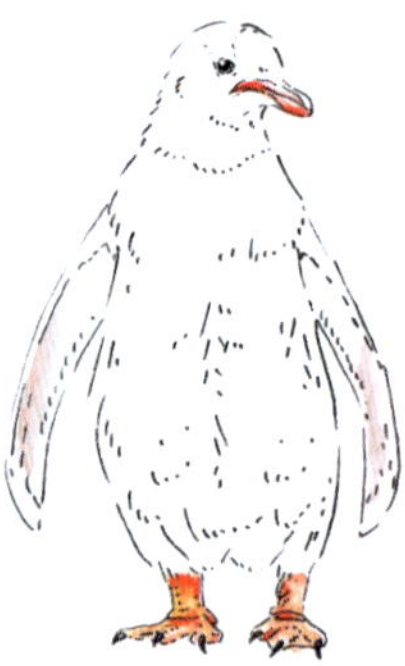

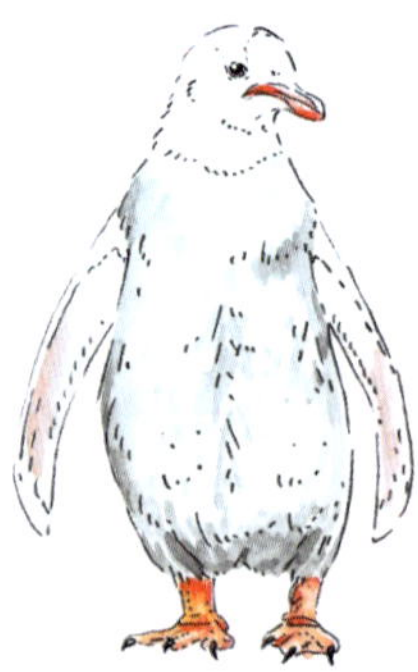

3. Start colouring from the red beak and legs. Differentiate the value of the colour depending on the parts. Add some pinkish hue on the inside parts of the wings.

4. Show the volume of the body by adding some bluish-grey mixture on different parts of the breast and the belly. The darkest part is at the bottom between the legs.

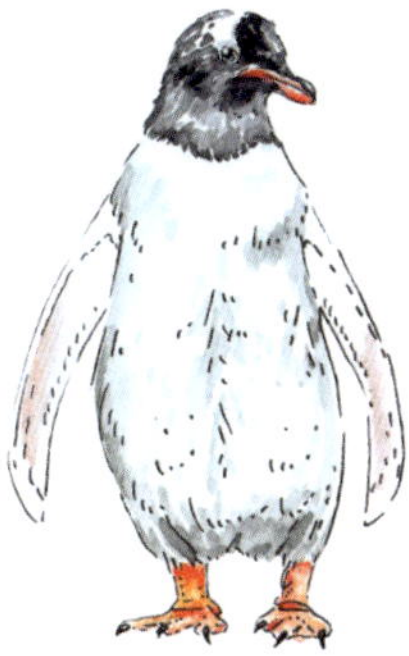

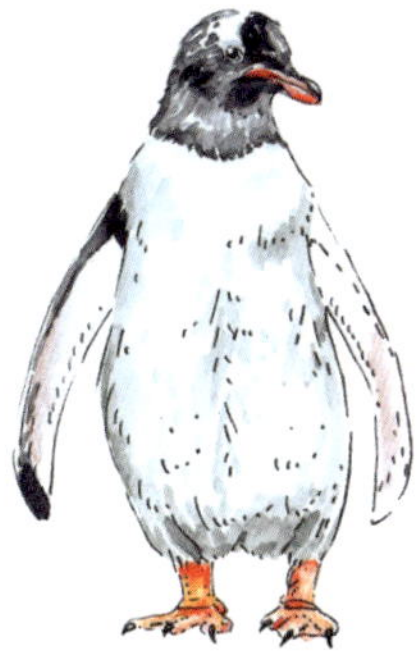

5. Add the black on the beak and head, showing the main white patches above the eye with this spotted pattern. Darken the bottom part of the head oval.

6. The black parts on the wing also have different volume. Make it darker on the top part, showing the "armpit" of the bird and lighter grey on the sides.

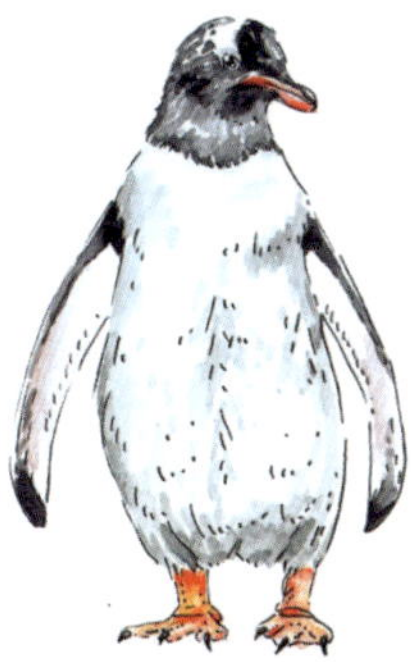

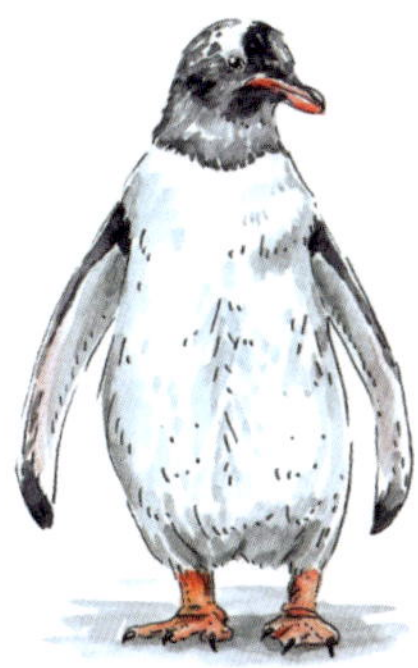

7. Same goes for the second wing. The texture of the greyish pattern can be different depending on the bird.

8. Darken some parts to create contrast: add shadows under the wings, on the legs and, of course, under the bird itself.

Shorebirds

Plovers, sandpipers, curlews, oystercatchers, avocets and others

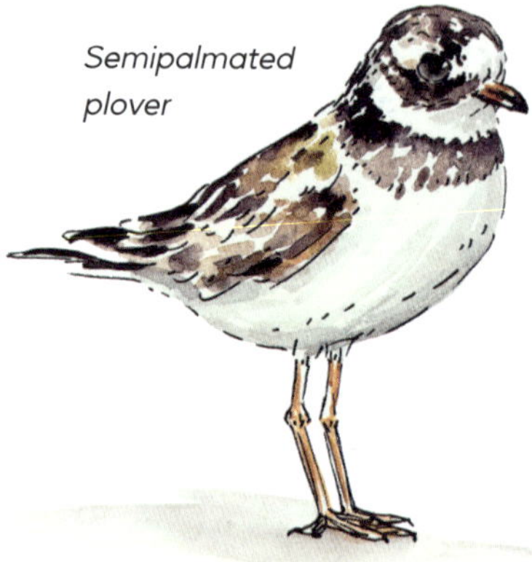

Semipalmated plover

Shorebirds, as the name suggests, live along shorelines. This habitat offers the main food source of insects and invertebrate animals hiding in the sand. For this, shorebirds have a variety of bill shapes, helping them to hunt.

The plumage of these birds is usually not colourful – but can have interesting patterns, which helps them blend with rocks and limited vegetation. They have a distinctive tall posture because of comparatively long and thin legs.

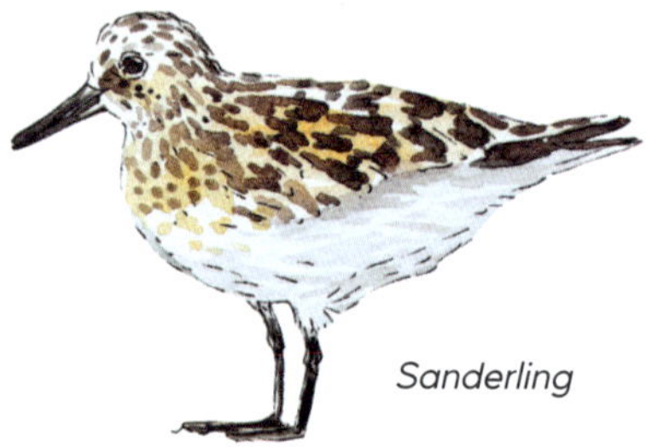

Sanderling

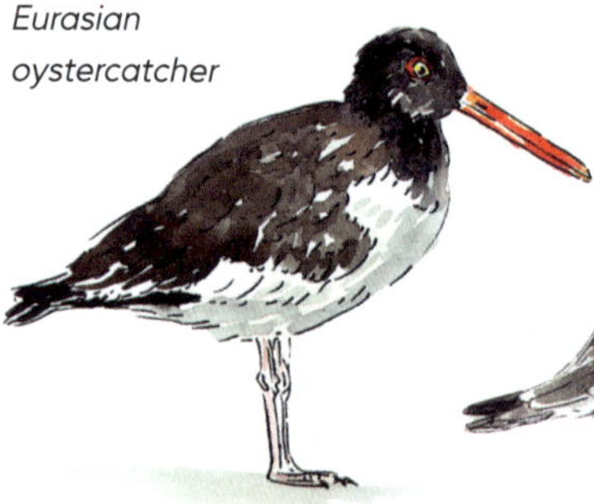

Eurasian oystercatcher

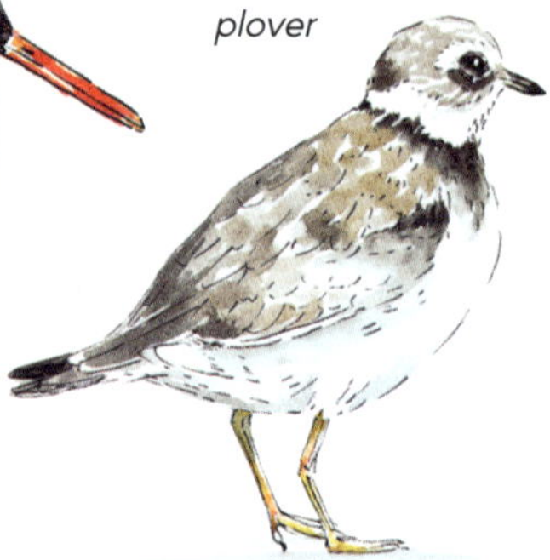

Ringed plover

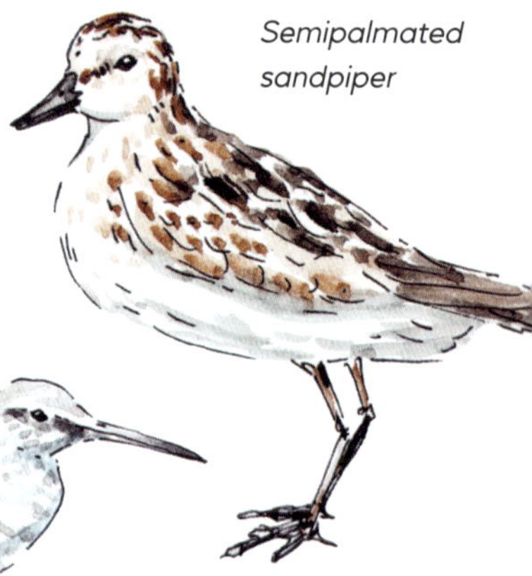

Semipalmated sandpiper

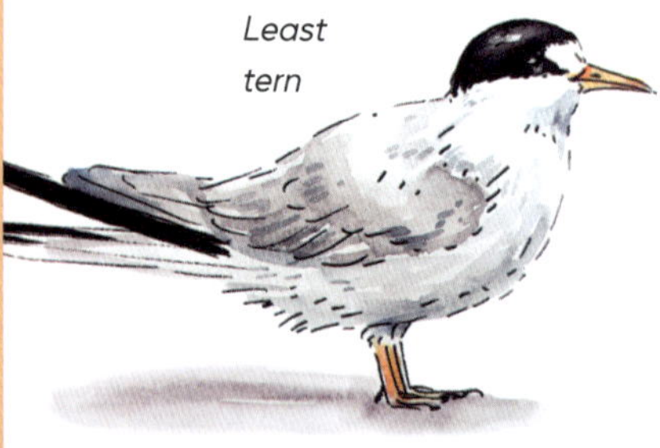

Least tern

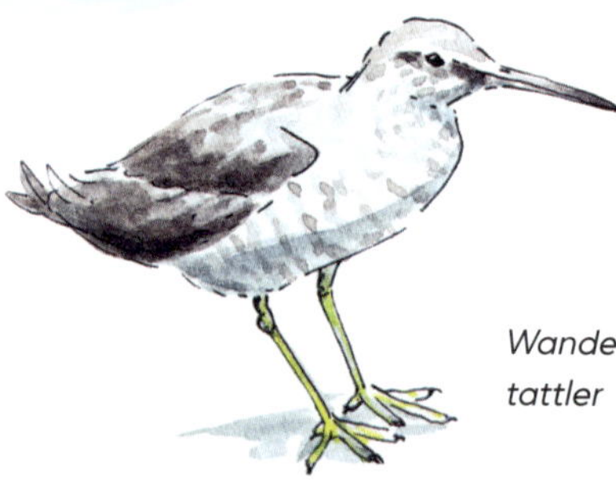

Wandering tattler

Ruddy turnstone

Arenaria interpres

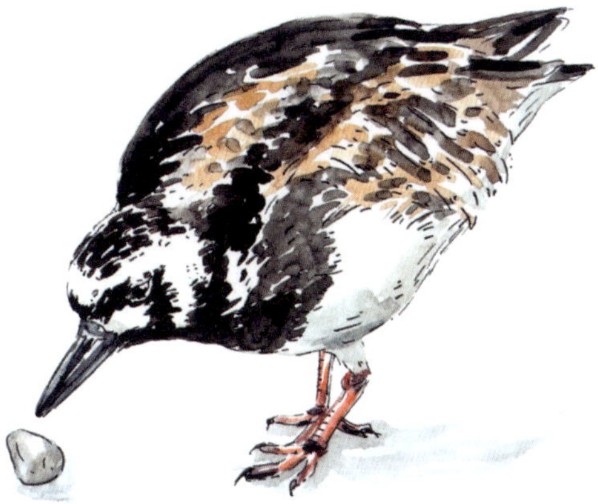

This bird from the sandpiper family is widespread and is often known simply as the turnstone. The name is a literal description of the bird's method of foraging: it turns stones and shells on the shore to find small invertebrates and insects hiding underneath. For this, the turnstone has a thick beak. The body might seem more compact and sturdy compared to some other shorebirds.

It has an interesting plumage that changes throughout the year. The breeding look is more striking, of course, with a beautiful contrast between black and white patches.

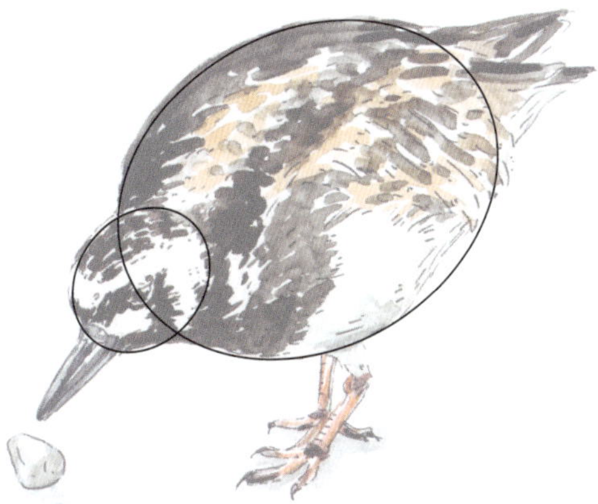

Key feature

We could draw it from different angles, but to show the action in the best way let's try the three-quarter view with the head almost at the ground. The neck is very shortened and the small tail is slightly popping out from behind.

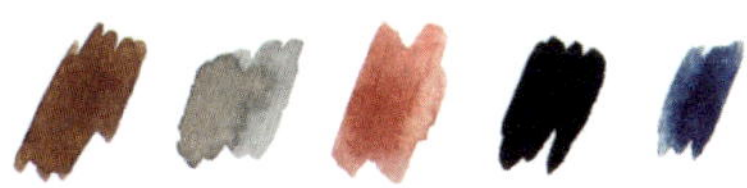

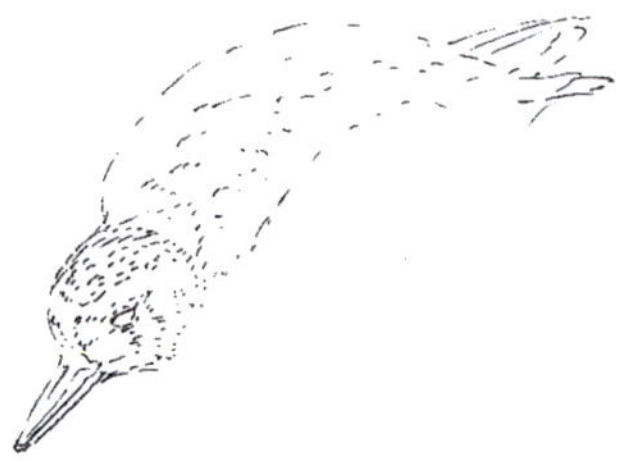

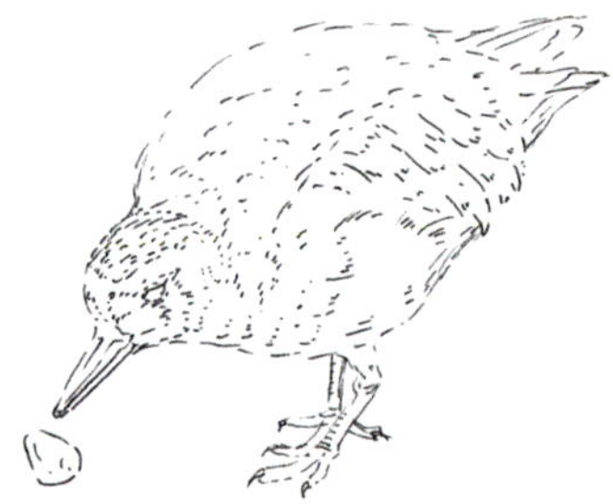

1. Start from the tip of the beak and continue to the top part, which here is the tail. Add texture, showing the main colour patches on the head and on the back.

2. Finalize the oval of the body and add legs. I thought it would be nice to draw this bird with the small stone it is turning.

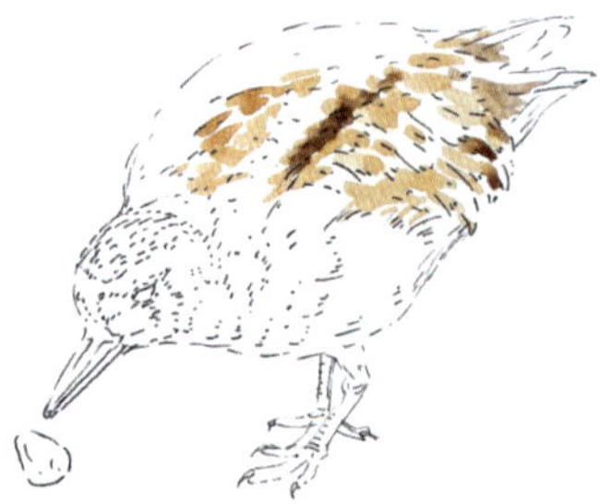

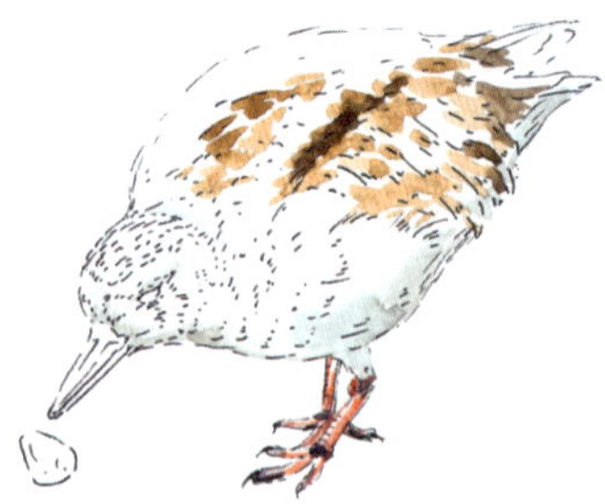

3. To make the interesting pattern this bird has, we'll make several layers. The first one is this brownish colour of different shades.

4. Give some volume to the white parts of the bird by making a graduated wash from bottom to top. Colour the legs with red. Notice the dark spots.

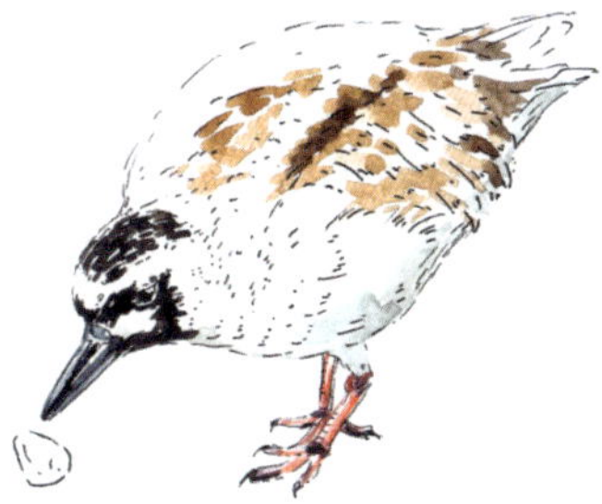

5. Drawing this black pattern isn't difficult – it's fun! Just show the most distinctive shapes with short strokes. Colour the eye and the beak, which might seem more bluish than the main black pattern.

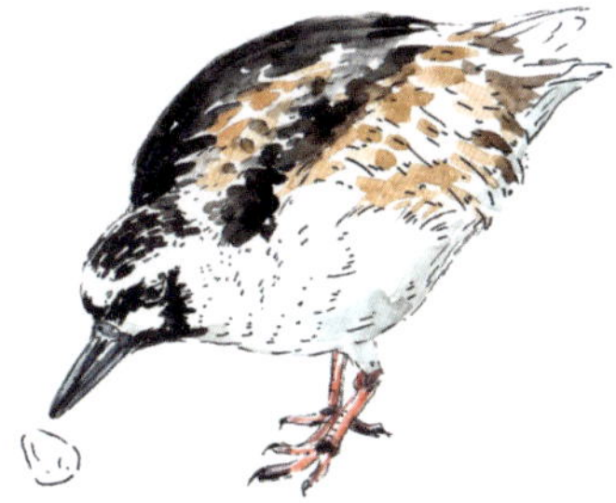

6. Continue adding black. The number of the dark spots on the back can vary, so don't overthink it – add some here and there to resemble the texture.

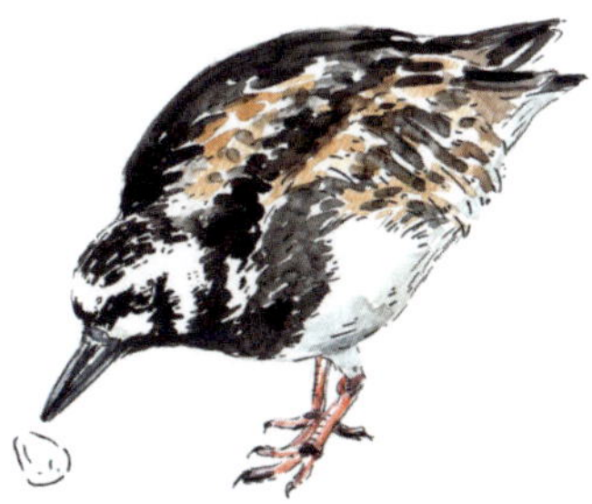

7. Finish the black pattern by adding a collar on the neck and across the breast up to the shoulder. I also added a few diluted black strokes to the wing that is overlapping the body.

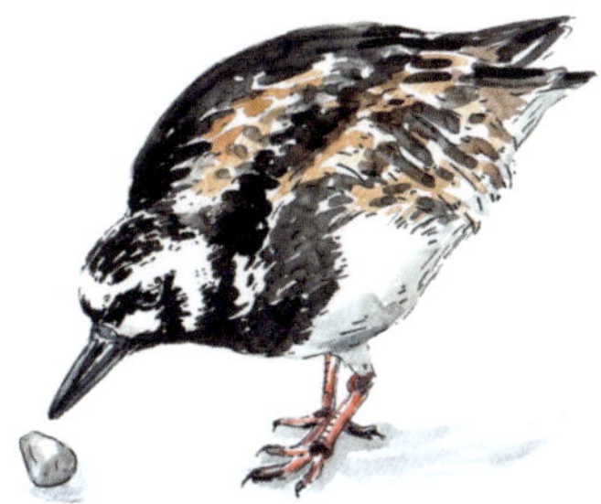

8. Add shadows under the bird, and colour the stone. Give it some shadow also, to connect it with the bird. Does it look like your turnstone is going to turn the stone?

Wading birds

Herons, egrets, ibises, spoonbills and allied species

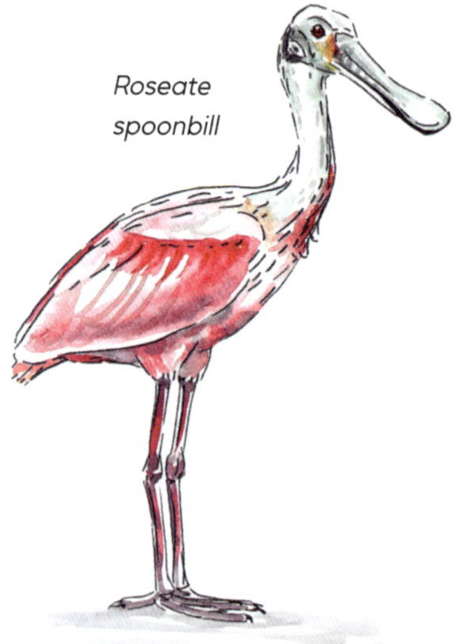

Roseate spoonbill

The line between shorebirds and wading birds is very thin. I prefer to think about wading birds as those that like freshwater ponds, lakes and marshes, while shorebirds live on salty beaches. However, many birds can be found on both kinds of shores.

But let's focus now on birds that have long legs and necks, and search for food not in mudflats but directly in calm shallow water. Their skinny legs with elongated toes help them move around. And a long beak in combination with an extended neck is the perfect tool for catching fish.

White-breasted waterhen

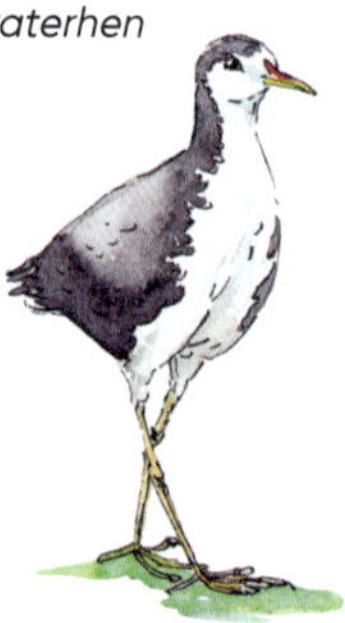

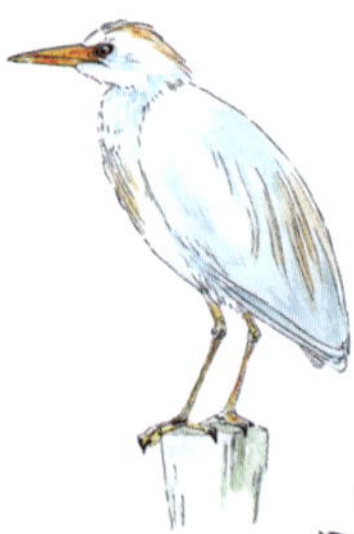

Cattle egret

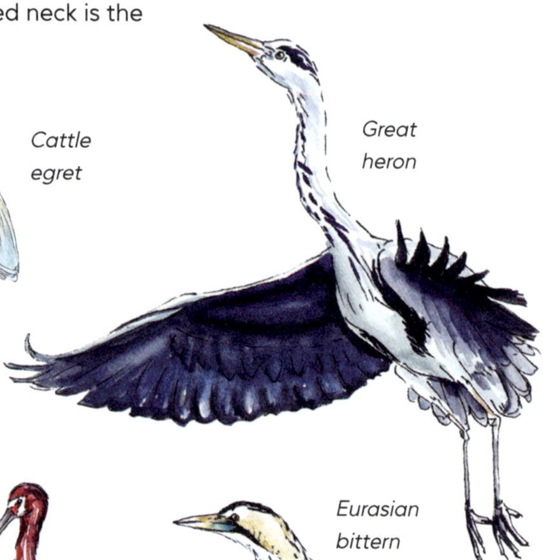

Great heron

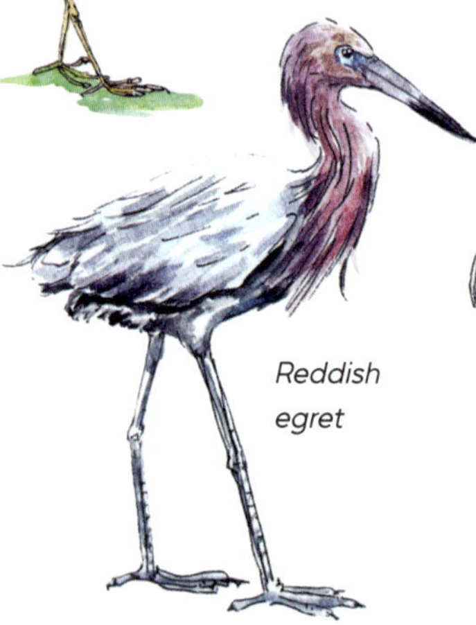

Reddish egret

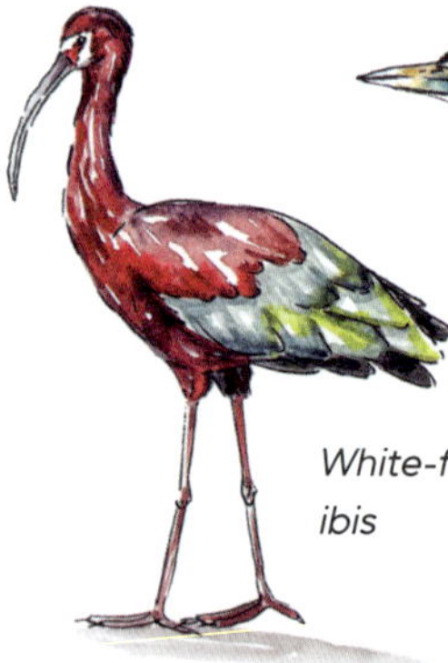

White-faced ibis

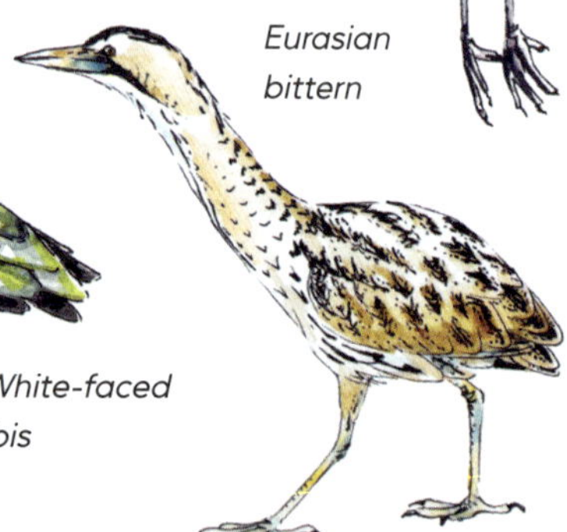

Eurasian bittern

Great egret

Ardea alba

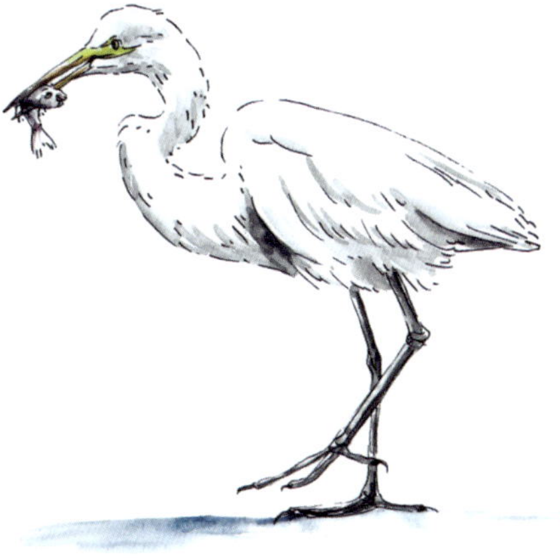

The great egret can be found in Europe, Asia, Africa and the Americas. It's a big white bird with a prominent yellow-orange beak.

In breeding plumage, great egrets have a stunning fan of feathers on the back, and the skin between the beak and the eye becomes greenish. Some subspecies also change the colour of the beak from orange to black during the mating season.

Key features

We'll learn how to draw a bird not just with such specific proportions but also while feeding. Plus I'll show you how to make a white bird stand out on the page.

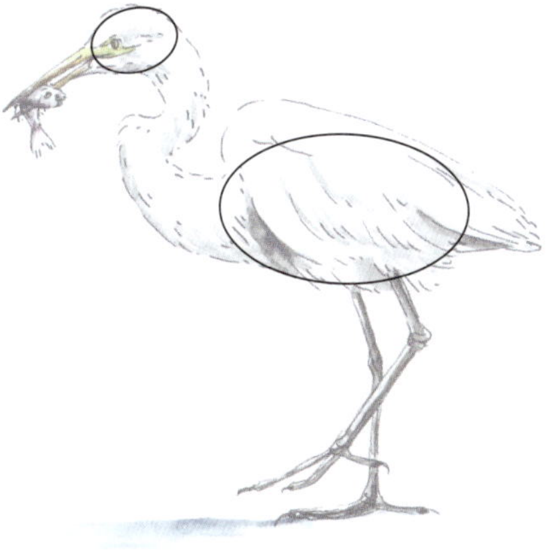

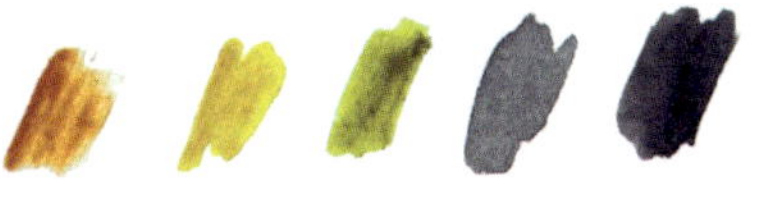

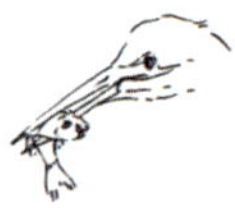

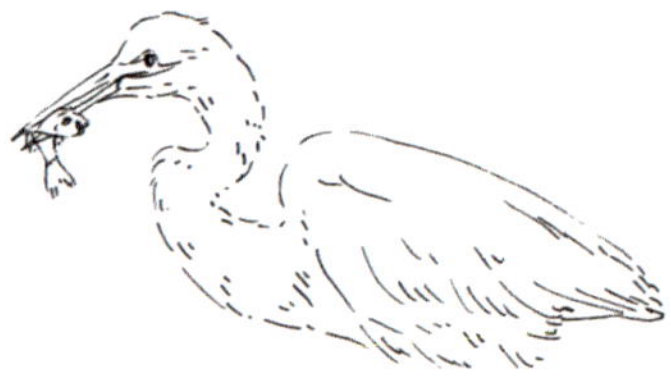

1. Begin with the top part of the beak, then draw the closest part of the fish, then the bottom part of the beak and finally the rest of the fish.

2. Draw the long S-shaped neck with short strokes and add the oval of the body, which in this pose is mostly covered by the wing.

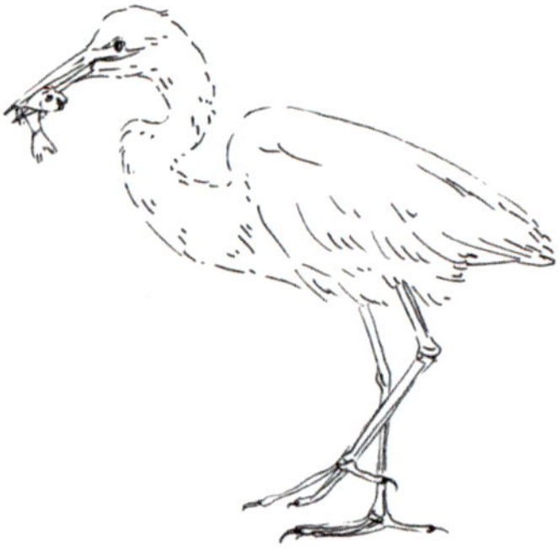

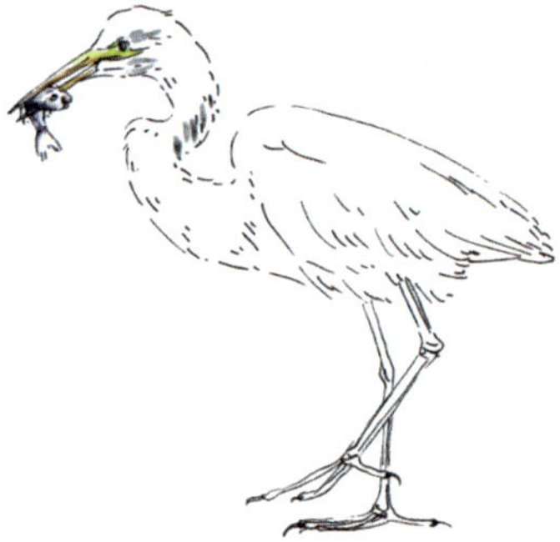

3. Finalize the line art by drawing the legs, which are really long – and we can see the upper part, which is usually hidden in most birds. Don't over-detail them though.

4. Paint the beak with orange and greenish yellow. Give some volume to the fish. For the neck, add a few bluish strokes on the darkest parts and move to the next step before the paint dries.

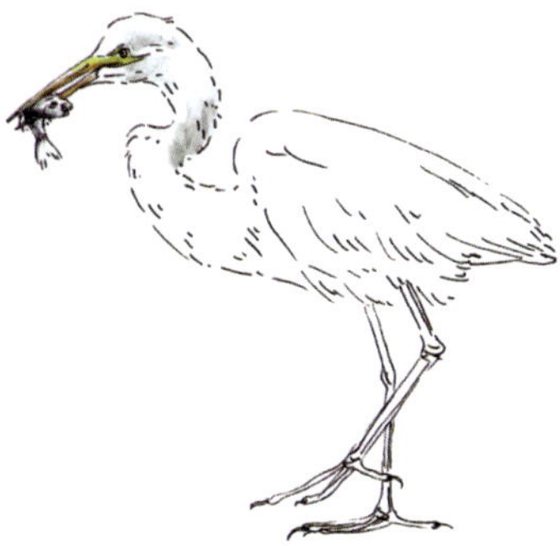

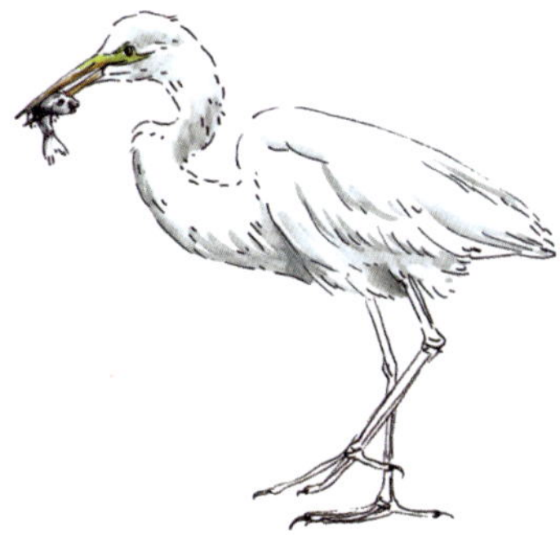

5. While these parts are still wet, smooth them to create a graduated wash. Now we have a white bird with volume that is clearly visible on white paper – that's a success!

6. Proceed in the same way when colouring the rest of the neck and the body. The darkest parts are at the very bottom of the bird and on different feather groups of the wing.

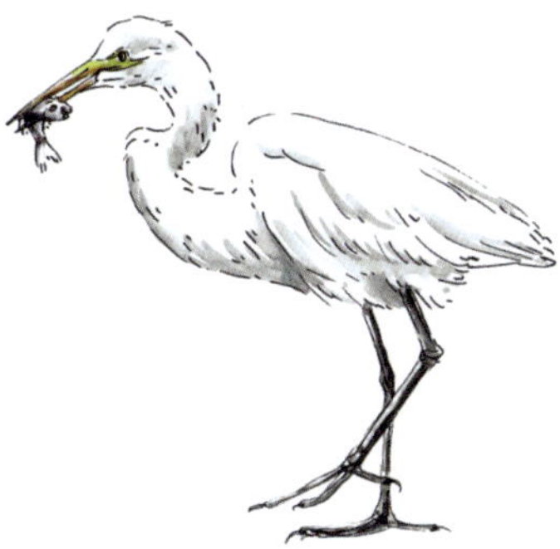

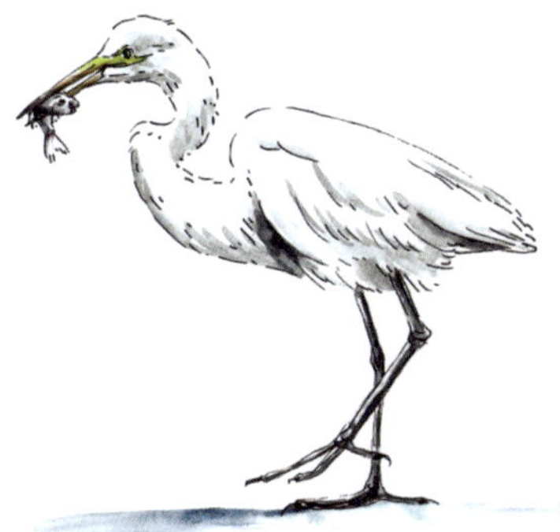

7. To colour the legs, just add a few dark strokes, keeping some space white to make it look like skin. Slightly darken the legs under the body.

8. Give more contrast to the bird by darkening the space on the neck and tail under the wing. I made the surface the bird is standing on more bluish than usual to resemble water.

Waterfowl

Ducks, geese, swans, teals, eiders, mergansers and others

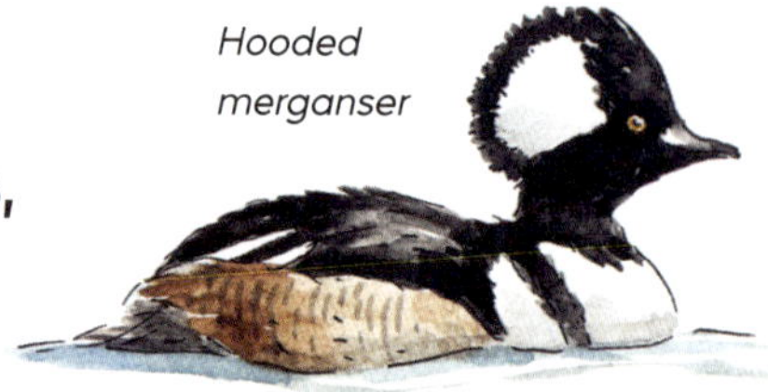

Hooded merganser

There are around 180 species in the order Anseriformes, also known as waterfowl. These aquatic birds are usually found in freshwater habitats. Many of them live in large colonies, and some are famous for forming long-term pair bonds.

They have adapted to spend the majority of their lives on the water. To do this, most of them have developed webbed feet, waterproof feathers, and broad beaks for filtering food and to eat vegetation specific to this habitat.

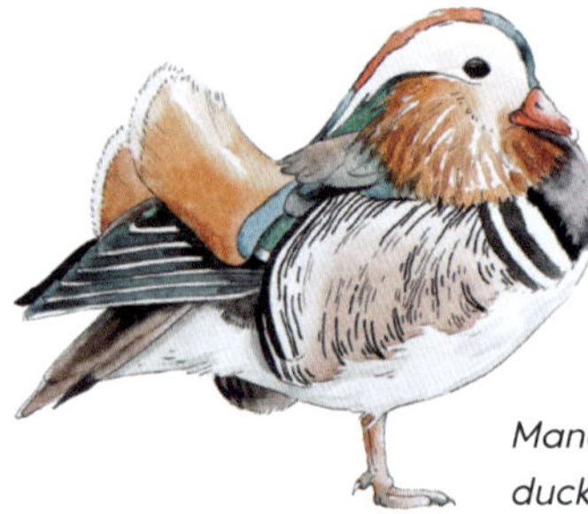

Mandarin duck

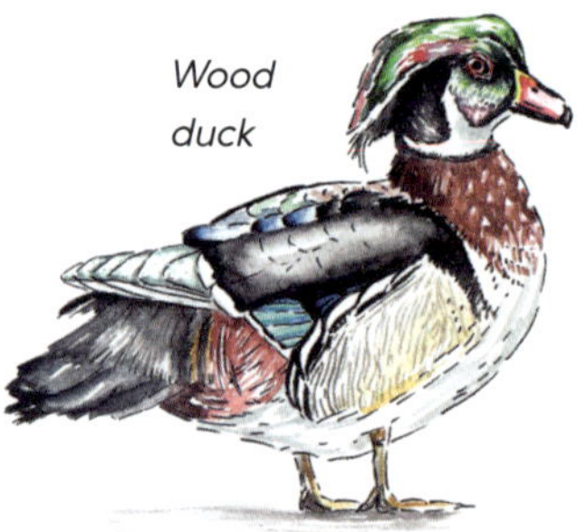

Wood duck

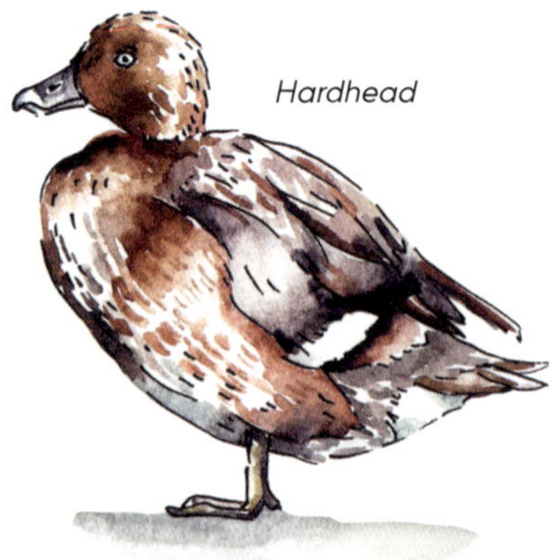

Hardhead

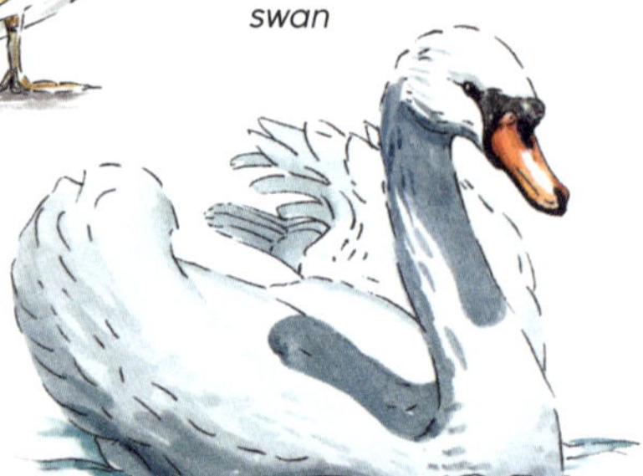

Mute swan

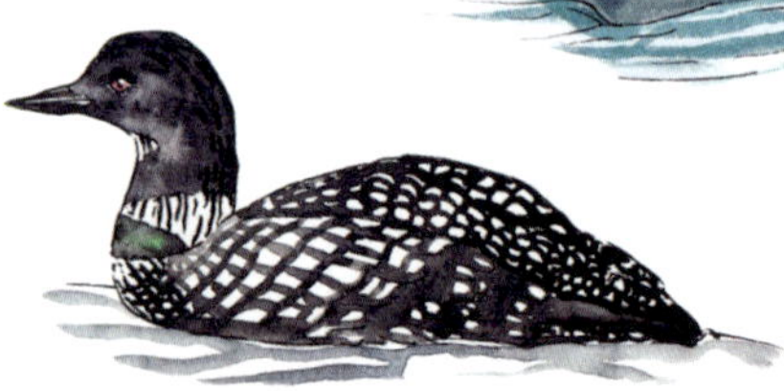

Common loon

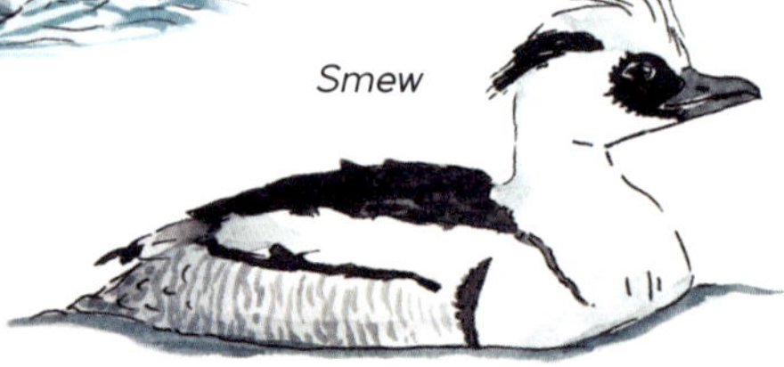

Smew

Mallard

Anas platyrhynchos

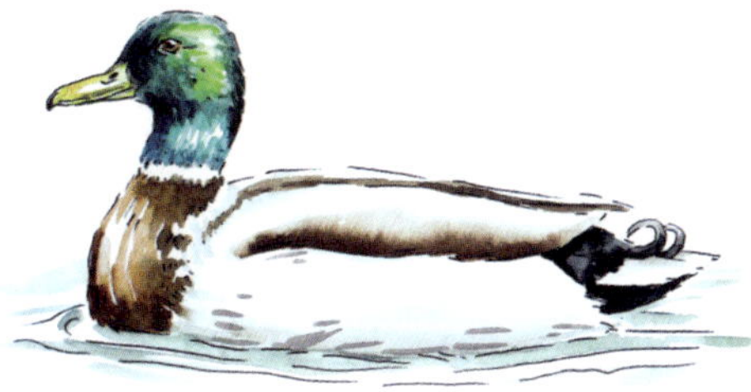

The most widespread duck in the world is the mallard, also known as the wild duck. If you have ducks on a nearby pond or lake, it's probably this one. Males and females look so different that some people think they are two different species. But males wear this gorgeous plumage only during breeding season – the rest of the year you can recognize them only by the colour of the beak.

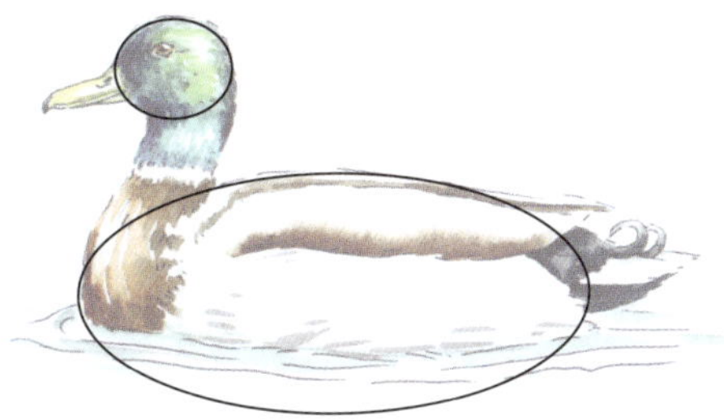

This bird has a very interesting anatomy and behaviour that became an object of scientific study, but we will focus on the plumage of the male bird for now.

Key feature

Drawing birds in water isn't as hard as may seem. To keep the proportions right, we just need to keep in mind that part of the bird isn't visible above the water line.

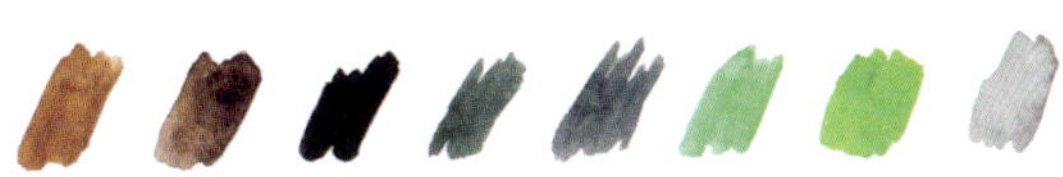

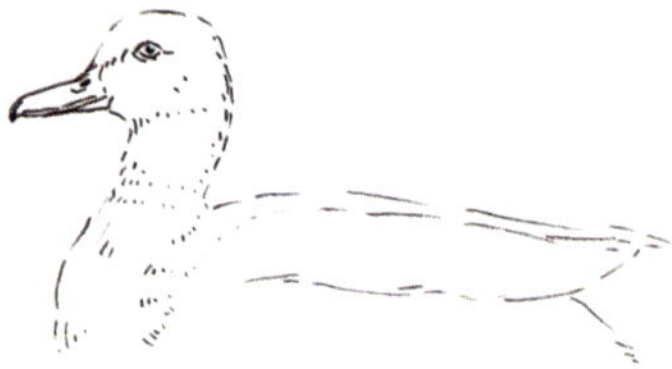

1. Focus on the beak – it's a very prominent feature of the bird. Show the direction of the feathers on the neck and breast and how the feathers of the belly are overlapping the wing.

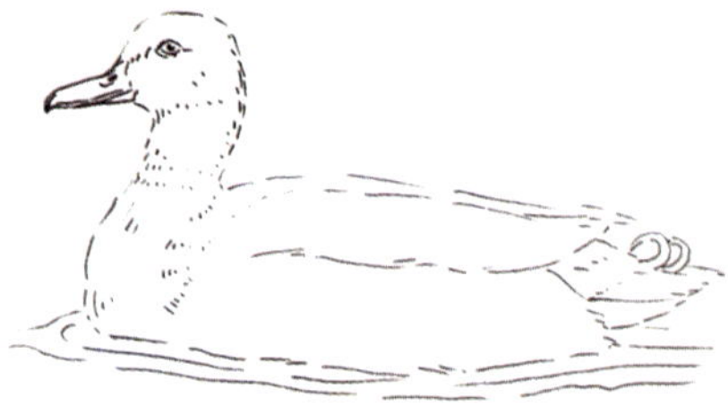

2. The oval of the body is partly hidden under the water. And the water shouldn't be a straight line – it also creates an oval around the bird.

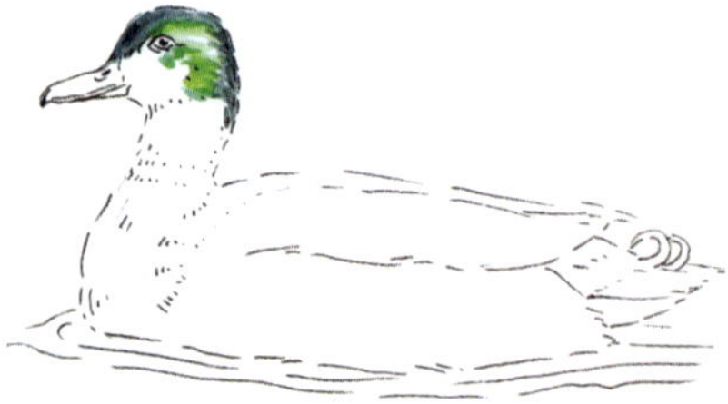

3. The head of the male mallard has various shades of green and blue. Use short strokes to show all the variety and values.

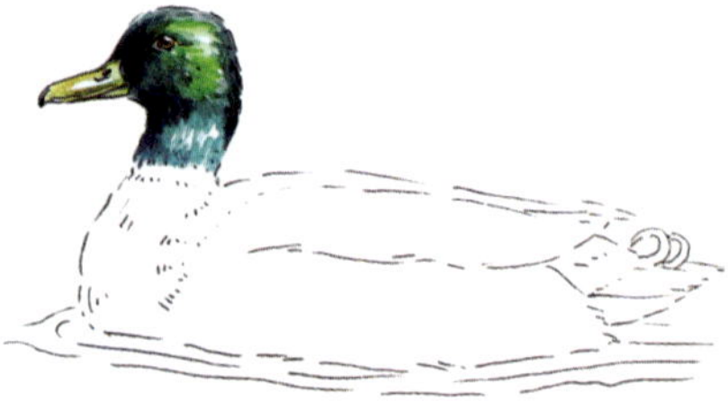

4. Finish colouring the head by creating a nice contrast, with dark blue in the shadowy parts and empty white space in the lightest. Colour the beak and eye.

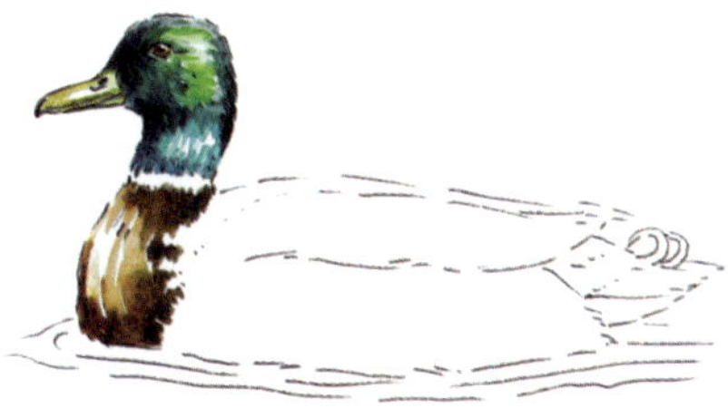

5. Don't forget to leave the white collar on the neck. Use some brownish shades to paint the breast, keeping the lightest part highlighted.

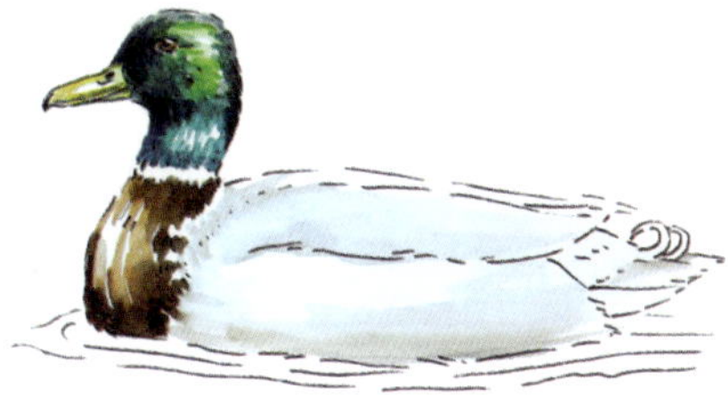

6. For the rest of the body and tail, let's make an underpainting to show the volume of the bird. The wing also has its darkest part on the bottom.

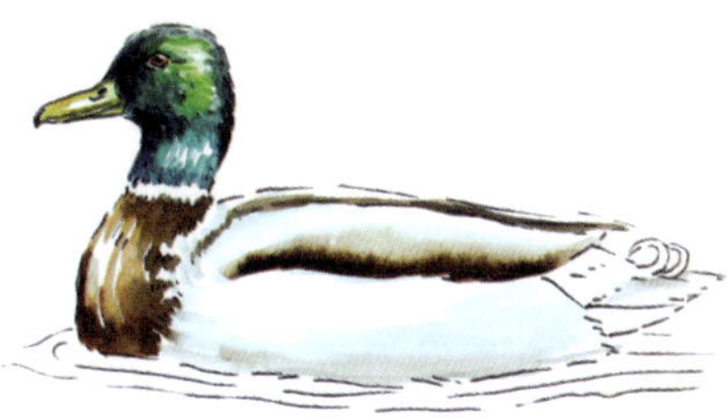

7. To finish the wing we just need to add some brownish strokes. My underpainting was still wet, which created a beautiful flow of pigment.

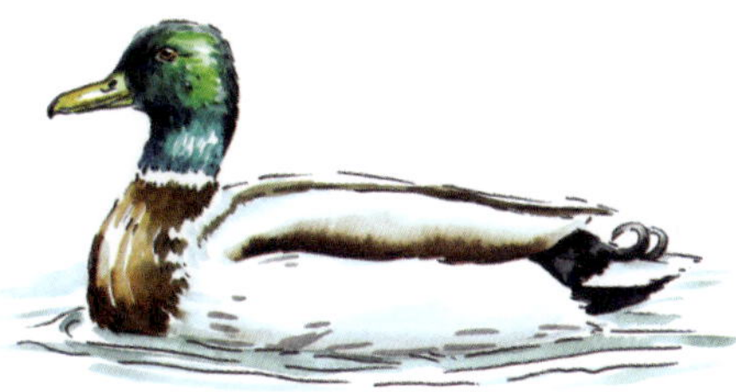

8. Colour the tail by covering the black parts with paint. Add a few dark strokes to the belly to show the texture of the feathers and give some colour to the water.

Seabirds

Gulls, albatrosses, terns, petrels, shearwaters, cormorants and many others

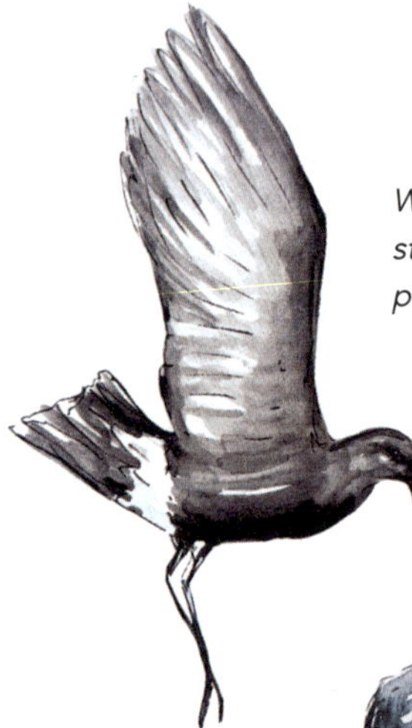

Wilson's storm petrel

One more group of birds living by water are seabirds. What's specific about these birds is that they spend time flying above the sea and catching fish. Some of them spend most of their lives far from any shores over deep oceans, returning to the ground only to breed and raise their chicks.

To spend so much time in flight most marine birds have long wings. Wandering albatrosses have the biggest wingspan in the world – more than 3 m (9¾ ft)! Seabirds also have webbed feet. Similar to shorebirds, they have less colourful plumage than terrestrial birds.

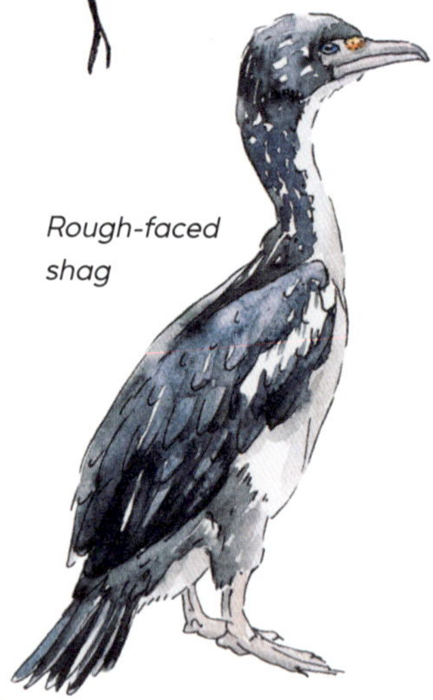

Rough-faced shag

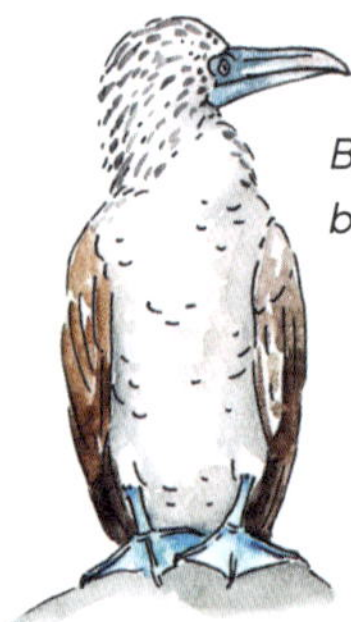

Blue-footed booby

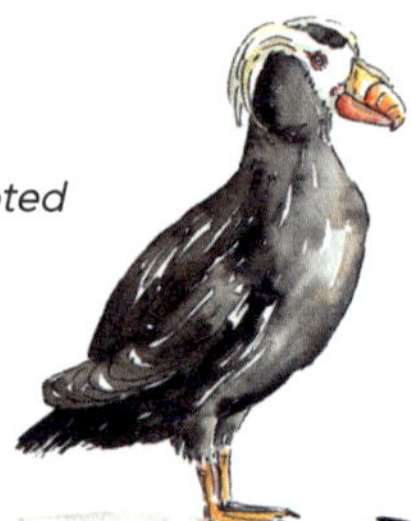

Tufted puffin

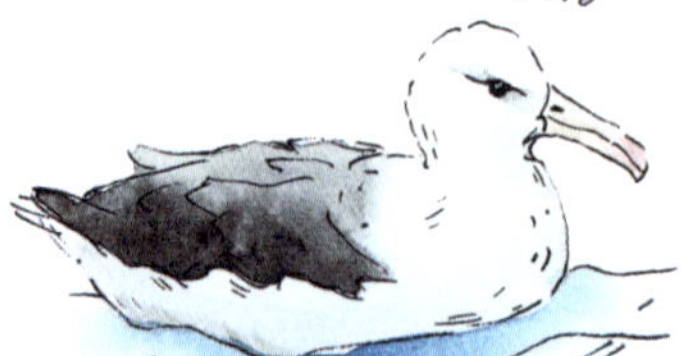

Great albatross

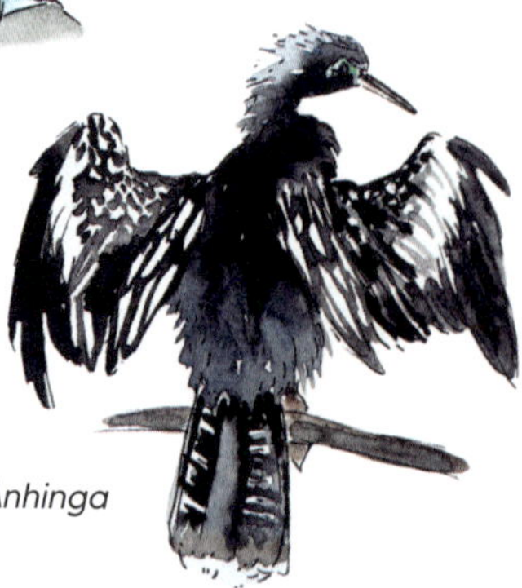

Anhinga

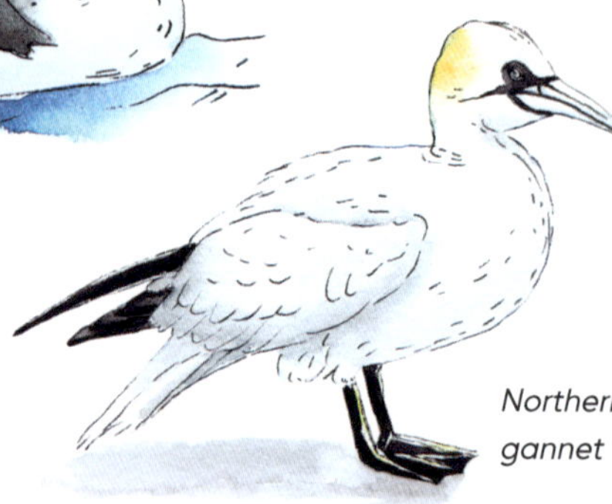

Northern gannet

Herring gull

Larus argentatus

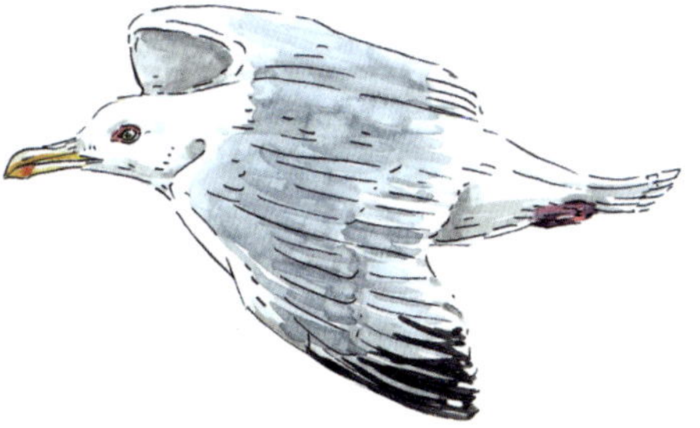

If we had to choose the most widespread or common seabird, it would be a shearwater or petrel, but seeing these birds requires going out to open sea, so let's take a look at the seabird that lives much closer to us – the seagull. Technically there's no such bird as a seagull; what people usually call "seagull" is the herring gull or other similar-looking species.

This bird has all the features common to seabirds – big wings, plain plumage, webbed feet and a strong beak for catching fish.

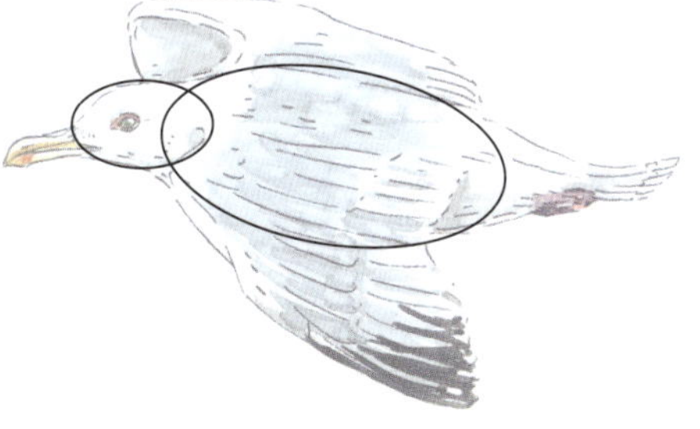

Key feature

There are different approaches to drawing flying birds, but you can just focus on what you see instead of diving deep into anatomy and wing mechanics. Here, we mostly see just one wing, so it's a great pose to start drawing birds in flight.

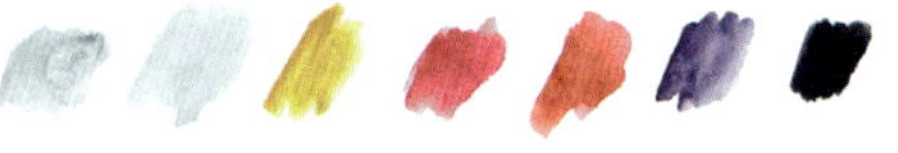

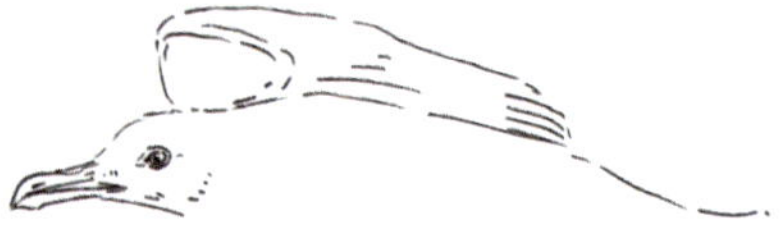

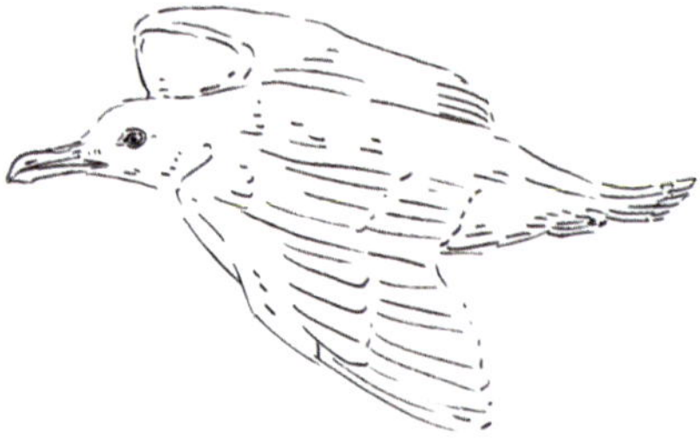

1. Begin from the strong beak the gull has. It has a specific shape – try to copy it. Outline the contour of the back and draw the wing that we see behind the bird.

2. Add the wing that's closest to us. It's slightly folded, but we can see some of the feather blocks. The tail is short. And we see just a couple of toes popping out of the belly feathers.

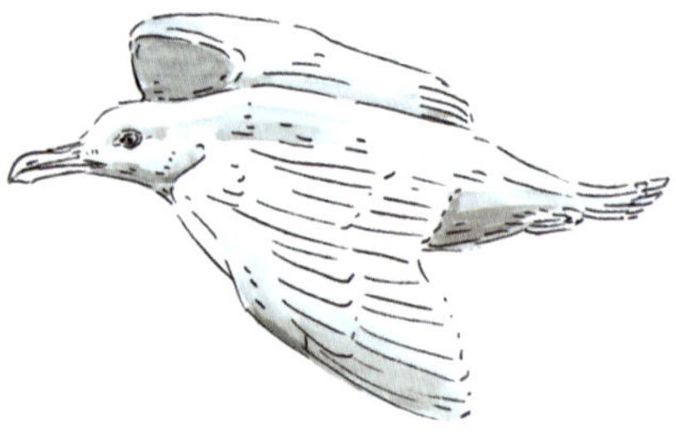

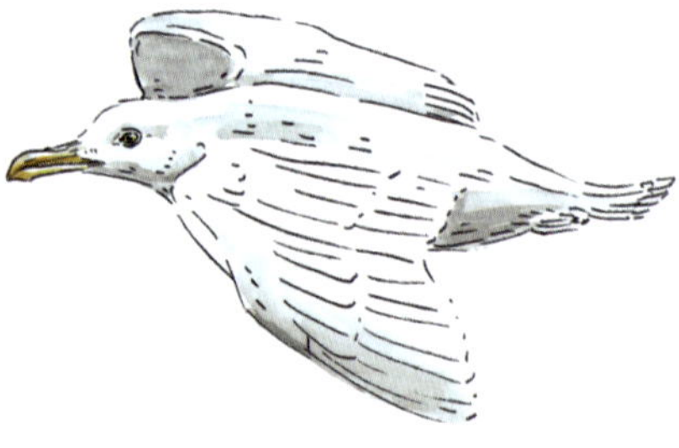

3. The bird is mostly white, so we can start by creating underpainting. Add shadows in the darkest areas and gently blend towards the lightest.

4. Colour the beak and the eye, which are yellow. If you can manage it, add different shades of yellow and orange on the beak – that will be perfect!

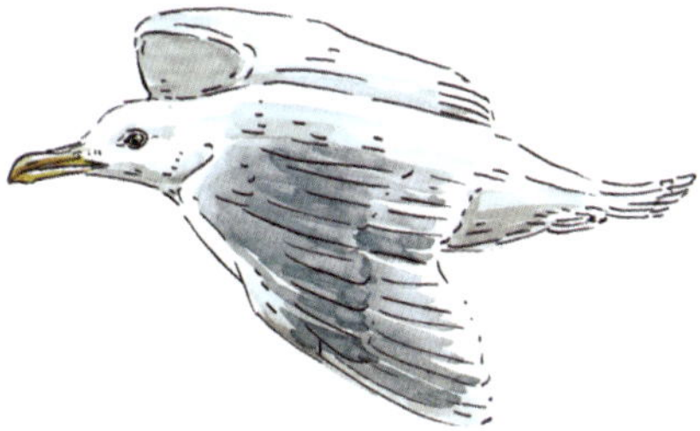

5. The top part of the wings and the back have a greyish-blue colour. Start applying it by working from the bottom of the closest wing, which is darker, to the top part. Keep the edges of the wing white.

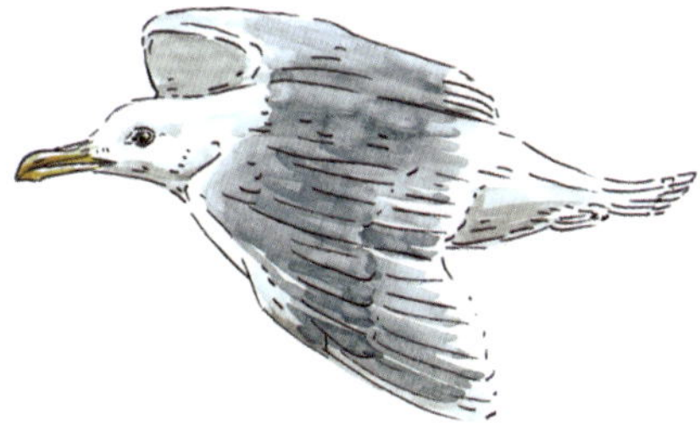

6. Finish this colour patch by painting the back and the second wing. Note how the top part of the second wing is much lighter than the bottom part of the first one.

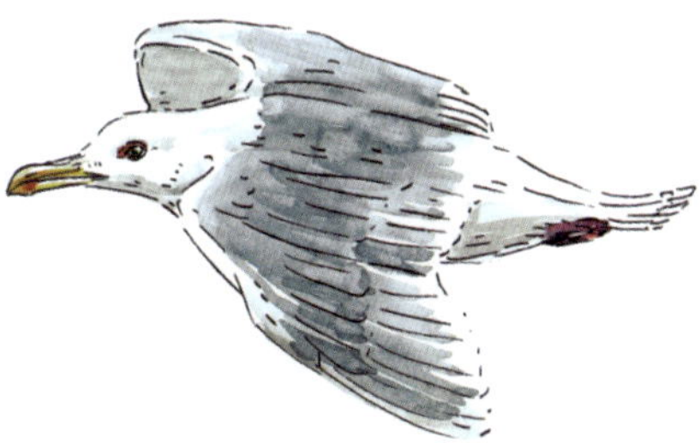

7. Add some cold red colour to the eye-ring and to the legs. And don't forget to make a bright red spot on the beak – it's an important detail.

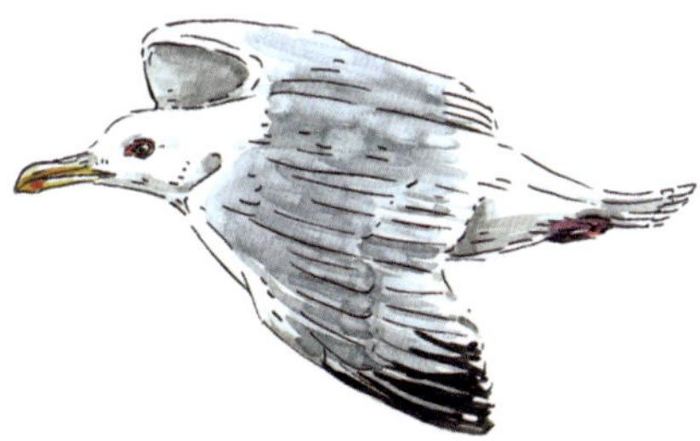

8. Last touch: the black tips on the wing. I also noticed that the contrast of the shadows isn't strong enough, so I added another layer of shadows underneath each wing.

Swifts and swallows

Along with needletails, saw-wings and martins

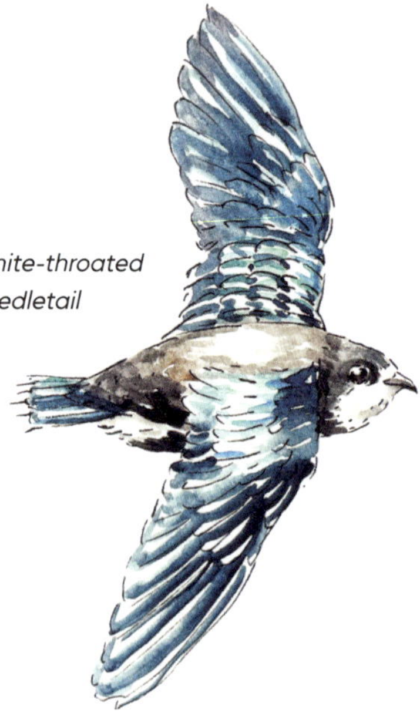

White-throated needletail

It's not scientifically correct to combine these birds in one section, because swallows belong to a completely different bird group from swifts, but they are often mistaken for one another due to their similar lifestyle and appearance, so it's only natural to look at them together.

Like seabirds, they spend a lot of time in flight. Swifts, for example, not only eat, but also sleep and mate in the air! Both swifts and swallows have slender bodies with long wings, very small feet and short, wide beaks that open wide to catch insects in midair.

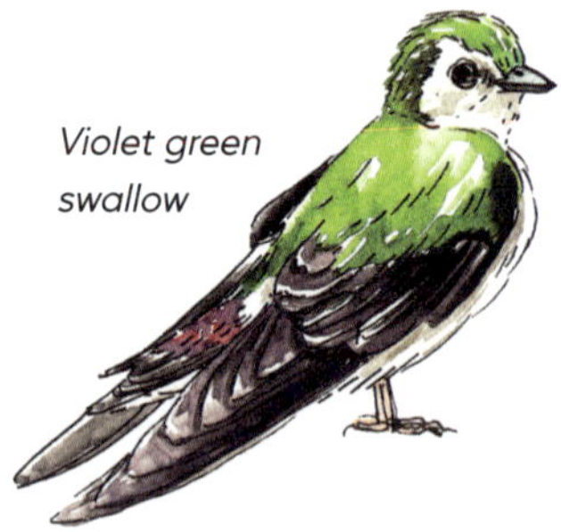

Violet green swallow

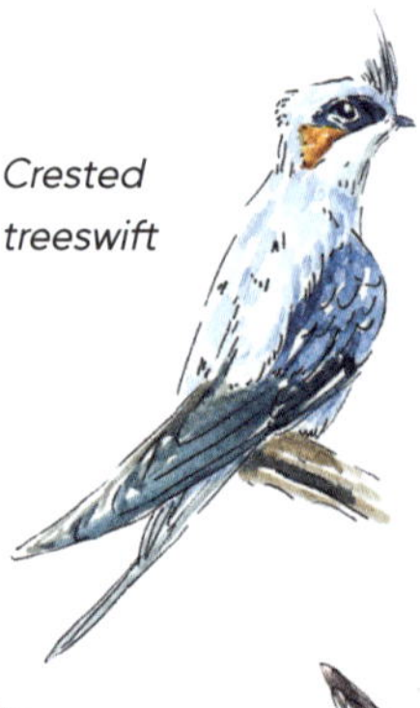

Crested treeswift

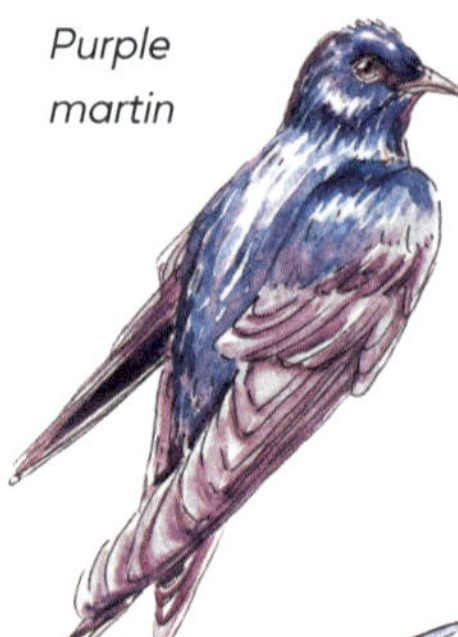

Purple martin

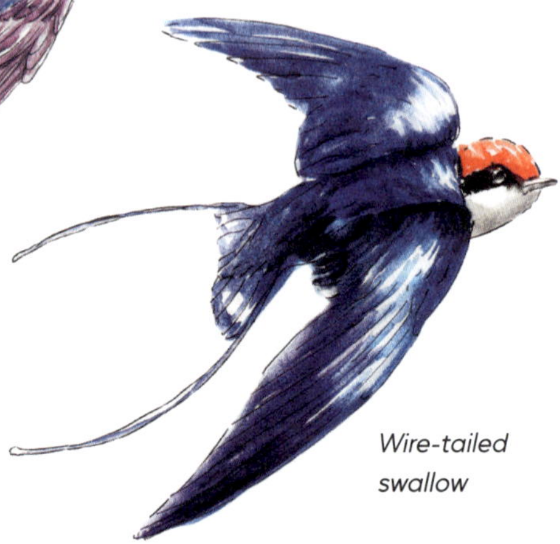

Wire-tailed swallow

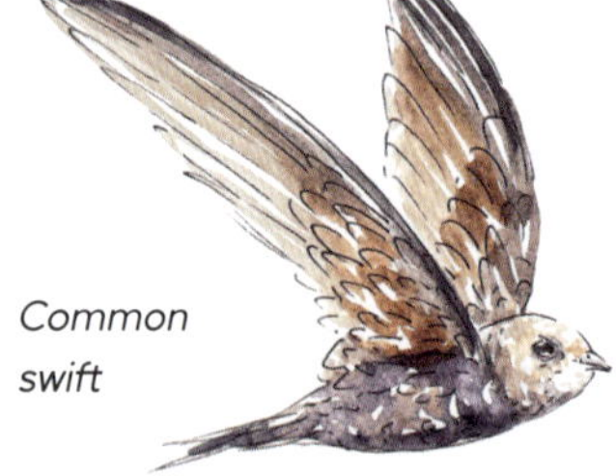

Common swift

Barn swallow

Hirundo rustica

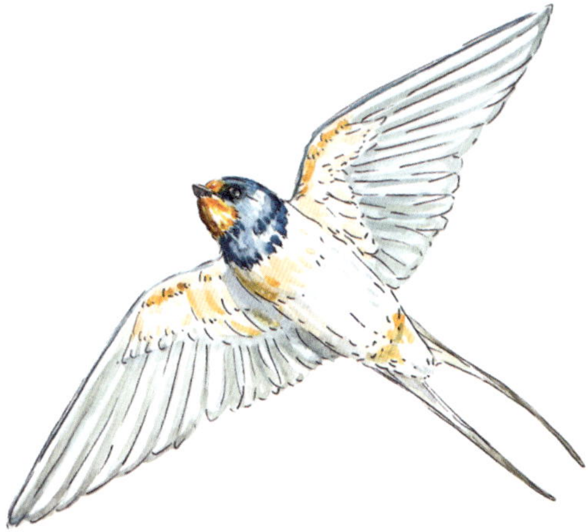

This is the most widespread swallow in the world. It has long wings and the small beak typical of swifts and swallows. The forked tail can be fanned or folded, which changes the look of the bird when seen in flight and might confuse birders unfamiliar with this feature. Females choose males during breeding season by the length of the tail.

Barn swallows living close to humans became a source of different beliefs, with some cultures considering them a symbol of love and hope.

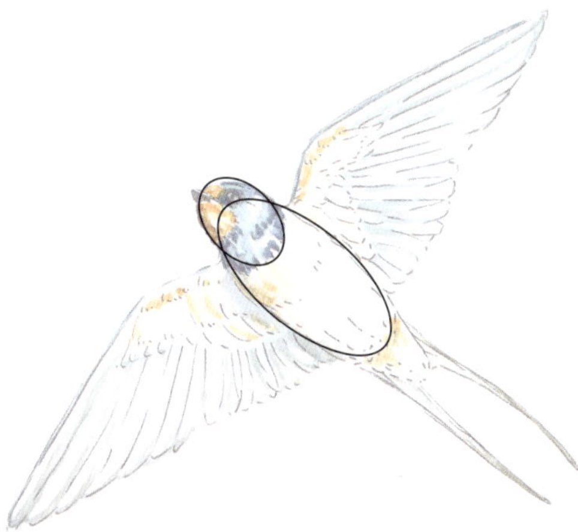

Key feature

This time we'll draw two wings, and from another angle. Note how the body of a flying bird usually looks more elongated because it's stretched, and the undertail coverts look like part of the body's oval.

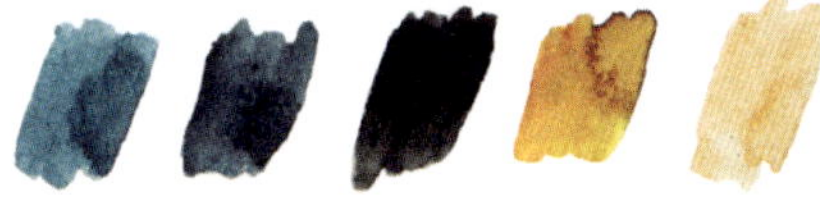

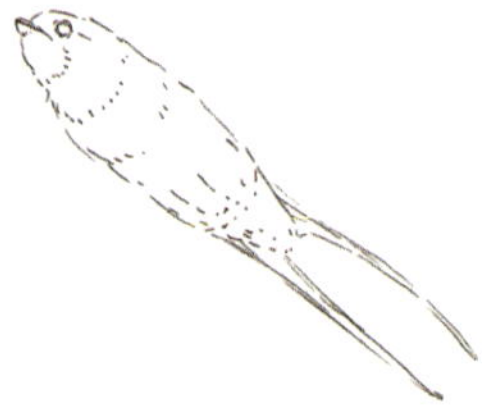

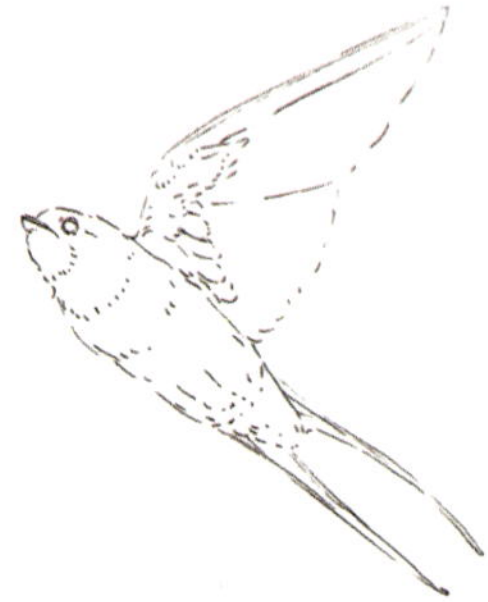

1. In this pose the head seems very small, so add just the main features. Continue drawing by indicating the body oval and the pointy streamers of the tail.

2. To draw the wing, start by capturing the overall shape, noting where the top and bottom parts are connected to the body.

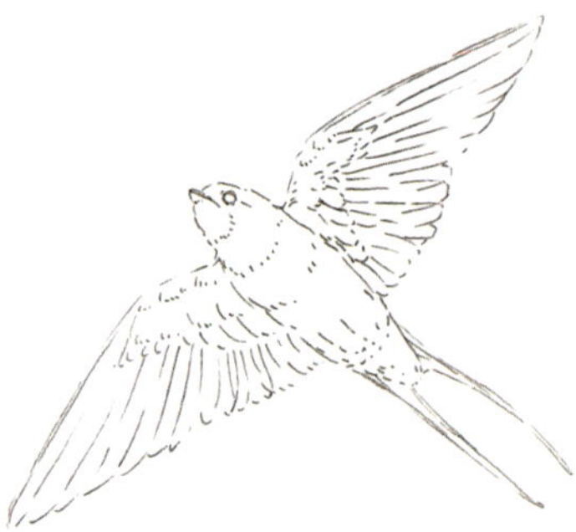

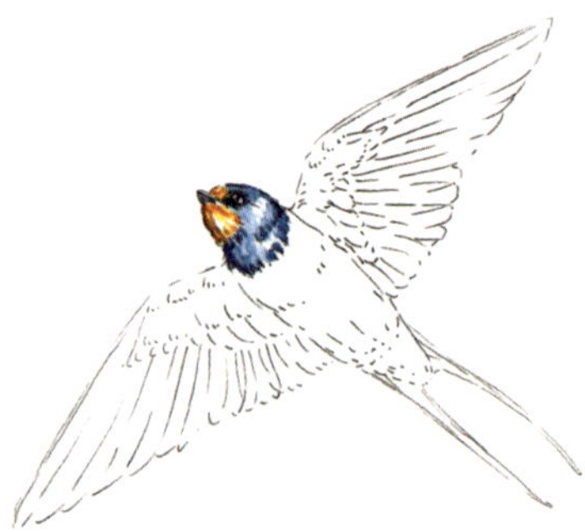

3. No need to draw each feather; just show the main blocks and the direction. And don't worry about making the wings completely equal – in this pose one looks longer than the other.

4. Swallows have very glossy feathers, so leave a lot of white space when colouring the head. The blue band on the top of the breast can look different depending on the subspecies.

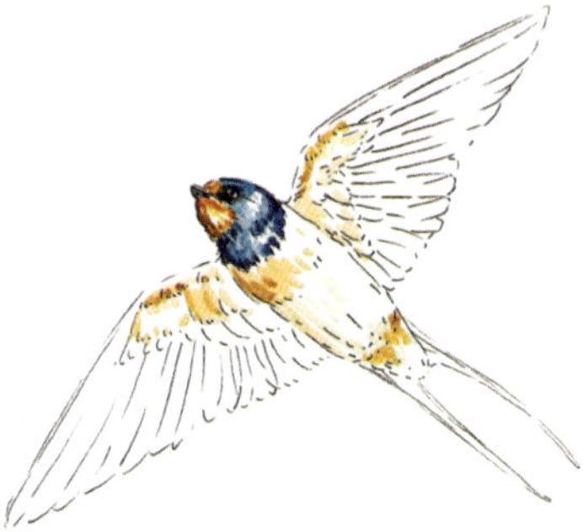

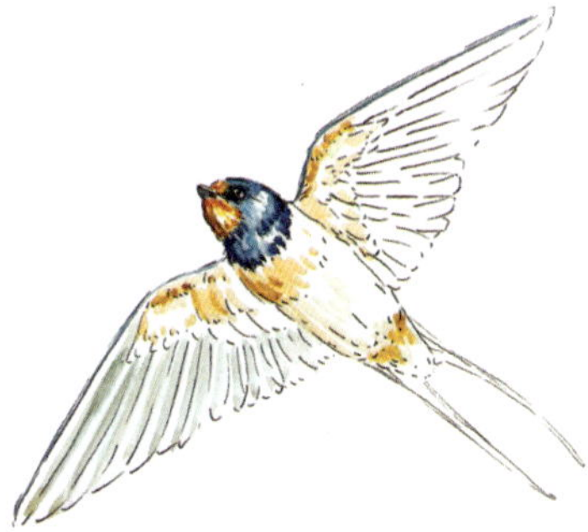

5. Colour the body and parts of the wings closest to it by applying some ochre pigment to the darkest areas. Blend it with paper, working gradually.

6. Make a dark blue edge on the wings to show the colour of the upper side. To paint the long feathers, just follow the lines you created with your drawing pen.

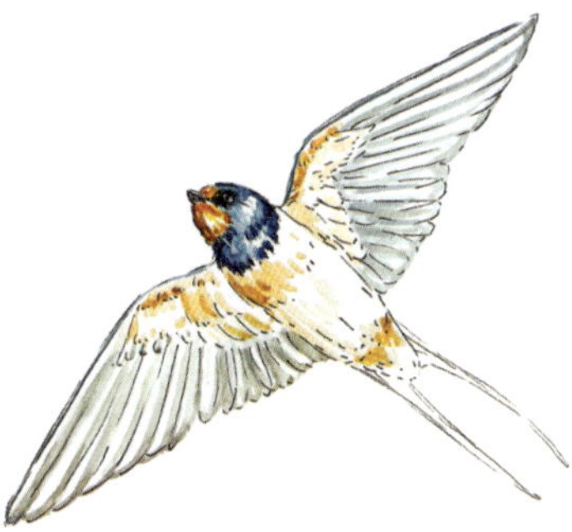

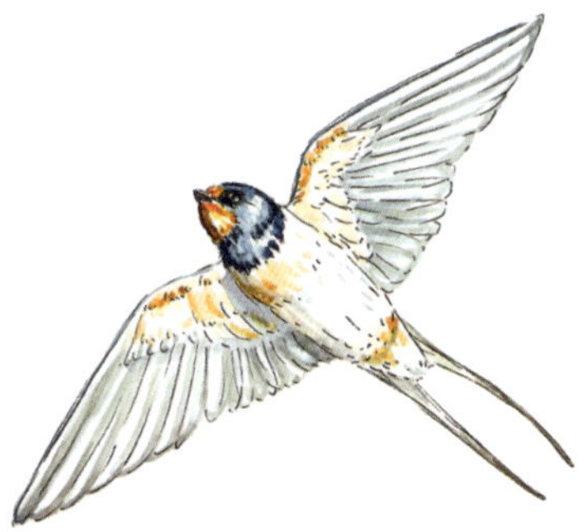

7. Add a second layer of paint to define the feathers on one wing more clearly. Repeat on the second wing.

8. Finally the tail! Add just a few strokes to give it a colour. And give some extra volume to the bird by adding shadows on the body and lower wing.

Raptors

Eagles, falcons, harriers, hawks, vultures and others

Predatory birds are the birds that mainly hunt and eat other animals such as mammals, reptiles or smaller birds. For this, they usually soar high in the sky and dive to the ground when they find their prey. Some raptors, such as vultures, feed on carrion, playing a significant role in their ecosystems.

Birds of prey are powerful and fast, with broad wings, amazing eyesight and strong claws. Sexual dimorphism in raptors is notable, with females typically larger than males. Usually, raptors have a very prominent cere at the base of the beak.

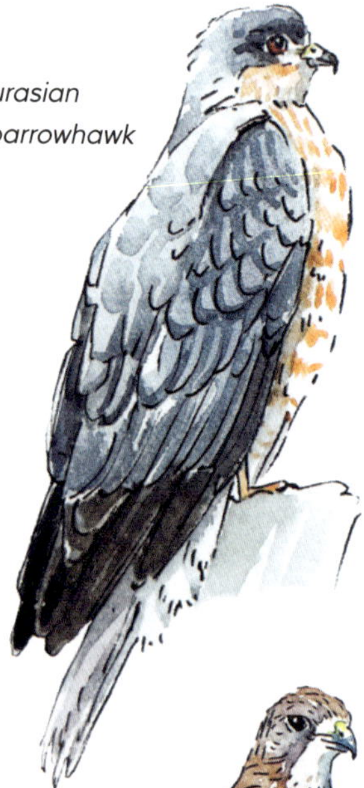
Eurasian sparrowhawk

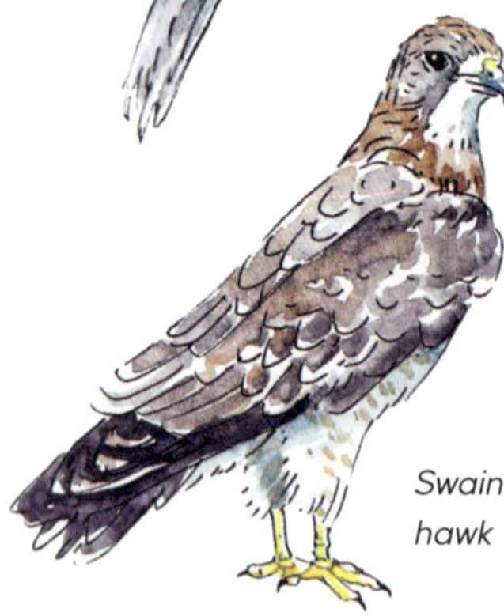
Swainson's hawk

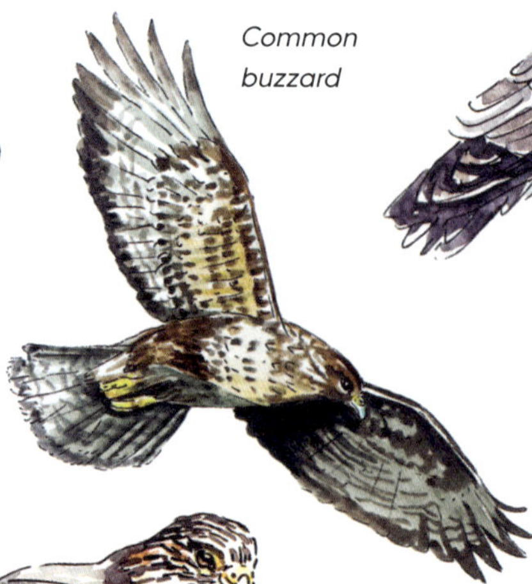
Common buzzard

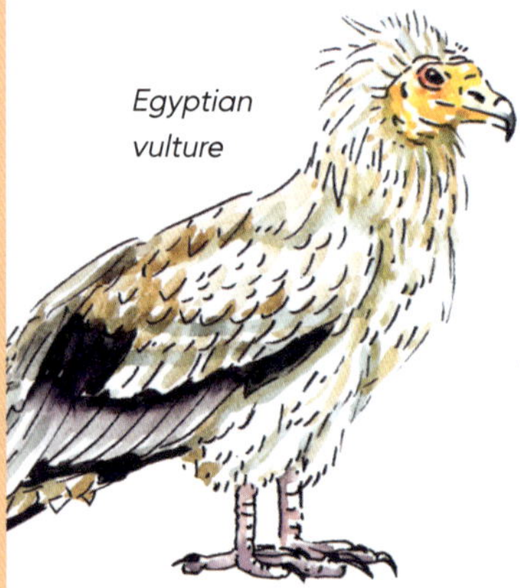
Egyptian vulture

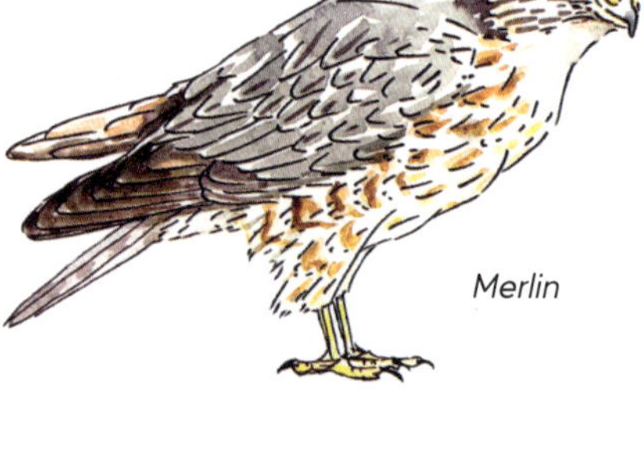
Merlin

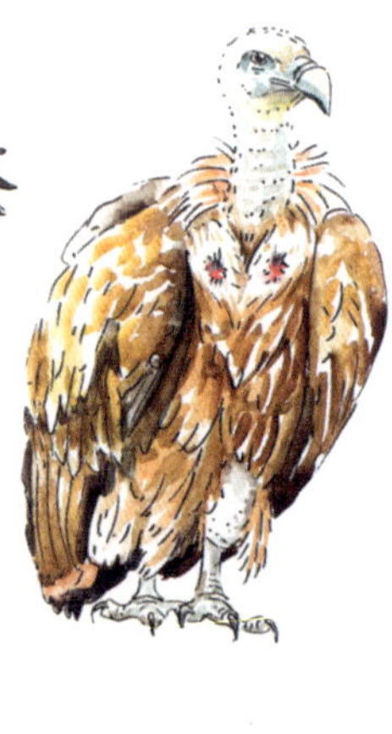
Griffon vulture

Peregrine falcon

Falco peregrinus

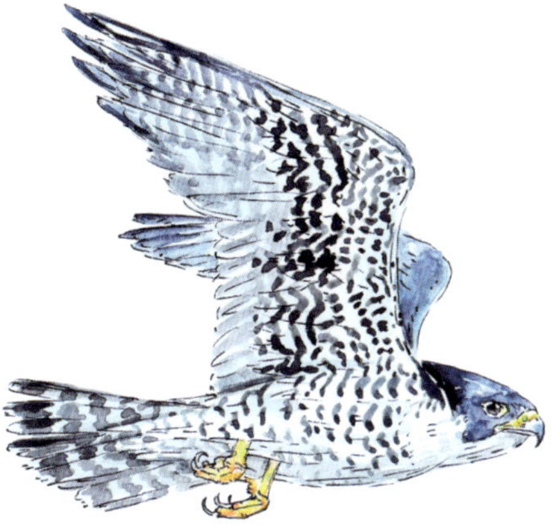

The peregrine is not only the fastest bird but the fastest animal in the world – when diving to catch its prey, it can reach speeds of more than 300 kmph (186 mph). It's also the most widespread raptor and can be found almost everywhere except Antarctica – a range that no other wild bird covers. However, it has become endangered in some areas due to the use of pesticides.

This bird has striking plumage with a dark bluish-black back and outer wings, and bars crossing most of the lightly coloured underside. Yellow legs and cere create a beautiful contrast with the rest of the plumage.

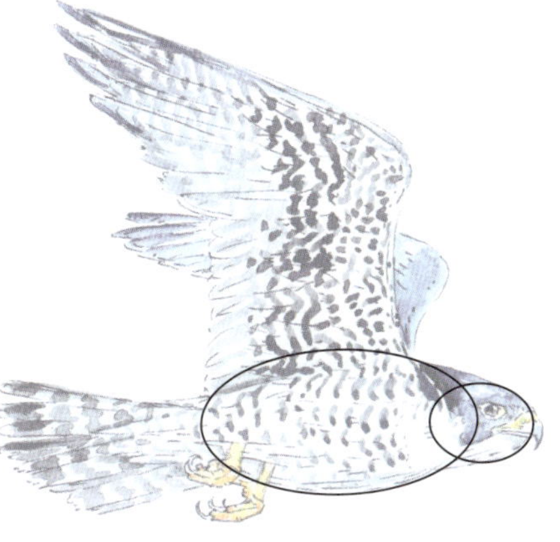

Key feature

Let's combine the two flying poses seen on pages 67 and 71. The bird is in profile but with the wings open, showing the striped plumage.

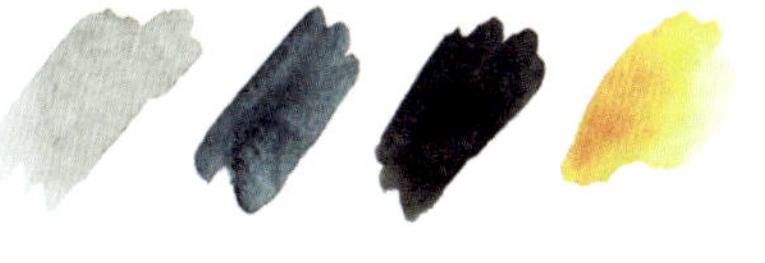

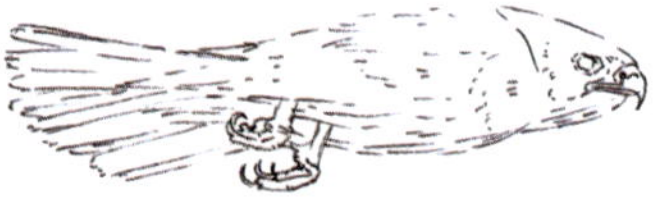

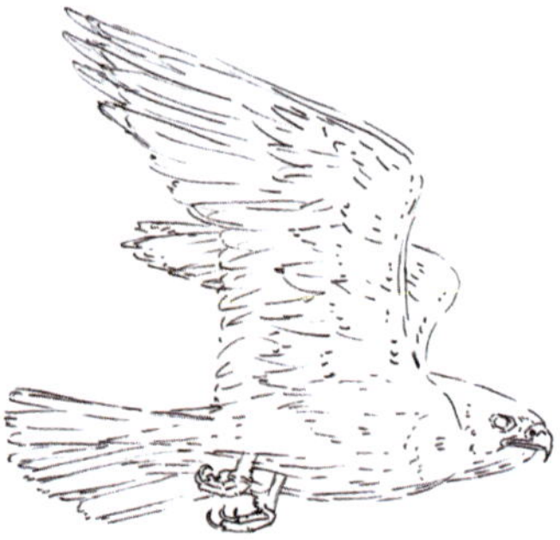

1. Draw the ovals of the body and the head, which here look like just one shape because of the neck. Add the fanned tail and the legs with their massive claws.

2. The wing might seem a bit messy, with all the feathers popping out here and there, but the main blocks are still visible. Don't forget to draw the second wing, too.

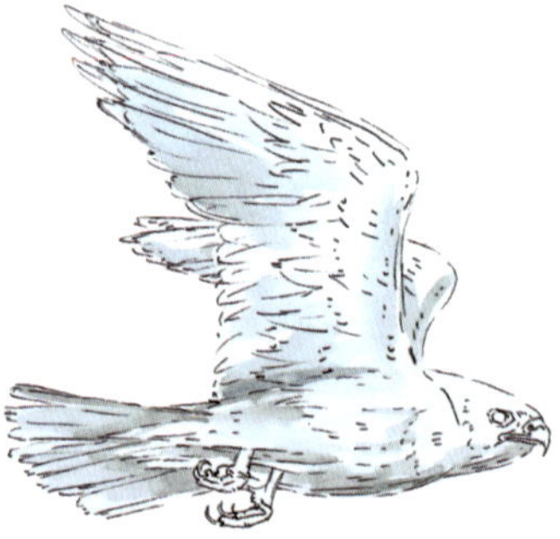

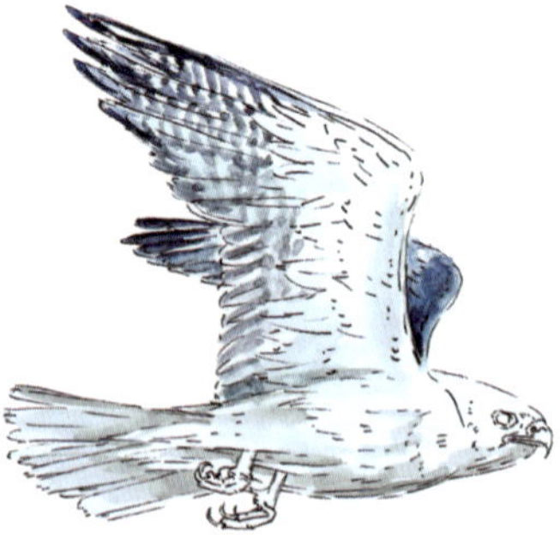

3. Same as we did for the great egret (page 59), create the volume of the bird. The darkest parts are the bottom of the wing, the tail and the lower parts of the body and head.

4. Colour the second wing with some dark blue. Then start creating the pattern on the closest wing by colouring the tips of the top feathers and drawing some bars on the left side of the wing.

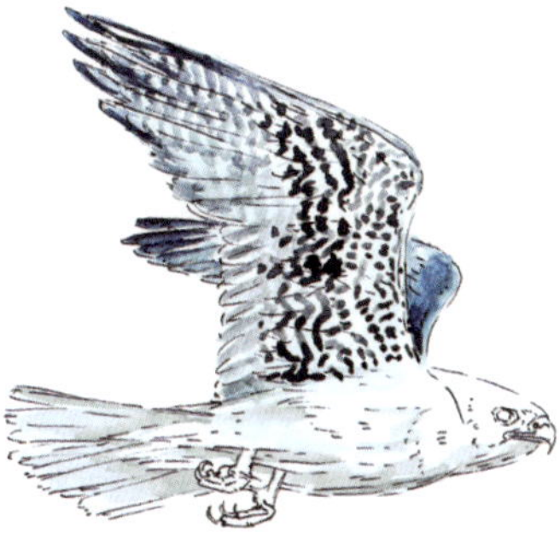

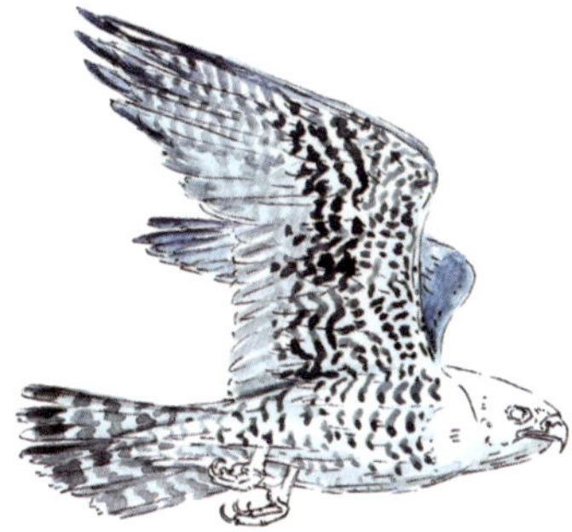

5. The rest of the wing has bolder lines, which become shorter closer to the bird's head, so they look almost like dots.

6. There are bigger bars with dark tips on the tail. Smaller stripes go across the body of the bird, stopping before the top part of the breast.

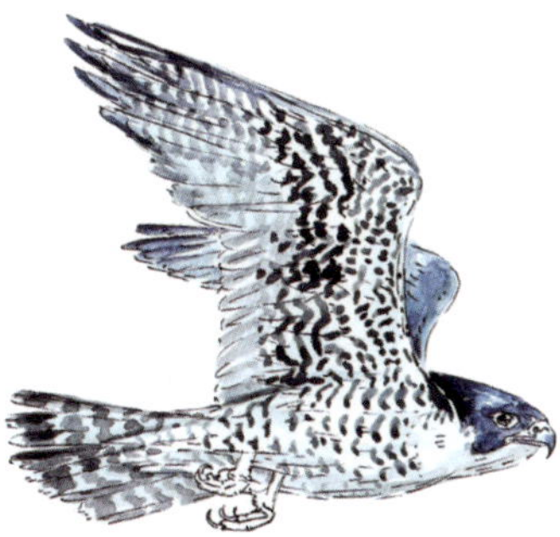

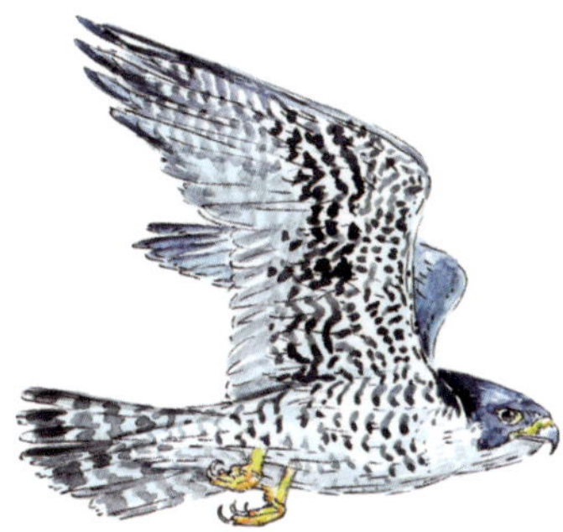

7. Colour the head with the darkest shade of blue you can create, but leave some white space on top to show the glossiness of the feathers. Colour the tip of the beak with a bluish shade, too.

8. Add yellow to the top part of the beak, the eye-ring and the legs. You can also add a little bit of orange on the legs to create some volume for each claw.

Nightbirds

Nightjars, poorwills, nighthawks, potoos, frogmouths and similar

Nightbirds can be found in almost every part of the world, but it's not that easy to find them! Active at night, they have become masters of camouflage so they can hide from predators in the daytime. Most of these birds have intricate patterns in earthy tones, helping them hide among leaves on the ground or even mimic a stump.

Night life led these birds to develop big eyes that reflect light. An insect-based diet led to a wide beak that opens into an enormous gape. They don't walk much, so their feet are quite small.

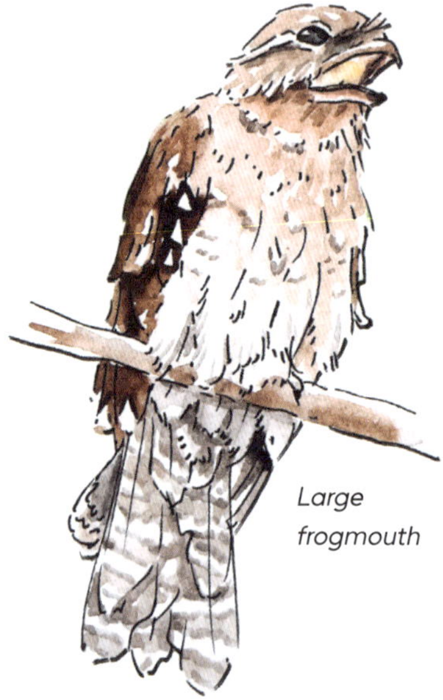

Large frogmouth

Chuck-will's-widow

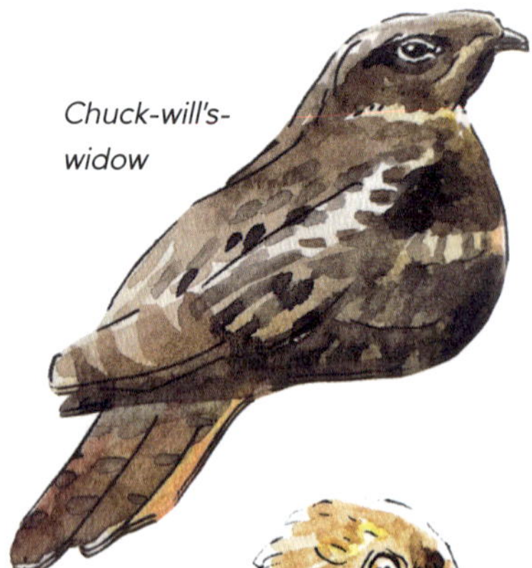

Rufous potoo

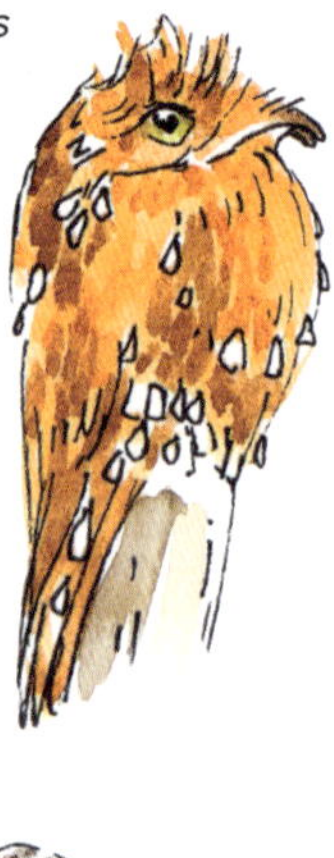

Great eared nightjar

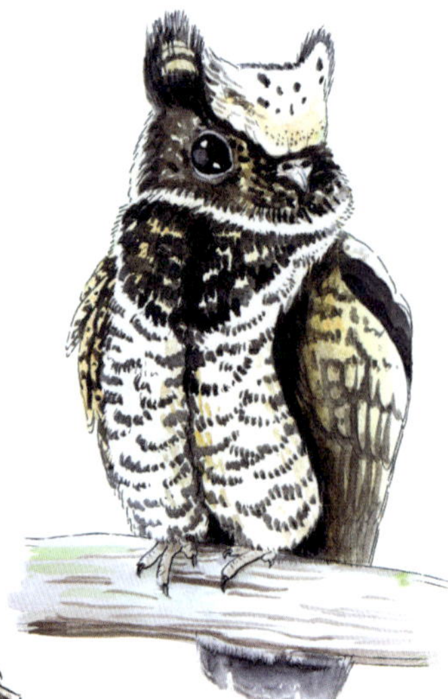

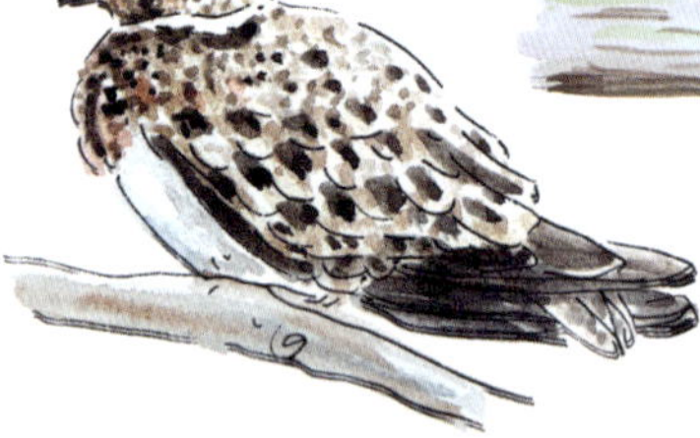

Nacunda nighthawk

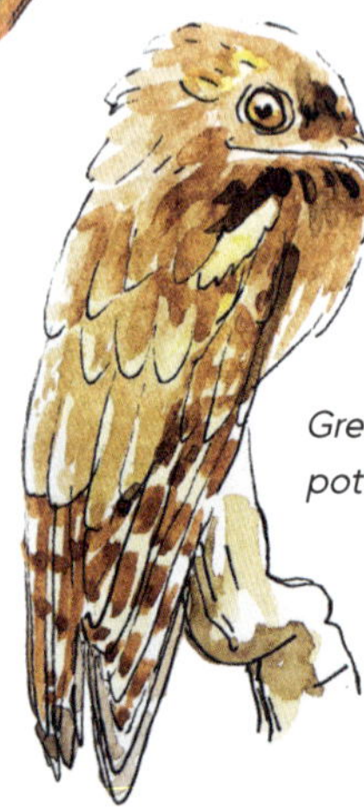

Great potoo

Common nighthawk

Chordeiles minor

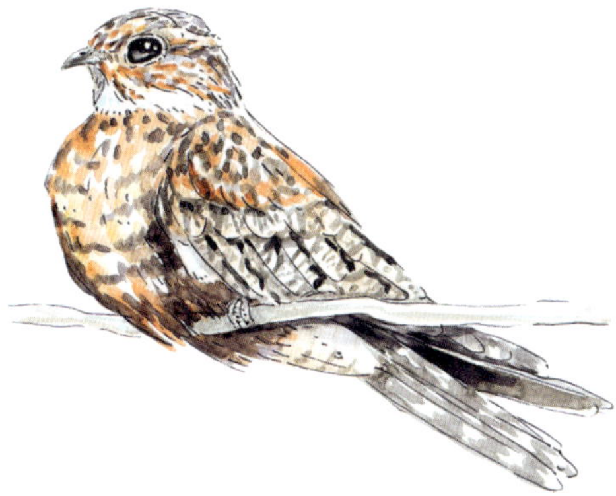

This typical nightjar occurs throughout the Americas and is as hard to find as the other nightbirds. Common nighthawks have perfect plumage for hiding on the forest floor amid rocks and leaves.

It's known for long-distance migratory habits and the amazing call it produces, piercing the night with short nasal beeps.

Key feature

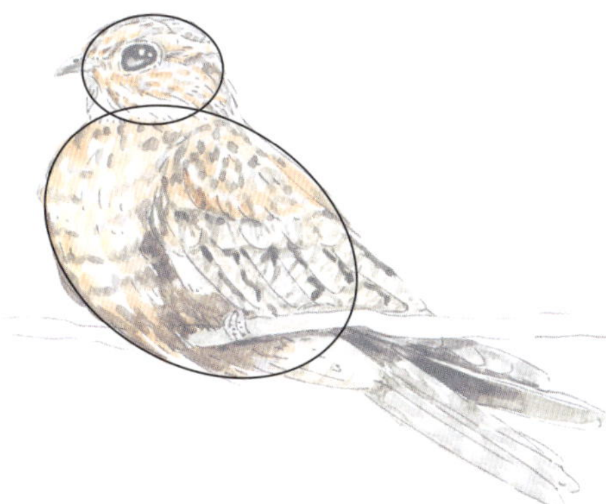

This is a typical pose of a resting nightjar. The ovals of the head and body are overlapped, long wings pointing slightly further than the tail. The white band on the neck is clearly visible.

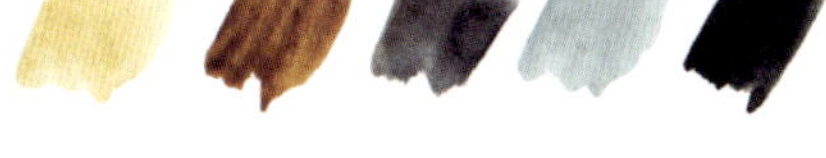

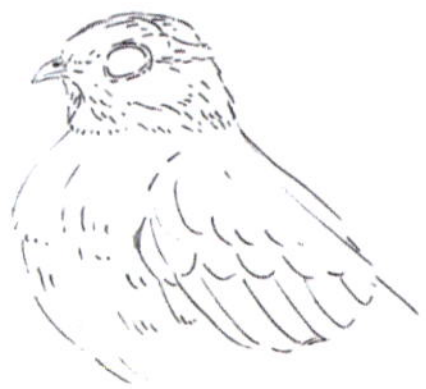

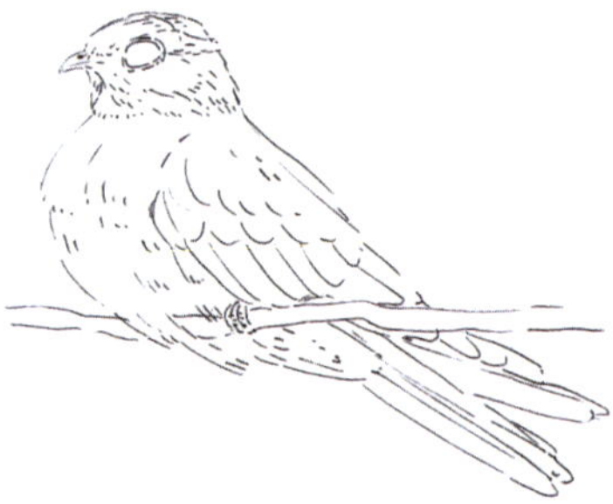

1. Begin with the small beak and the giant eye. Outline some feather blocks on the head. Continue by building the oval of the body and top part of the wing.

2. Show how the front belly feathers and the legs are covering the branch. Under the branch we see the longest feathers of the wing, the undertail and the tail itself.

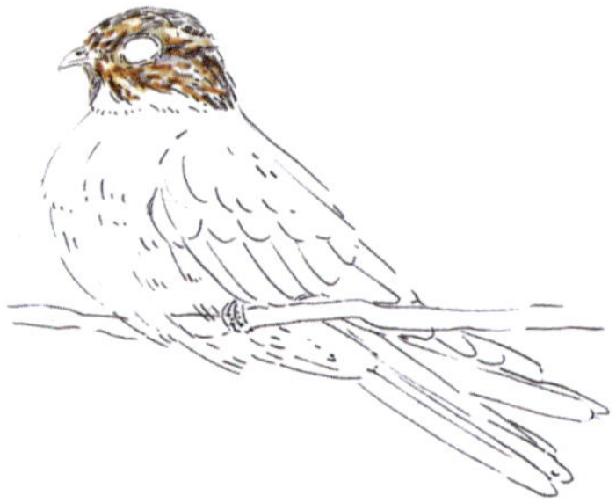

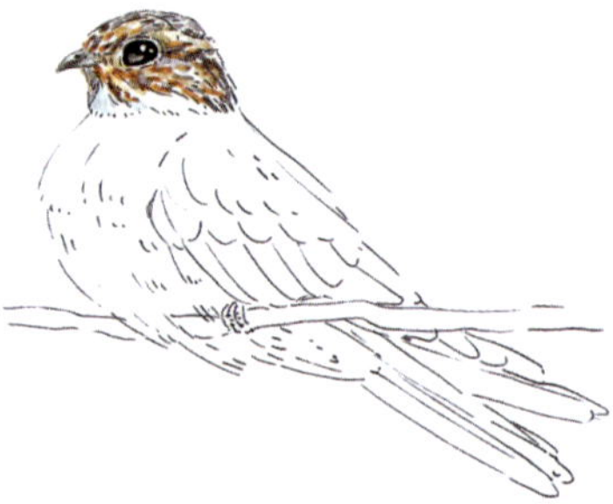

3. To create the texture on the head, use really short strokes and a variety of colours from ochre to brown and dark purple shades. Leave some white space as usual to let it breathe.

4. Colour the beak slightly and pay extra attention to the eye. Since it's big, we can make it more lively and interesting. Add a few bluish strokes on the neck to create shadow.

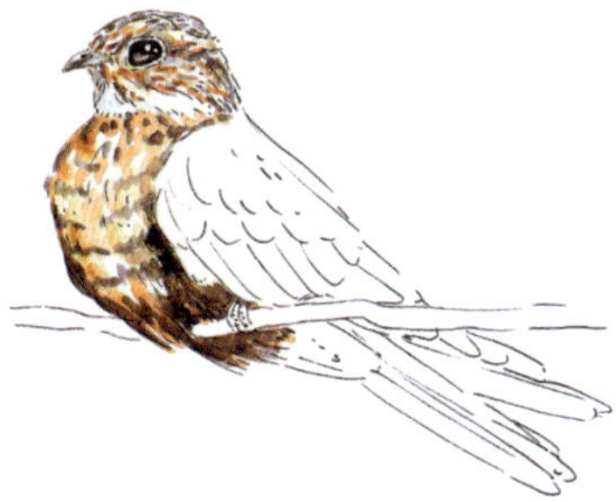

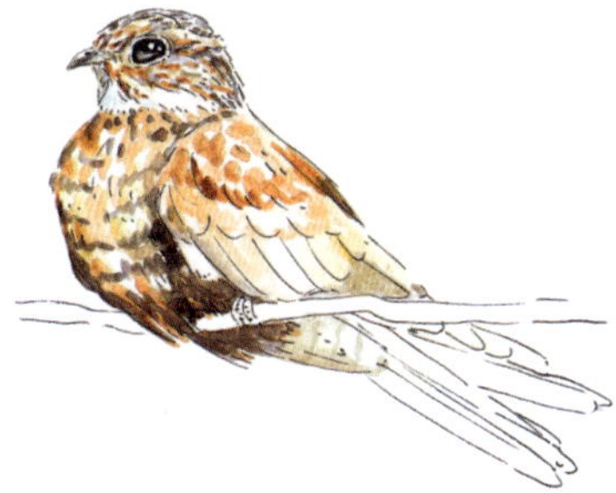

5. Paint the rest of the belly by applying several layers of colour: start from the lightest and finish with the darkest, while creating the pattern of the bird's plumage.

6. Colour the undertail coverts and the top part of the wing, but not the white feathers popping out on the left. Add diluted dark bars on the undertail and a few rufous strokes on the shoulder.

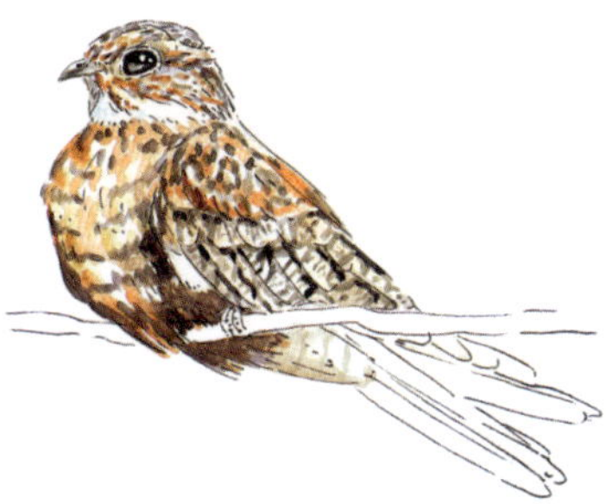

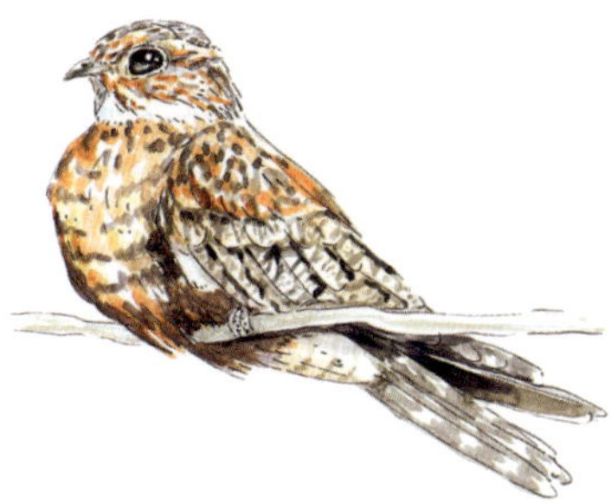

7. To create the intricate pattern the nighthawk has, add small spots on the shoulder in a darker colour and draw whimsical lines that look like veins on the rest of the wing.

8. Paint the tips of the longest feathers under the branch, darkening the bottom part. Create bars on the tail and colour the legs slightly, along with the branch the bird is sitting on.

Owls

Along with boobooks, eagle-owls, hawk-owls and owlets

After nightbirds, the other nocturnal birds that are famous and widespread are owls. Their ability to fly silently and use echolocation to orient at night is fascinating. There are over 200 species in the order Strigiformes, with size of the birds ranging from 12 to 70 cm (5 to 28 in)!

Most owls have cryptic plumage, similar to other nightbirds, offering camouflage during the day. But owls are predators themselves: when hunting small mammals and birds, they are easier to locate due to the alarm calls of other birds noticing them nearby.

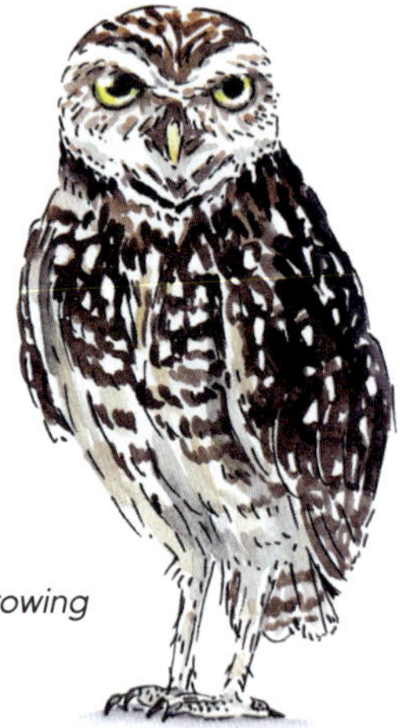

Burrowing owl

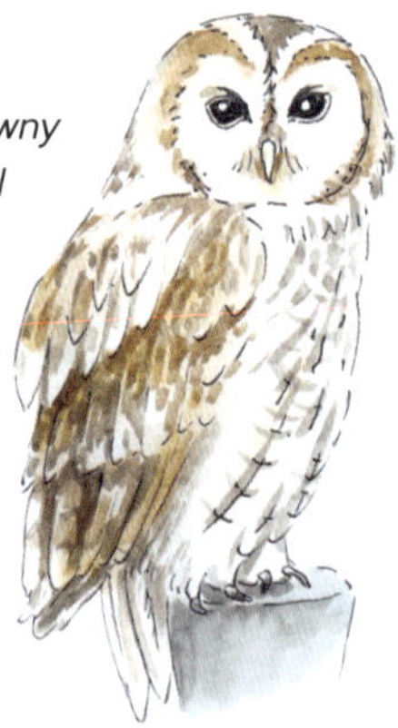

Tawny owl

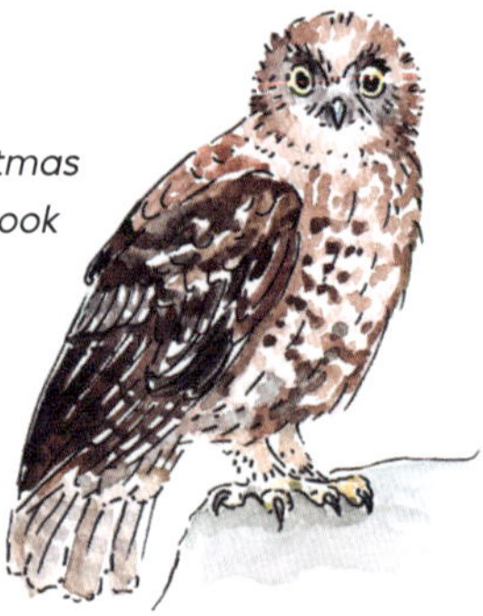

Christmas boobook

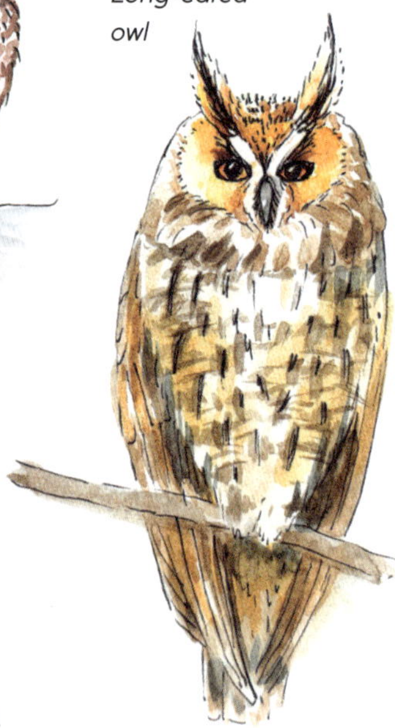

Long-eared owl

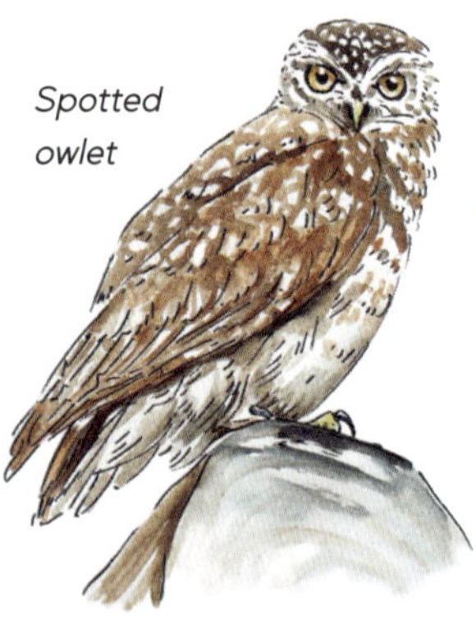

Spotted owlet

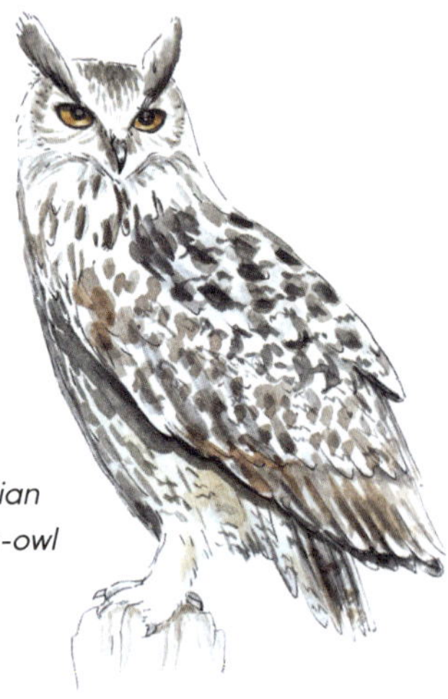

Eurasian eagle-owl

Barn owl

Tyto alba

This cosmopolitan bird is sometimes classified as three different species depending on its range, since it is the most common owl worldwide.

The heart-shaped facial disc is one of the characteristic details of these owls. The birds have light-coloured feathers with various kinds of speckles, and a rusty back and head. Strong feet with big talons are tailored to catch prey. The legs are covered with feathers to keep the bird warm in cold environments and make their movements as silent as possible.

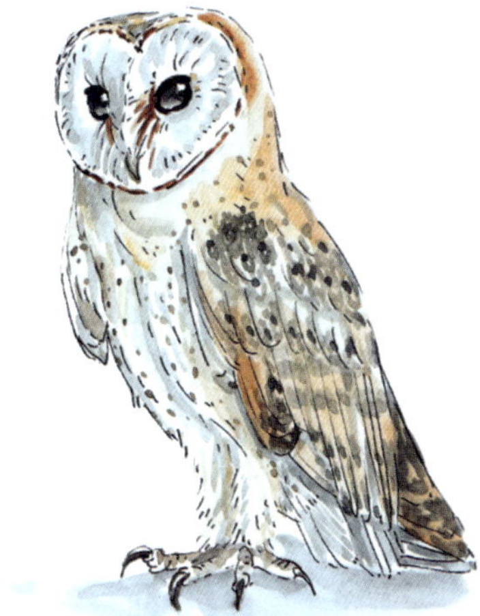

Key feature

This three-quarter view helps us see not just a flat profile or front view but the overall shape of the head. We can also compare the light colour of the breast and belly, which contrasts with the brownish wings.

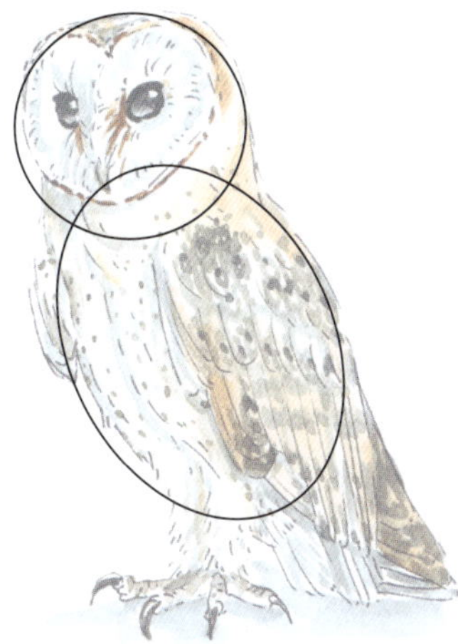

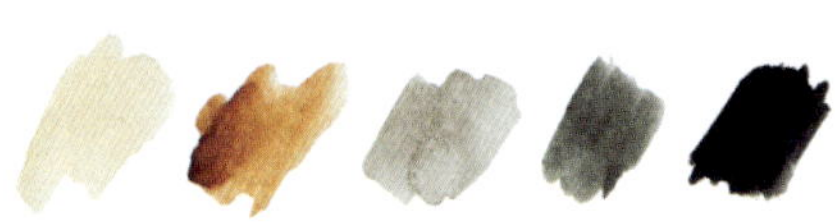

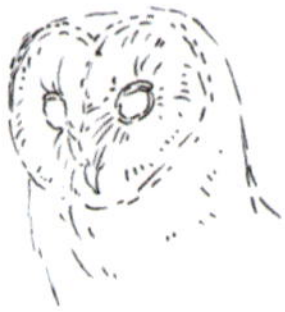

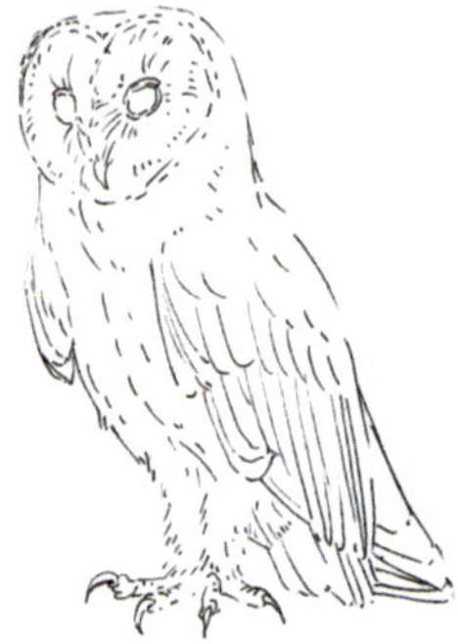

1. Create the heart-shaped face and add additional lines to finalize the oval of the head, which is somewhat squarish. Draw the middle line crossing the face, the eyes and the beak.

2. Define the main blocks of feathers on the wing and draw the body of the bird with a vertical line in the middle. Make the legs extra fluffy and the claws curved and sharp.

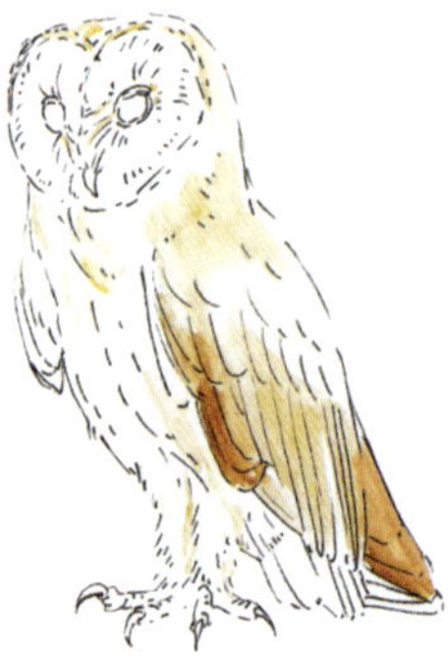

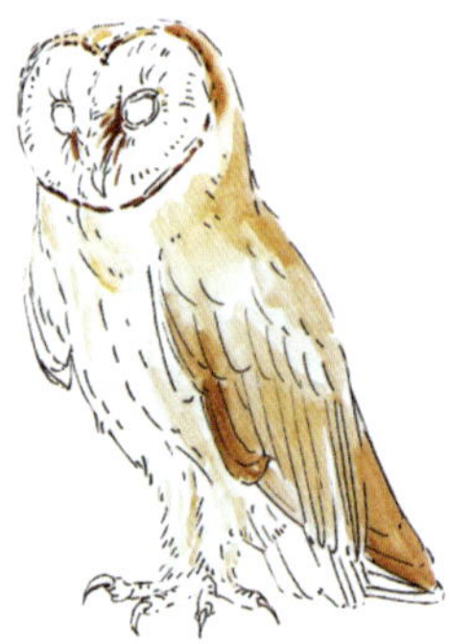

3. Paint most of the bird with a base colour to create the underpainting. Note how it's much lighter on the breast and belly, and darker at the tips of the wing feathers.

4. Add dark feathers on the head between the eyes and the beak, and around the heart-shaped face. Smooth the colour a little to the back of the head.

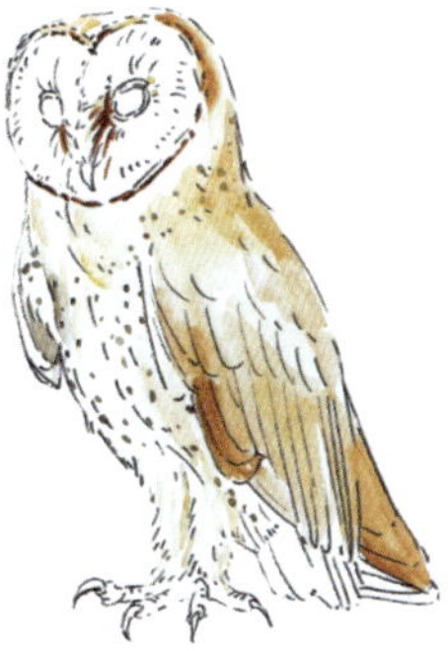

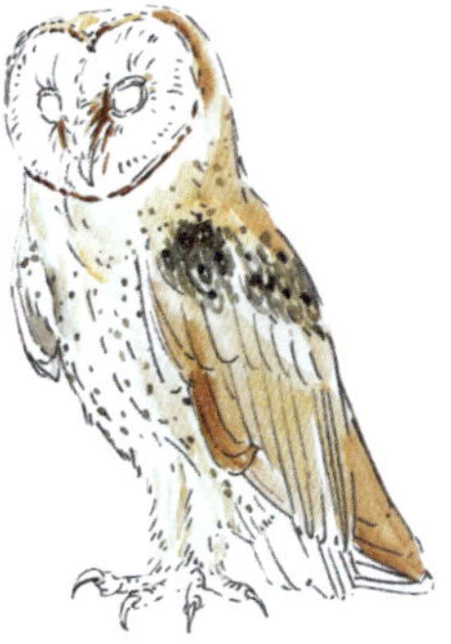

5. Start with the simplest pattern: the bird has small dots going across the neck, breast and belly. You can also see some dots under the far wing.

6. To make the markings on the wing, apply a layer of slightly diluted dark colour, leaving some white circles. Then add an additional layer of darker colour around those circles.

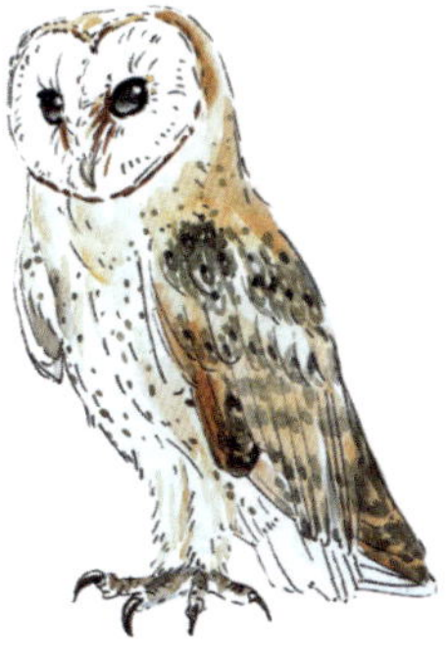

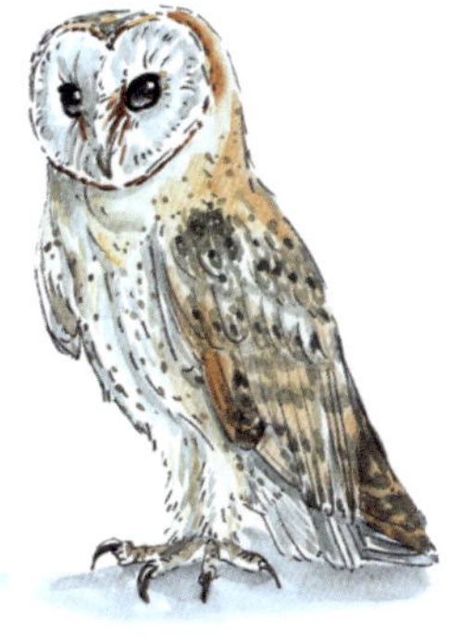

7. Finalize the wing in a similar way. Colour the legs and the eyes of the bird, which have really dark contours around them that slightly resemble eyelashes.

8. Give more depth to the bird's face by shading some parts and creating a contrast between the head and the neck. Add some shadows under the wings, on the tail and under the bird.

Landfowl

Junglefowl, grouse, partridges, turkeys, peafowl and many more

Landfowl are a group of terrestrial birds from the order Galliformes, which consists of almost 300 species. Some of them were domesticated, and some are known as game fowl. Males typically have more expressive plumage and perform courtship displays during the breeding season.

These are chicken-like birds, mostly ground-dwelling, relying on their feet more than on their wings. As a result, their legs are quite massive and the wings, in contrast, are shorter than those of most other birds.

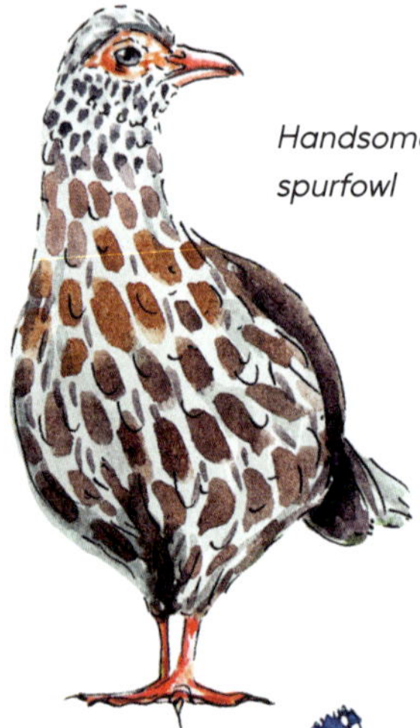

Handsome spurfowl

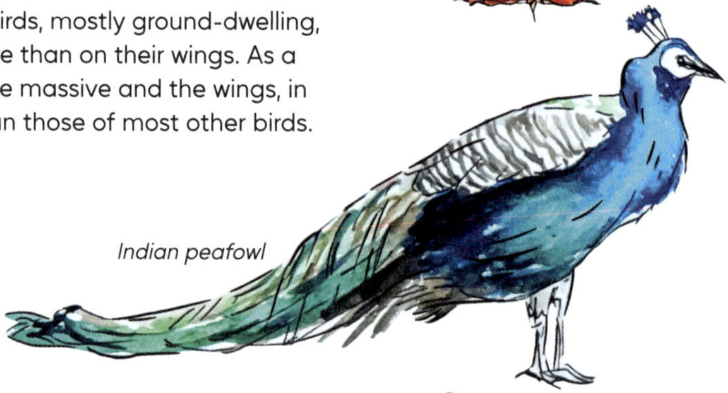

Indian peafowl

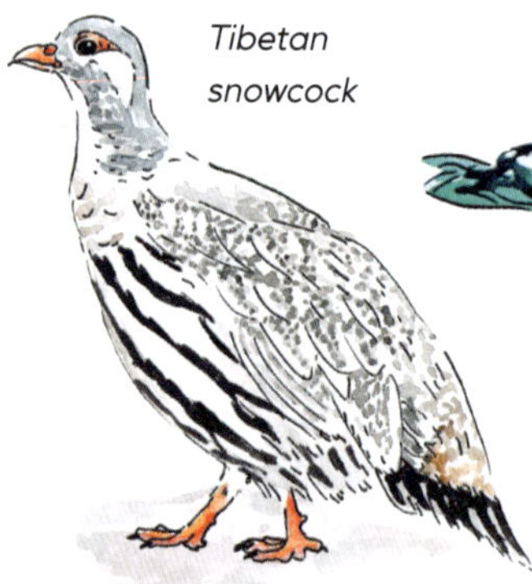

Tibetan snowcock

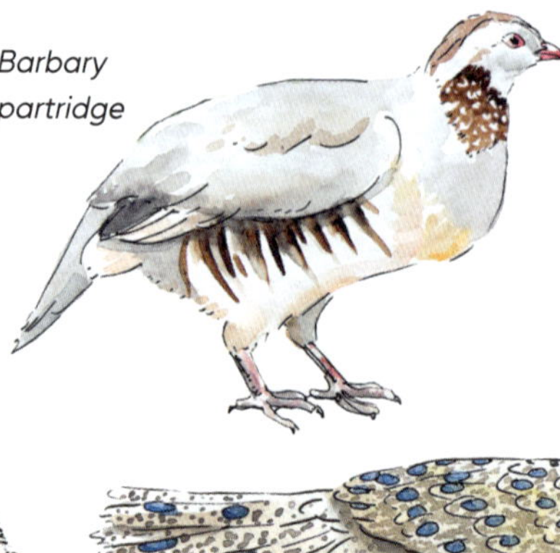

Barbary partridge

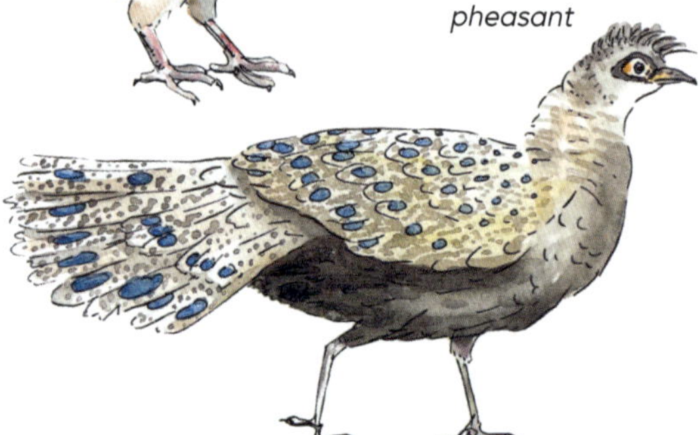

Malayan peacock-pheasant

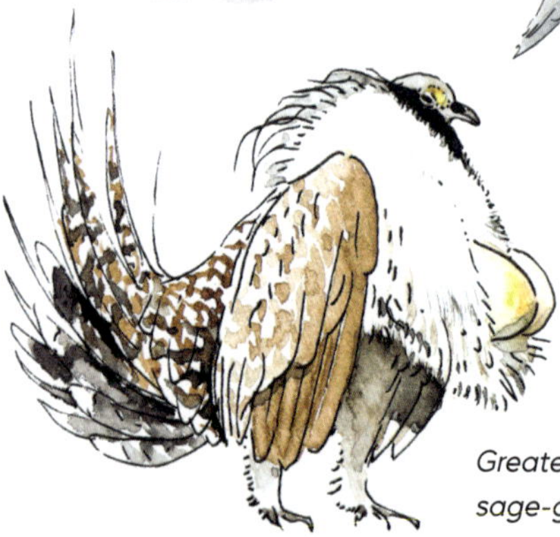

Greater sage-grouse

Common pheasant

Phasianus colchicus

This species, also called the ring-necked or blue-headed pheasant, is an amazing example of how intricate a bird's appearance may be. Different colour combinations, patterns, extensive tail feathers and even ear-tufts – male pheasants have it all! The red fleshy skin patches on the face become brighter and bigger during breeding season.

Having originated from Asia, this bird was widely distributed across the world by humans. Due to selective breeding, there are different variations of plumage within this species.

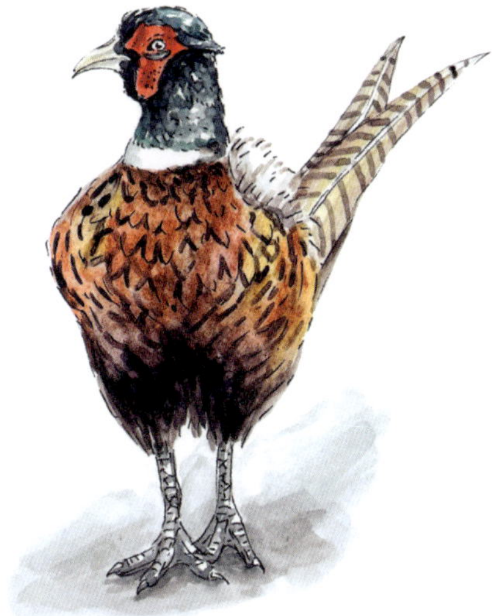

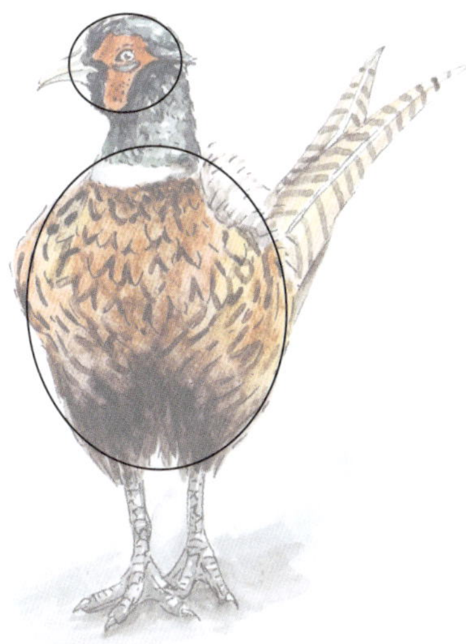

Key feature

This bird looks gorgeous from any angle, but we'll practise this front view of the body to keep it manageable. The head is in profile, so all the details of the plumage are clearly visible.

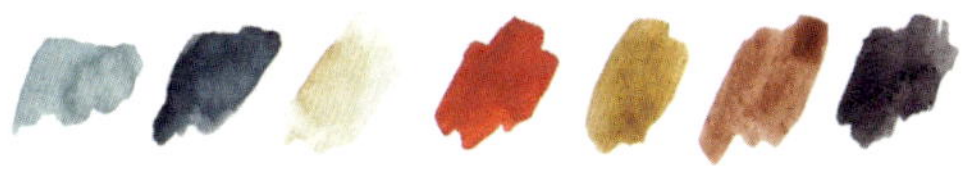

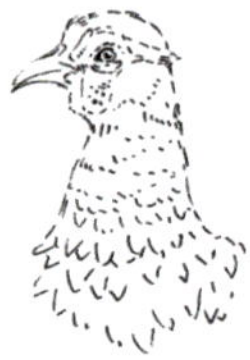

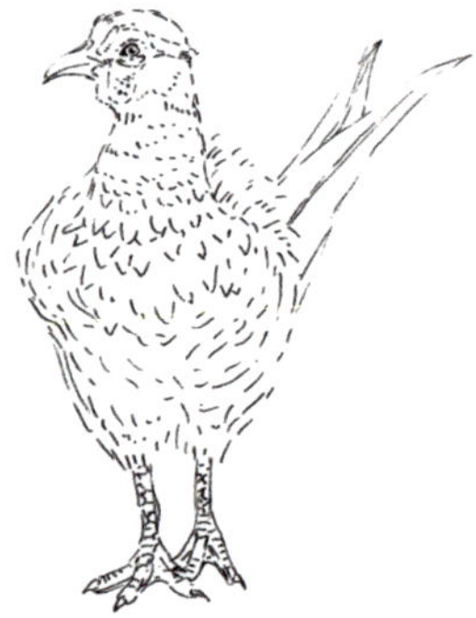

1. Outline the colour patches on the head – you'll need this guidance later. Draw the texture of the feathers on the neck and the top part of the breast.

2. Continue adding texture down the breast, flattening the shapes closer to the belly and legs. Map out the rump feathers popping out behind the back, the pointy feathers of the tail and the legs.

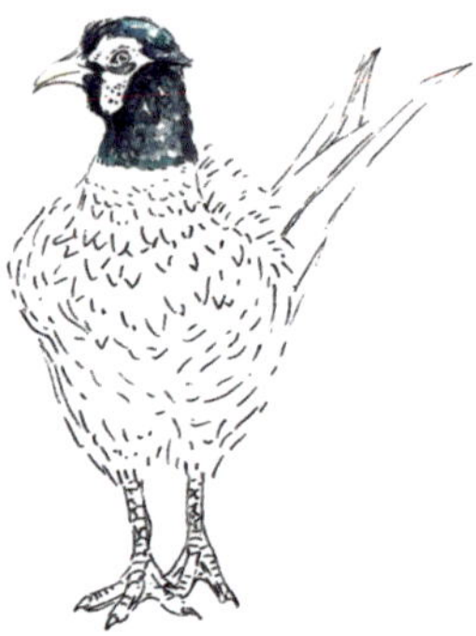

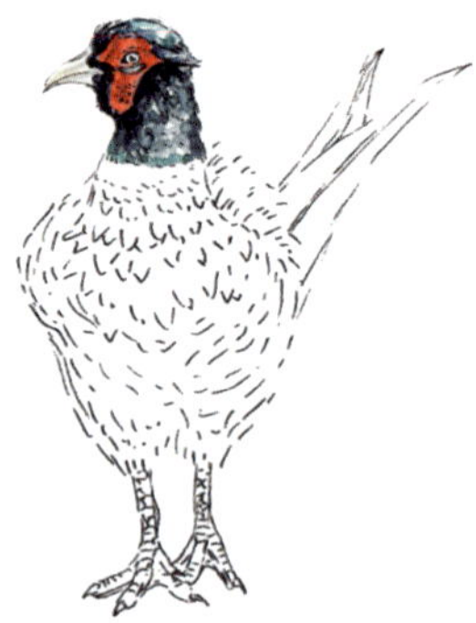

3. The main colour of the head has different shades of blue. Create volume and show how shiny the feathers are. Also, paint a small patch under the eye.

4. Complete the head by colouring the beak with diluted yellowish paint. Colour the red skin around the eye, but don't make it flat – create a slight graduated wash to give it depth.

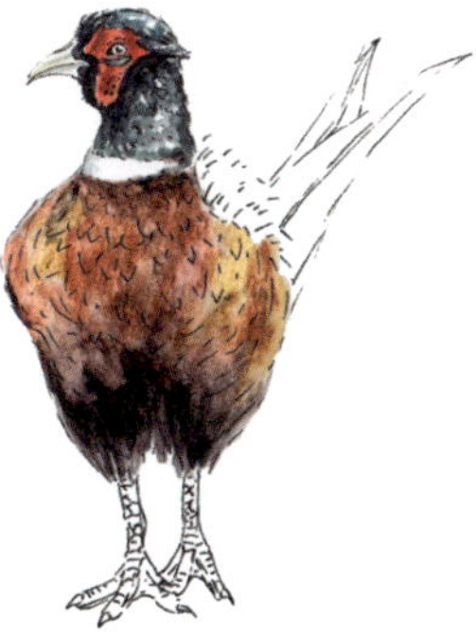

5. Add a little shadow on the white ring on the neck to show volume. To colour the rest of the body, make a colourful wash with darker parts on the bottom, deepening it between the legs.

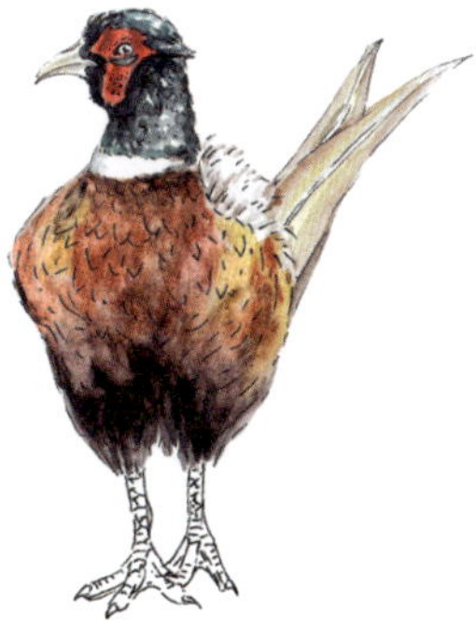

6. Paint the light-coloured feathers of the rump. For the pointy tail feathers, create underpainting, leaving the white lines across each of the feathers.

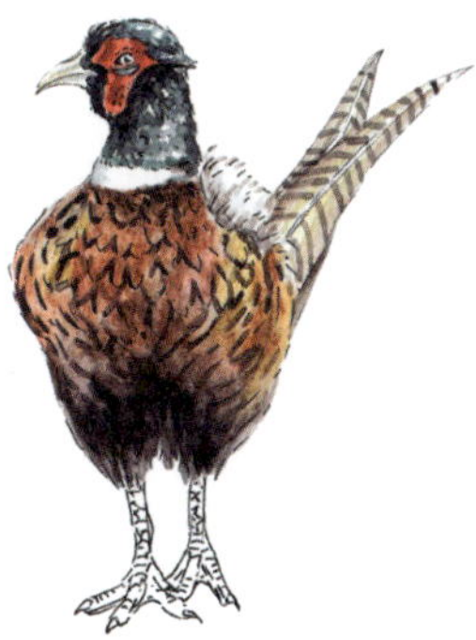

7. With a darker colour, repeat the texture of the feathers on the body of the bird and draw the bars on the long feathers of the tail.

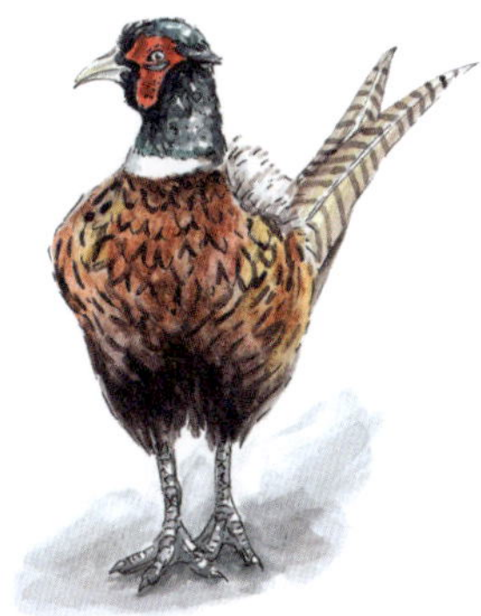

8. Check if you need to add any extra value to the drawing. Paint the legs, showing the scaly texture, and create the shadow under the bird itself.

Ratites

Ostriches, emus, rheas, cassowaries and kiwis

These birds belong to an ancient lineage that split from other avian species around 80 million years ago! They kept some traits of their ancestors and the biggest birds alive in the world are in this group. Ratites have short wings, which lack a keel – a special bone that is essential for flight.

They have other anatomical characteristics in common; they typically have strong legs for running instead of flying, and many ratites have a unique foot structure. The feathers are also built differently than those of other birds – they look soft but dense at the same time.

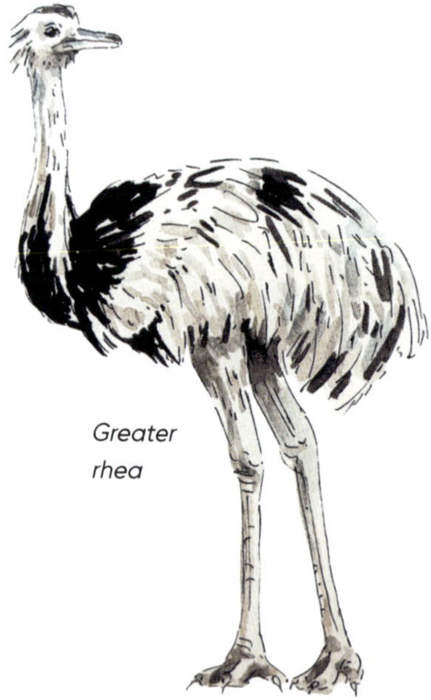

Greater rhea

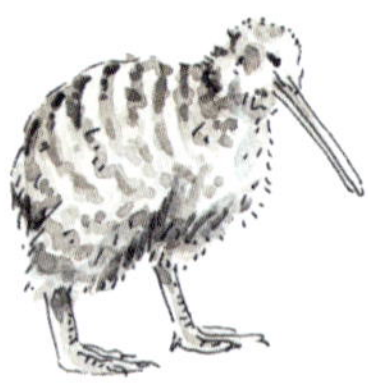

Little spotted kiwi

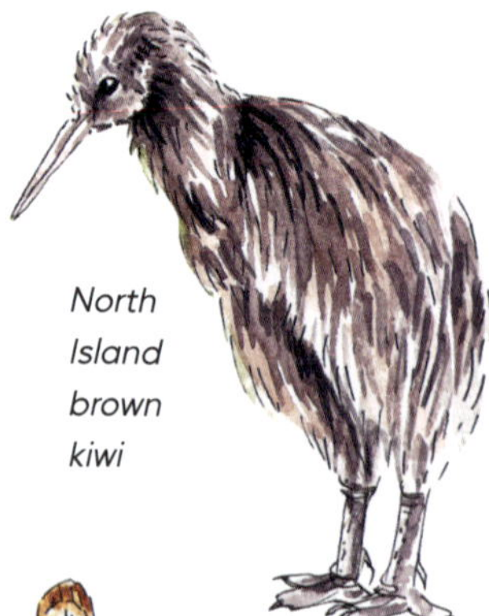

North Island brown kiwi

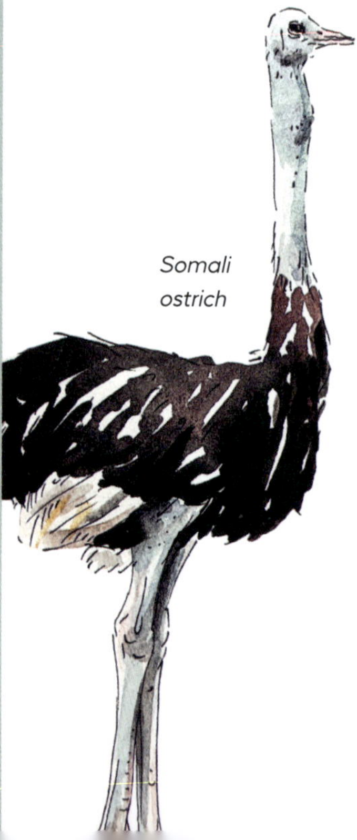

Somali ostrich

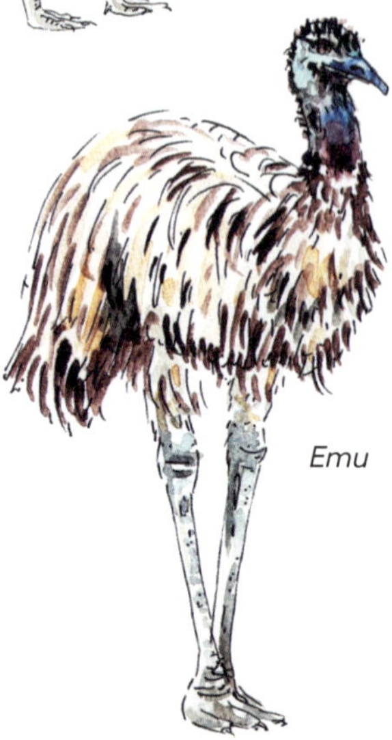

Emu

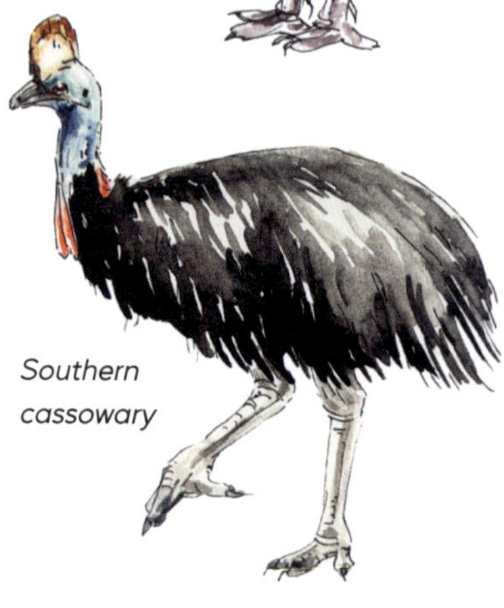

Southern cassowary

Common ostrich

Struthio camelus

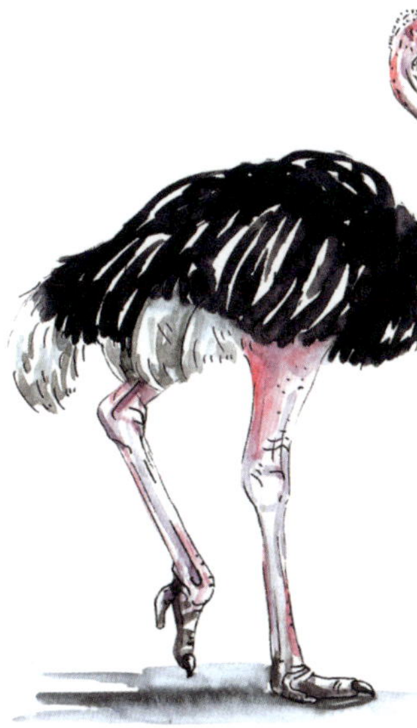

This African bird is the tallest and heaviest in the world, with a height of more than 2 m (6½ ft) and a weight of around 100 kg (220 lbs) or even more! Compared to other ratites, the ostrich has larger wings, which it uses in courtship displays.

They are great runners, and over long distance can outrun a horse. When attacked, they can kick with their massive legs. Unlike most other birds, which have four toes, ostriches have only two – one big toe with a nail and one smaller toe without a nail.

Key feature

We'll be drawing a male ostrich. Since the head is relatively small, let's focus on the strong legs of the bird and try to replicate the structure of the feathers, which is very specific to ratites.

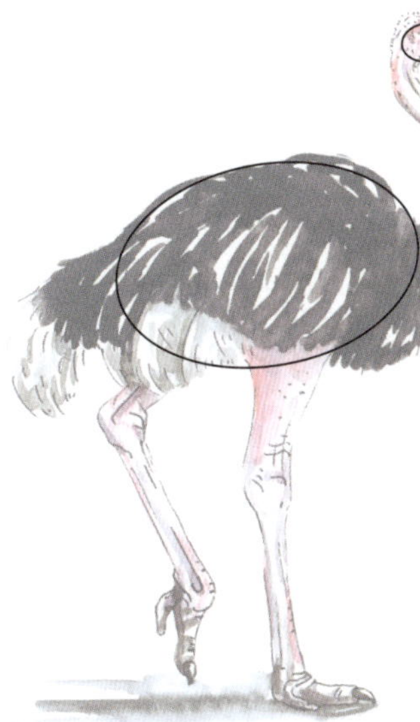

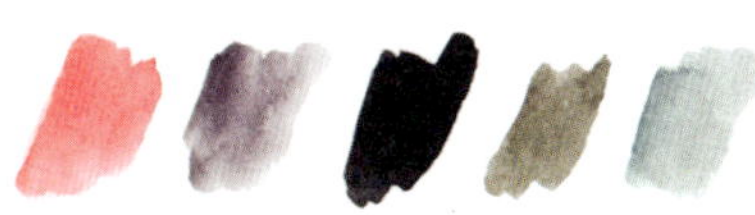

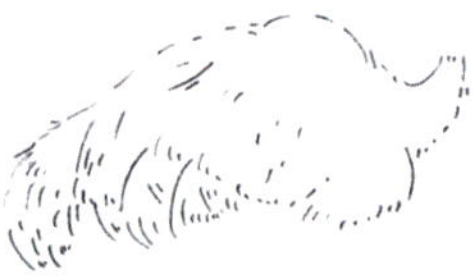

1. Begin by drawing the tail, body, wing and the bottom part of the neck. The bird has long feathers falling heavily down. Try to show this in your sketch.

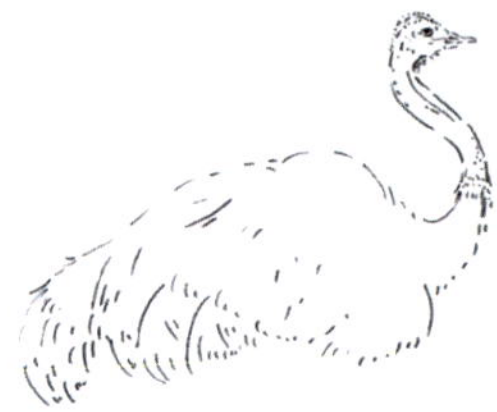

2. Draw the rest of the neck and the head. Focus only on the main parts, such as the eye and the beak. Use dots to show the fluff on the bare skin of the head.

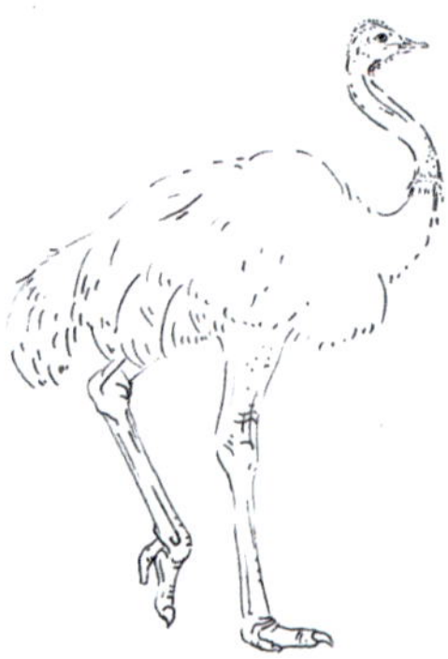

3. Finish the line art by drawing the massive legs. We can make them more detailed than usual. Show the texture of the skin and the two giant toes. Note that only the bigger one has a toenail.

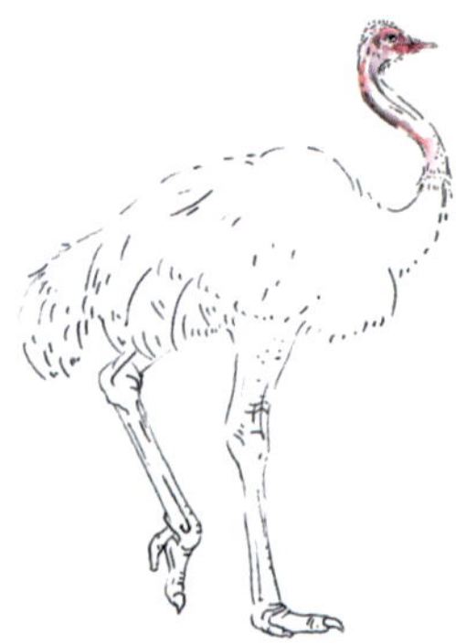

4. To colour the head and neck, apply some pinkish shades to the darkest parts and blend them gently with the paper. Add a few violet strokes to give more contrast to the areas that are in shadow.

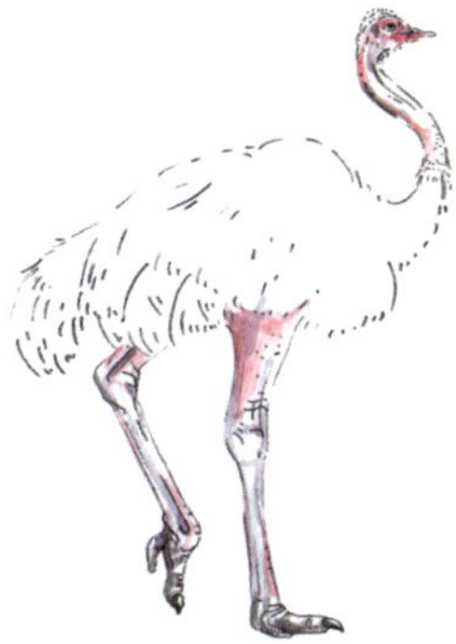

5. In the same way, colour the legs of the bird, but add darker strokes to the bottom part of the legs. Don't forget to paint the claws too, leaving white lines on the top parts to show the glossiness.

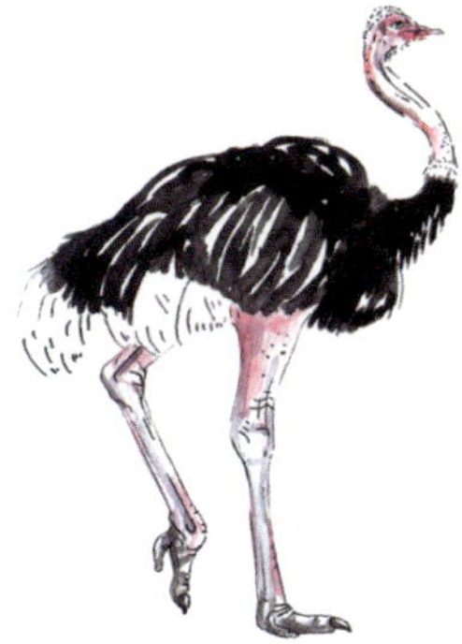

6. We can paint the black parts in just one layer if we keep a lot of white space, showing different values between the body, the wing and the tail.

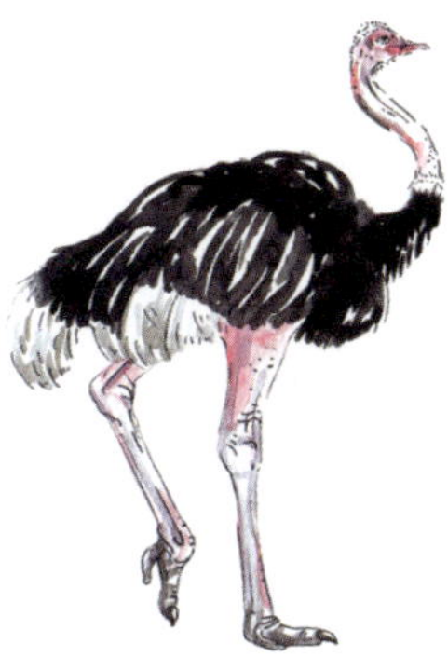

7. The tips of the wing and the tail are white but have a slightly dirty shade, which you can create with a diluted brownish pigment.

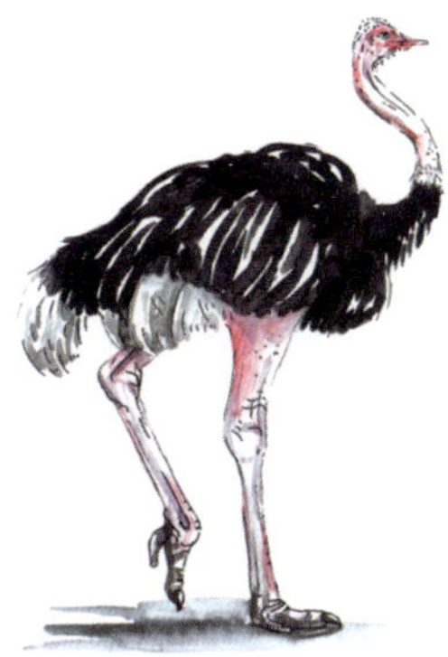

8. Add extra shadow to these white feathers and on the legs. With a few strokes highlight the white feathers on the neck – between the pink and black parts. Create a shadow wash under the bird as well.

Parrots

Parakeets, macaws, lorikeets, cockatoos, corellas, kākās and others

There are around 400 species in the Psittaciformes order, with most of them found in Oceania and South America. Despite such diversity, a third of parrots are on the verge of extinction due to hunting and habitat loss. As extremely intelligent birds, which are able to imitate human speech, they became very popular as pets – and trapping for the pet trade is one of the threats they face.

Most parrots are vividly coloured. They have a strong, curved beak to forage for seeds, nuts and fruits – this is their main diet. The head is large, with eye placement giving them a visual field unlike that of other birds. Some parrots have the longest lifespan among birds, living 80 to 100 years in captivity.

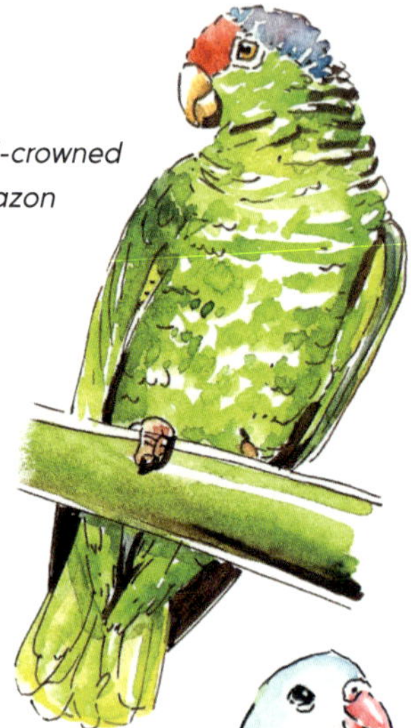

Red-crowned amazon

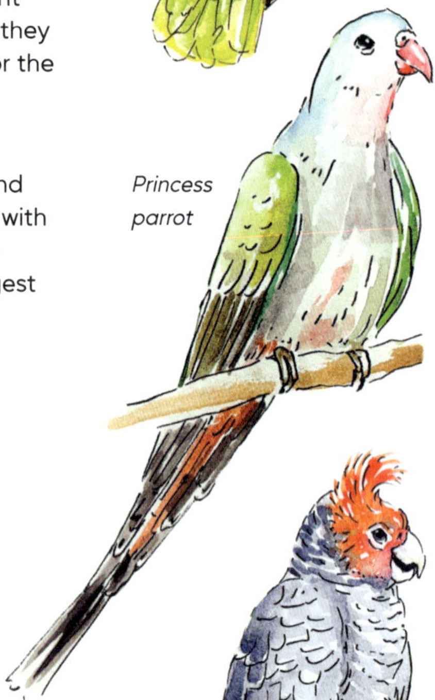

Princess parrot

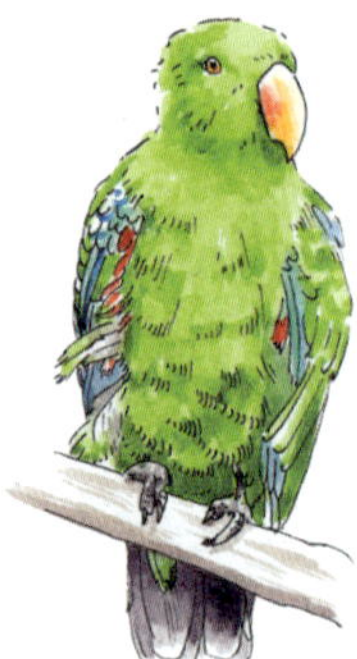

Eclectus parrot

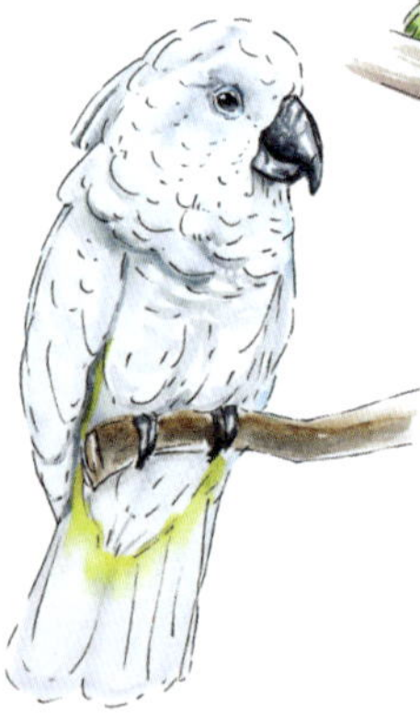

Blue-eyed cockatoo

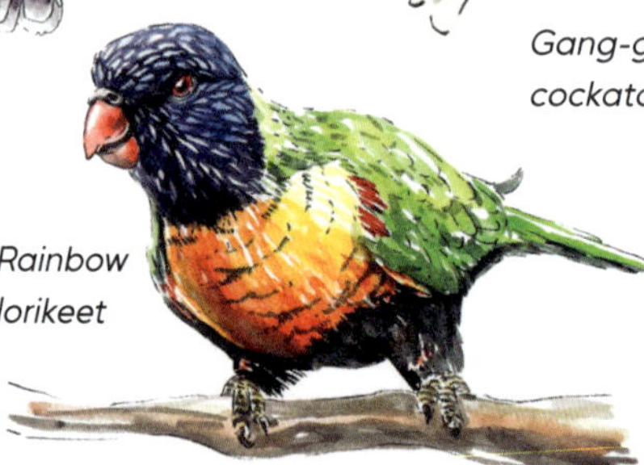

Rainbow lorikeet

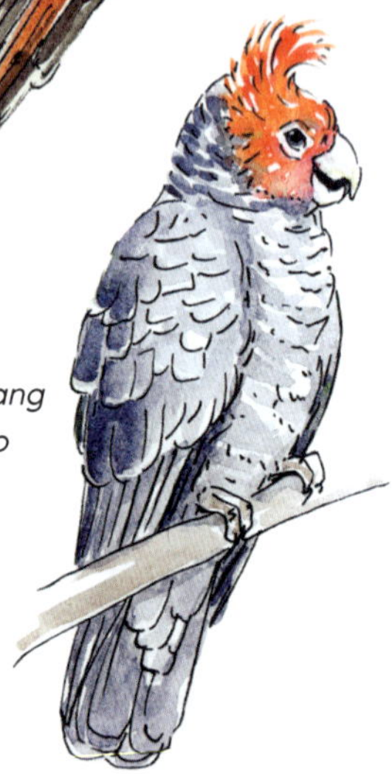

Gang-gang cockatoo

Monk parakeet

Myiopsitta monachus

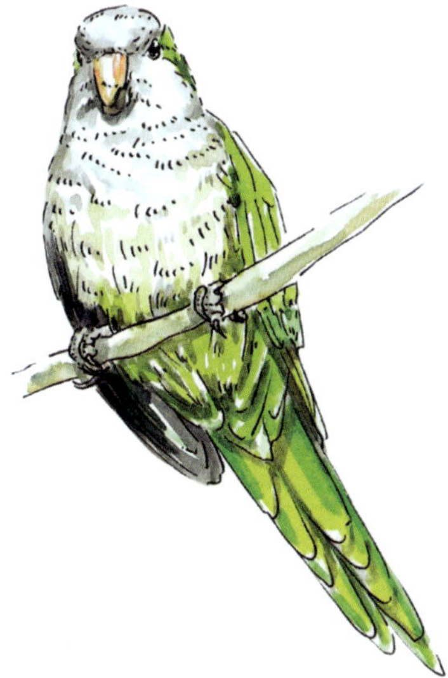

This bird, also known as the Quaker parrot, originates from South America – but after being introduced as a pet to other parts of the world, has created stable feral populations in Europe and North Africa. Monk parakeets are social birds, which breed in colonies and build large nests suitable for many pairs.

Like other parrots, monk parakeets have two toes facing forward and two backward, which they use for perching, climbing and manipulating objects, much like humans use their hands.

Key feature

This pose is similar to the cuckoo (see page 47), but we'll explore the way the bird looks with its head facing almost forward – a tricky angle to draw.

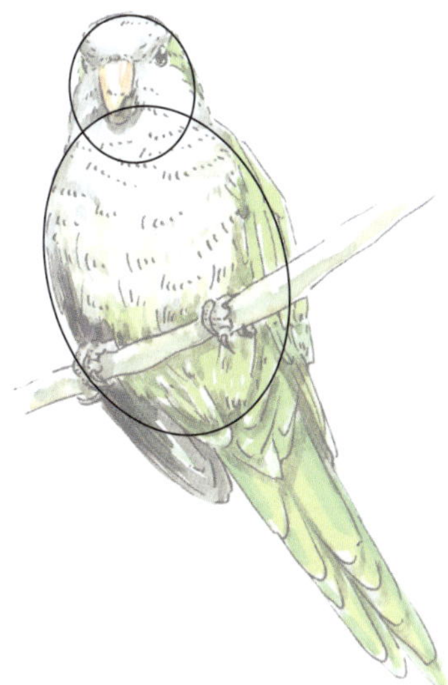

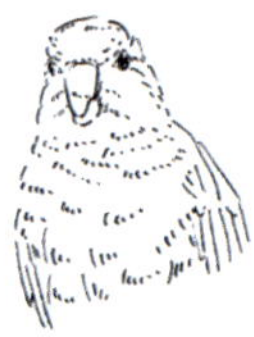

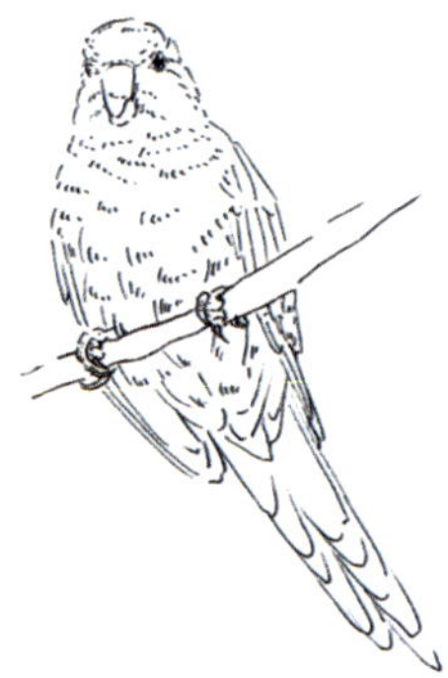

1. The head oval looks squarish from this angle, and the beak seems almost flat, so pay extra attention to how you draw it and the eyes. Map out the top part of the body.

2. Make the toes of the bird cling clearly to the branch and pay attention to the structure and the length of the tail.

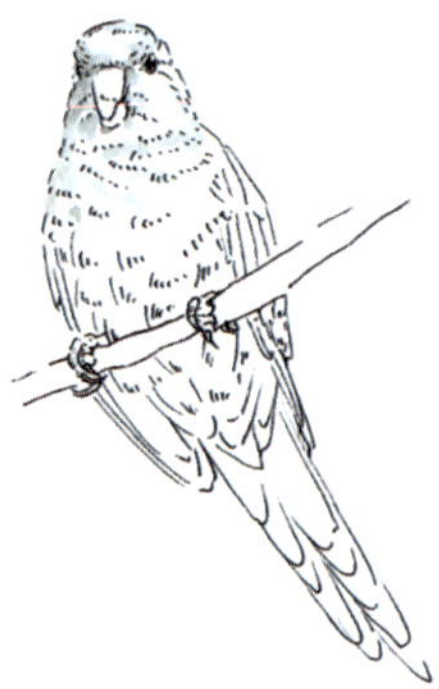

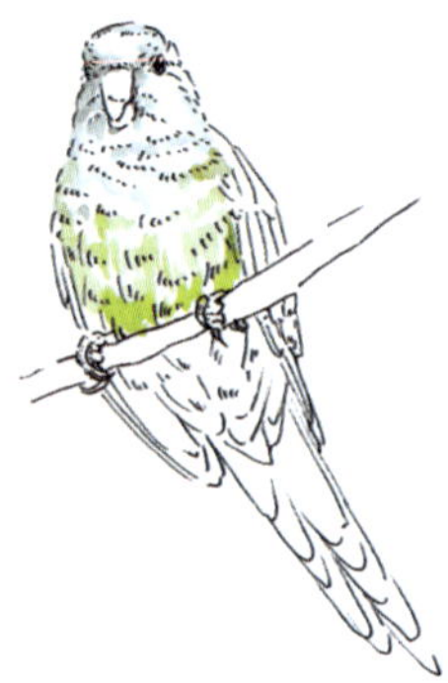

3. The front part of the bird is really light in colour, so you can just create the volume by adding shades. The left part of the head is darker because the light is coming from the top-right corner above the bird.

4. To colour the belly I recommend using a mix of green and yellow. Blend it nicely with the blue shades on the head by overlapping the layers.

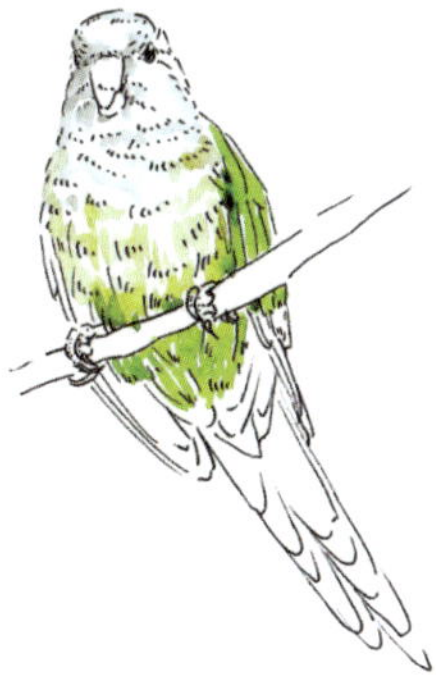

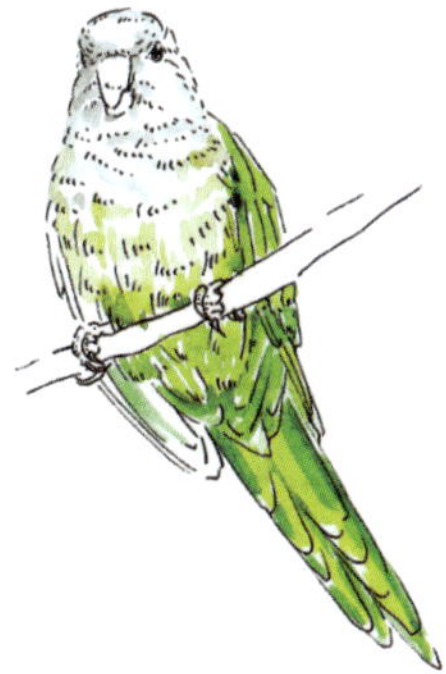

5. Paint the bottom belly with a more vivid green colour. You can use the same colour to paint the right wing, making it slightly darker on the left where the breast feathers cover it.

6. Mix some cool shades into your green to colour the lowest feathers, and create layers of different shades of green on the tail of the bird.

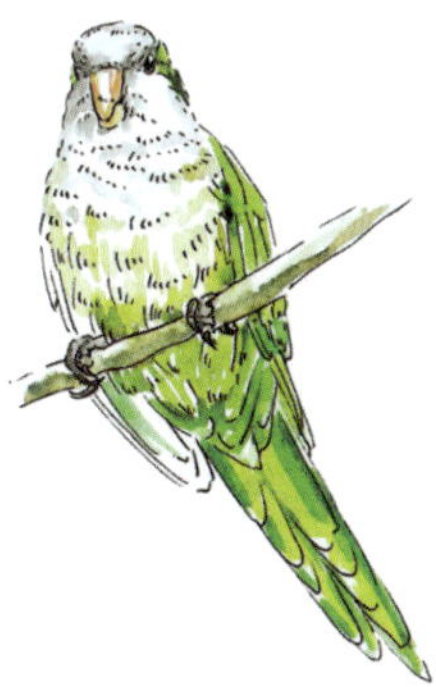

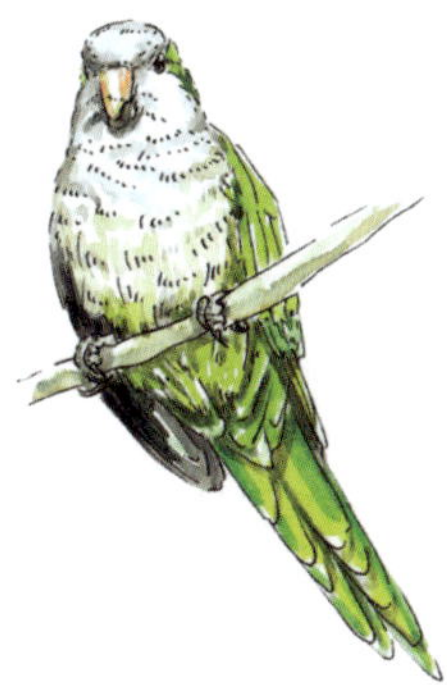

7. Give some colour to the beak, darkening it on the sides and leaving a white space in the middle. Colour the patches going from the eyes to the back of the head, then the toes and the branch.

8. Add shadows to the head, bottom parts of different feather groups across the body and under the feet on the branch. The darkest part should be under the left wing.

Kingfishers

Along with kookaburras

These birds from the family Alcedinidae are distributed across the world, with most of the 118 species found in tropical regions of Asia, Oceania and Africa. However, some of species live in the Americas and Europe, making this family very cosmopolitan. They are typically colourful, showing some interesting patterns in their plumage.

The key characteristics of these birds are small bodies with short legs and massive long beaks. As the name suggests, their diet consists mostly of fish, and this is what their anatomy is built for – to dive into the water from perching branches. Some species in the family, use this hunting technique to feed on small invertebrates rather than fish.

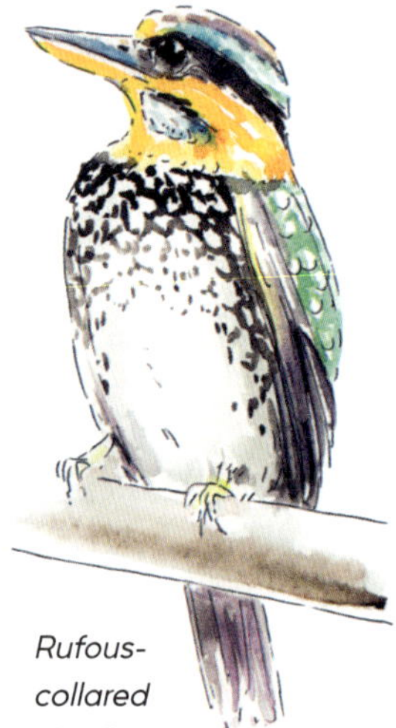
Rufous-collared kingfisher

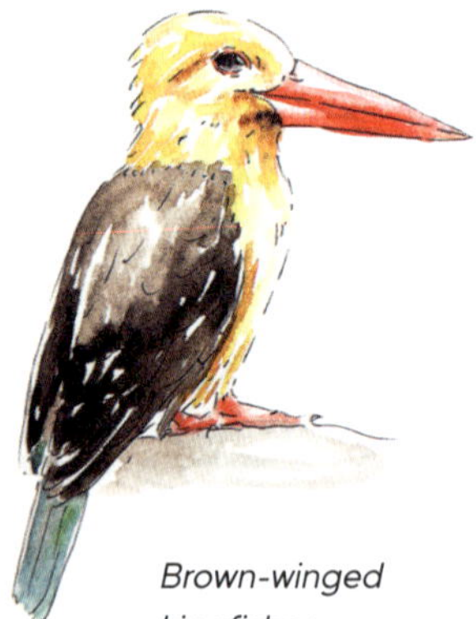
Brown-winged kingfisher

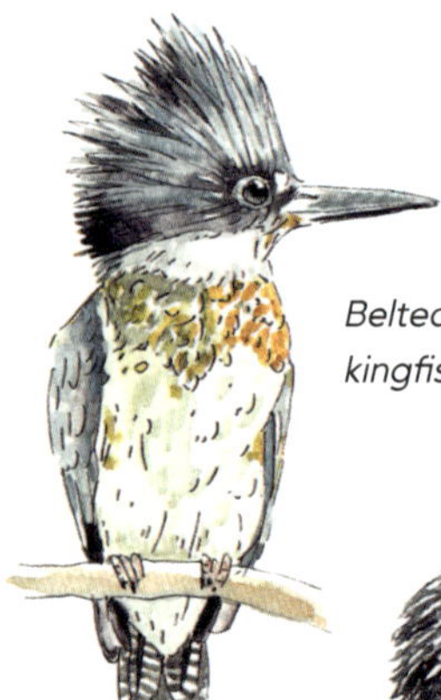
Belted kingfisher

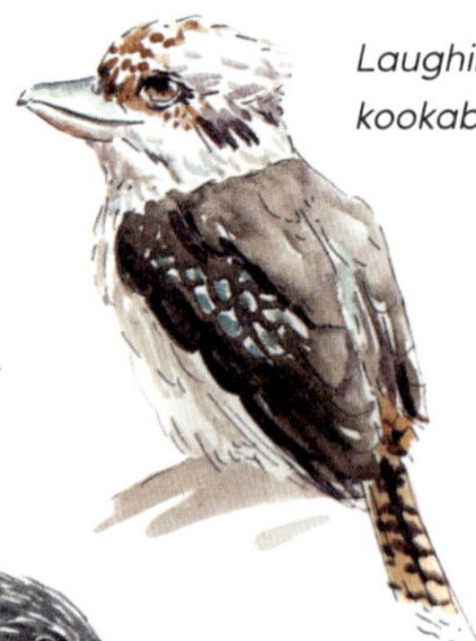
Laughing kookaburra

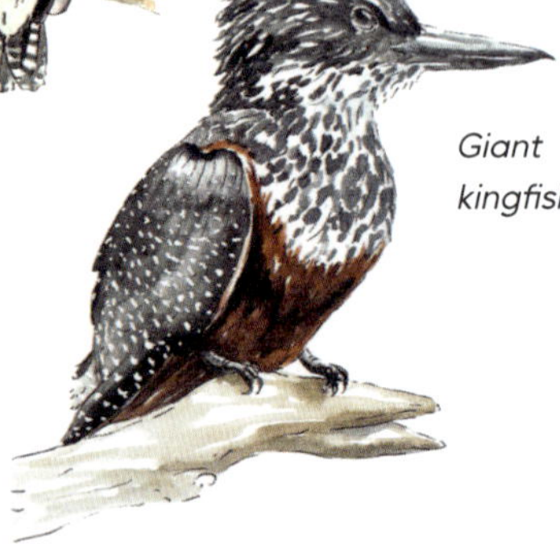
Giant kingfisher

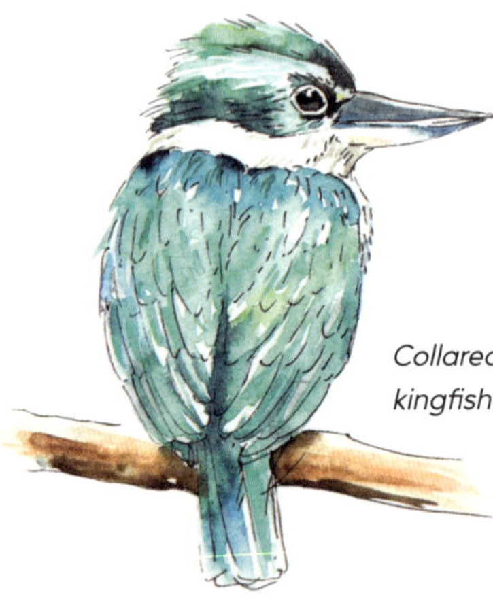
Collared kingfisher

Common kingfisher

Alcedo atthis

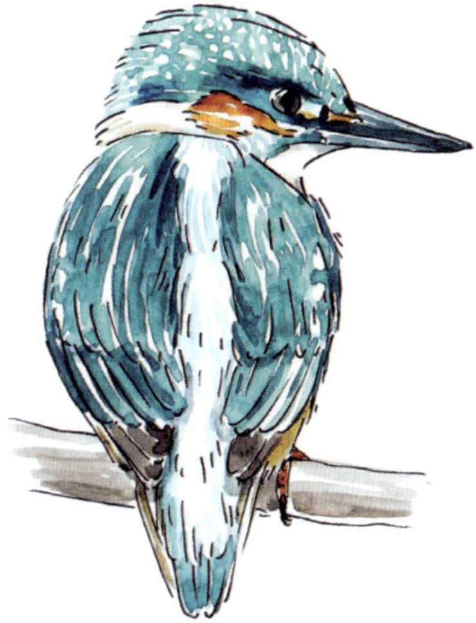

Another name for this bird is the Eurasian kingfisher, since it lives mostly in Europe and Asia, with wintering grounds in North Africa. It's the only kingfisher that can be found in Europe and is definitely one of the most colourful birds in this area.

It lives by shallow open water and has a special vision adaptation that allows it to see underwater. Common kingfishers build nests in burrows they excavate in steep riverbanks.

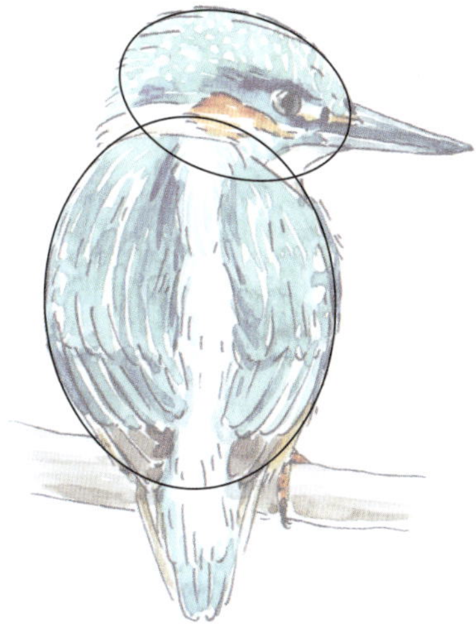

Key feature

The bird has a very distinctive orange breast and belly parts, but let's practise drawing a back view. I'll also show you how I make this spotted pattern on the head.

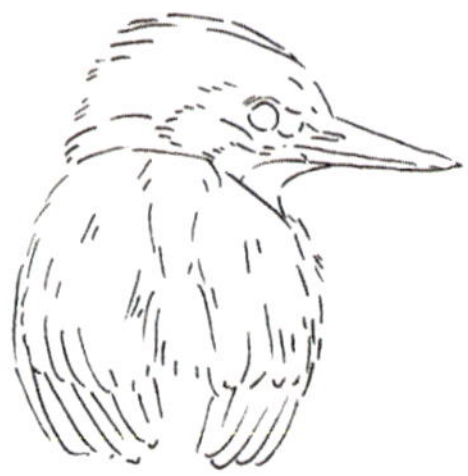

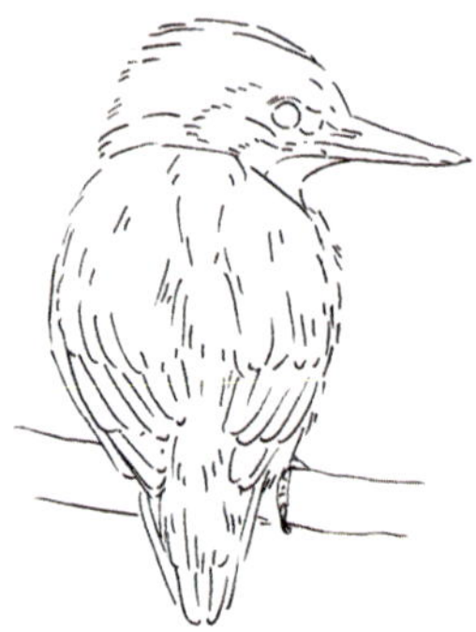

1. Draw the slightly rectangular shape of the head and a really big and strong beak. Note how, although we see the bird from the back, the wings are not totally symmetrical.

2. Finalize the wings and add the short tail as a continuation of the back. We also see a small toe on the right and the branch it is sitting on.

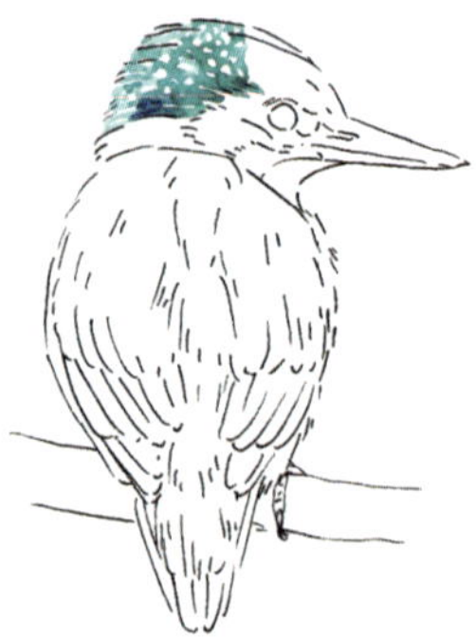

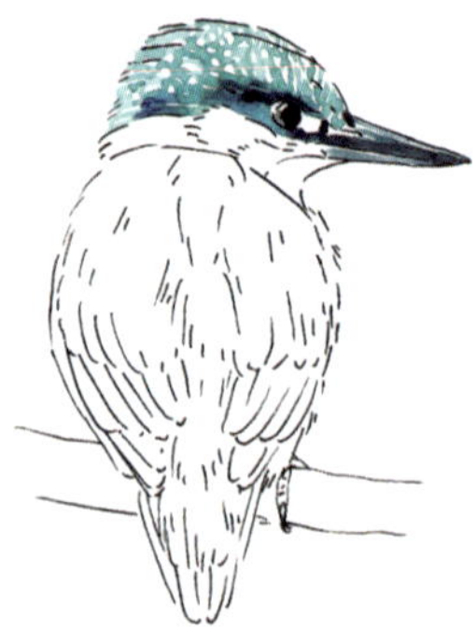

3. To create the pattern on the head, draw small empty circles and – before the paint dries – colour the space between them. Use different shades of blue and aqua to show the volume.

4. Finalize the head. Note how the circles turn into bars closer to the beak. Colour the beak, the dark patch around the eye, and the eye itself, but leave a white spot between the eye and the beak.

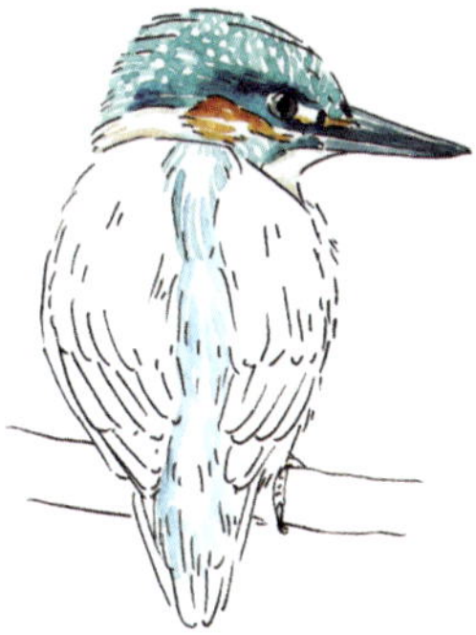

5. Paint the rufous cheek and the small patch between the white spot and the beak. The neck is almost white, but with a bit of ochre. Paint the back of the bird from top to the rump above the tail.

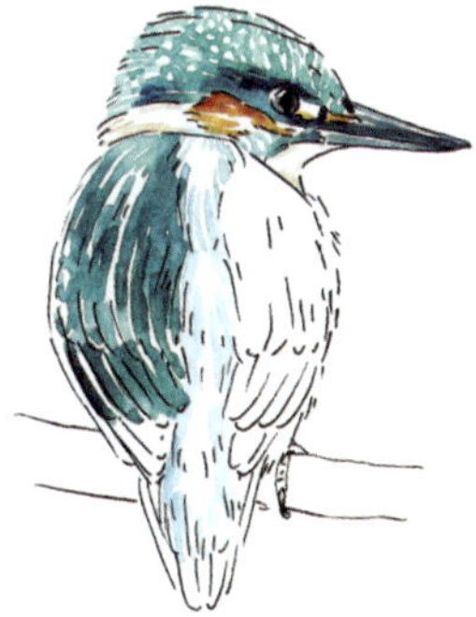

6. Cover the left wing with similar shades to those we used for the head. The direction of your brush strokes should repeat those you made with the pen.

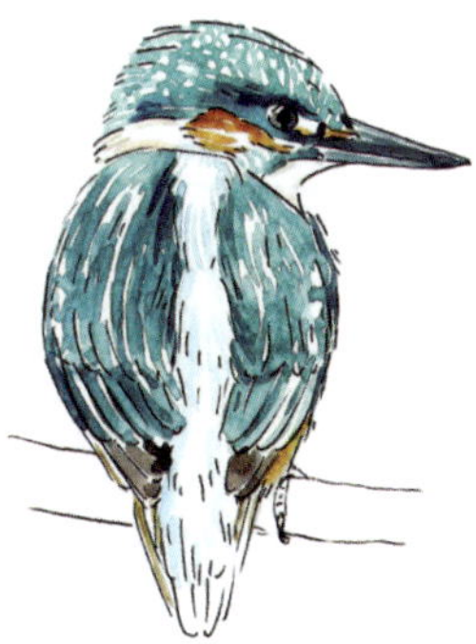

7. Paint the right wing the same way. Colour the tips of both wings, a few belly feathers we see on the right, and the further tail feathers, with shades of brown.

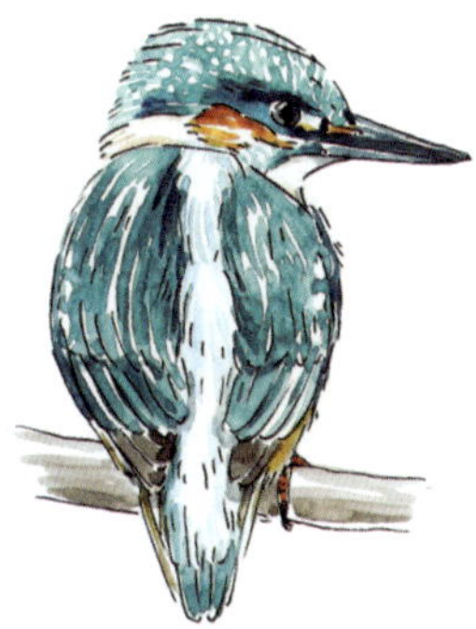

8. Complete the tail by adding aqua to the tip. Paint the toe with an almost red rufous colour. With a few diluted brown strokes, depict the branch under the bird.

Hummingbirds

Jacobins, pufflegs, sunbeams, brilliants, coquettes, gems and others

These rapid tiny birds are beloved by many people for their cute and colourful appearance. The family they belong to, Trochilidae, consists of 375 species, with most of them distributed across Central and South America. Hummingbirds are highly adapted to speedy flight and hovering. Their wings flap so fast that they produce a humming sound, which the birds are named after.

The smallest bird in the world is a hummingbird measuring only 5 cm (2 in) long. With such compact bodies, they have comparatively long, thin beaks for feeding on flower nectar. They also eat insects. Hummingbirds have very small and short legs, which they hide in their feathers when flying to be more manoeuvrable.

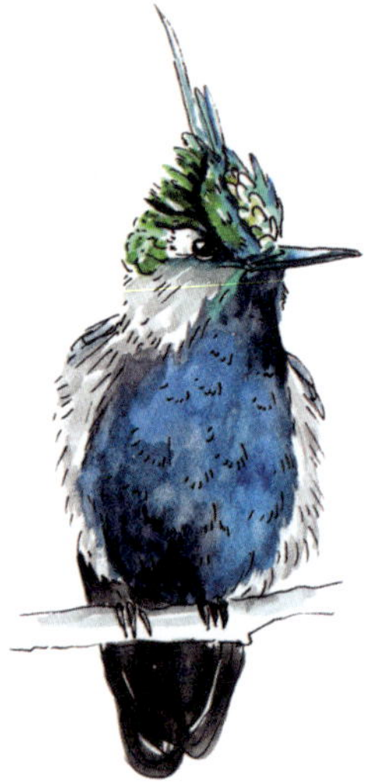

Green-crowned plovercrest

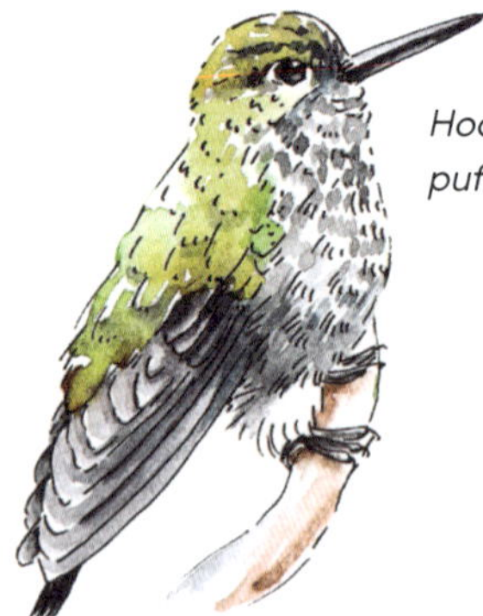

Hoary puffleg

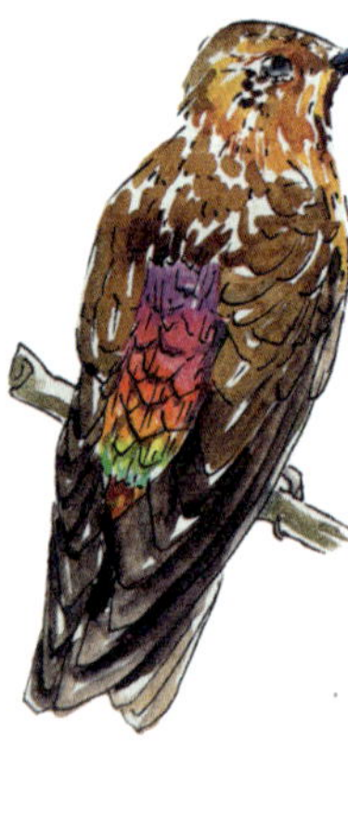

Shining sunbeam

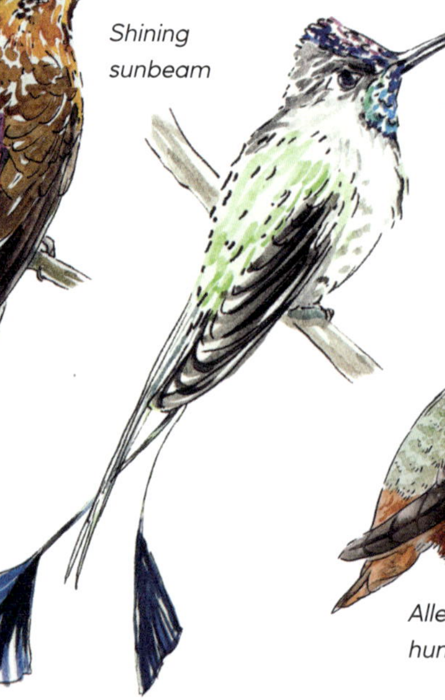

Marvellous spatuletail

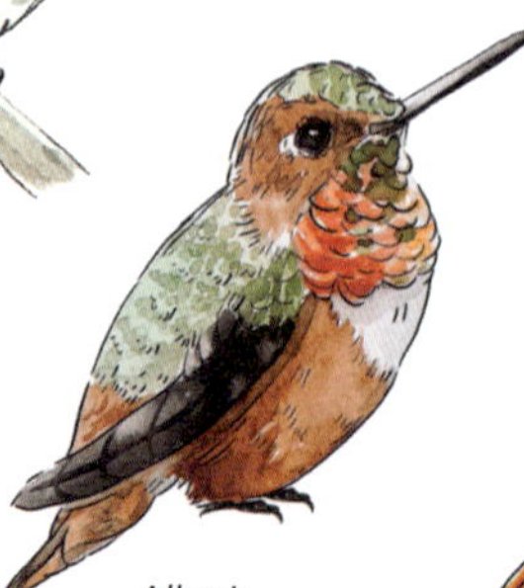

Allen's hummingbird

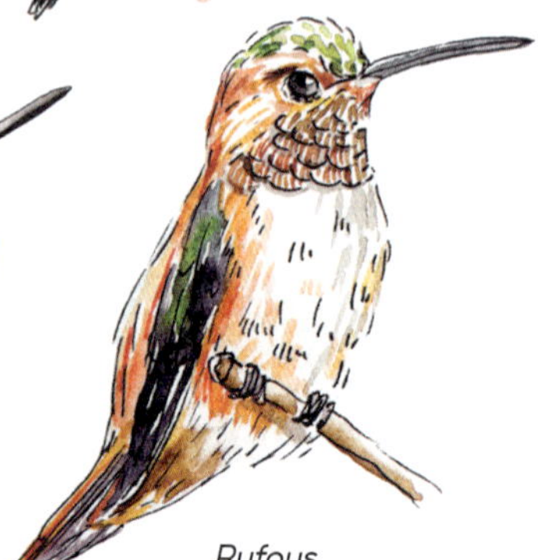

Rufous hummingbird

Ruby-throated hummingbird

Archilochus colubris

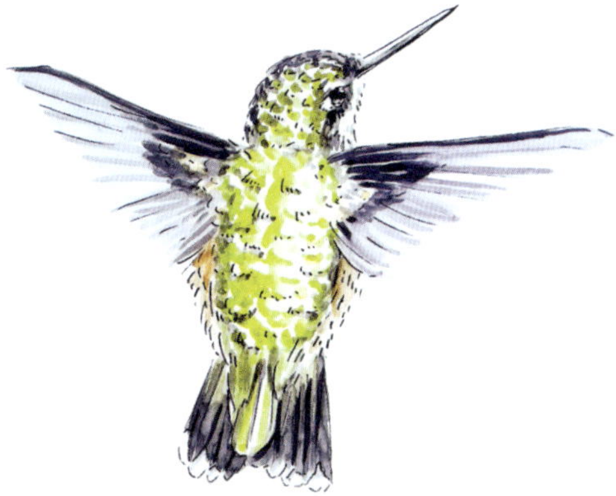

The most common hummingbird of North America migrates across the whole continent to winter in Central America. On this journey, they fly non-stop across the Gulf of Mexico for more than 1,000 km (620 miles).

The bird's name comes from the appearance of the adult male, which has an iridescent ruby-coloured throat patch that looks almost black in low light. Males also lack white tips on the tail, which females have.

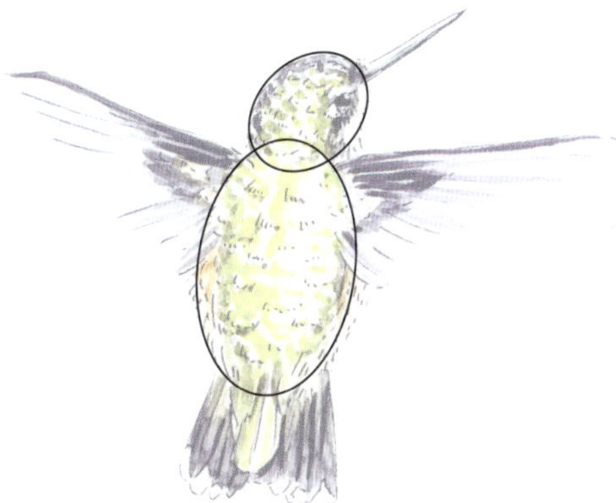

Key feature

We'll be drawing a female, focusing on the appearance of the shiny green back and quickly flapping wings.

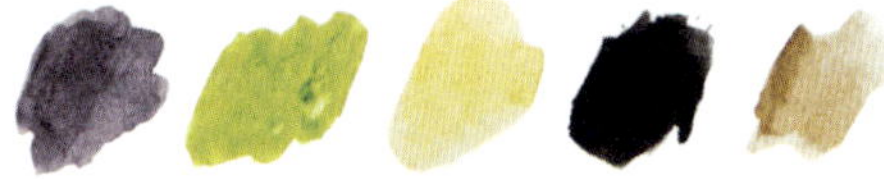

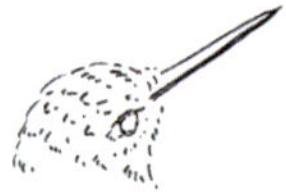

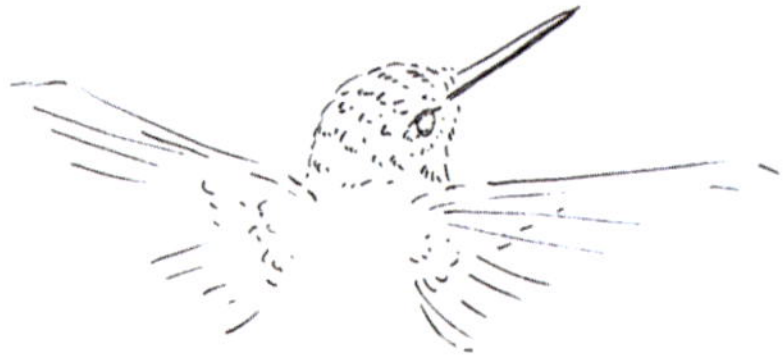

1. Draw the texture of the feathers on the back of the bird's head, and the long and sharp beak. From this angle, the eye appears slightly flattened.

2. Don't focus on the structure of the wings too much – we see them mostly as a blur. Indicate the direction of the feathers, and leave plenty of space between the lines.

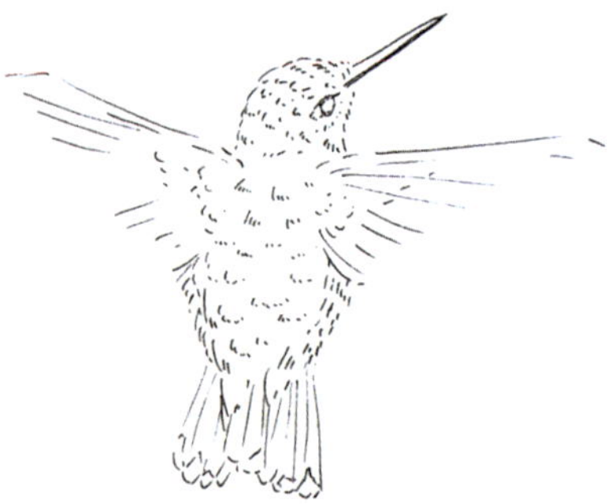

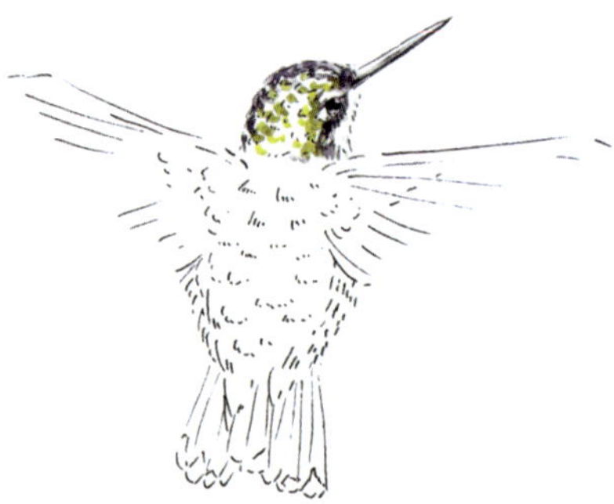

3. Define the body of the bird by creating the texture of the feathers on the back, the puffed flank on the sides, and the tail of the bird, which is slightly fan-shaped.

4. To show the iridescence, use short strokes with colours from very dark to olive green and yellowish shades. Colour the eye and beak, leaving the white patches on the left side of the eye and neck.

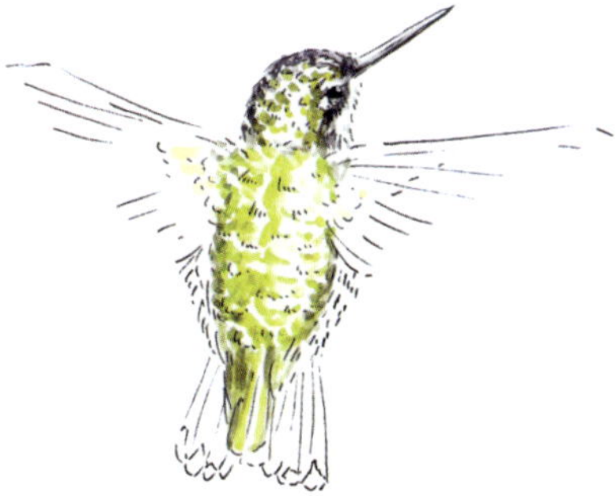

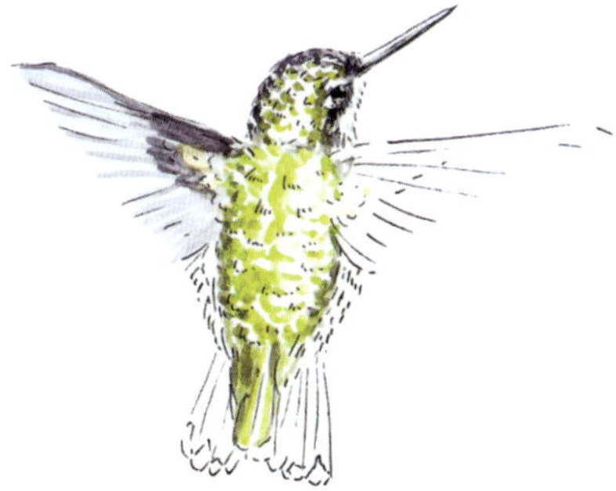

5. The back and rump have the same olive green shade we used on the head. Create texture by making quick strokes, and leave a lot of white space on the right side, where the light reflects on the feathers.

6. Colour the left wing by adding some dark brown or violet near the bird's body and in the direction of the feathers. Wash it gently to imitate the movement of the wings.

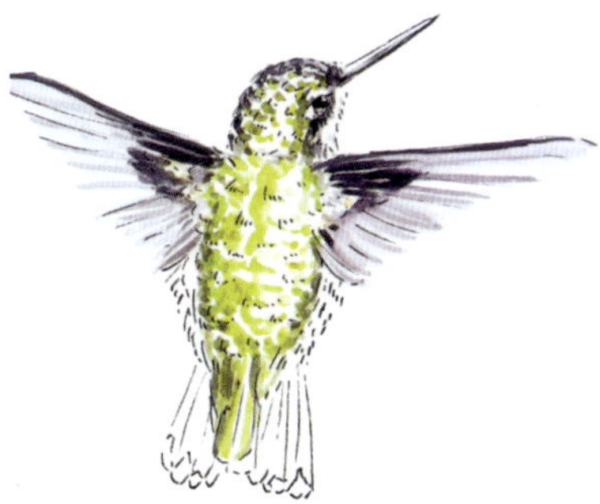

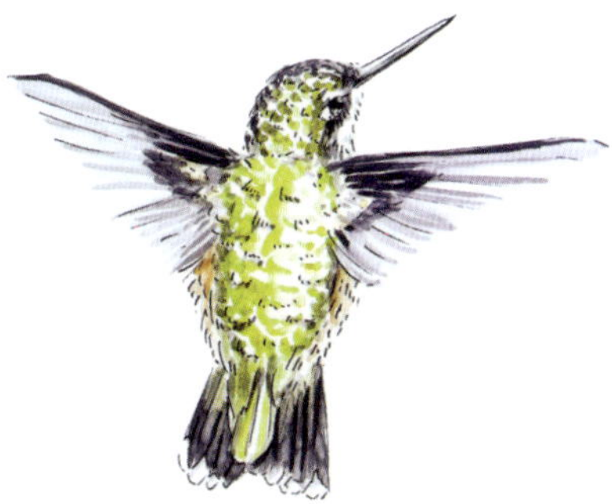

7. Repeat for the second wing. I made it a bit darker to add contrast, and adjusted the first wing to match.

8. Colour the flank feathers that pop out below the wings with some warmer tones, and paint the tail with dark colour, leaving the tips of the tail feathers white.

Other tropical birds

Toucans, birds-of-paradise, tanagers, turacos, cotingas and many more

We talked about parrots, hummingbirds and kingfishers, but there are other amazing-looking birds in tropical forests. This habitat is full of life and biodiversity, including a wealth of bird species – each bird has evolved to be distinct from other species.

The craziest plumages and exaggerated features can be found among these birds. Their colourful appearance helps them hide among bright flowers and fruits but also stands out during courtship displays, with dense vegetation as a background.

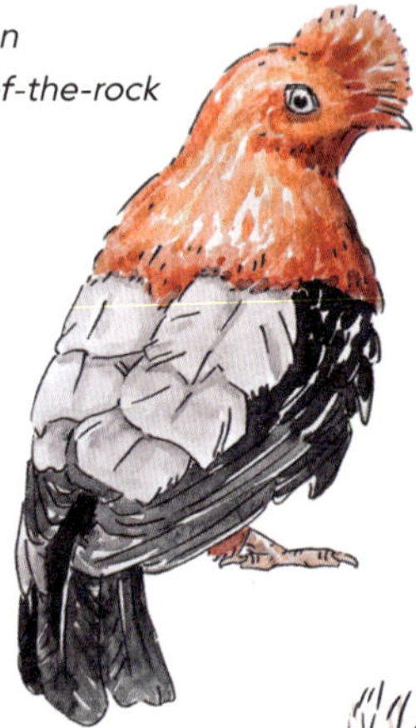

Andean cock-of-the-rock

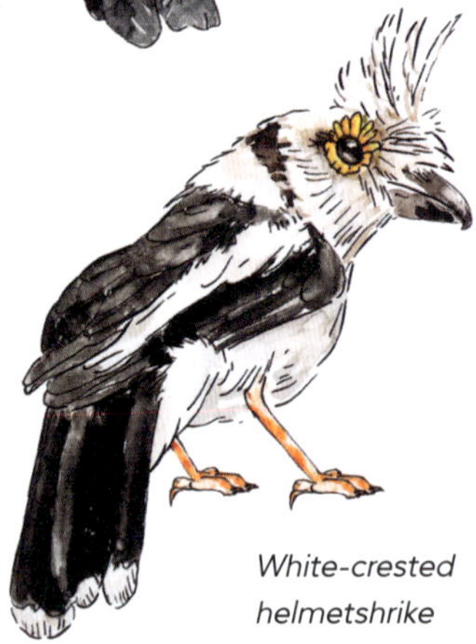

White-crested helmetshrike

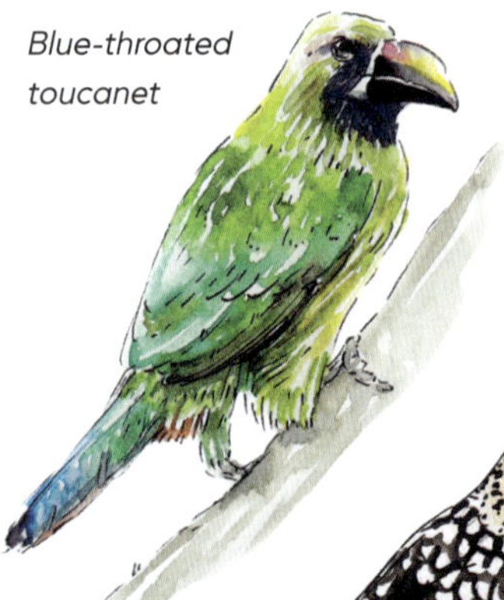

Blue-throated toucanet

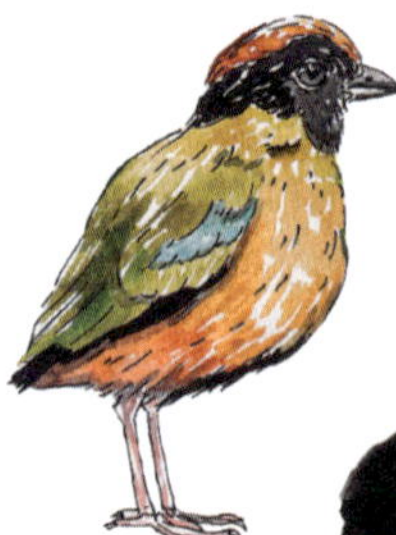

Noisy pitta

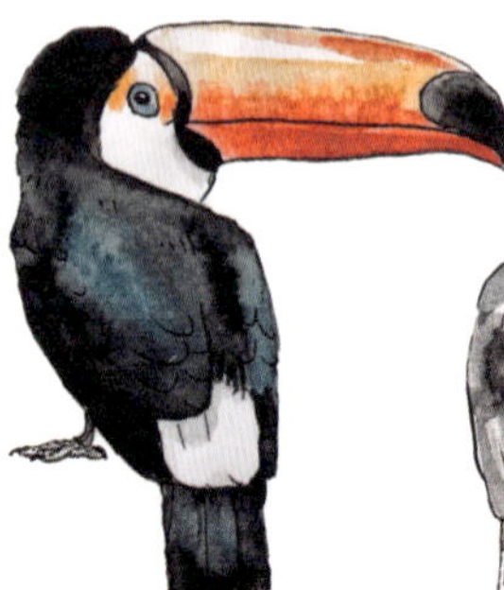

Toco toucan

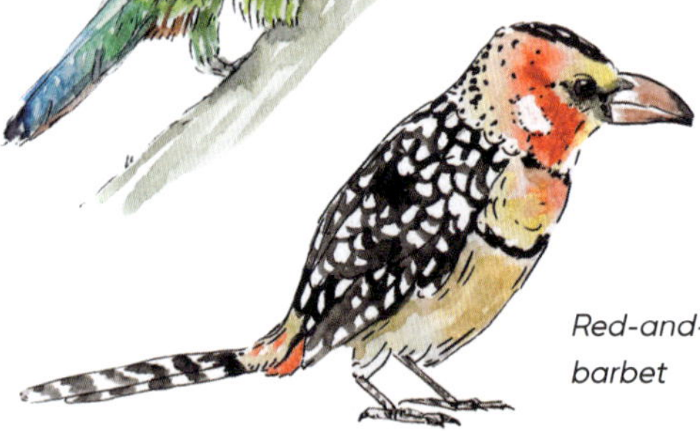

Red-and-yellow barbet

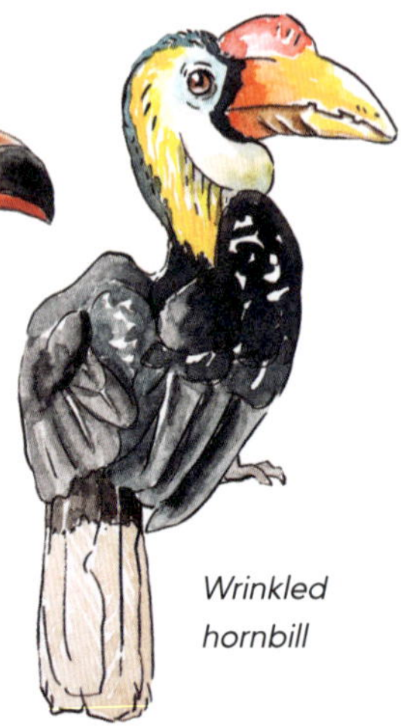

Wrinkled hornbill

Resplendent quetzal

Pharomachrus mocinno

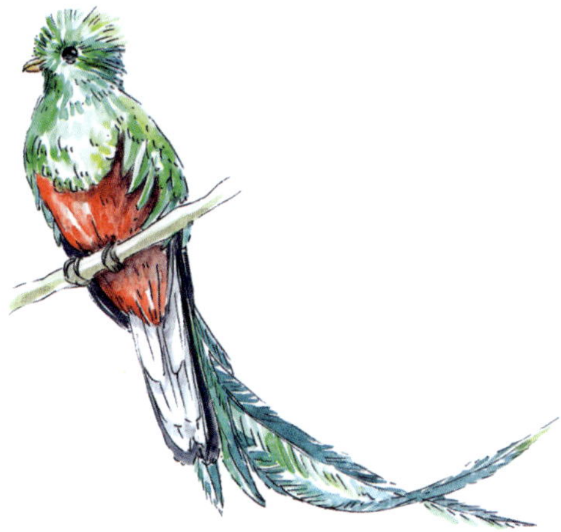

The national bird of Guatemala can be found in the warm forests of Central America and parts of Mexico. Males have marvellous, mostly green and red plumage with extensive upper tail coverts, around 50 cm (20 in) long.

The green parts of the bird can change colour depending on the light, sometimes looking more bluish and sometimes golden. They are in fact mostly brown, and show these variations due to the structure of the feathers, which creates this optical effect.

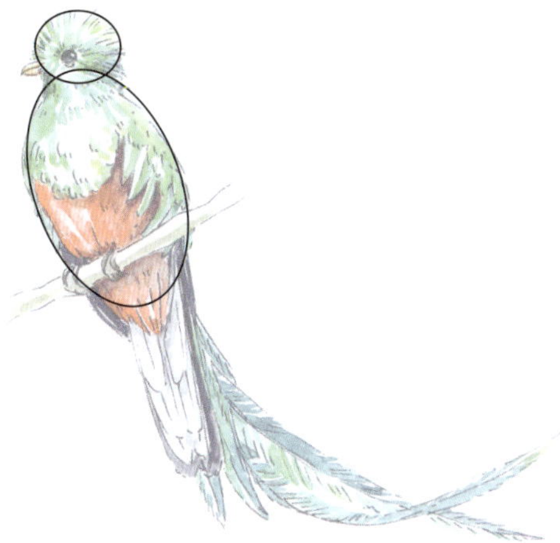

Key feature

Our goal is to capture the beauty of the stunning tail and other specific features of this amazing bird. Let's dive in and see how unusual and distinctive a bird can look!

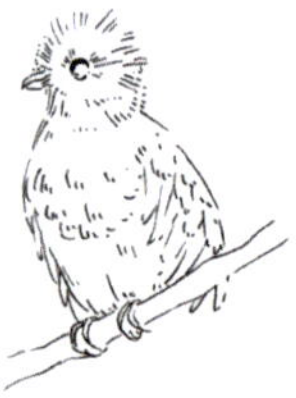

1. The feathers on the head radiate around the eye in different directions. Another thing to pay attention to is the wing feathers covering the breast from both sides.

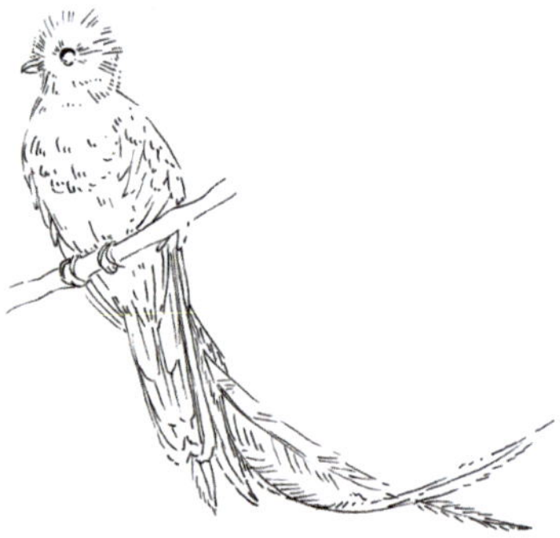

2. To draw the long tail feathers flowing behind the bird, start from the middle parts of these feathers, then add volume with short strokes around them.

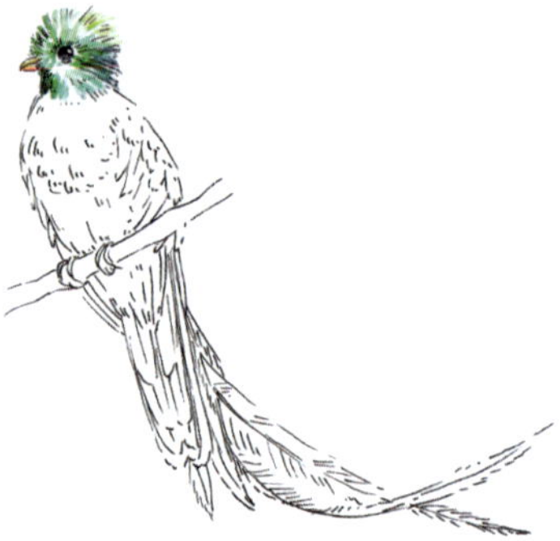

3. With long confident strokes going from the eye, apply various colours to shape the head. Leave plenty of white space to make them look glossy. Colour the beak and the eye as well.

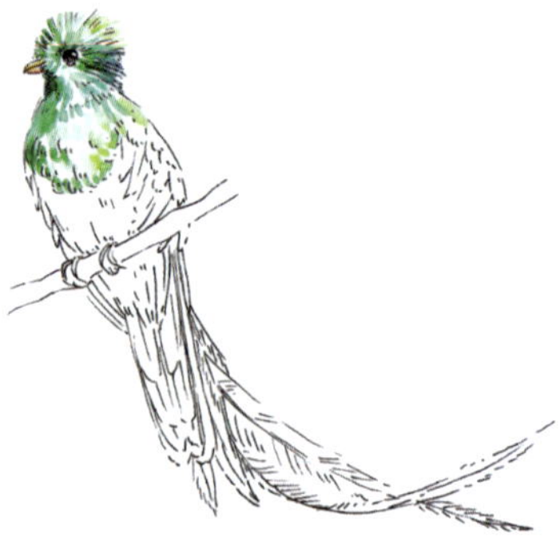

4. Using the same colours, continue painting the breast of the bird. Show the difference in texture by making short strokes.

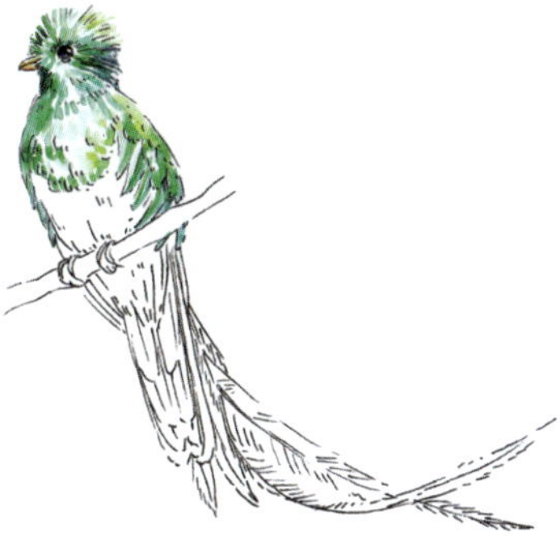

5. Create a graduated transition from the long wing feathers that cover the breast to the back of the bird, making the back lighter.

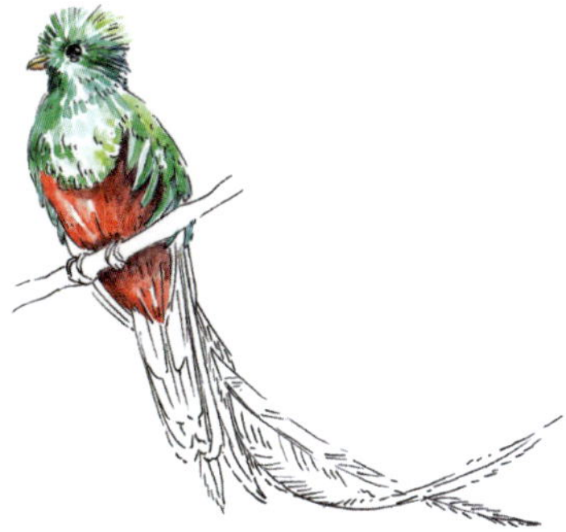

6. The belly and undertail have a bright red colour. Use different shades, making it much darker under the wing and under the branch, since these parts are in shadow.

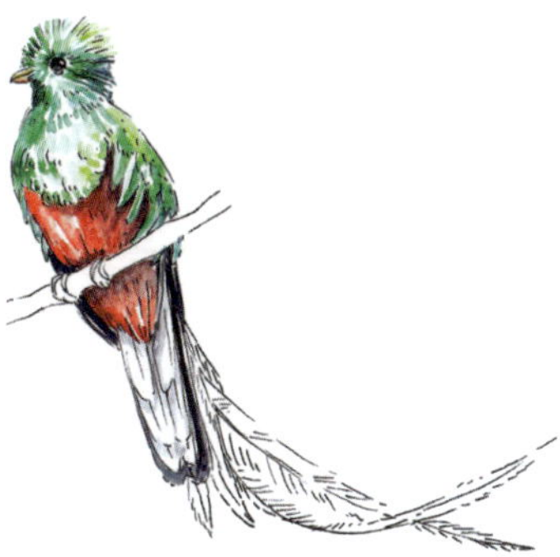

7. The darkest parts are the longer feathers of the wing. The tail feathers closest to us are almost white, but there are a few dark ones behind.

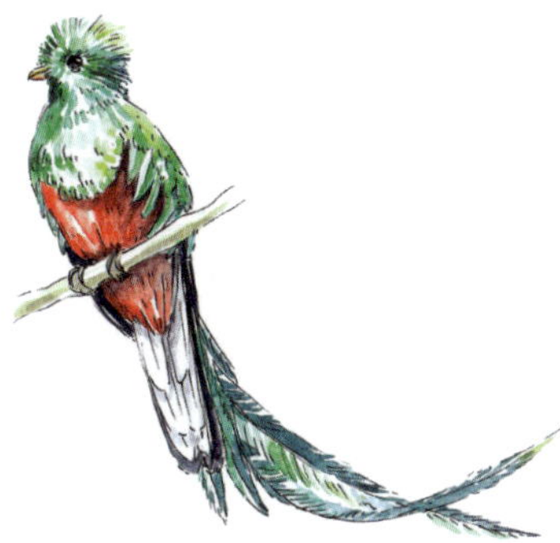

8. For the longest feathers of the tail, use different shades of green and blue to show iridescence. Copy the feather texture when making brush strokes. Colour the feet and the branch.

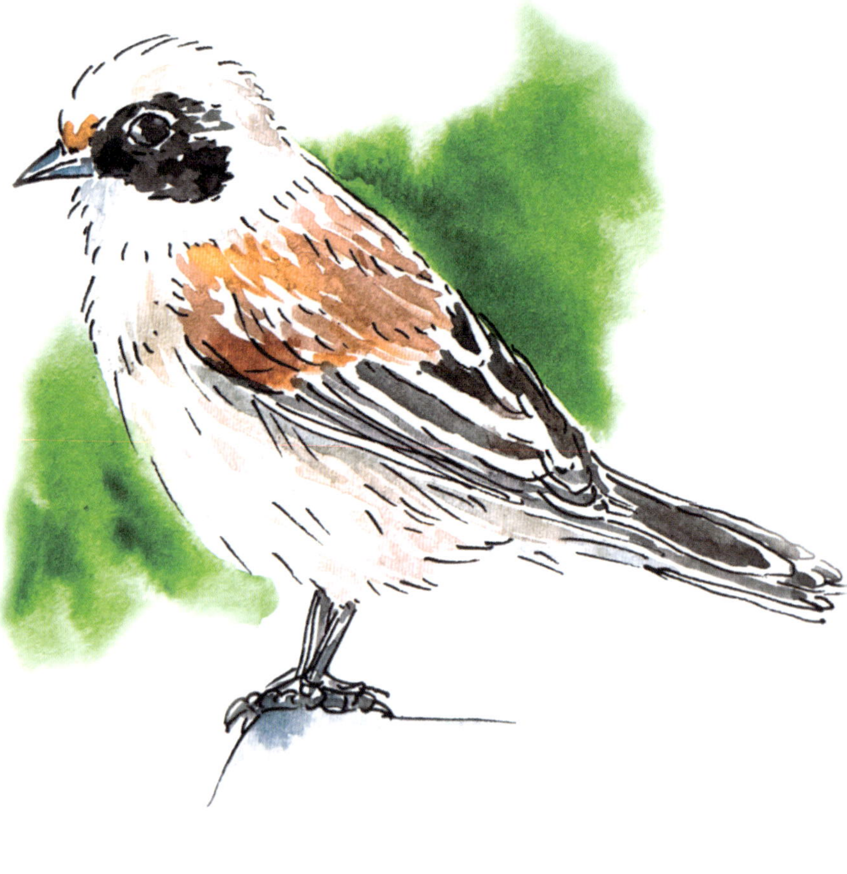

Chapter three

More than a drawing

Turn your bird drawings into a powerful tool for learning about birds and their lives. Let's find out what you can add to your sketch to make a beautiful informational page.

Background

Adding washes and abstract shapes

Even a simple and abstract background can serve a specific purpose on your page. It can set a mood, add depth and context to your drawing, show light direction and create contrast. Depending on the function of your background, you can choose a different colour palette and a technique for it.

You can also connect different pages of your sketchbook by creating a series of drawings with the same background style. Using a limited palette keeps sketches cohesive.

To create an abstract background, use techniques you already know:

- Graduated wash
- Colour transition
- Layering
- Wet-on-wet

I usually combine graduated wash or colour transition with the wet-on-wet technique to create a smooth background that doesn't take over the drawing, keeping the bird the main subject. Play around to see what works best for you.

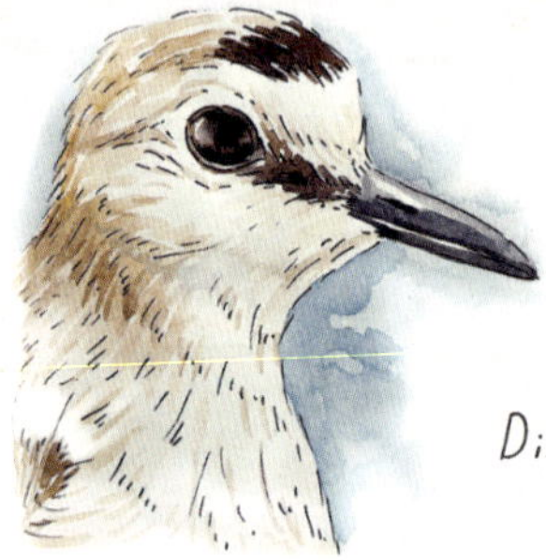

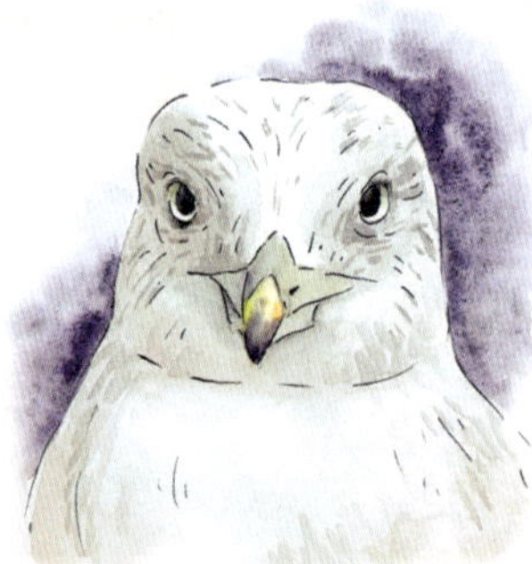

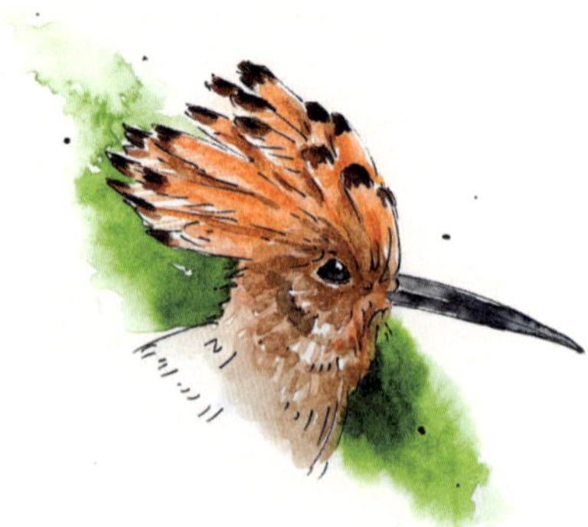

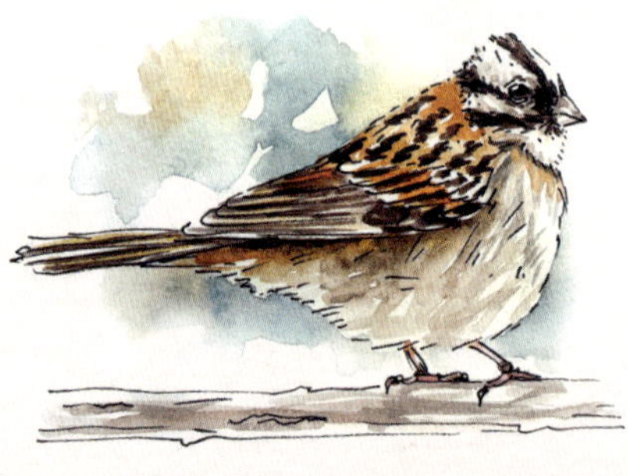

There are some additional techniques that we haven't discussed yet, but which can be very useful:

- A flat wash that creates a simple one-colour background or can be used to draw geometric shapes around the bird.
- Using salt to add an interesting texture to the wash.
- A splatter of colour for a more expressive background – just be careful not to cover the bird with paint.
- Masking with special fluid or tape to keep some parts uncovered.

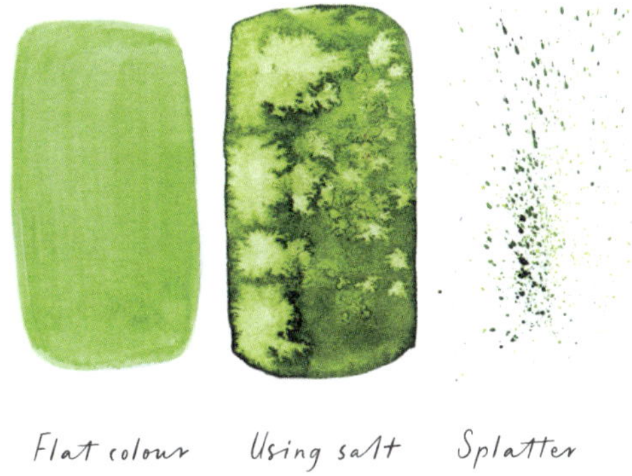

Top tip

You can also use all of these techniques to create a still abstract but more organic background, resembling foliage, sky or water. It won't be a proper landscape behind the bird, but it can suggest its habitat.

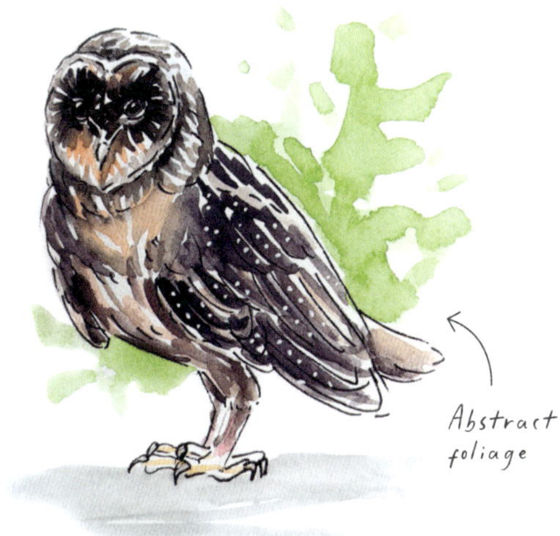

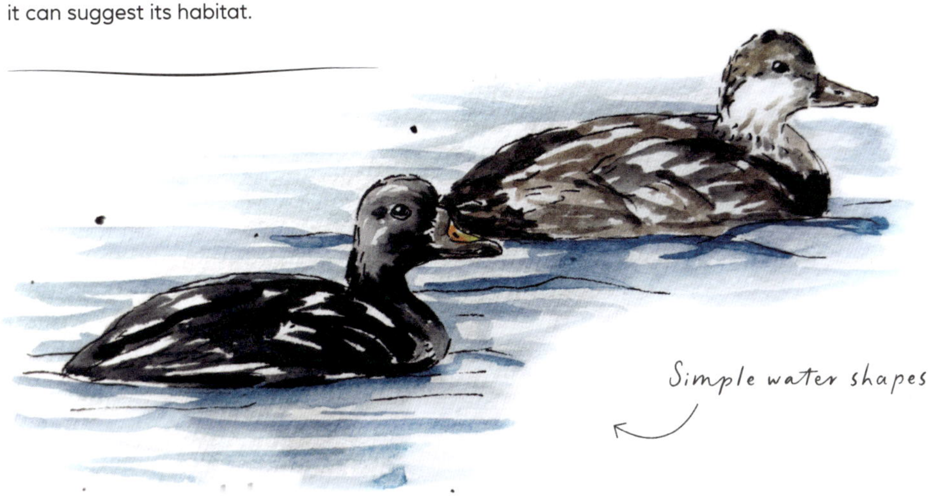

Typography

Text and other visual elements as part of the composition

Adding notes and additional text elements to your sketches can enrich your pages with extra information. You can write down things you can't draw, making the drawings more meaningful and personal.

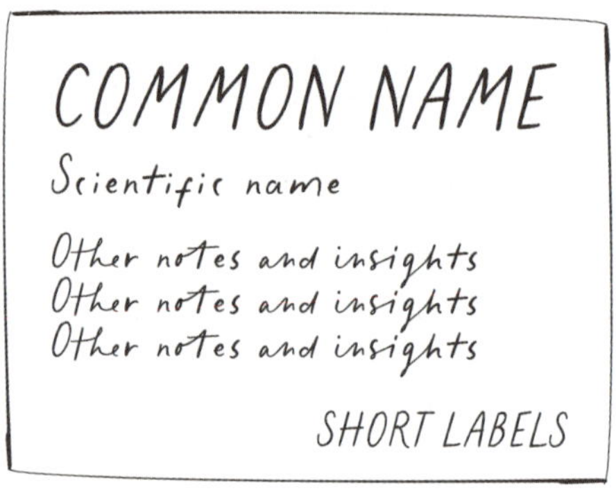

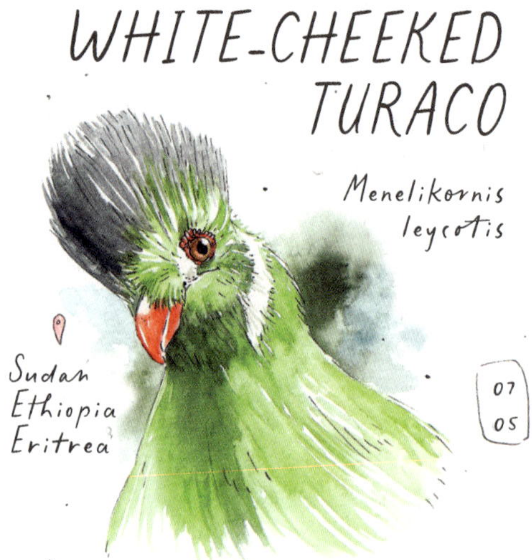

Include some factual information or your personal observations and thoughts. Both directions are great but a combination of the two is best – this creates an in-depth study of the bird.

Writing the name of the bird is crucial. There is, of course, the common name (and sometimes more than one), but I believe that documenting the scientific name is also important. I usually write the common name as the page title in big capital letters and the scientific name in my own handwriting, as you can see in my page on the black-headed gull opposite. I also use my handwriting for any other notes.

When writing in your sketchbook, play around with text elements. Find fonts that are easy to replicate, and be consistent when making a series of bird sketches.

Have you ever found an old drawing and can't remember when it was made? Making it a habit to add a date in your sketchbook is an essential part of the process. There are other numerical data you can record alongside your sketches: size, weight, distance, population, you name it!

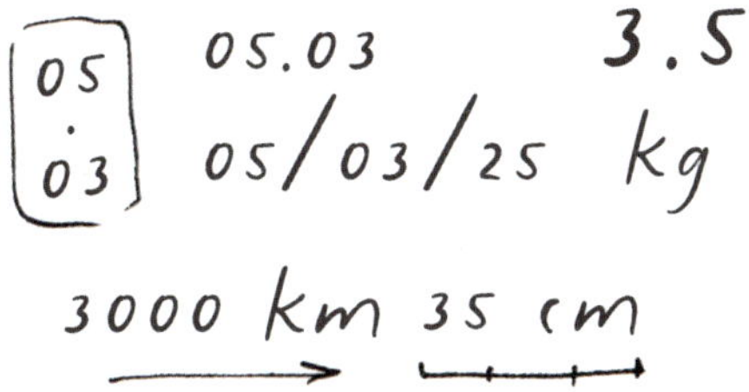

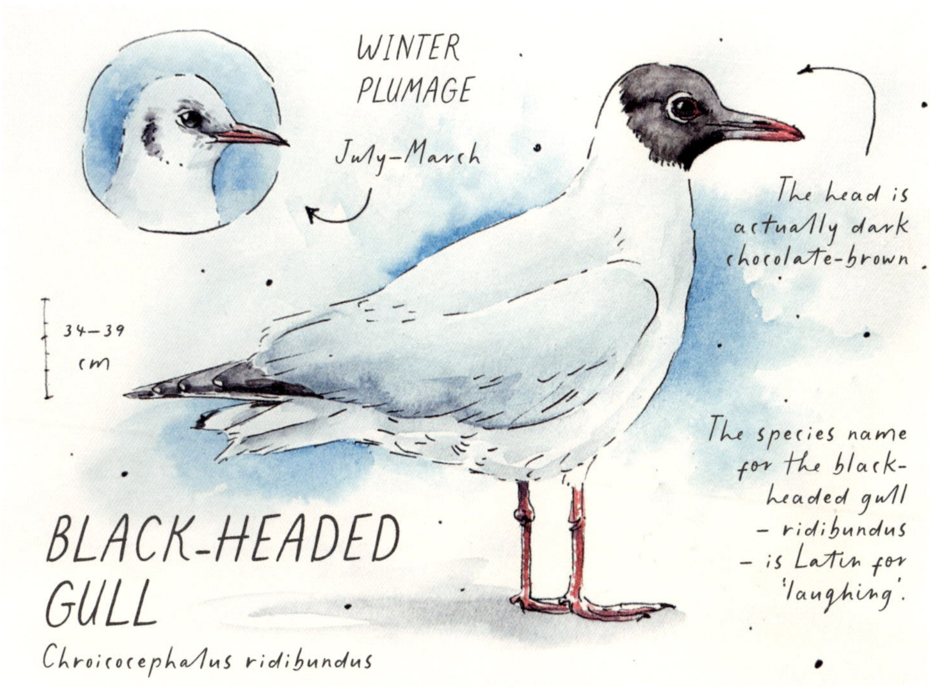

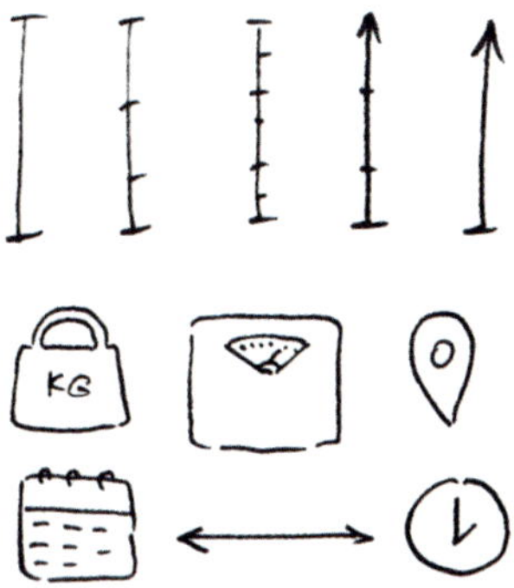

Feel free to add icons to some parts of your text. There's no need to overload the page with symbols, but if there's information you provide about most birds you draw, using a graphic element will create a helpful visual clue and add uniformity to your pages.

Other stylistic elements you can integrate into your sketchbook pages are frames, arrows, dividers and other graphics, to fill space and create a connection between your drawing and written notes.

I'm always on the lookout for how other artists create sketchbook layouts. There's nothing wrong with copying what you like. Over time you'll transform them and keep only those that reflect your personal style and vision.

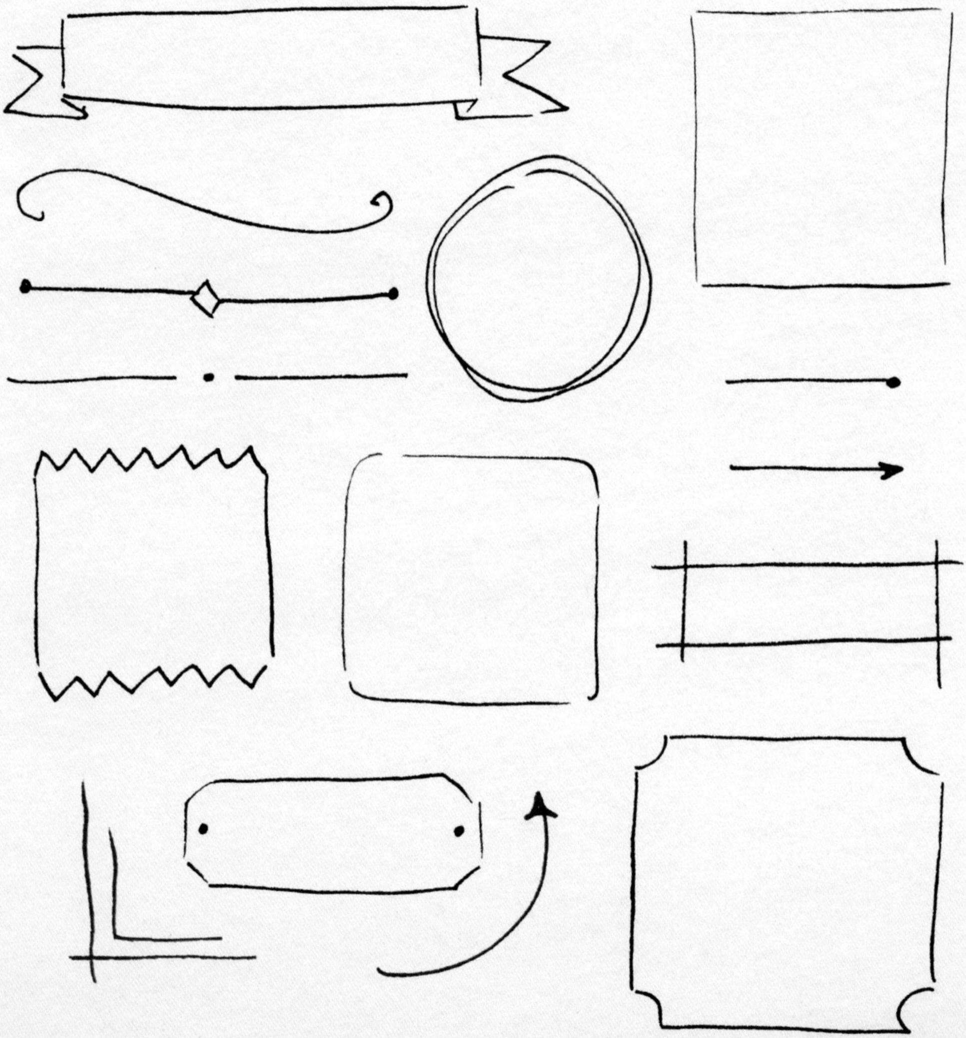

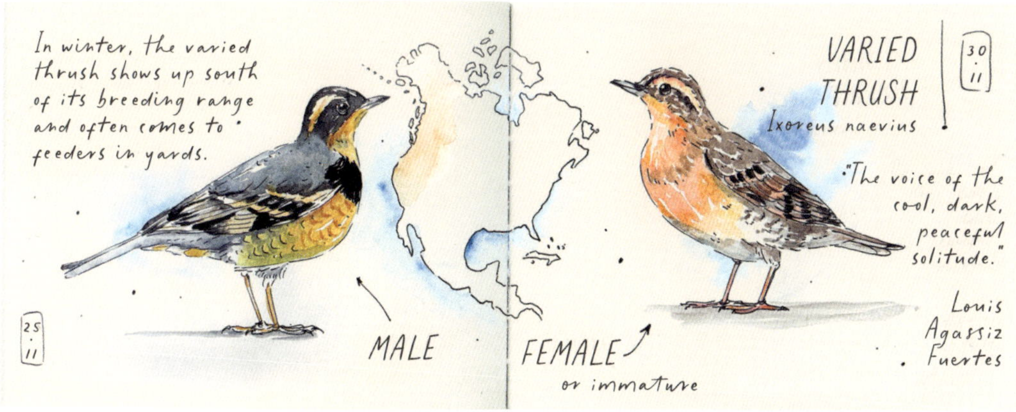

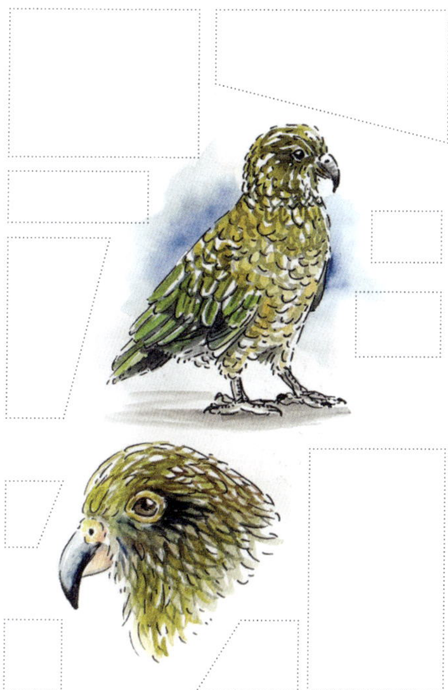

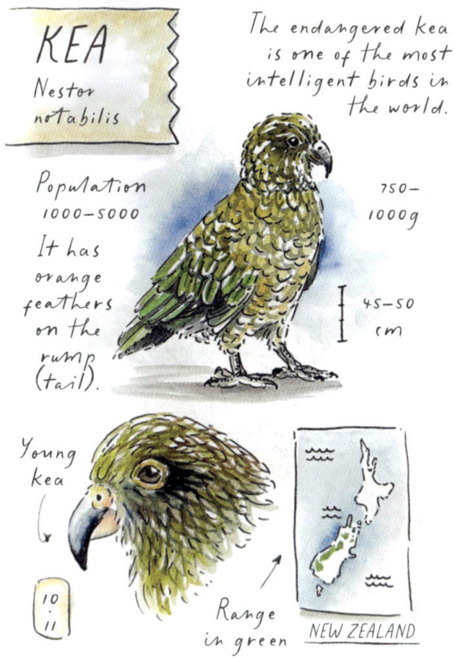

To keep visual rhythm, don't place all of your elements and notes in one cluttered block. Split them into parts and scatter them across the page, creating an appealing composition and flow.

After making the main drawings of the bird, I arranged all the pieces of information around the sketch, adding various graphical components to balance the page.

Genders

Sexual dimorphism and breeding plumage

The difference between the appearance of male and female birds of one species is called sexual dimorphism. They can have distinguishing colours, body shapes, extra feathers on the head or the tail, markings and variations in overall size. Some birds have a very clear and striking difference in their look, while others require more precise observation to notice the characteristics that set males and females apart. Some species have males and females that look different all their lives, while others display such distinction only during breeding season.

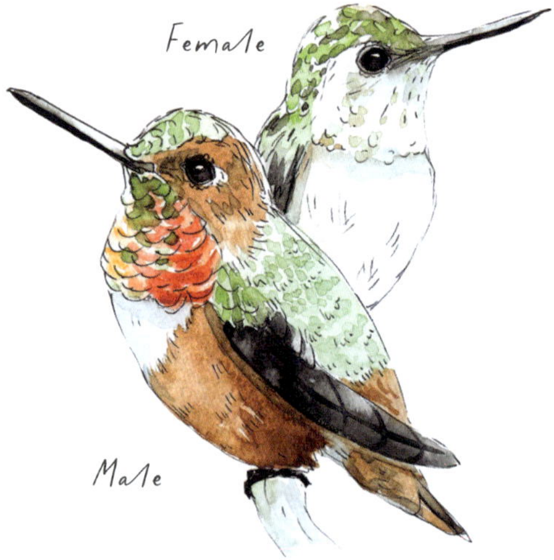

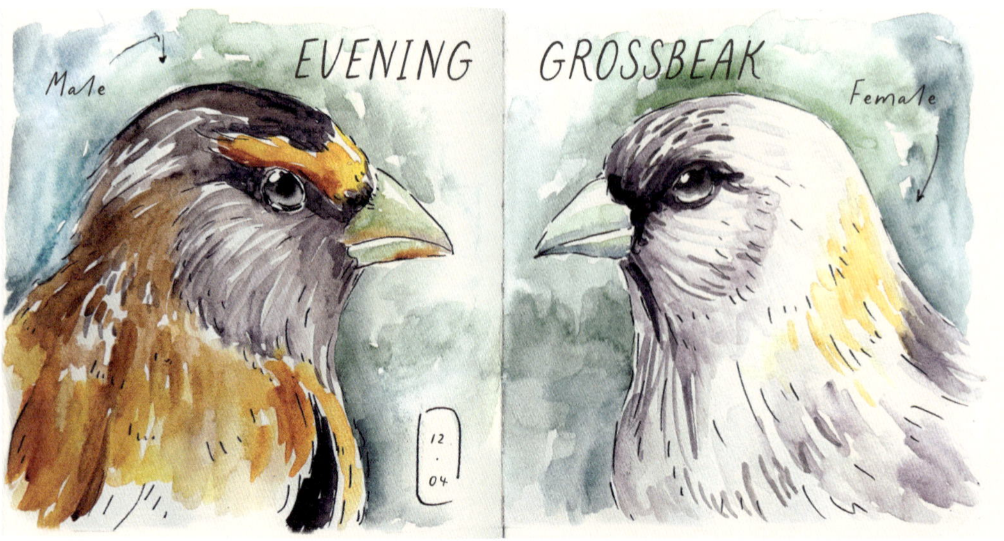

You can compare genders in your sketchbook or, if a bird shows its interesting plumage only during the breeding season, you can draw the same gender but in its breeding and nonbreeding plumage.

To show such differences, you can draw both birds in full, side by side, for an easy comparison. Or, if the birds mostly look alike, you can draw only one gender and indicate the features that differ in the other gender with highlighted details nearby.

Top tip

A deeper study of the seasonal plumage changes can also be made by drawing moulting stages. If you can observe a bird during this transition, you have the chance to capture a unique appearance.

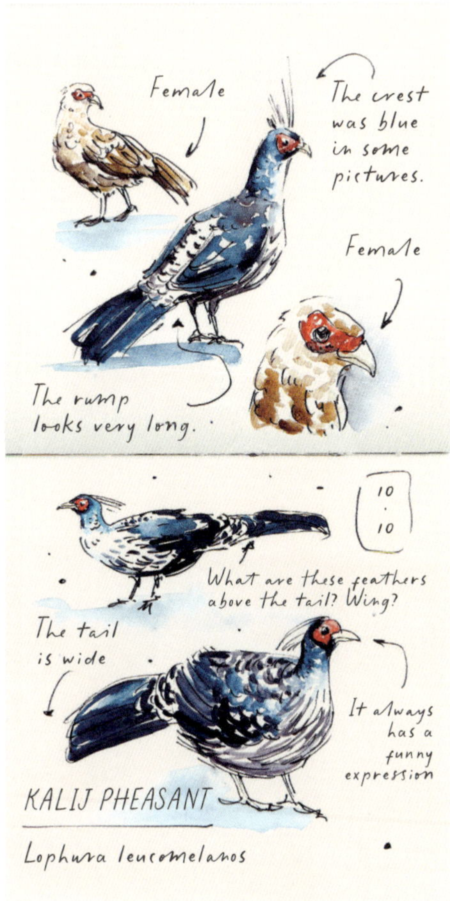

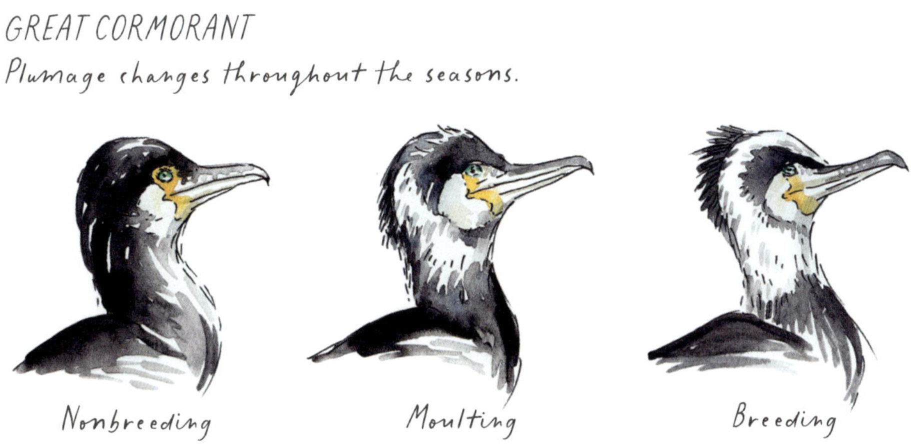

Mating and nesting

Rituals, nests and eggs

During the breeding season, many birds change their appearance and engage in various behaviours to impress a potential mate. They sing complex songs, make gifts, fight with each other and build intricate nests.

One of the most spectacular behaviours is the courtship display. Some birds perform solo, such as the male pin-tailed whydah, while others create a whole show by dancing together.

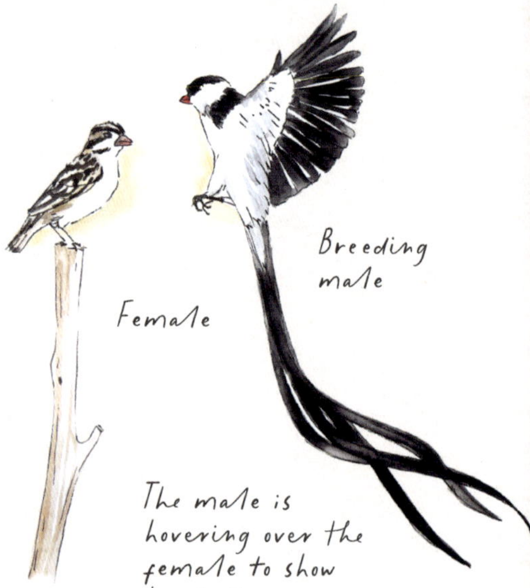

Pin-tailed whydah's courtship flight display.

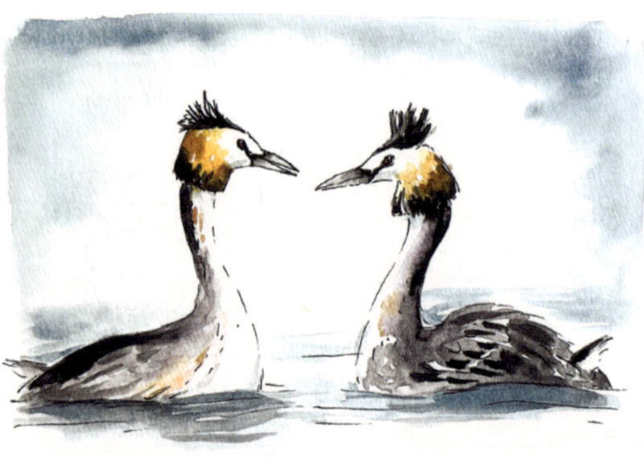

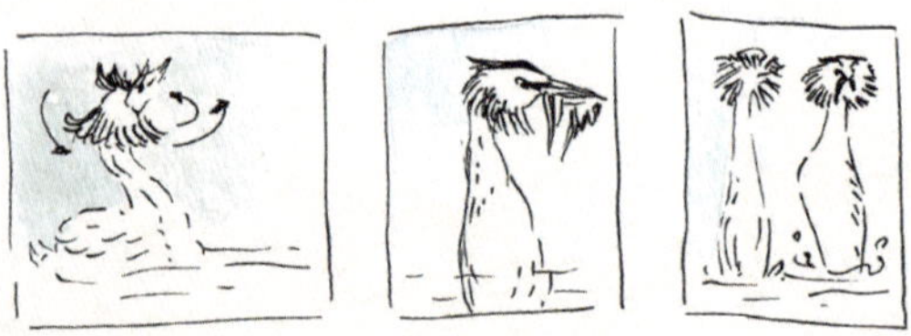

Top tip

Create a small storyboard capturing different poses the birds make during the dance. Draw arrows to show the direction of movements.

Great crested grebes have one of the most amazing courtship dances! This is also a great example of a feeding display, since they bring weed to each other during the dance.

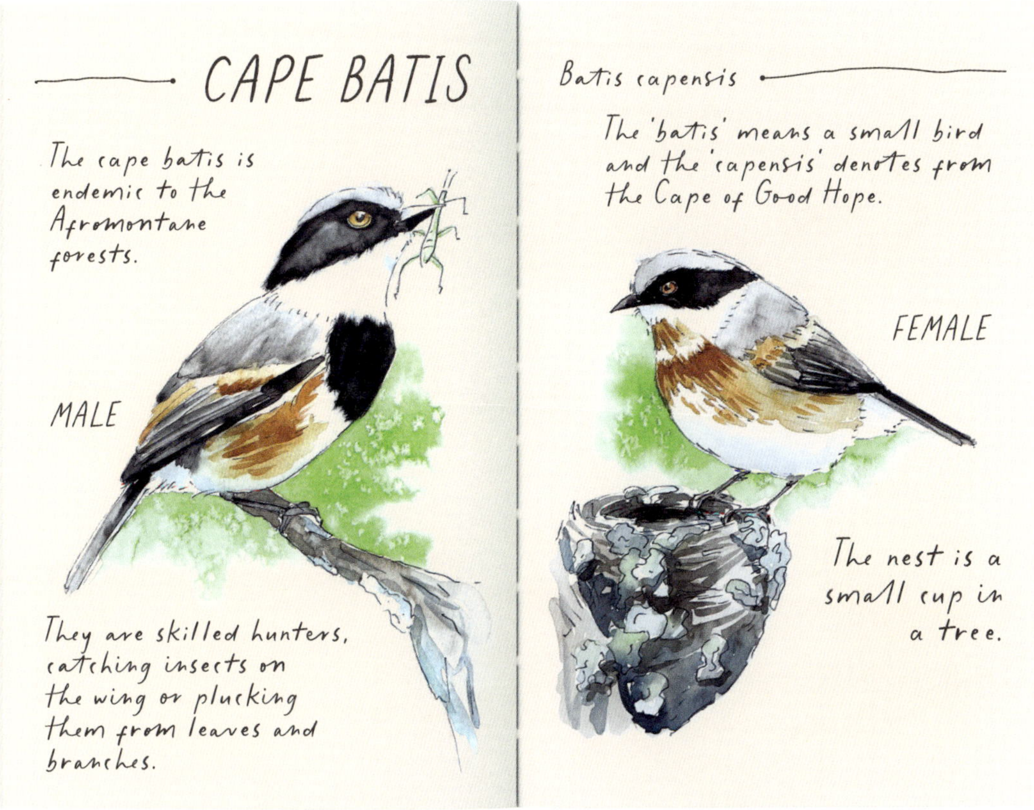

You can combine the mating display of the bird and the nesting habits of this species on the same double spread. For example, the male Cape batis offers food to the female as part of its courtship display. If they form a couple, they build a nest. Tell their story by drawing both of these important steps in their lives.

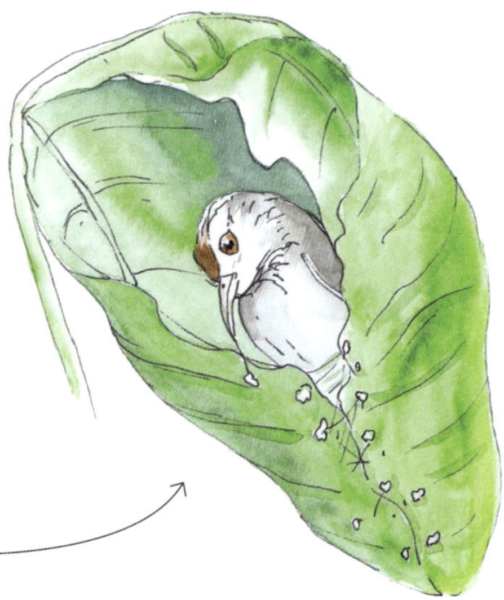

The tailorbird got its name because of the nests it creates by stitching leaves together with plant fibre or spider silk.

THE MOST COMMON TYPES OF NESTS

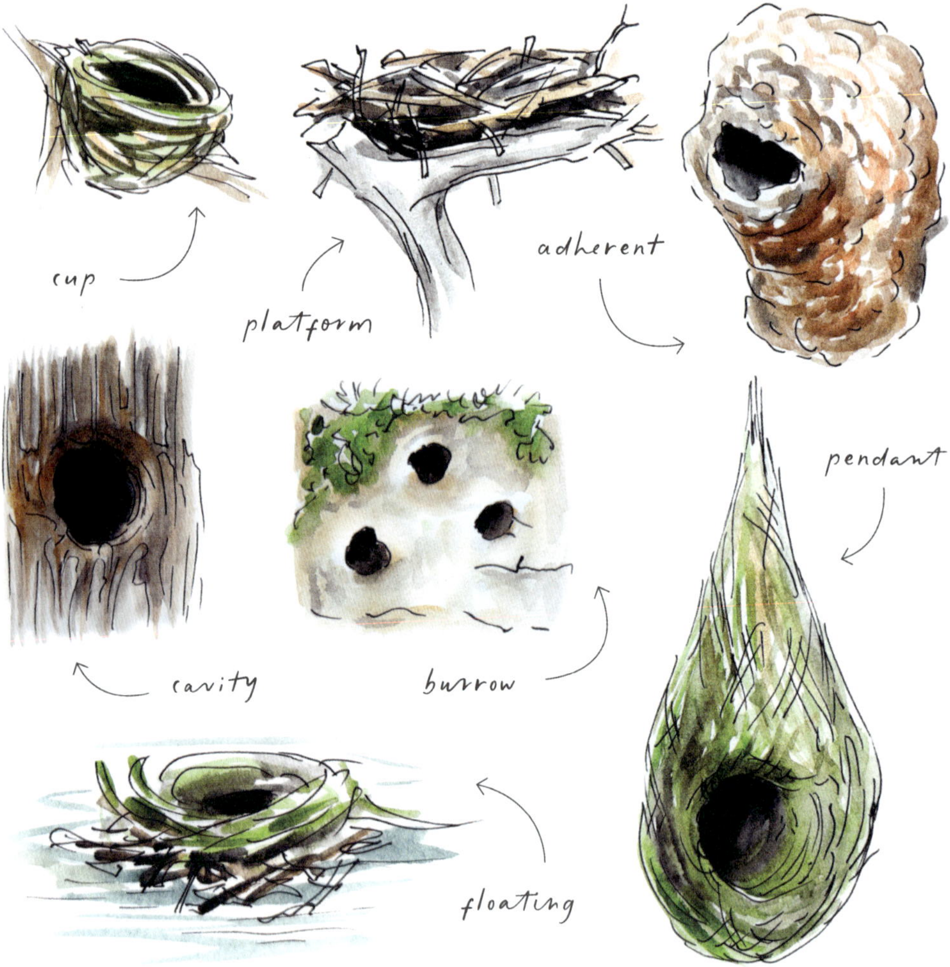

There are many different types of nests. Usually, we imagine a nest as a cup, which is very common among small birds. However, some other birds create scrapes, burrows, mounds, pendants and other amazing structures. The form of the nest depends on the characteristics of the habitat, the potential predators, climate and the availability of nest materials. Some birds that live together in colonies create specific kinds of nests based on their social behaviour. And for other birds, nest building is a part of their courtship display.

Egg-laying is the way dinosaurs reproduced themselves, and birds preserved this approach through evolution. Bird eggs can vary in size, colour and pattern. Learning the differences between the eggs of bird species is an amazing opportunity to unveil this sacred part of a bird's life.

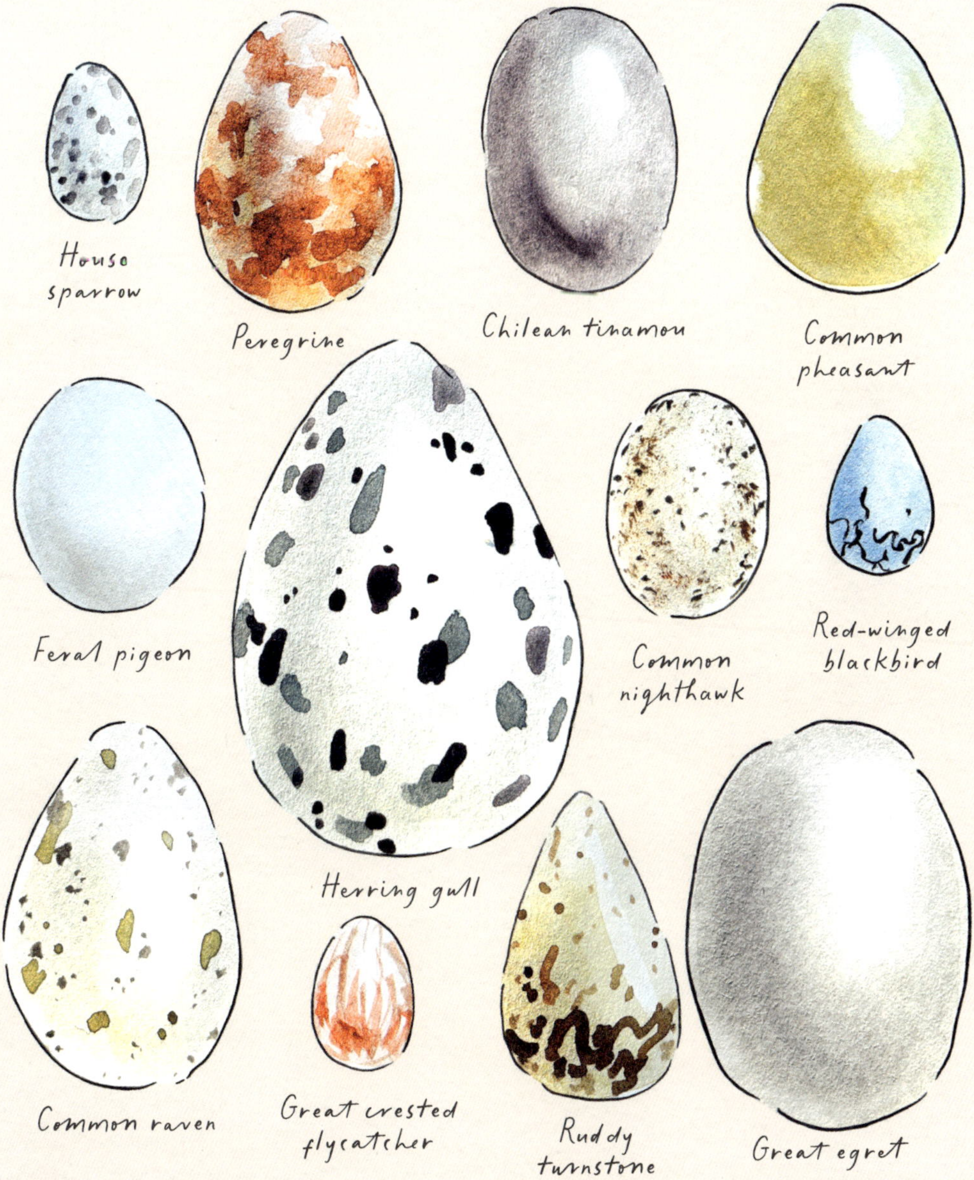

Growth

The bird's changing appearance from chick to adult

There are different bird ages that you can study. After a chick hatches from an egg, it becomes a fledgling – non-flying toddler, so to speak. When it grows up and starts to fly, but isn't sexually mature and usually still has some distinctive visual differences from an adult – this is a juvenile bird. This stage can be quite long for bigger birds. For example, you can differentiate a second-year juvenile herring gull from the three-year one by the moulting markings. When the bird is fully grown, it's the last version of its look (not counting the breeding plumage, of course). By capturing a bird at different ages, you can follow the transition of the body proportions, growth of different feather blocks and change in the plumage of the bird.

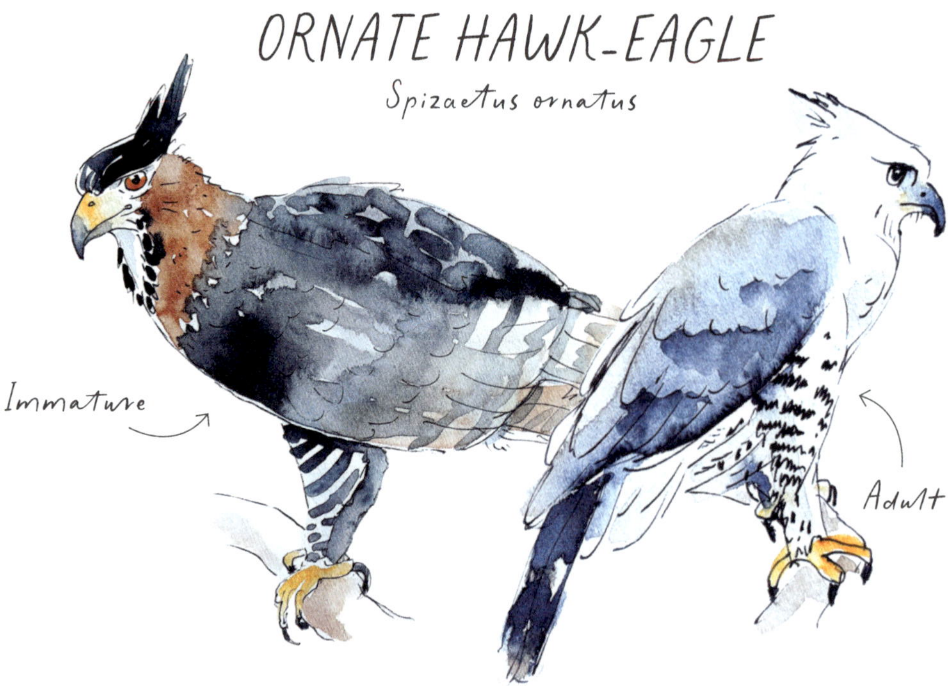

How to draw a chick in 4 steps:

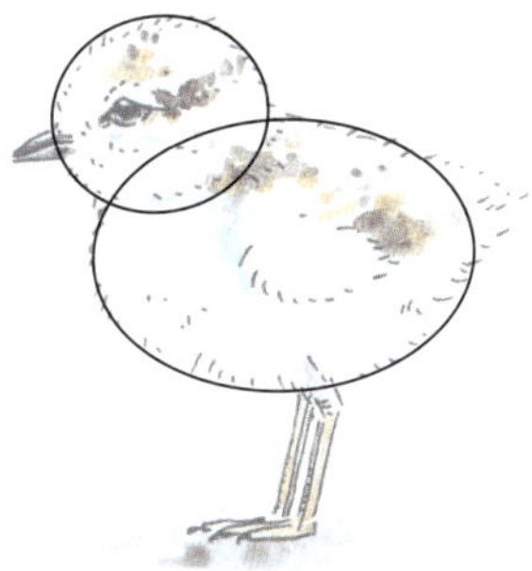

1. Chicks, similar to small songbirds, have comparatively big heads. Keep these proportions when defining the head and body ovals.

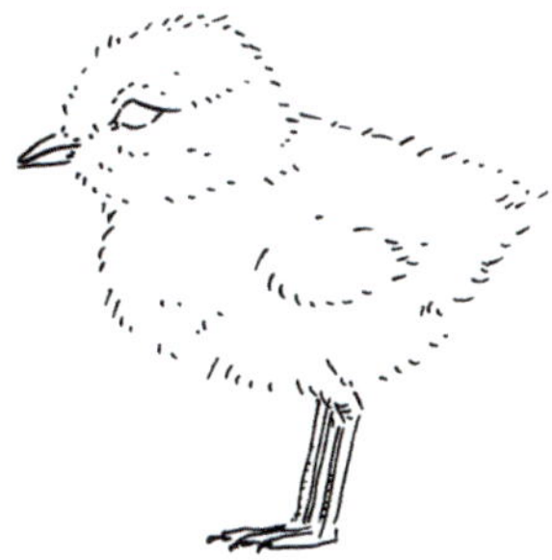

2. Use short strokes popping out in every direction to show the fluffy "fur" of the chick. A lot of white space between the strokes will make it glow.

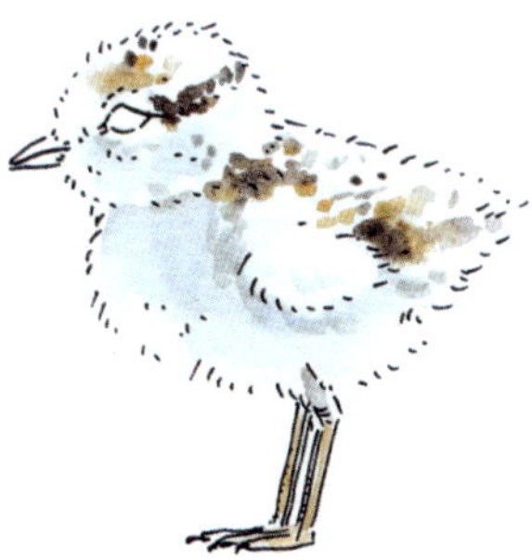

3. Colour the chick from the darkest part, gradually blending the colour towards the edges, where the feathers are almost transparent.

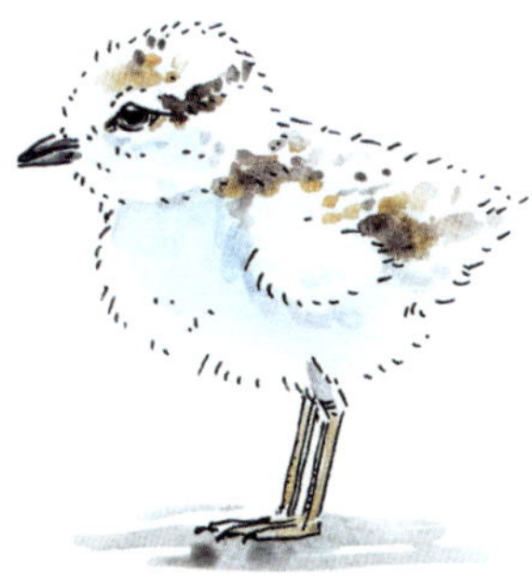

4. Drawing wings is much easier with chicks, since you don't have all these blocks of feathers yet. But give more detail to the eye and beak.

These steps work for any chick, but each species has its own traits, like this piping plover chick's colourful spots and long legs.

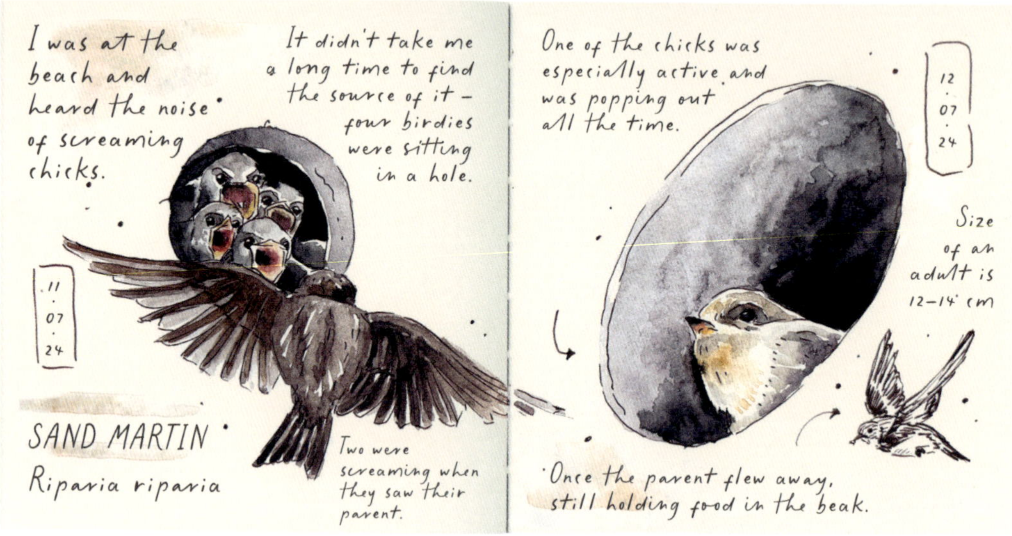

One of the interesting scenes to capture is the interaction of fledglings and juveniles with parents. There are various moments to draw – from feeding rituals to flight or swimming lessons. Choose the most characteristic for these species and show them in your sketchbook. This is the way to represent not just an adult and chick separately but the connection between generations.

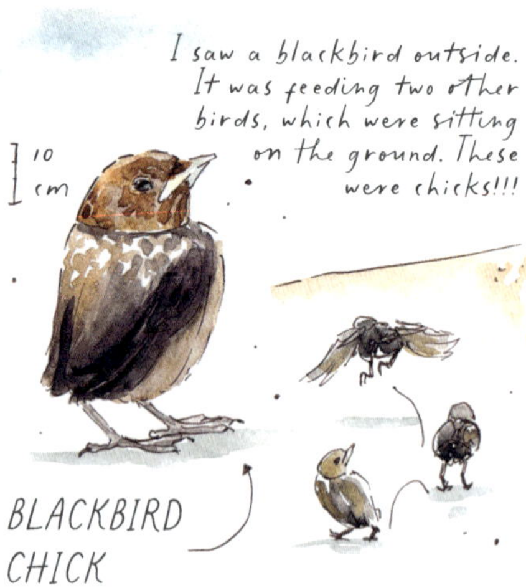

Most birds lay several eggs, and relationships between siblings are also an amazing opportunity to draw several birds in different poses, studying their habits while sketching. Is it the way young birds act in the nest, when begging for food or simply looking out in wonder? Or the way they play with each other, sometimes synchronize their movements or mimic their parents' activities? Everything is worth drawing!

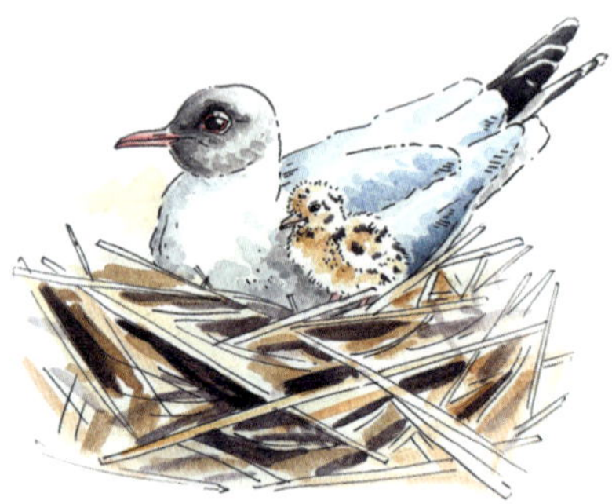

Different angles

Poses, flight, portraits

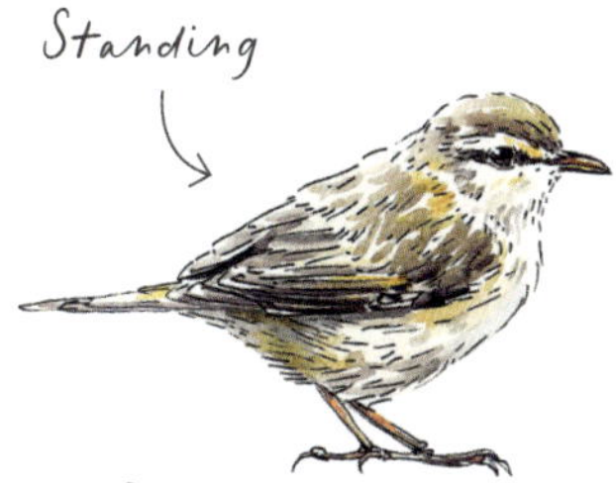

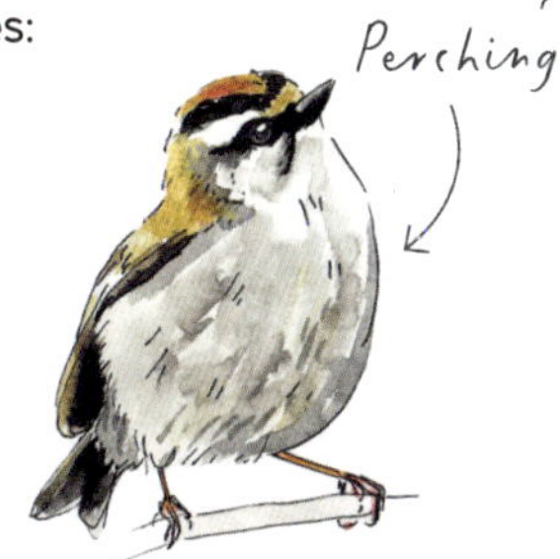

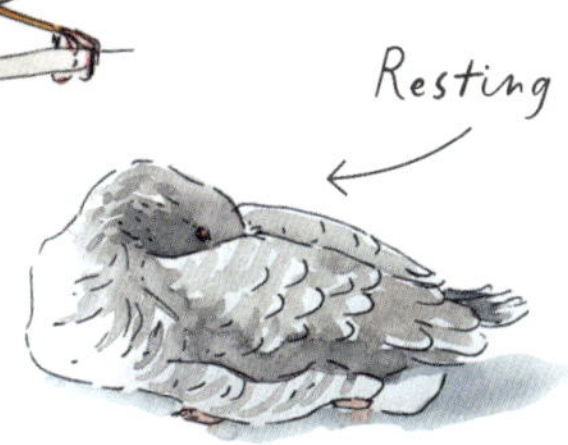

The variety of poses that birds can make is an endless source of inspiration! Not only can they do almost everything that most mammals do, but many species also fly and/or swim. Start by capturing the most common stationary poses: standing, perching and resting.

Top tip

Stationary poses are easy to capture, but have you tried to draw a bird in the same pose from different angles? Note how the main shapes become more elongated and change position when we look at the bird from other sides.

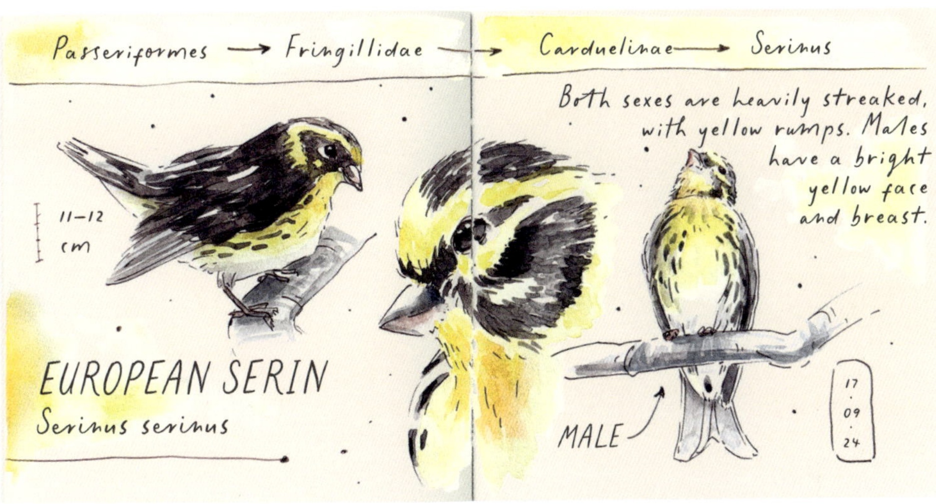

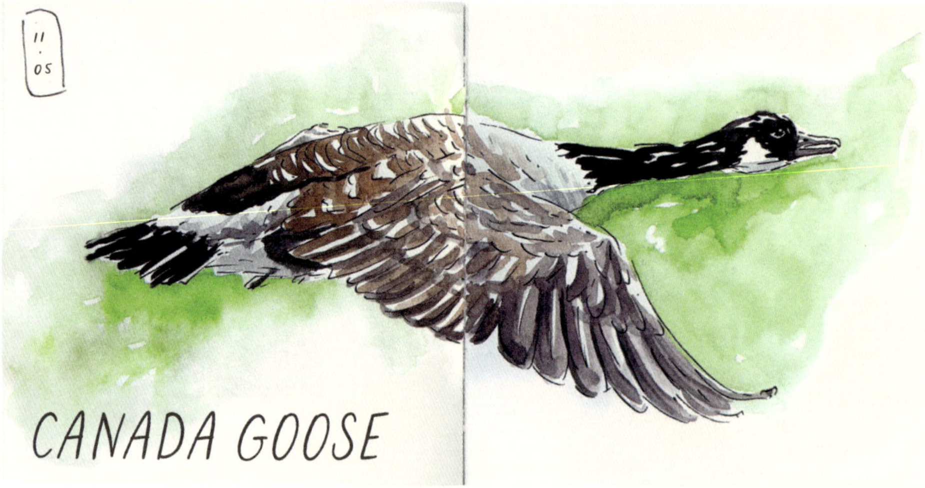

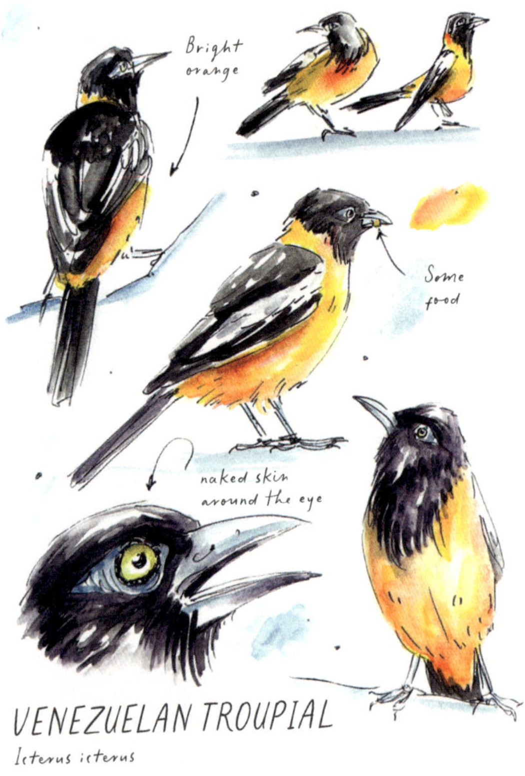

Of course we can't forget about two special activities: swimming and flying. You can make a simple study of the silhouettes or do proper research on how birds use wings and legs, extend necks and erect tails, to do such incredible activities. Don't be scared – jump into this, just as a bird jumps into swimming or flight to catch its prey!

I have always thought about a bird portrait as a special kind of sketching. It's another level of capturing the bird's details. You can be more precise with the shape of the beak, eye placement and understanding of different feather groups layered around the face.

Finally, a bird portrait is an opportunity to show some expression on the bird's face, representing it not as a mindless animal, but as a beautiful living creature with its own personality.

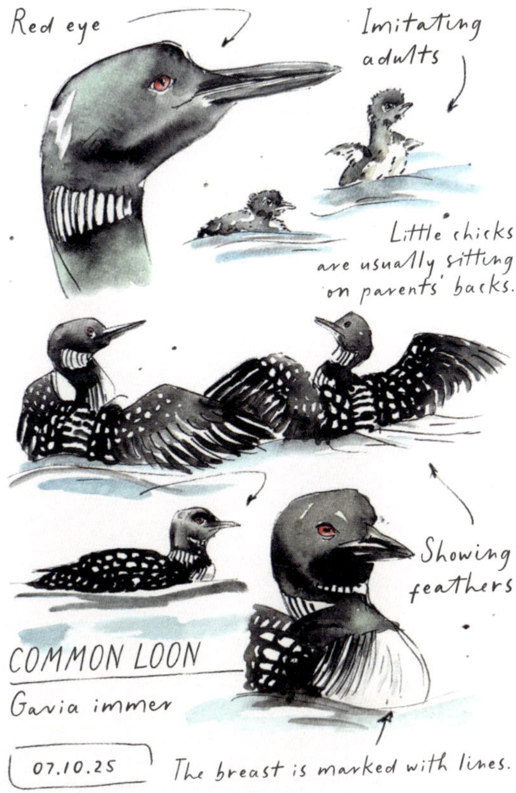

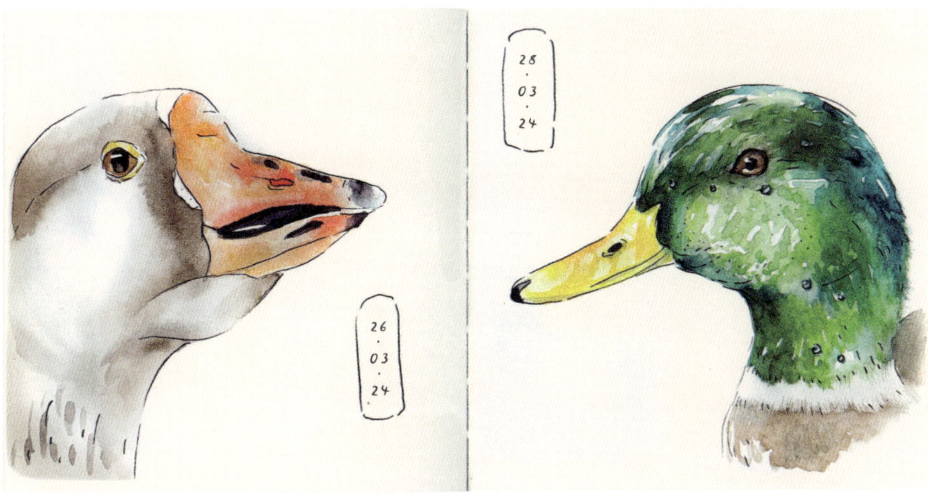

Diet

Plants, insects and other food

Beside feeding being an essential part of any bird's life, the study of the diet of a specific bird can help with understanding how the food it eats shapes its anatomy and behaviour.

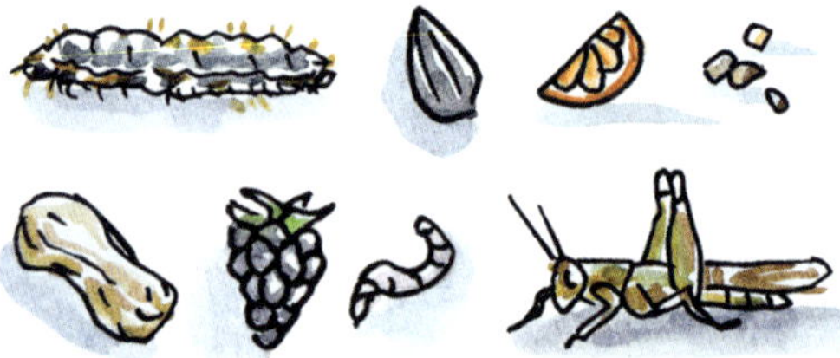

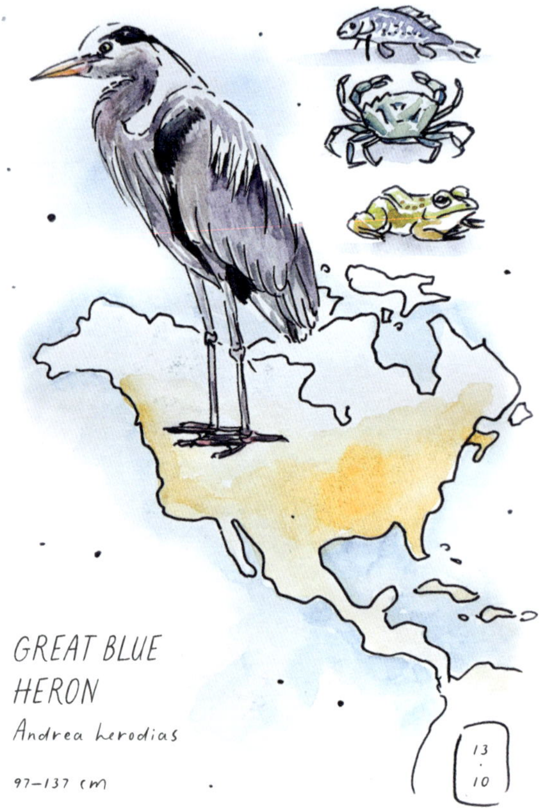

Most birds can be assigned to one of these groups:

- Carnivores, which mostly eat other animals such as insects, fish and small mammals.
- Herbivores, which eat plants such as seeds, nuts, fruits, nectar and leaves.
- Omnivores, which eat both animals and plants.

One way to show a bird's diet is by simply drawing the food it eats next to your bird illustration. You can be as detailed or as simple as you like – it's totally up to you! You'll learn about it while researching, which makes it very interesting anyway.

LITTLE PENGUIN

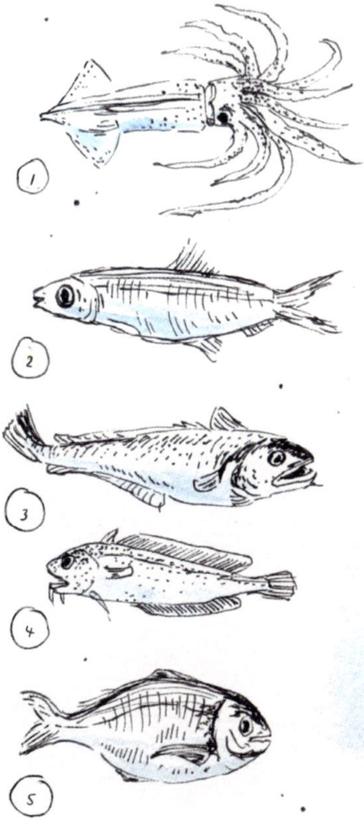

Captures prey by means of pursuit-diving. Dives to depths of c. 50 m.

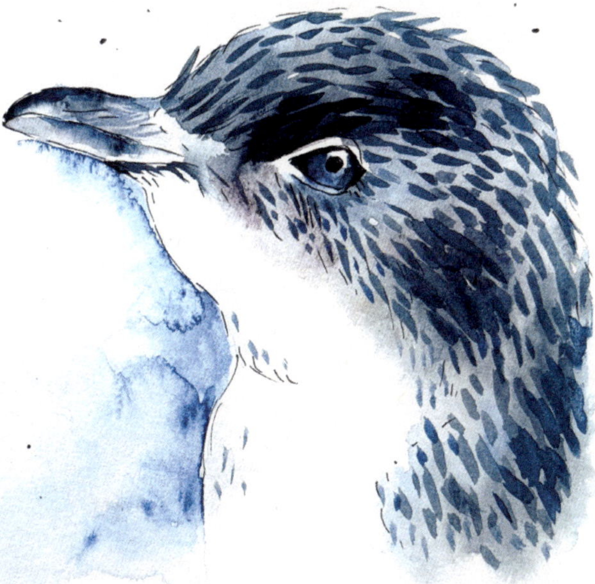

DIET: 1. Arrow squid 2. Slender sprat
3. Red cod 4. Ahuru 5. Blue warehou

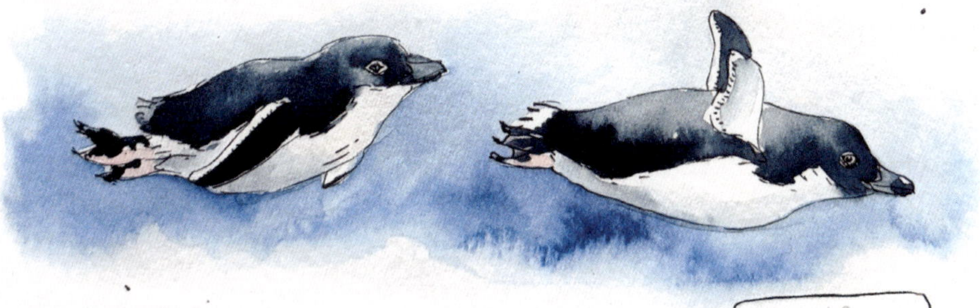

27.10.25

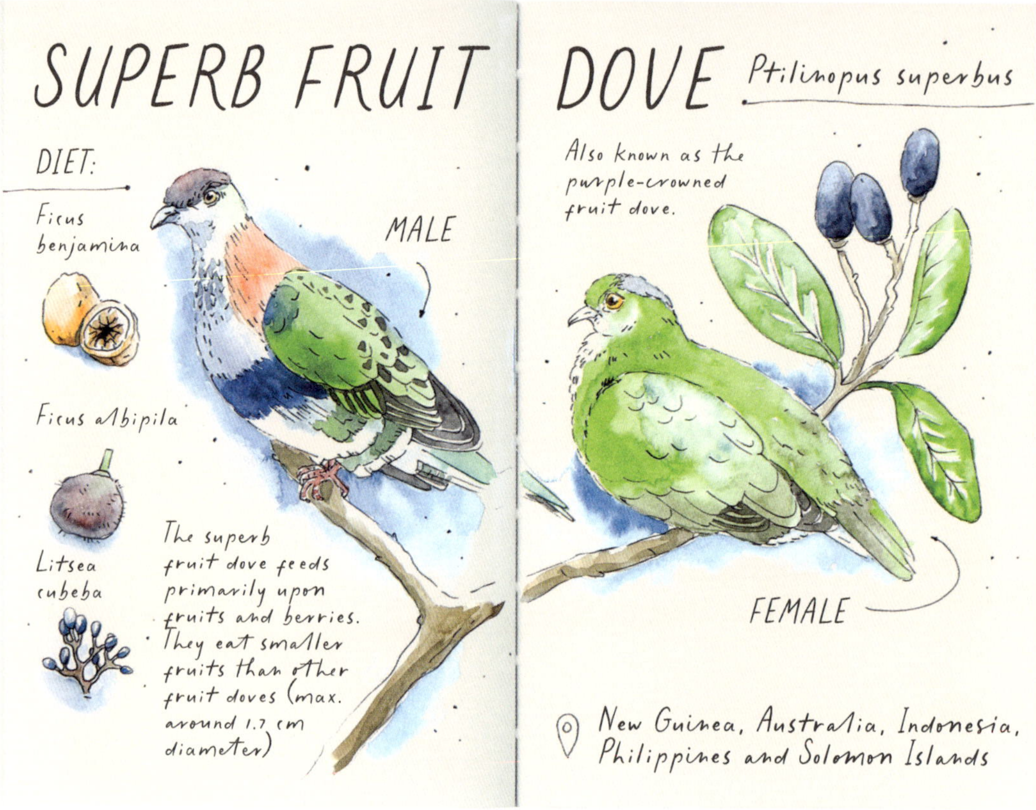

Another way to approach this topic is to capture birds in action by drawing hunting and feeding scenes. It's an effective method to combine the drawing of the bird in different poses with showing its diet at the same time.

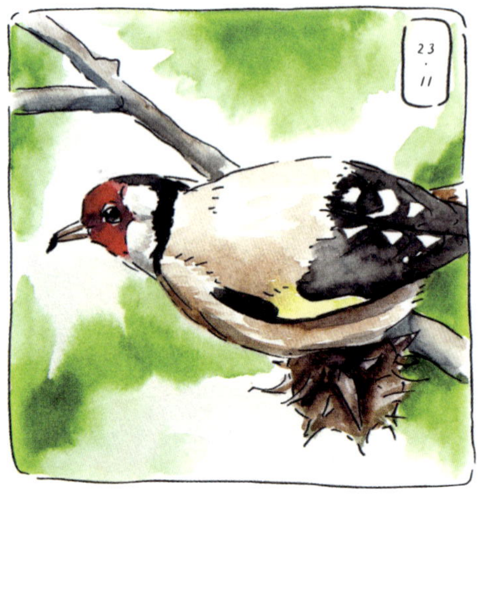

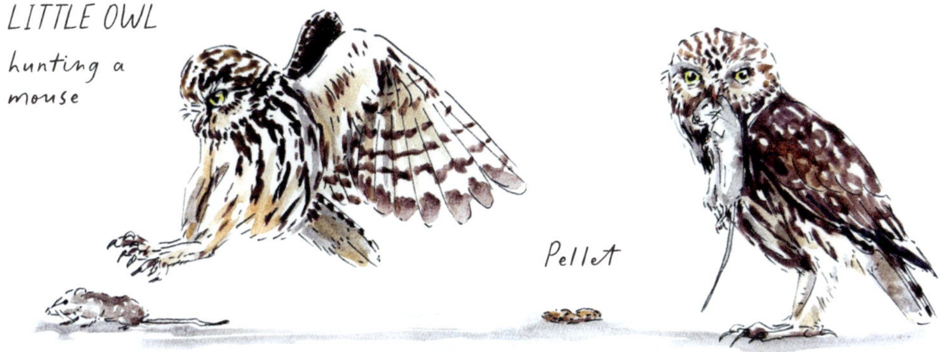

What about creating a whole sequence by showing the bird finding, catching and eating food? You can even add the pellets of the bird as a result of this process, if it's a bird of prey.

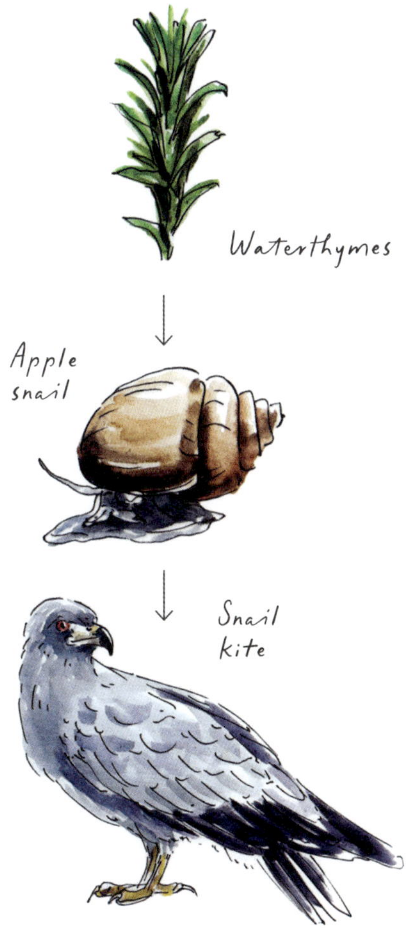

Top tip

Show a whole food chain! The bird can still be the main focus, but since it's a part of the complex environmental system, why not depict it on your page?

Details

Eyes, legs, feathers, and other parts

Remember how in the first chapter I highlighted some of the bird's features that are important to capture properly to make your drawing realistic? You can do the same in your sketchbook! But instead of simply writing notes to point out the main features, draw them enlarged in more detail.

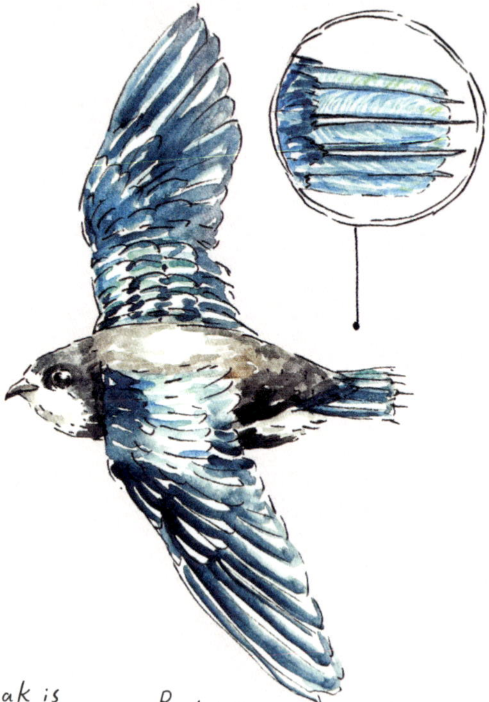

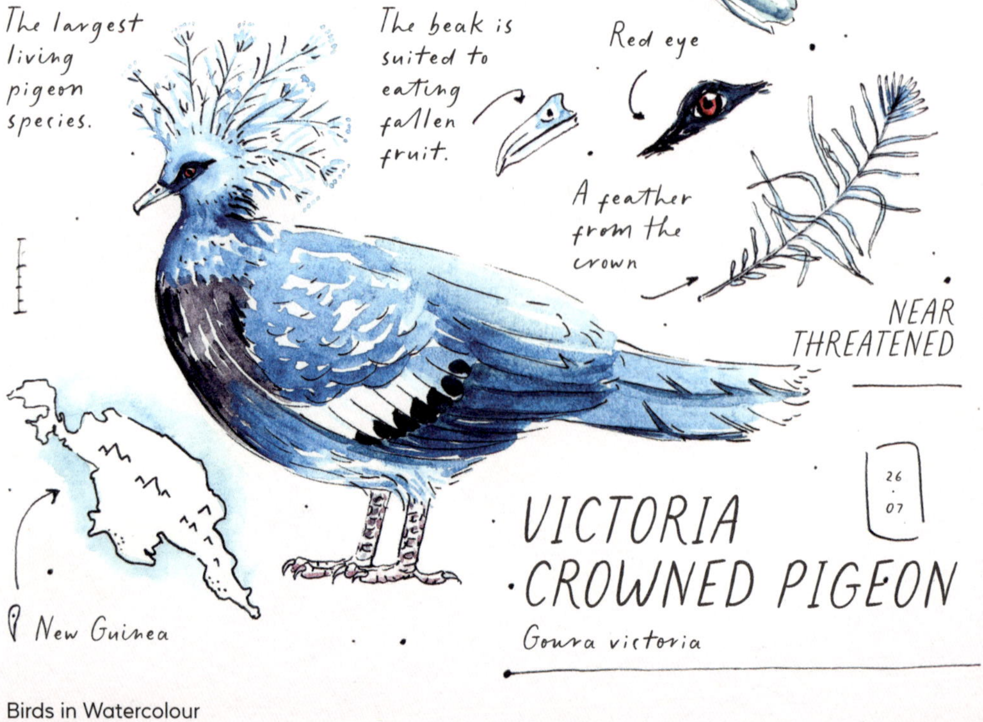

Feathers are a very specific bird attribute. They can vary in size, shape and pattern, but all have a similar structure. Let's draw the feather of the rainbow lorikeet.

How to draw a feather in 3 steps:

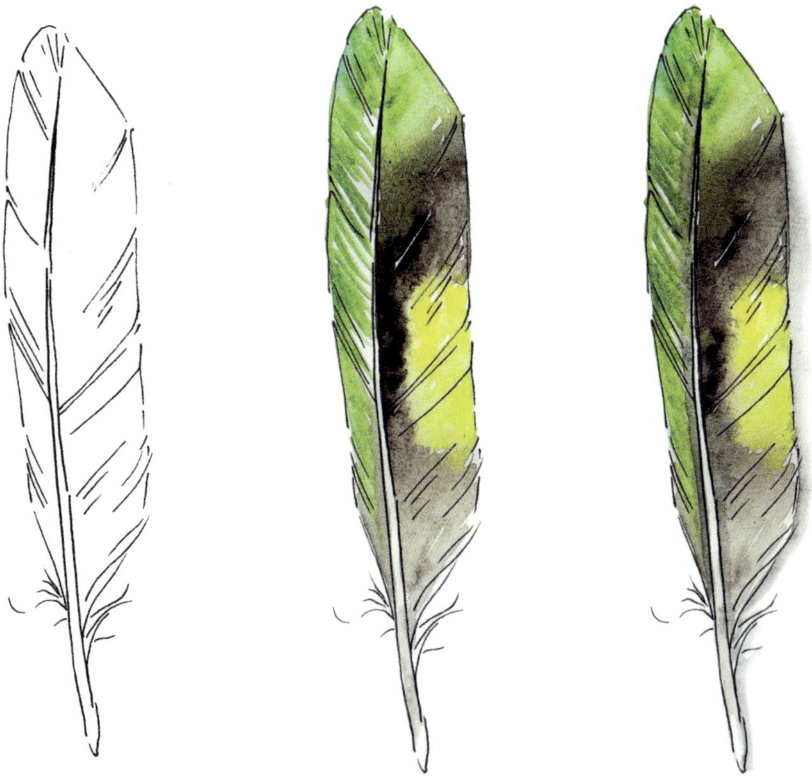

1. Draw the central part of the feather, thickening closer to the base. Build the shape by adding small strokes here and there. Note the fluffy part on the bottom.
2. Replicate the colour pattern. The middle part of each side is usually lighter, since it's slightly curved.
3. Finalize the drawing by deepening colours to suggest a nearby light source. You can also add shadow under the feather, so it looks like it's lying on the surface of the page.

Maps

From world maps to a garden scheme

Adding maps to your sketchbook pages can make your artwork even more engaging and informative. Drawing maps is a fun way to blend art and geography, while also showing the natural habitat and range of the birds.

Here's a double spread from my sketchbook about the Cuban trogon. It is endemic to Cuba, meaning it is found nowhere else in the world. A map provides this geographical context perfectly.

Drawing a map of an island is especially simple: open the location in Google Maps and carefully recreate its silhouette. Don't be nervous if you are not very precise – this is your artistic interpretation.

If this isn't just an island but also an independent country, you can add a flag to your drawing. The Cuban trogon is the national bird of Cuba, so here the flag was especially appropriate.

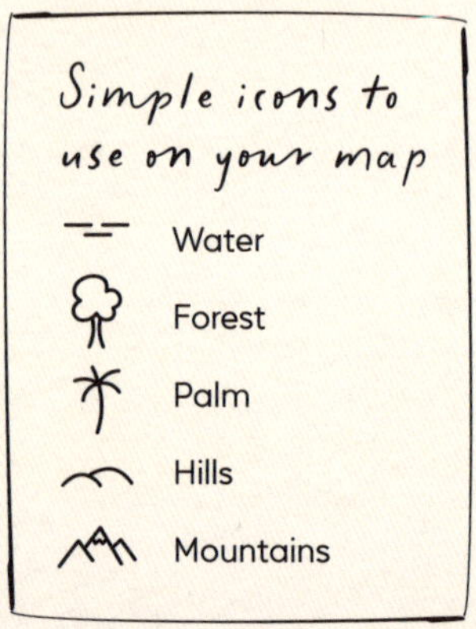

No need to colour the map completely; just add a hint of colour for different zones. I used a wet wash technique to accent the water and blend it with the page nicely.

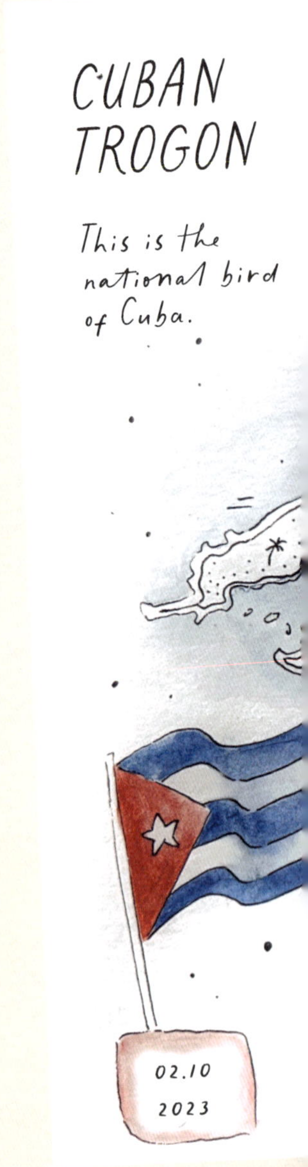

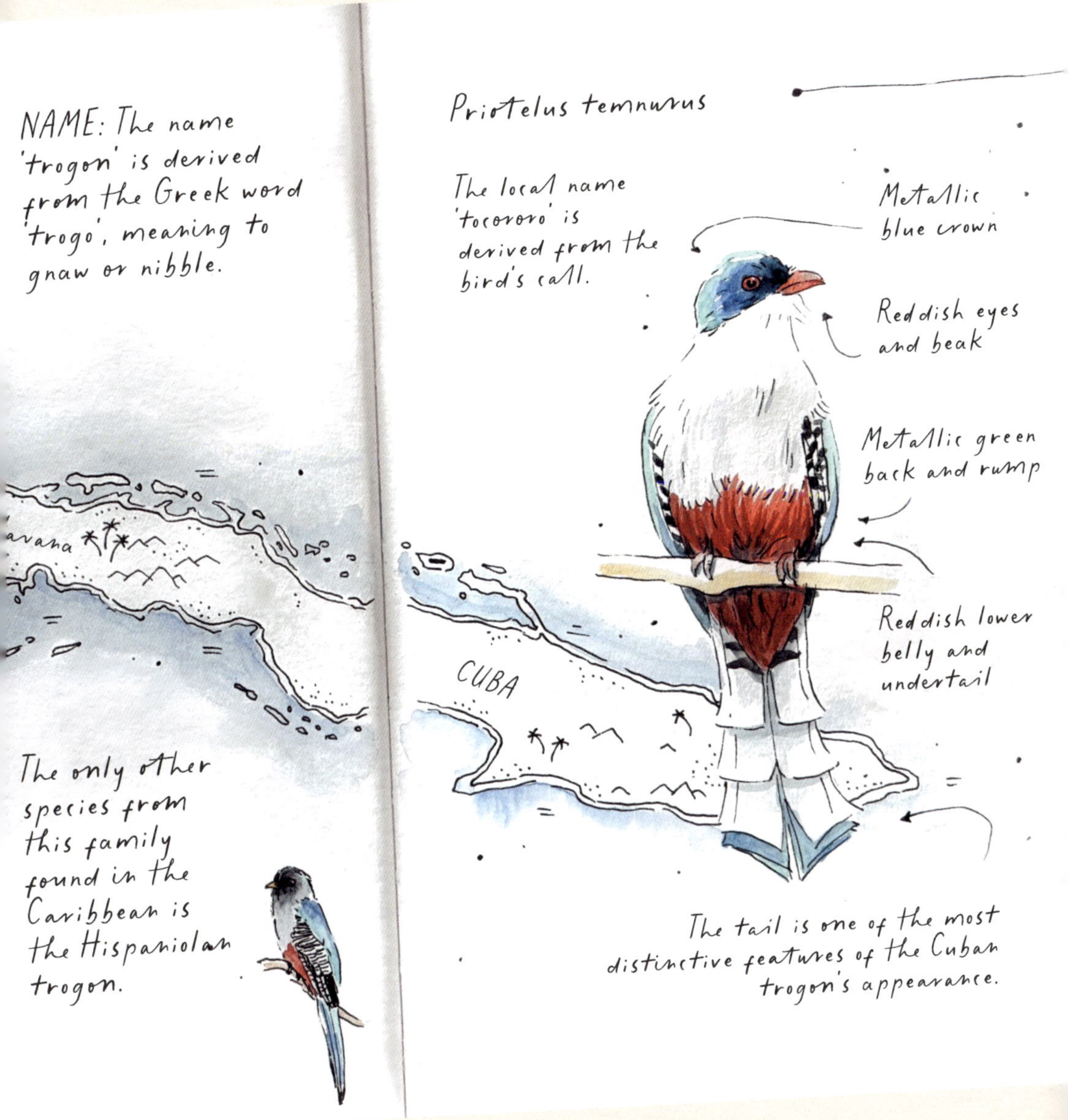

Avoid clutter by only including necessary details. A clean, simple map is easier to read. Beside, the bird should stay the main focus on your page. The map is just a supporting element.

You can give some texture and additional elements to your map. When it's an island, always make it clear that there's water around.

Showing the distribution of a bird that lives on an island is the simplest thing. What about the range of a species across a whole continent or a world map showing the migration paths of the bird?

Create different colour codes depending on the zone:

- Where the bird stays year-round.
- Where it breeds.
- Where it stays when not breeding.
- Where it can be seen only during migration.

Besides the legend, other visual clues can be placed on your map, such as decorative borders, grid lines, scale bars, inset maps and orientation symbols such as a compass rose.

What about making a map not for a single bird, but for all the birds you can find in one location? You will be drawing a whole micro-habitat. It doesn't matter if it's your backyard, favourite park or a whole city – it's totally up to you. It can be a long-term project or you can limit it to a specific time period.

You can make a map of your birdwatching walk or a trip you took to some natural spot. Show your route and what you saw along the way. How vividly this day will stick in your mind if you draw a map like this with all the observations summed up on one page!

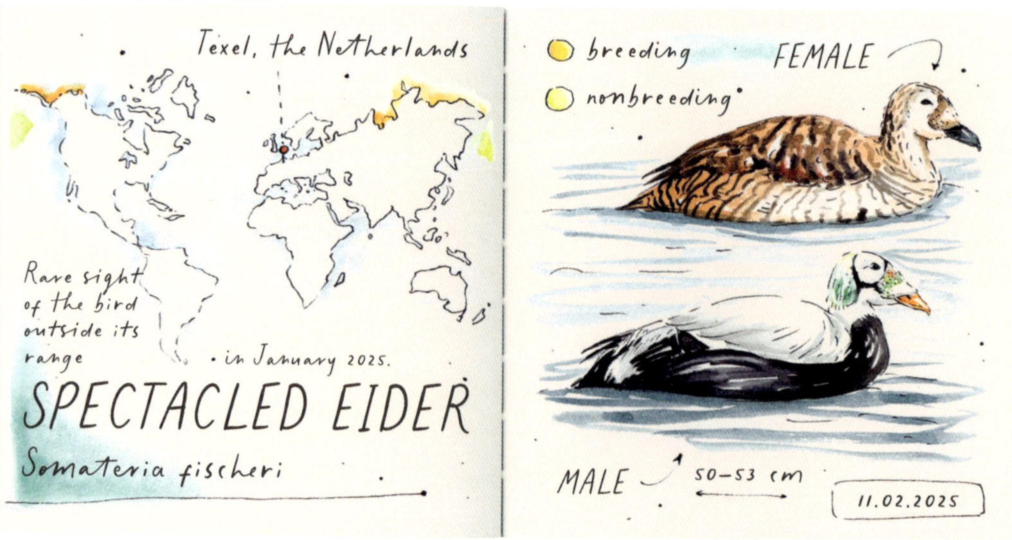

In January 2025 there was an extraordinary occurrence of the spectacled eider in Europe. I couldn't resist an opportunity to record this in my sketchbook.

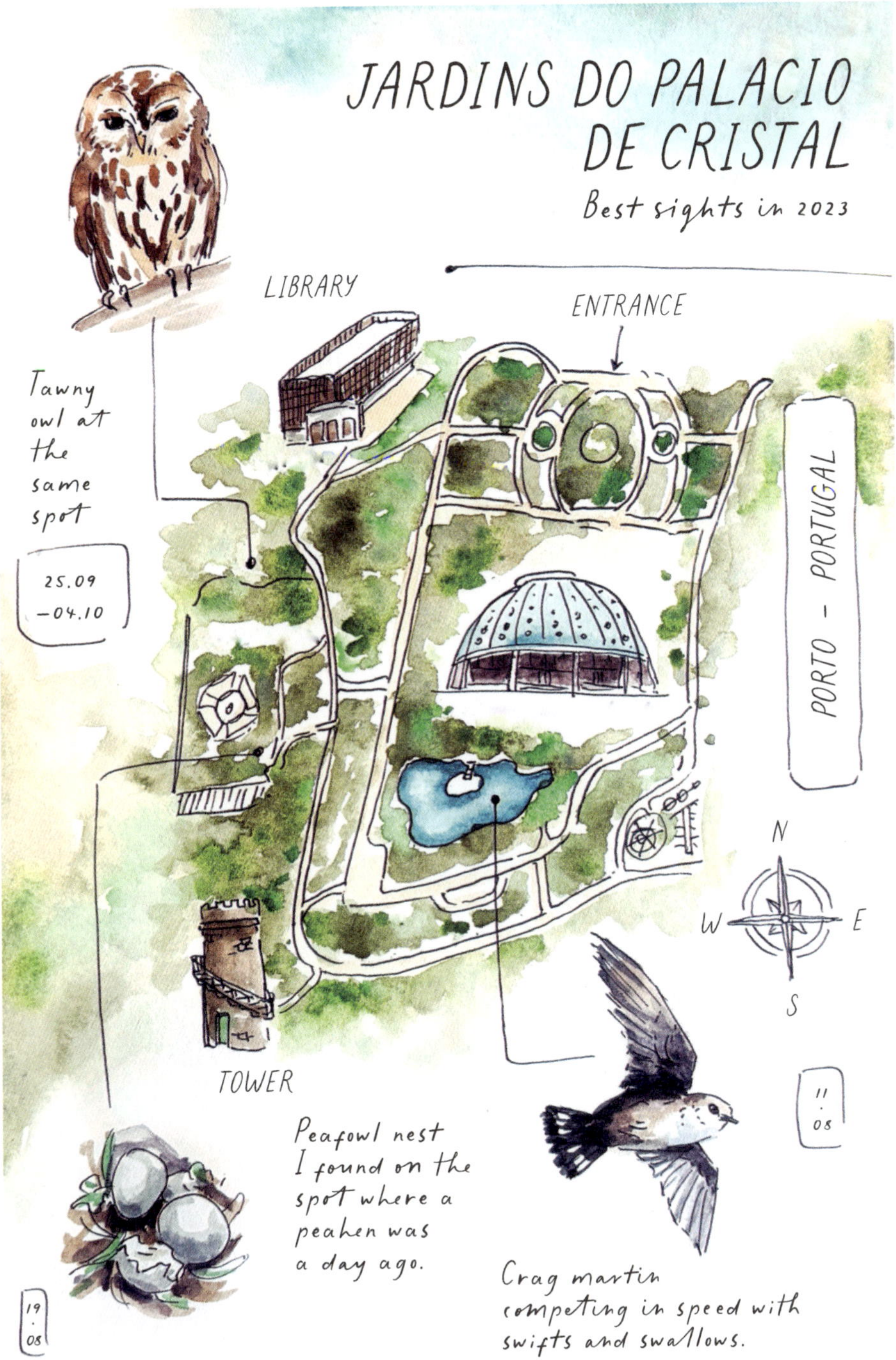
JARDINS DO PALACIO DE CRISTAL
Best sights in 2023
LIBRARY
ENTRANCE
Tawny owl at the same spot
25.09 –04.10
PORTO – PORTUGAL
N
W
E
S
TOWER
11 08
Peafowl nest I found on the spot where a peahen was a day ago.
Crag martin competing in speed with swifts and swallows.
19 08

Habitat

Drawing landscapes

Another way to give a sense of the location is, of course, to draw a bird's habitat. The importance of the environment in the bird's life is obvious and creating a whole scene featuring a bird with a beautiful background is a great idea for your sketchbook.

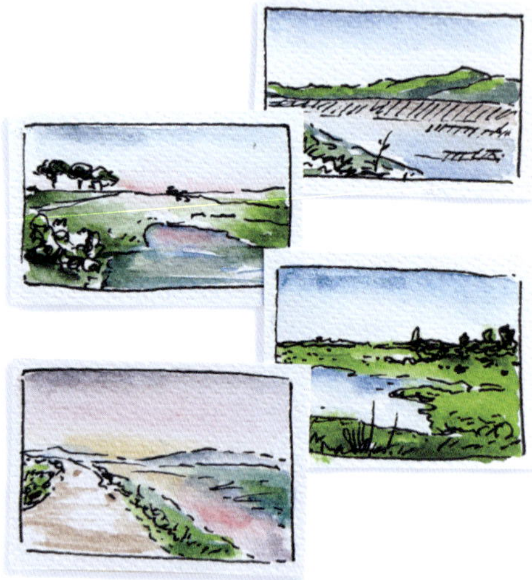

Top tip

For any landscape drawing you make, there's one strategy that will lead to success: draw the background elements less detailed than those in front. Basically, the closer the object is to the horizon, the blurrier it should be. I usually draw far objects with just watercolour to keep it simple.

Further objects are more simplified than those that are close.

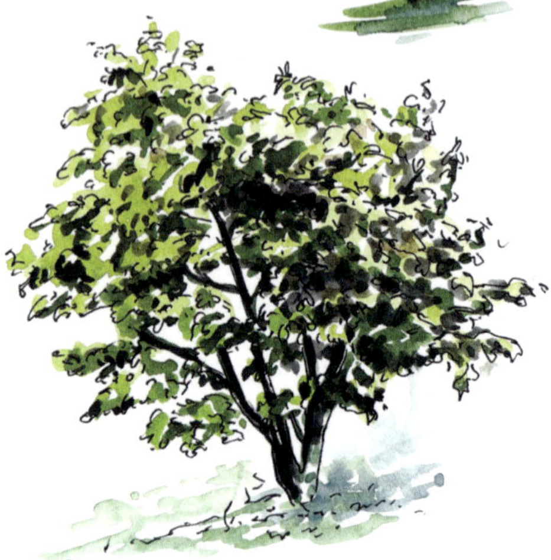

Sky

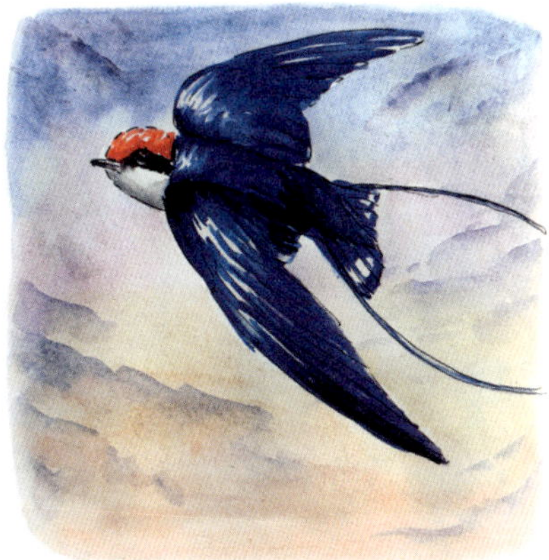

Drawing sky is the first thing to master if you want to add a landscape behind the bird. If we are not just adding colour as we did in the Background section of this chapter, we need to show the gradation of colours that the sky usually has. It depends on time of day and weather, of course – and the same goes for the shape and colour of the clouds. Play around to show what you see.

Woodland

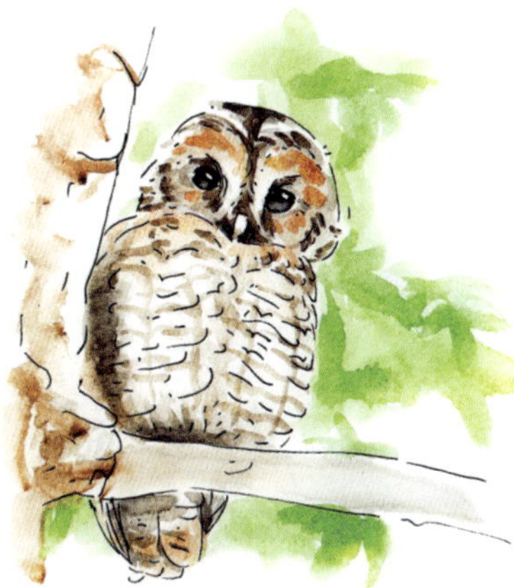

The first setting for a bird that comes to your mind is probably woodland. Layering technique will be helpful here to show depth. But don't overdo the background – it should be subtle even with the canopy and tree trunks.

You can dive more into details when drawing the tree where the bird is perched, to match it in clarity. But the bird should still be the main focus.

Wetlands

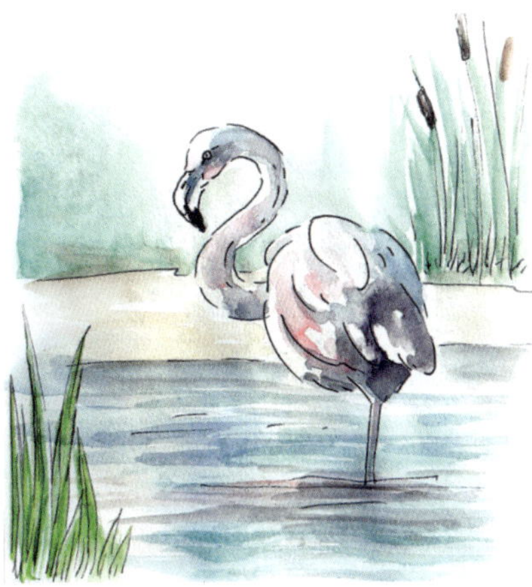

Wetland is another popular habitat for birds. When practising drawing water surfaces, pay attention to reflections and the shapes of ripples.

Coasts

What about the coastline with its soft sand, crashing waves and endless horizon? Watercolour is the best medium to show the contrast between white sea foam and dark rocks. You can see how the plumage of shorebirds fits perfectly in this landscape.

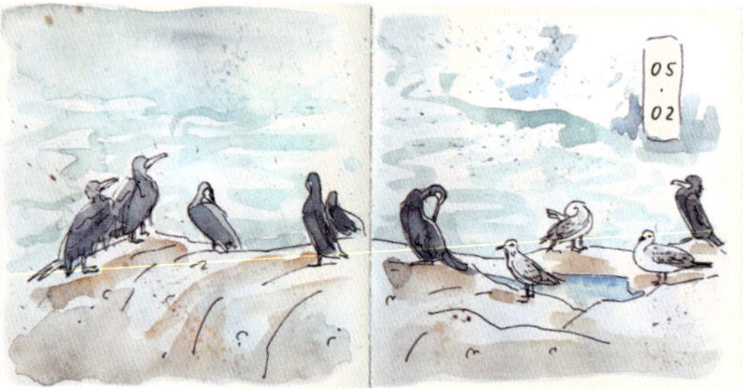

Mountains

The most incredible scenes with layers of colour can be found in mountainous regions. Cliff edges, hazy peaks, tree canopies and grassy fields at the base of the slopes – there are so many things to show!

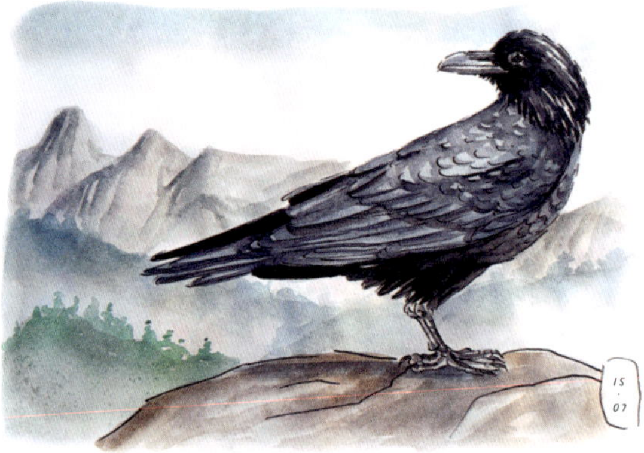

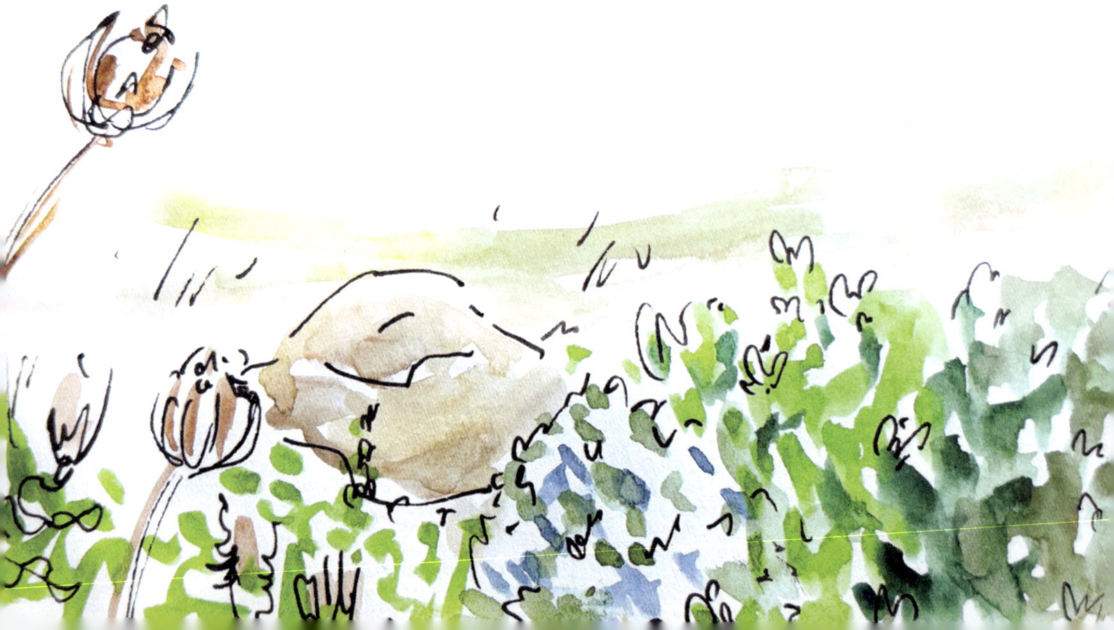

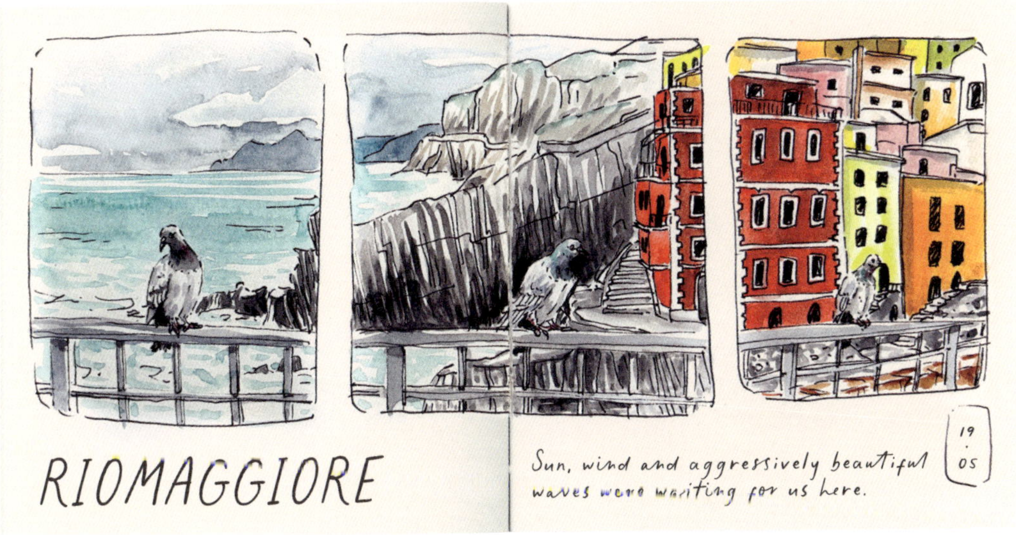

Other habitats

There are many other habitats where birds can be found, from snowy landscapes in the north to sunny deserts in the south, and from airy, wide grasslands to crowded urban scenes. Don't feel intimidated by the location, draw it simplified just to give a sense of the place. Think about it as giving your bird a home – let the scene hug and nurture it.

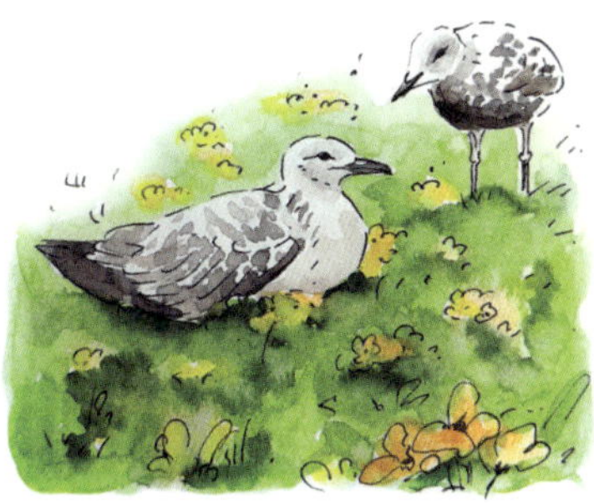

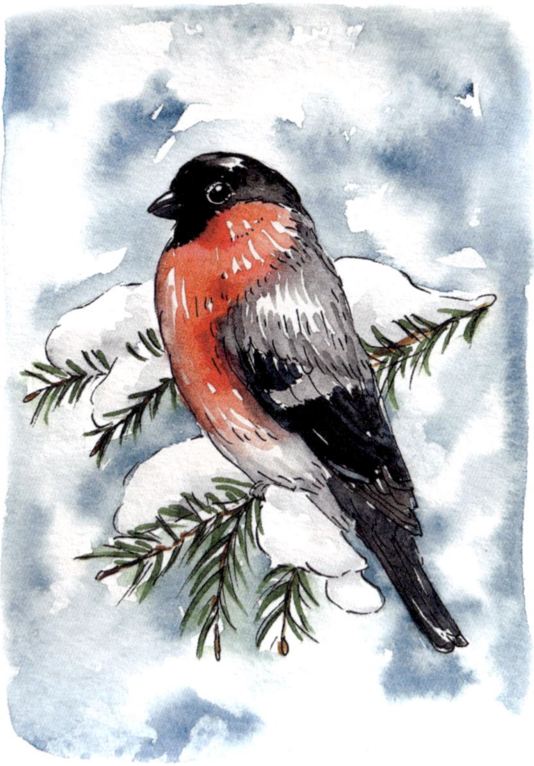

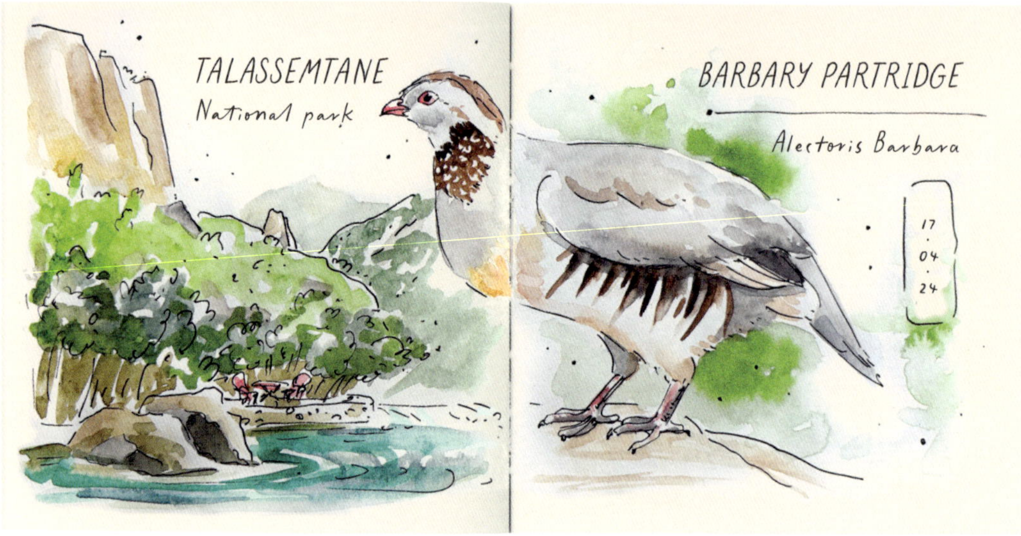

Combining birds and landscapes

In my previous examples the bird was always placed within the landscape, but on your page you can combine the two in different ways. Draw the bird and landscape separately if you want and connect the drawings with your notes.

A combination of these two approaches is a partial integration of the bird in the landscape. It's similar to the abstract backgrounds we created but with more detail, resembling a specific location.

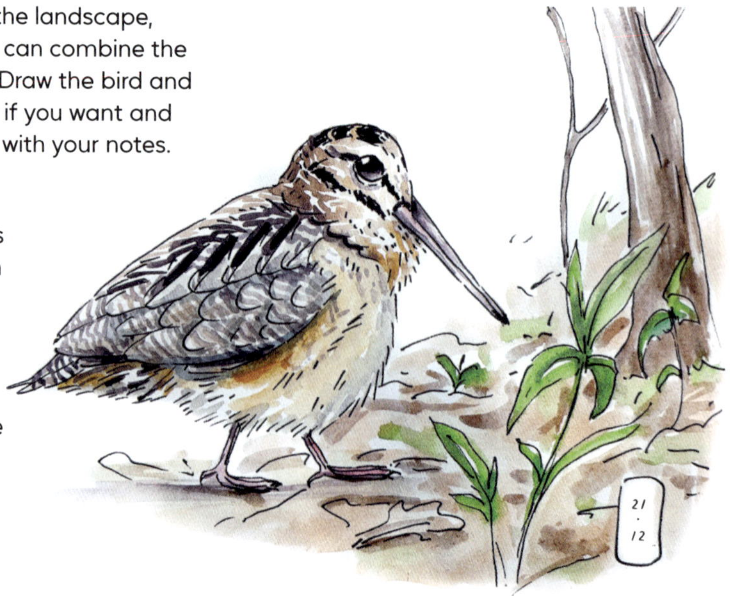

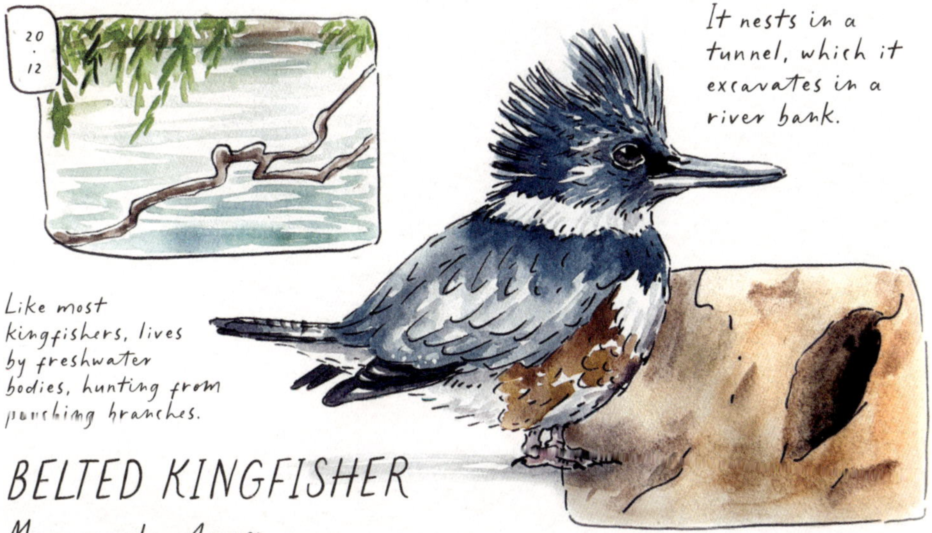

BELTED KINGFISHER

Megaceryle alcyon

I also love placing landscapes or birds in panels, so they feel connected yet separated at the same time. You can create many interesting compositions when using panels like these.

Top tip

One of the most advanced ways to show the habitat of a bird is by drawing a cross-section. Imagine that you cut the scene you see and turn it into a flat graphic. It's especially fun to do for burrowing or wading birds, making visible their underground or underwater world!

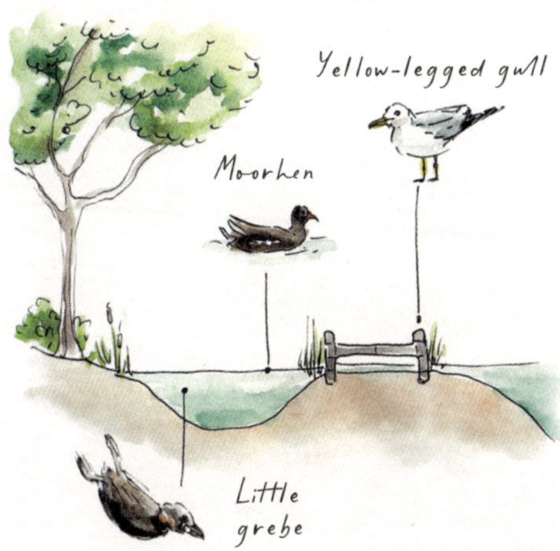

PARQUE DA CIDADE DO PORTO

Bridge across the pond

Other notes

Colour swatches, subspecies, ephemera and song charts

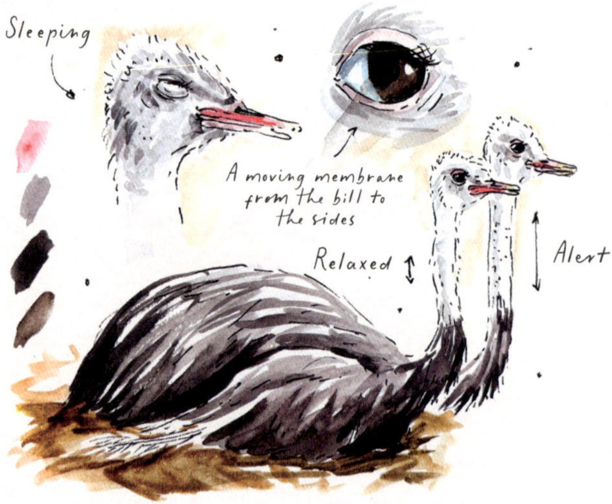

Are there any other elements you can add to your bird sketches to fill the space and make your page feel more complete? Of course! Here are a few more ideas for you to explore.

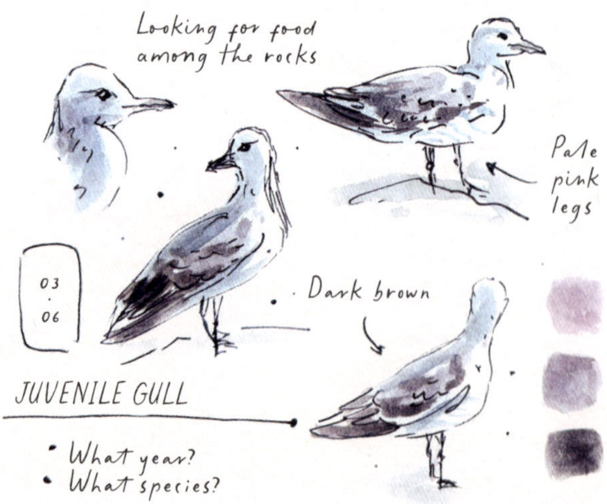

Colour swatches

One very simple thing to do is to test colours right on your sketchbook page before applying them to the drawing. This is not only useful for understanding how the colours will work with this specific page, but also gives another sense of the bird's plumage.

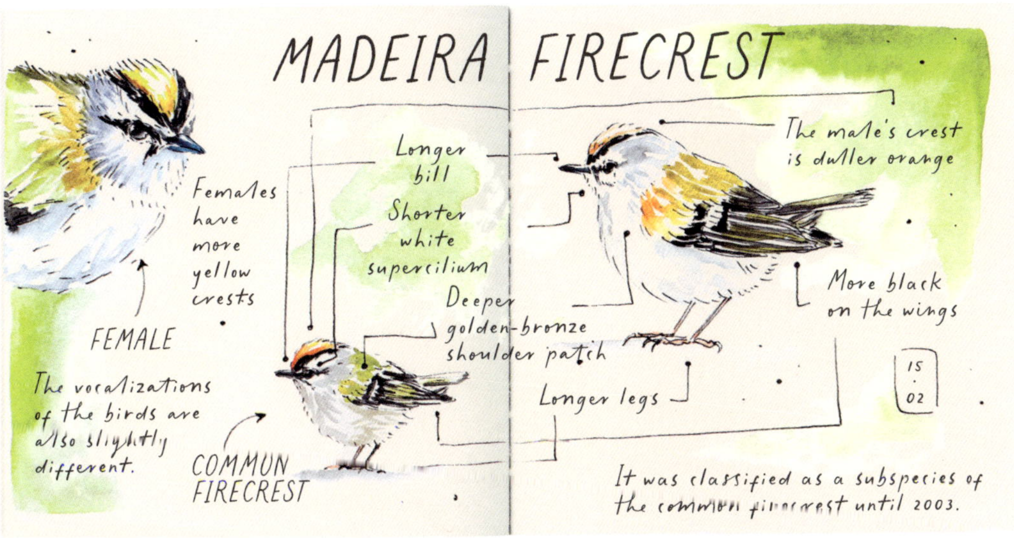

Subspecies

We learned about visual variety of the same species when it comes to genders and ages, but there is also a difference between subspecies with some birds. Not only does this need a pro-level of birdwatching skill to identify them, it's also an interesting thing to draw. Subtle markings that can be easily overlooked become the focus of your bird study – isn't it fascinating?

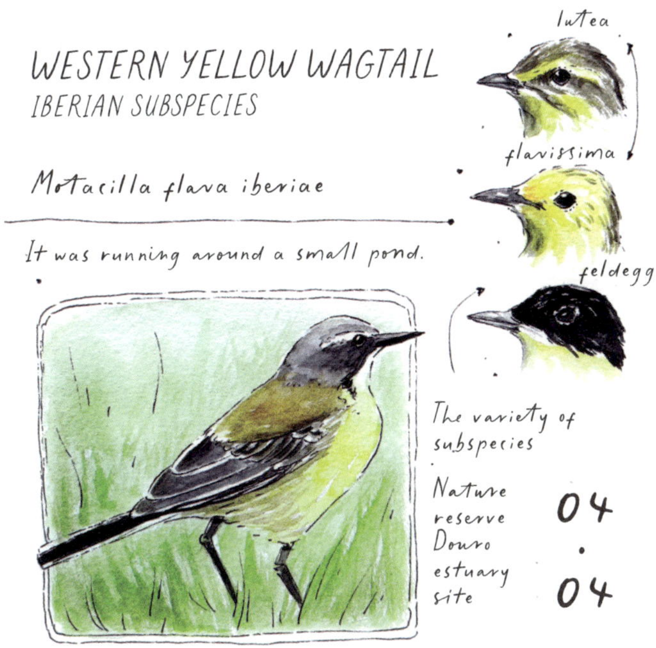

Song charts

Speaking of additions to your bird drawings without mentioning visualization of a bird's song would be a crime. I personally find it challenging to identify birds by song, so drawing the sound is especially hard for me, but it's always fun to try! Create your own system for translating the vocalization using lines, waves, letters or something else that works best for you.

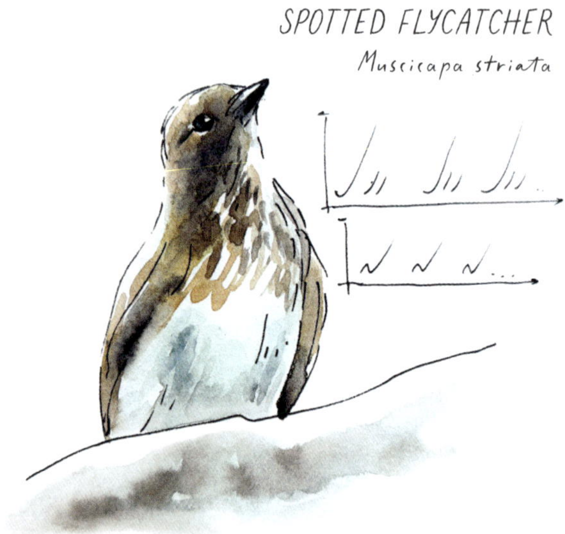

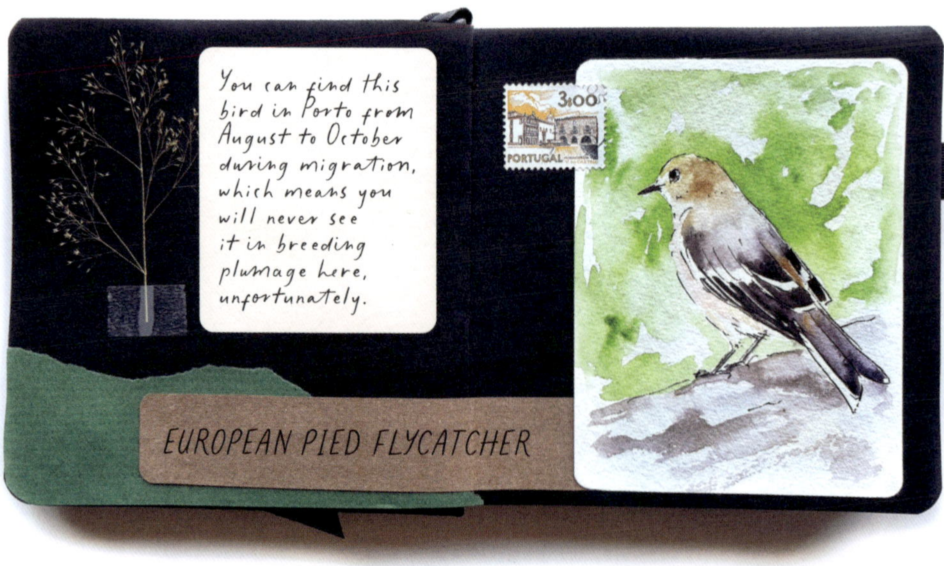

I tried a sketchbook with black paper, but didn't really like how my drawings looked there. It turned into a great junk journal.

Ephemera

Including various memorabilia is a whole other deal in the world of art and crafts. But who said you can't add something more to your bird drawings occasionally?

There are so many options of what can be included – leaves, feathers, park tickets, stickers, stamps etc. All these visuals can enrich your sketchbook. There's a problem, though, with this: the page is uneven and bulky. Here are my ways to deal with this:

- Use a sketchbook with thick paper and add only very thin and flat items.
- Use pockets and flip-out pages.
- Keep ephemera only on the left side of the double-page spreads, and carry a piece of cardstock in your sketchbook to cover it.
- Collect the things you'd like to include, but place them on the pages after you finish the sketchbook.

Using flip-outs

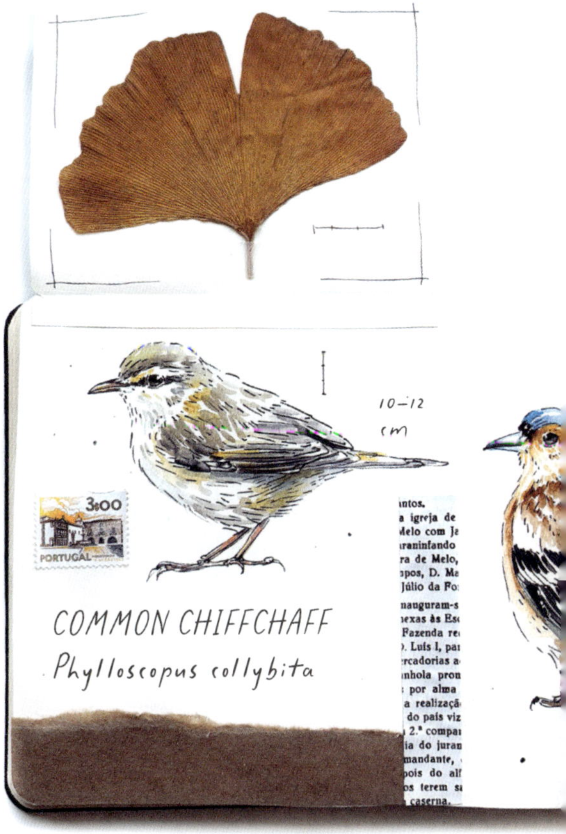

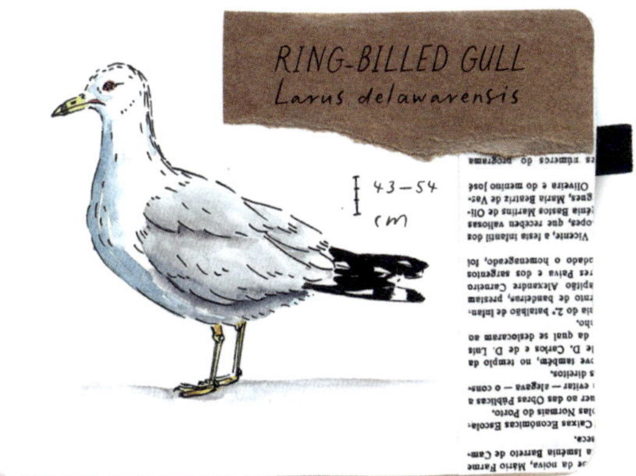

Thin and flat additions

Top tip

Dedicate a special sketchbook for nature junk journalling. Create drawings separately and glue them in just as you do with the other additions.

Composition

Building a layout of the page

Now let's bring together all the elements into one balanced composition. You might think that this is what we were supposed to start with, but my approach is usually based on drawing the main object and then filling the space around it with other components.

Look for the biggest empty space on the page – this is probably the one you need to fill first to balance the main drawing. Add notes and smaller elements around, creating visual rhythm without making it too symmetrical.

When you have one main object on the page, there are several approaches for placing it. Here are the most common ways to choose the location strategically.

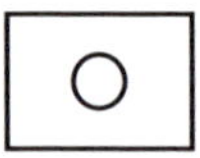
Bird in the middle of the page

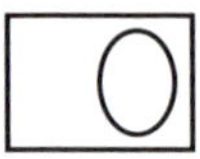
Closer view at the edge of the page

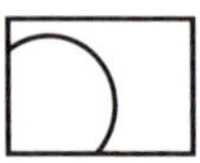
Asymmetrical composition

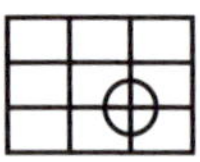
Use rule of thirds to place a bird

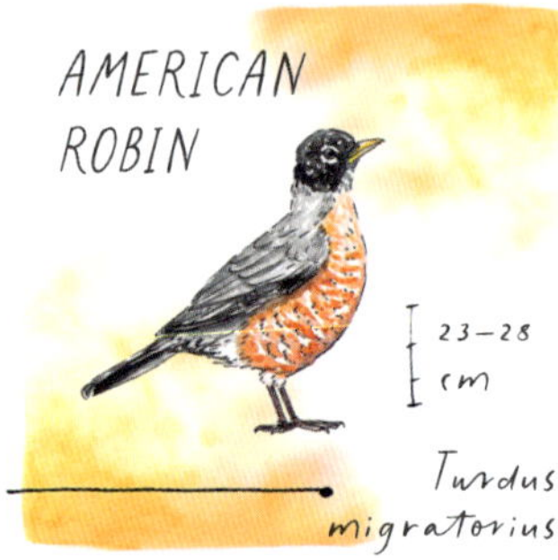

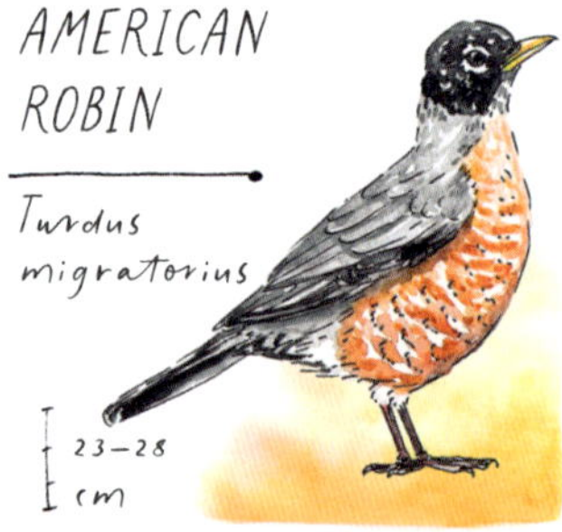

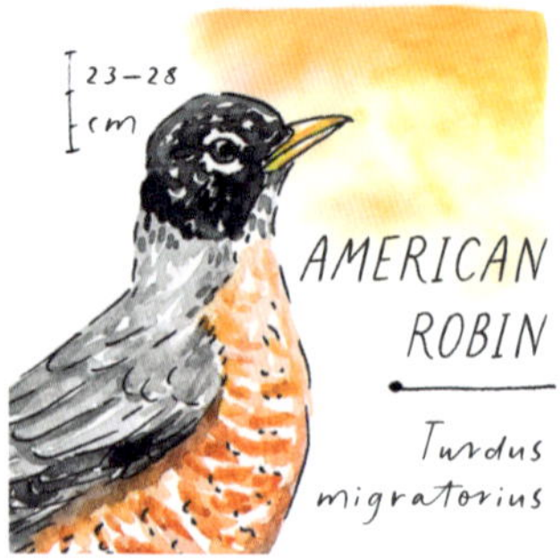

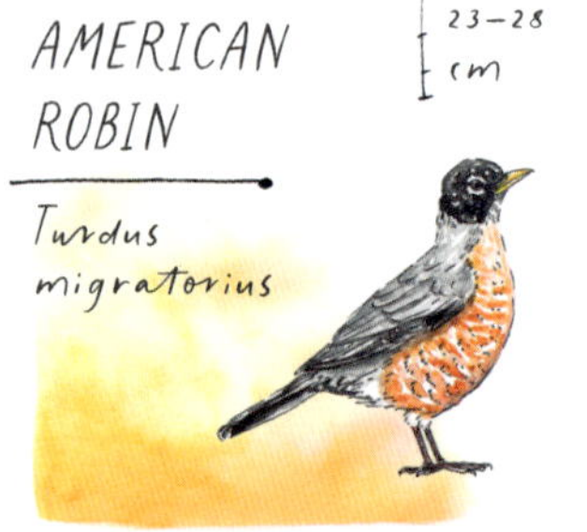

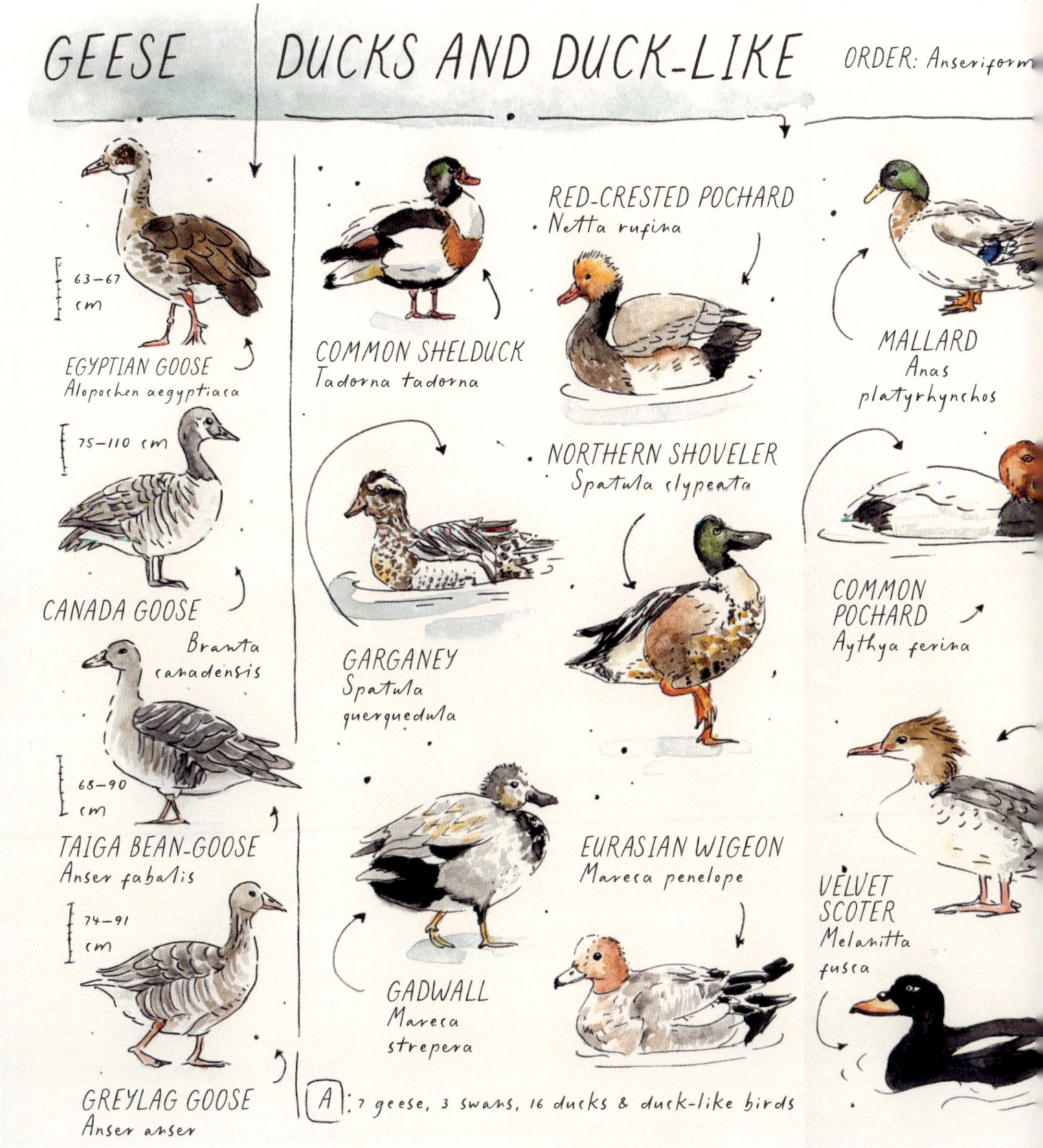

If you want to make several bird drawings on your page, the variety of compositions is almost endless! I shared many examples across this chapter and I'm sure you are now more than ready to come up with your own ideas. The only question left is how to choose which bird to draw...

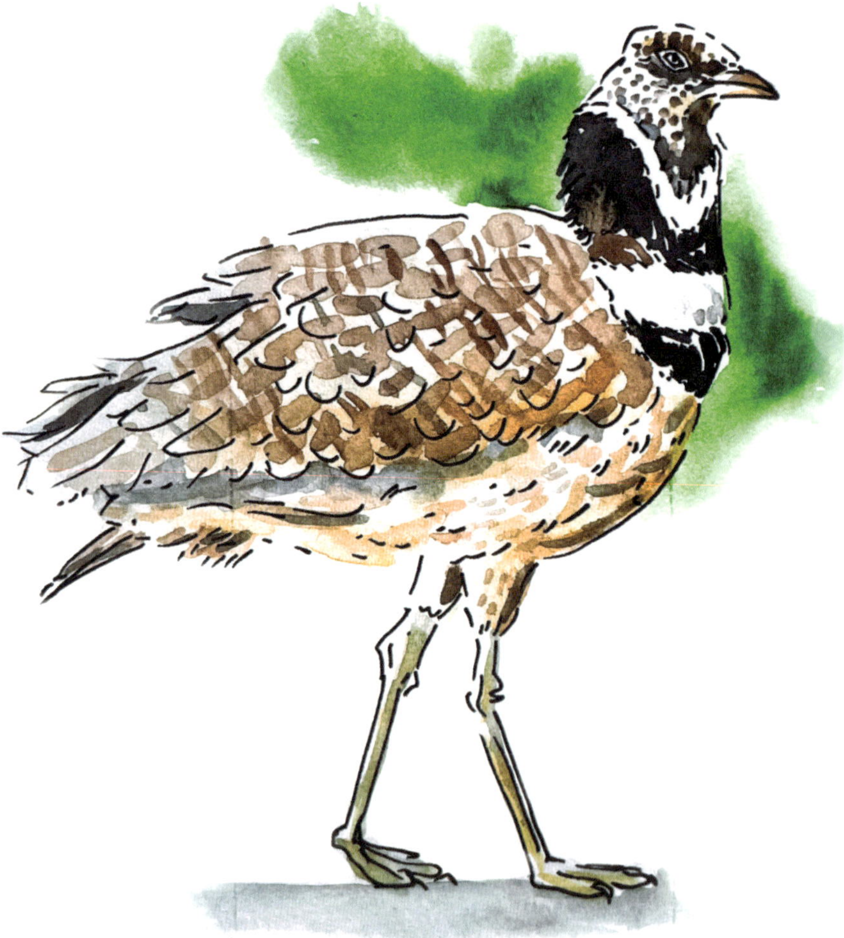

Chapter four

What's next?

There are more than 10,000 bird species in the world. How do you choose which one to draw? Let me give you some ideas.

Bucket list

Draw birds you are dreaming to meet

I don't know if you've ever tried to make a bucket list of the birds you'd like to see, but if you are a birdwatcher, you probably have a few birds in mind that would definitely be on such a list. However, just writing down their names probably doesn't seem useful.

The thing is that drawing is different from merely writing – when you draw birds, you learn much more about how to find them. This is extremely helpful when you want to observe a specific bird. So I highly recommend making a list like this if you've never tried it, and setting it as a kind of a goal for the next month or year, for example. Consider this your birdwatching vision board!

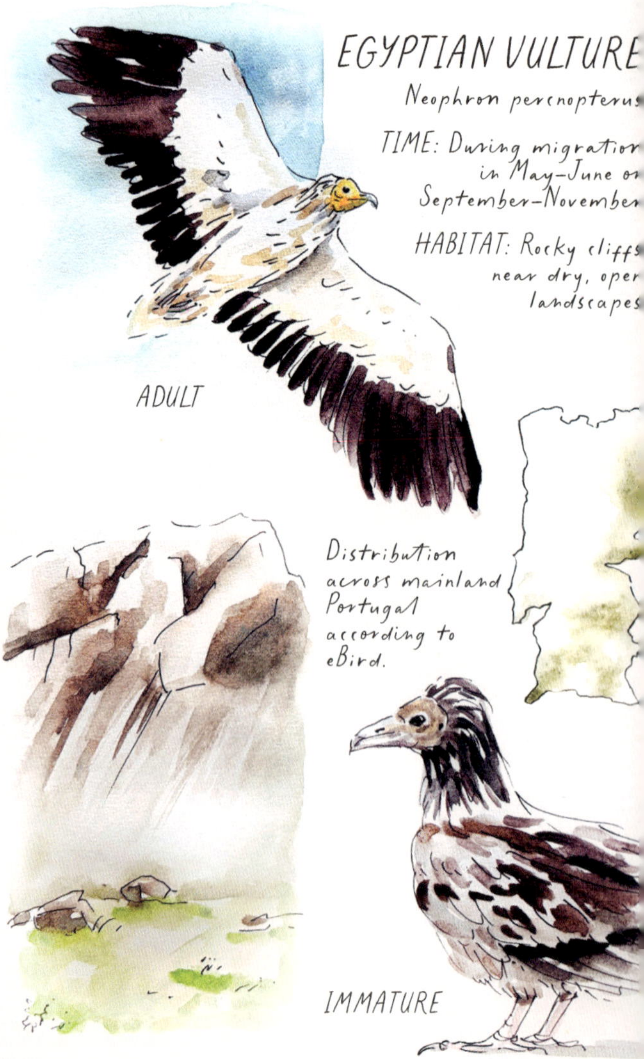

There are various ways to create such a list. It can be just a simple list of bird names with a small drawing nearby.

It can also be a more detailed study of the bird, where you try to figure out how it will look based on gender and age, when and where to find it and how to differentiate it from similar species, if applicable. Depending on how long your bucket list is and how much time you have, you can choose different approaches and go from there.

I find the most important thing in this kind of study is to focus on the habitat of the bird and the specific spots where I can find it, using eBird, for example.

You can also create a bucket list for a trip you are planning. A new place always means new birds. Learn about them before your trip just as you learn about local sightseeing. I'm sure you did this before, but when sketching is involved, the chance to actually meet these new species is much higher!

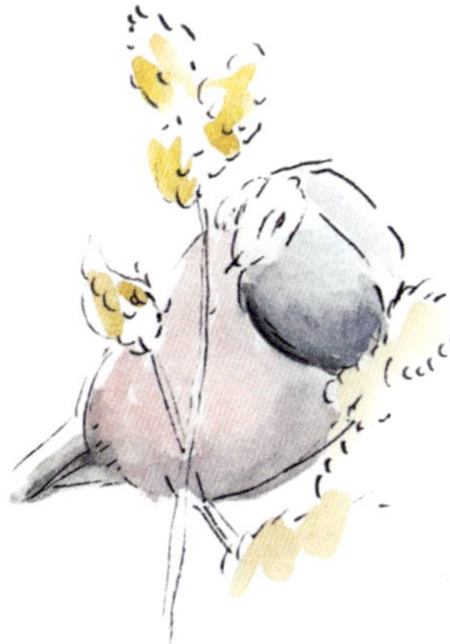

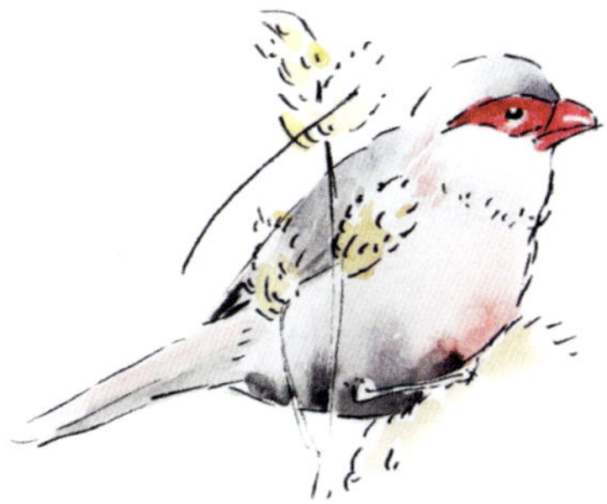

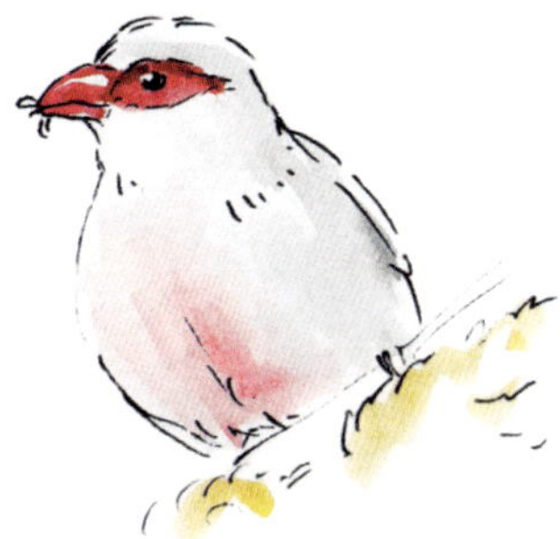

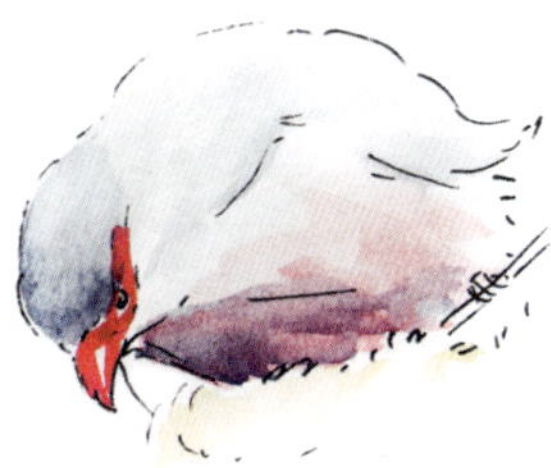

BUCKET LIST

Estuário do Douro
January–February 2025

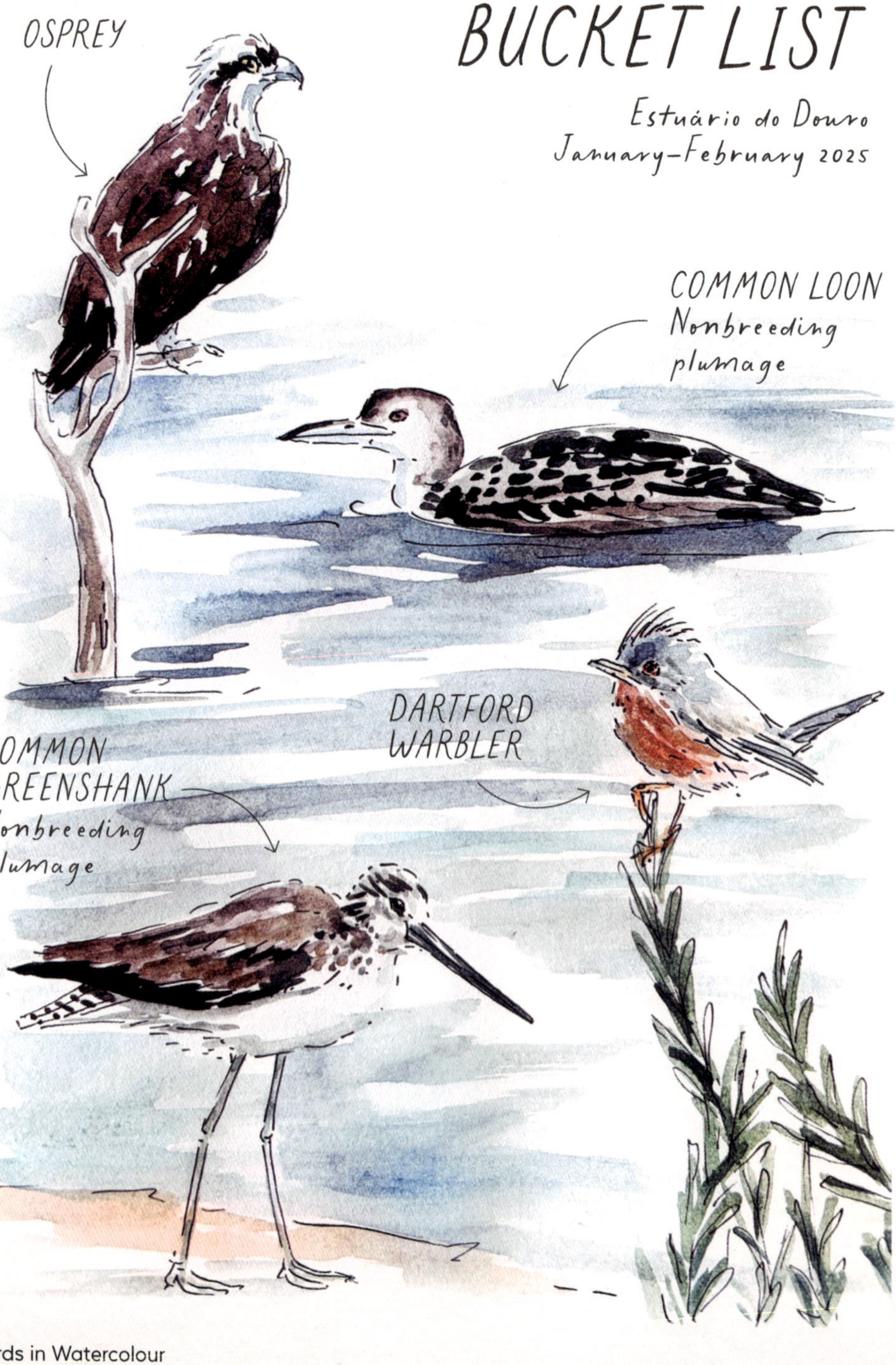

Lifers list

Keep a memory book of birds you have seen

A lifers list is one that a birdwatcher adds to after seeing a bird for the first time – it's an ongoing list that you keep throughout your life. To be honest, I didn't know it was a thing when I started birdwatching, and later I just didn't keep proper records of the birds I saw. It wasn't until a couple of years ago that I started it in the form of a sketchbook!

After seeing a bird, I was making a sketch of the exact scene and writing down some information about the moment. I was also making a detailed portrait of the bird based on references I could find on the internet – this way I could study the bird better.

Before seeing a bird, you only know it remotely, and you usually don't understand it that well. Of course, if it's a bird you really wanted to see, you will have looked at pictures of it and maybe even watched some videos. But after seeing it in real life, it's like you finally get to know this bird! And drawing it feels completely different.

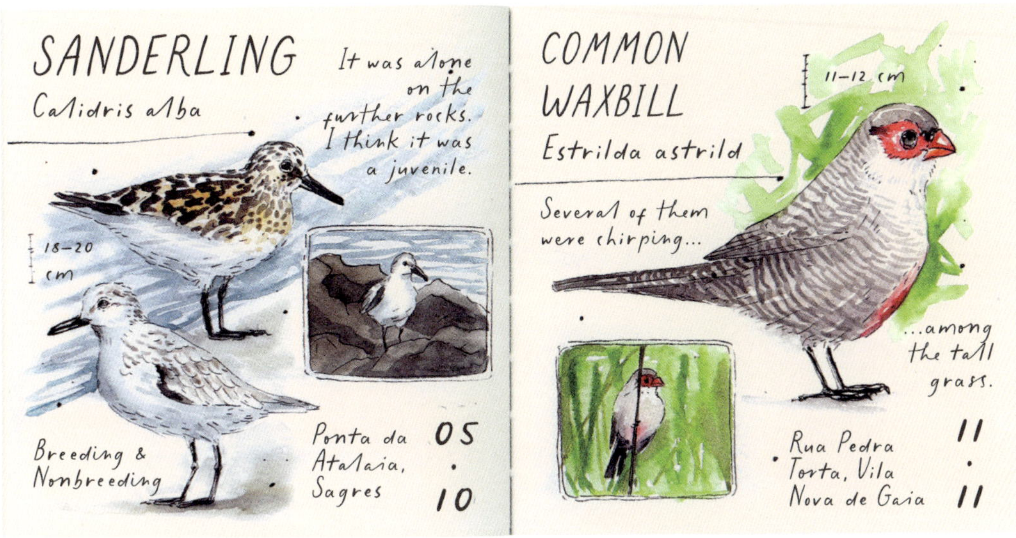

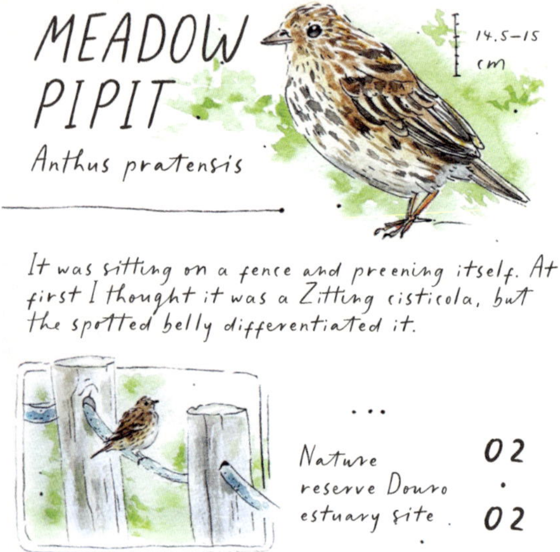

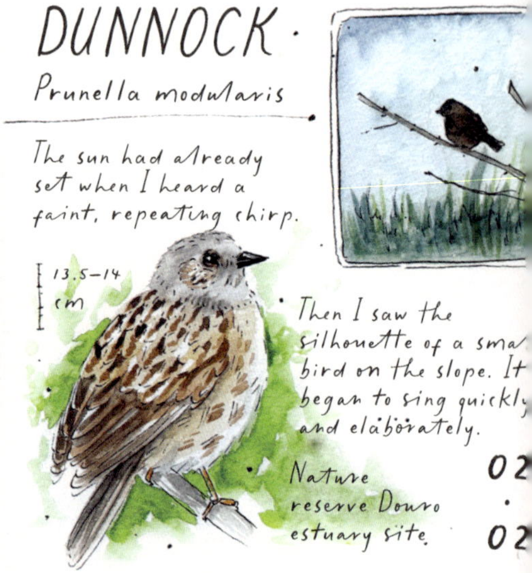

If you've never tried incorporating drawings into your lifers list, I highly recommend it. It can be simple, like a bucket list with just the bird's name, date and a small sketch, or it can be a richer record of your experience, with personal notes and additional sketches of the place or other birds you saw. Studying a bird after seeing it becomes much more meaningful this way.

Another benefit is that you don't always have your camera with you to take a picture. Sketching is priceless and preserves memories far better. You don't just end up with a dry list of bird names and dates – you get visual support that keeps your memories alive and vivid.

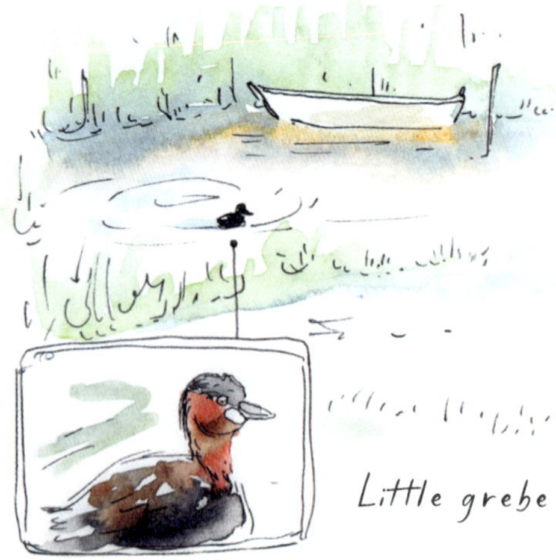

Little grebe

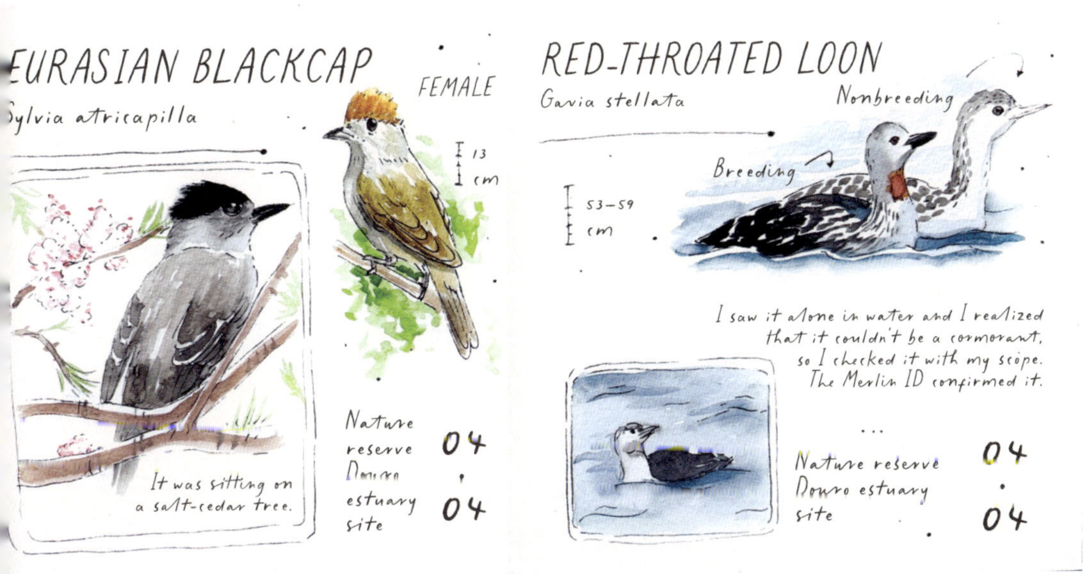
EURASIAN BLACKCAP
Sylvia atricapilla
FEMALE
13 cm
It was sitting on a salt-cedar tree.
Nature reserve Douro estuary site
04 . 04
RED-THROATED LOON
Gavia stellata
Nonbreeding
Breeding
53–59 cm
I saw it alone in water and I realized that it couldn't be a cormorant, so I checked it with my scope. The Merlin ID confirmed it.
Nature reserve Douro estuary site
04 . 04

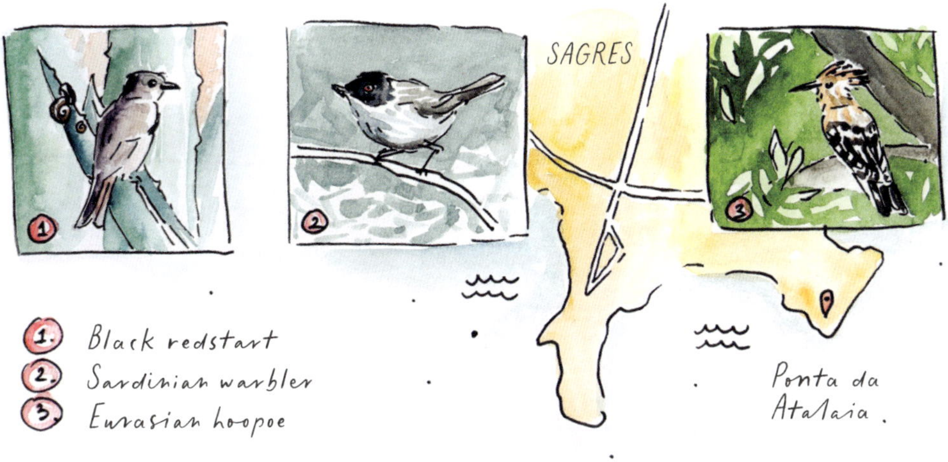
SAGRES
1
2
3
1. Black redstart
2. Sardinian warbler
3. Eurasian hoopoe
Ponta da Atalaia

Bird guidebook

Create your own guide to birds of your country, region or garden

When I finished my first Instagram challenge, where I was drawing birds daily, I needed a new project to keep myself on track. I couldn't come up with anything better than drawing all of the birds of Portugal! This seemed like the best way for me to draw birds for as long as possible. I think drawing the birds in your area is a great project if you want to practise drawing and learn about the birds around you.

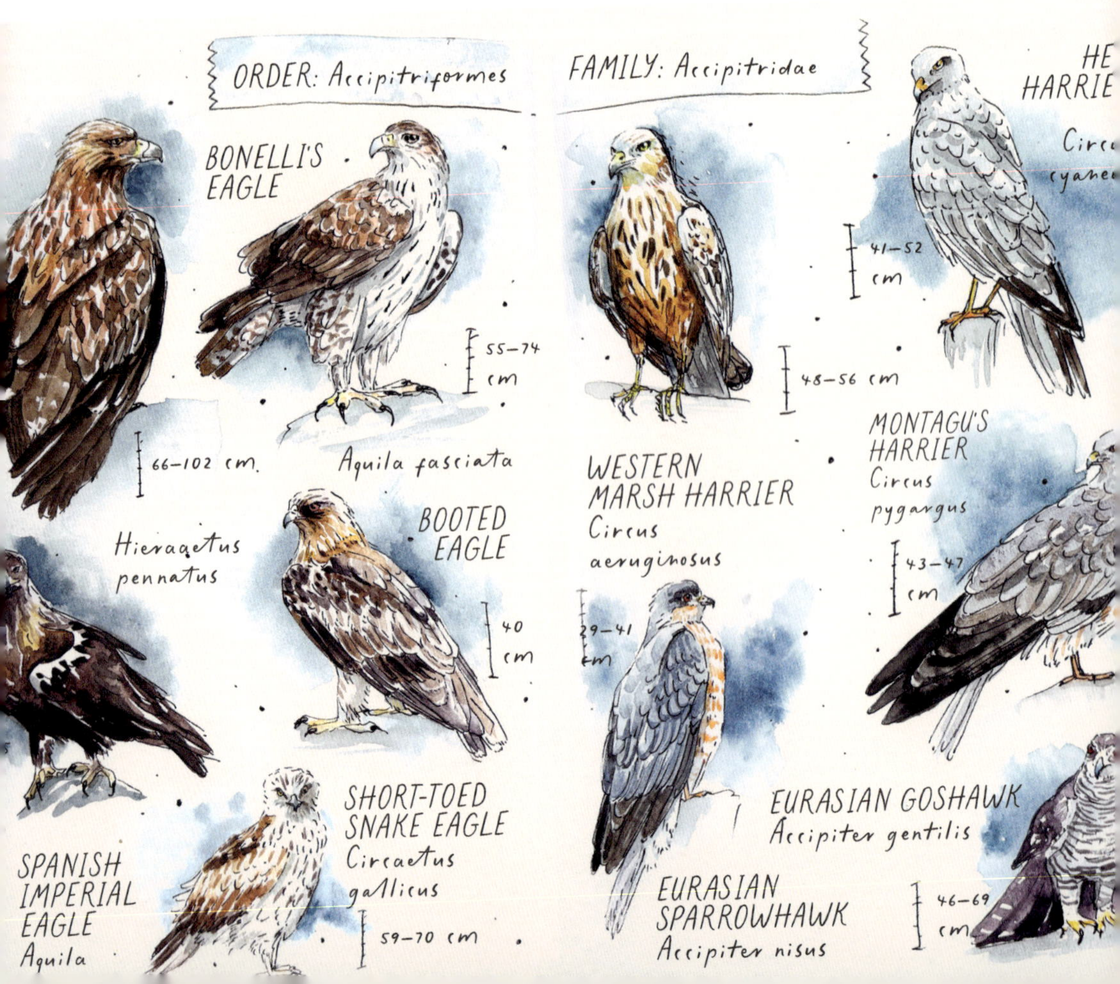

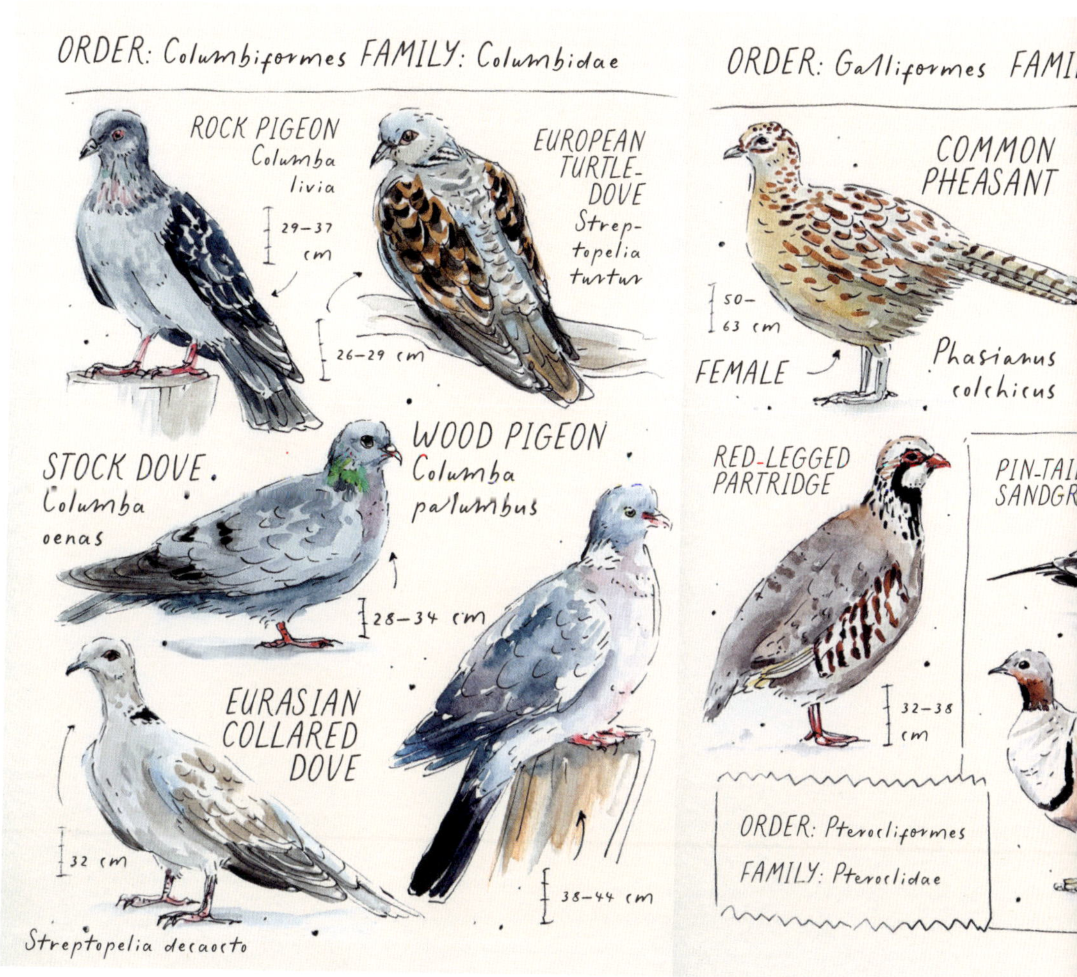

The difference between this and a bucket list or lifers list is that these aren't birds you've seen or necessarily want to see – they are all the birds of a specific place. Isn't it exciting? The area can vary – it could be your city, your state, a whole country or even a larger region like Europe or North America. It doesn't have to be where you live – it could be a place you just want to learn more about.

When making a guidebook, it's not practical to dive too deeply into details, because the list of birds might be huge. I usually draw one bird per species, choosing the most distinctive look of the bird so they are easy to tell apart.

Write the bird's common name and scientific name next to the drawing. To keep it structured, group birds by their order and family. This was very insightful for me because, as a non-biologist, I'm not that good with all these classifications. Keeping such a guidebook helps me with this a lot, and I really enjoy the process.

My bird guidebook of Portugal isn't finished yet, but I'm very excited to continue working on it. Whenever I have a spare moment, I just return to this guidebook and start a new drawing.

If you're looking for a big project, create your own bird guide like this. It will also help you learn a lot about the birds you might encounter. Some birds I couldn't add to my bucket list simply because I didn't know they exist! After I found out about them while making my guidebook, I added a few to my bucket list and am very excited to meet them.

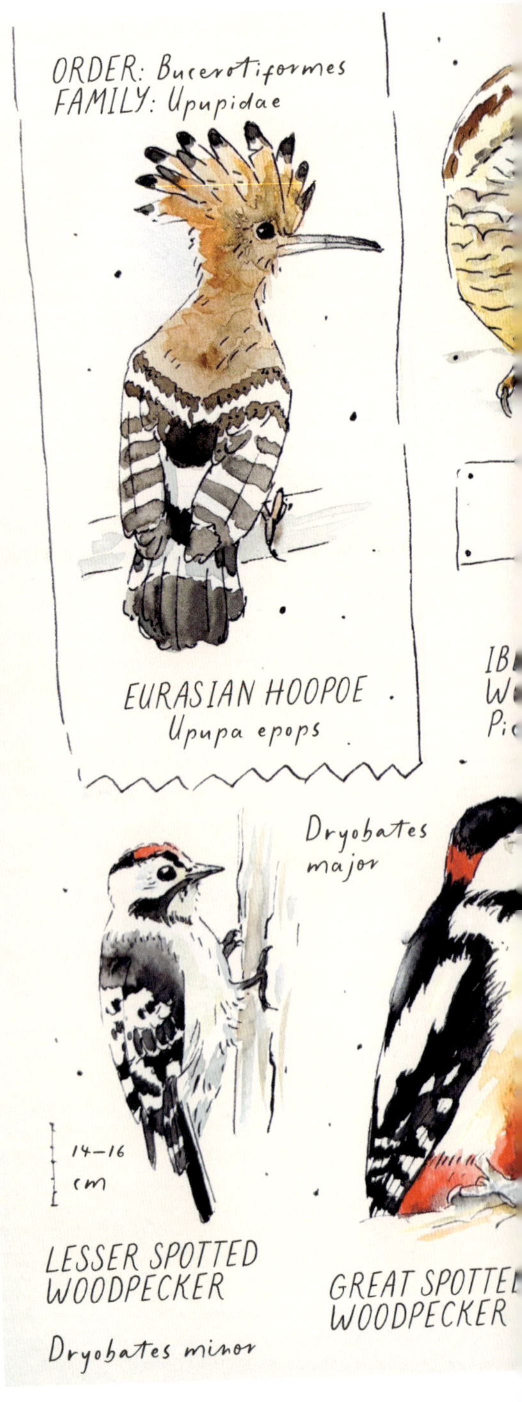

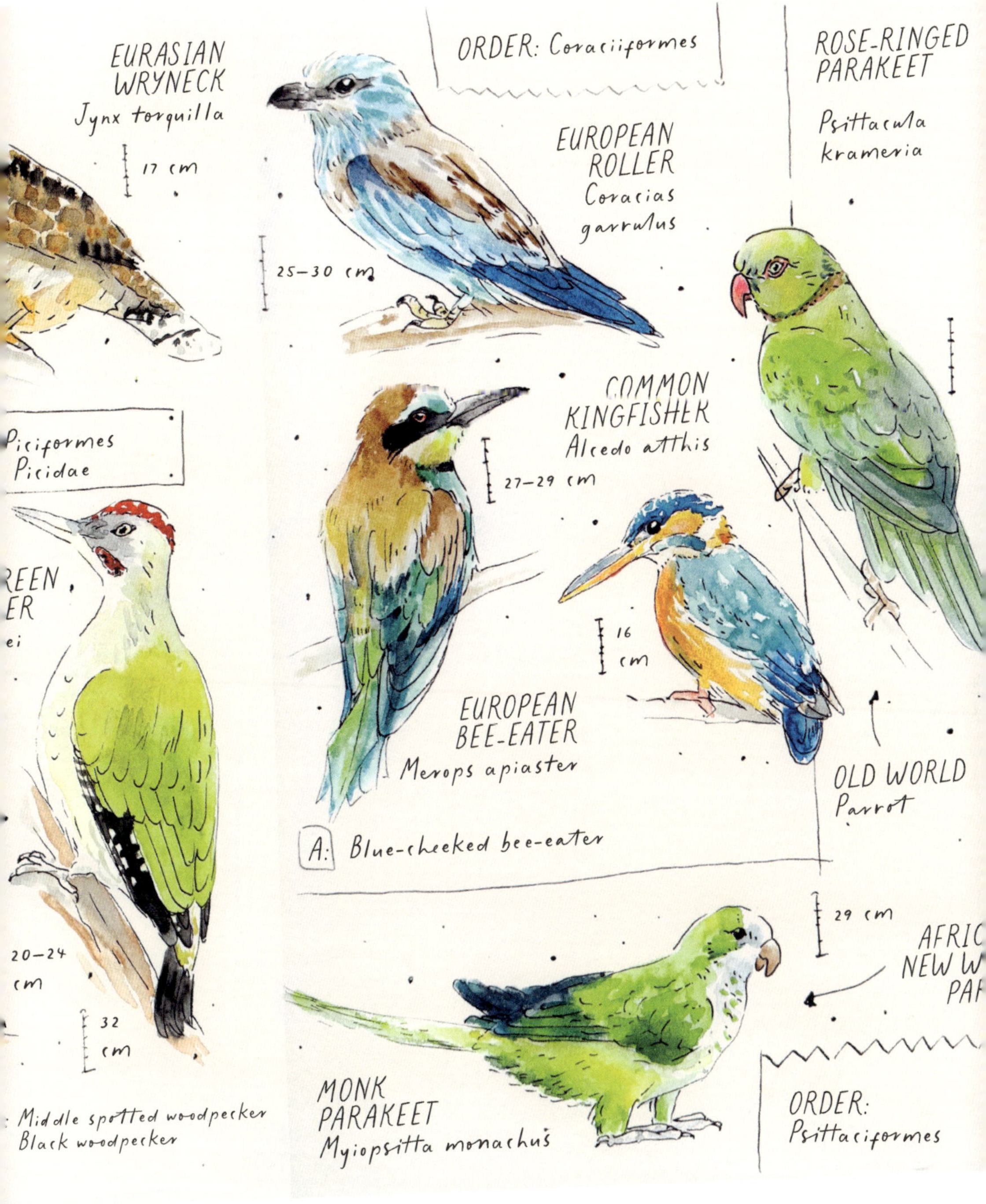
EURASIAN WRYNECK
Jynx torquilla
17 cm
Piciformes
Picidae
REEN
ER
ei
20–24 cm
32 cm
Middle spotted woodpecker
Black woodpecker
ORDER: Coraciiformes
EUROPEAN ROLLER
Coracias garrulus
25–30 cm
COMMON KINGFISHER
Alcedo atthis
27–29 cm
16 cm
EUROPEAN BEE-EATER
Merops apiaster
A: Blue-cheeked bee-eater
ROSE-RINGED PARAKEET
Psittacula krameria
OLD WORLD Parrot
29 cm
AFRIC
NEW W
PAF
MONK PARAKEET
Myiopsitta monachus
ORDER: Psittaciformes

Red bird book

Learn about endangered species and raise conservation awareness

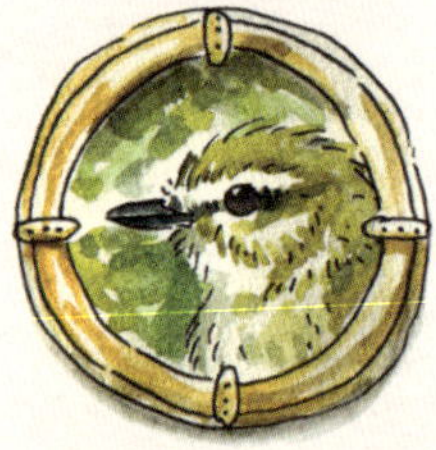

Alagoas tyrannulet

This is a project with extra attention to endangered birds. They face different types of threats, and you can approach this project in various ways. Focus on a specific location and learn about all the endangered species there, or concentrate on birds with a particular conservation status.

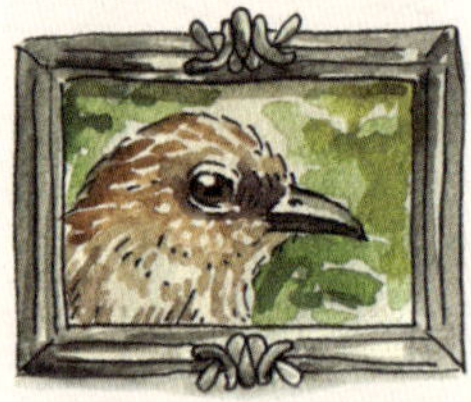

Socorro mockingbird

There are several categories of threatened species you can focus on:

- Vulnerable (VU)
- Endangered (EN)
- Critically Endangered (CR)

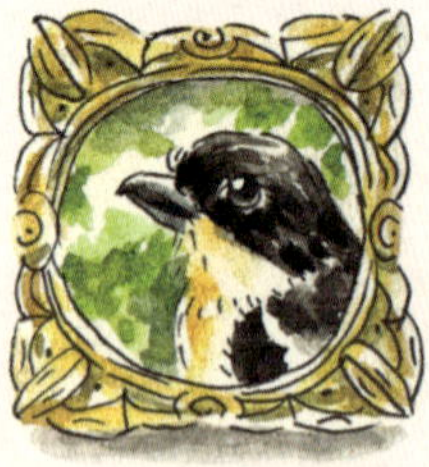

São Tomé fiscal

Find out about birds that live in your country and belong to one of these categories, or choose a specific order of birds to learn about and protect.

For example, I started drawing critically endangered birds from around the world as part of my appreciation to my new Patreon members. I don't make a big study of each bird, but at least I gain a basic familiarity with each species, which I will expand in the future.

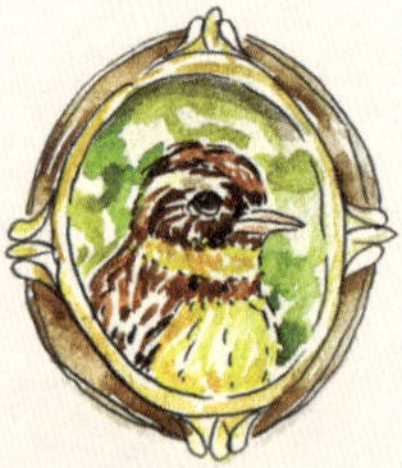

Yellow-breasted Bunting

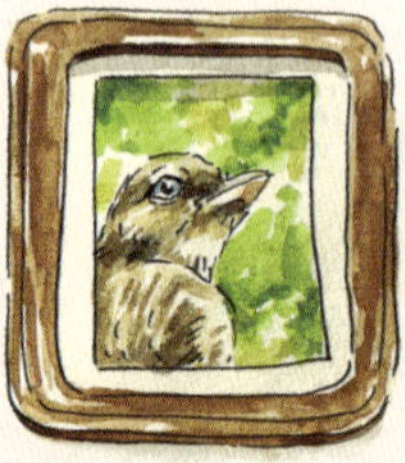

Sangihe whistler

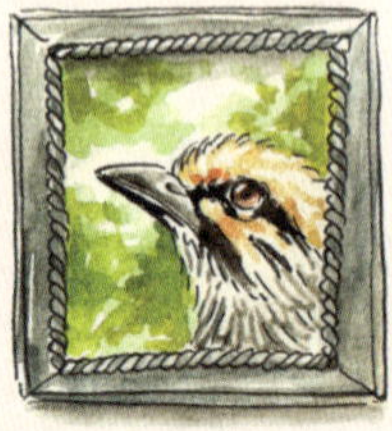

Straw-headed bulbul

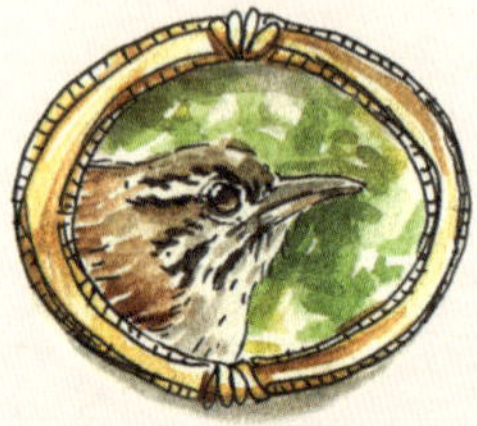

Niceforo's wren

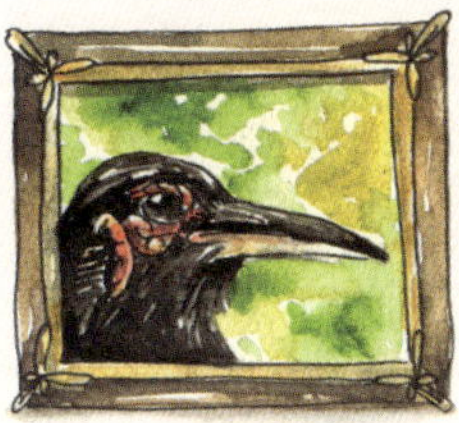

Crow honeyeater

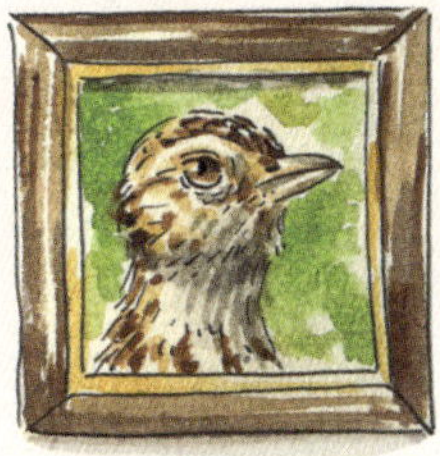

Archer's lark

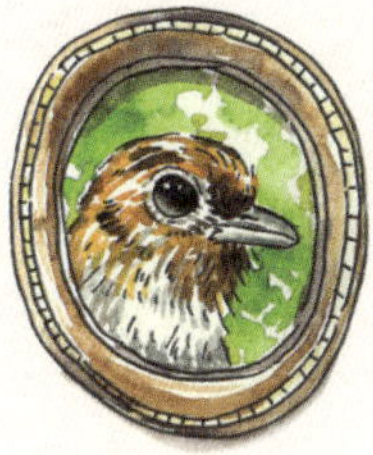

Urrao antpitta

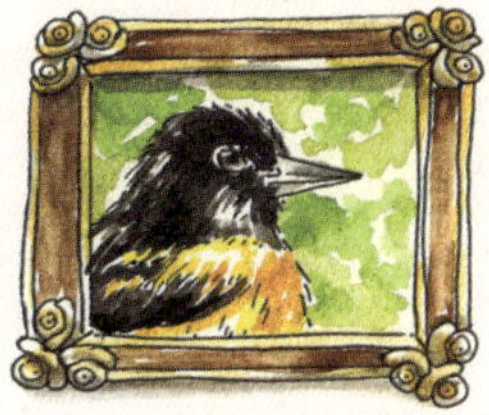

Bahama oriole

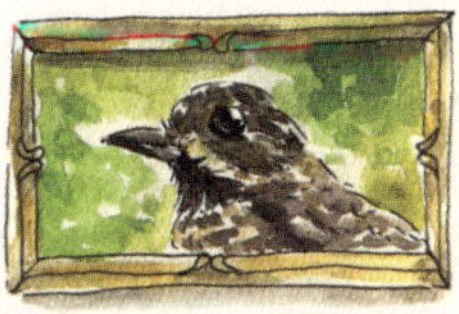

Tachira antpitta

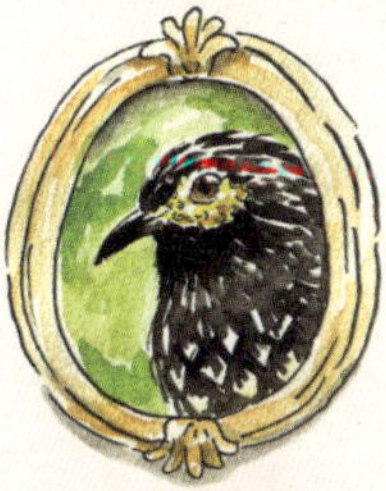

Regent honeyeater

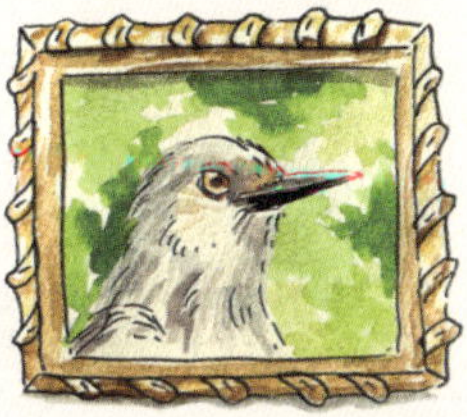

Long-billed forest warbler

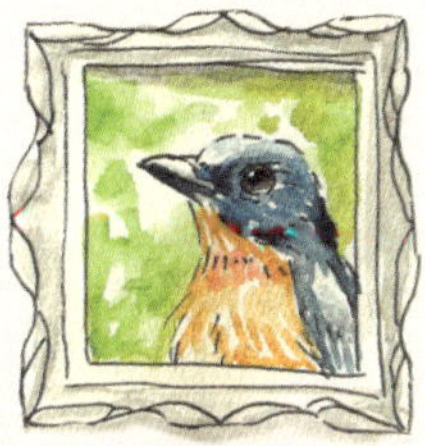

Javan blue flycatcher

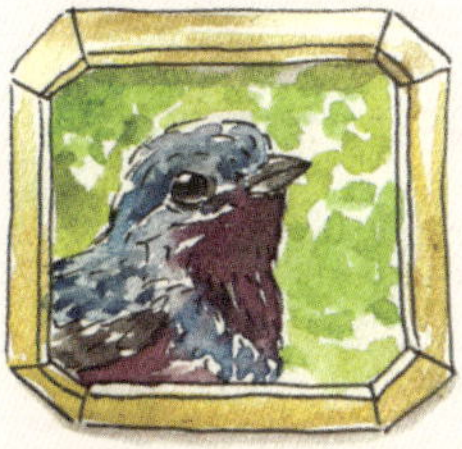

Banded cotinga

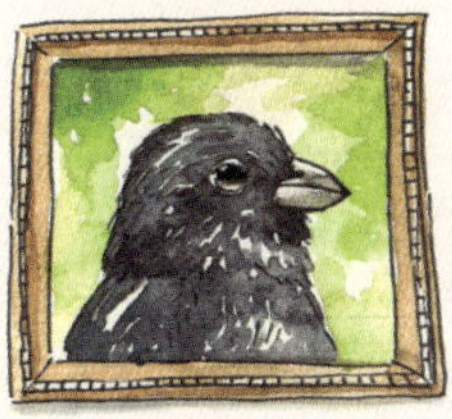

Carrizal seedeater

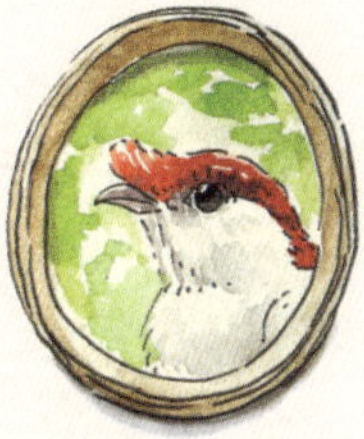

Araripe manakin

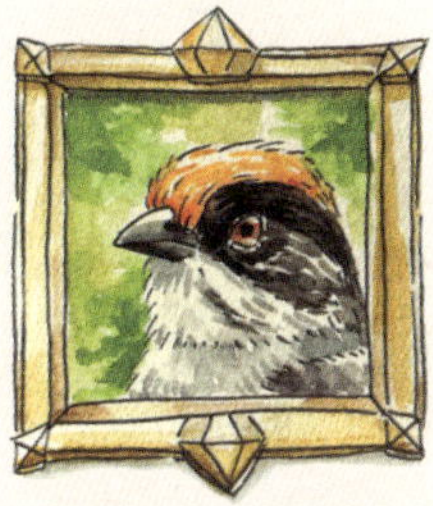

Antioquia brushfinch

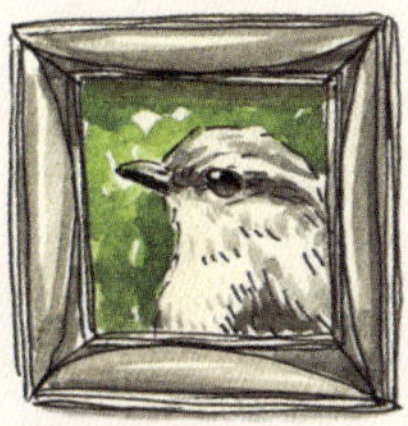

Réunion cuckooshrike

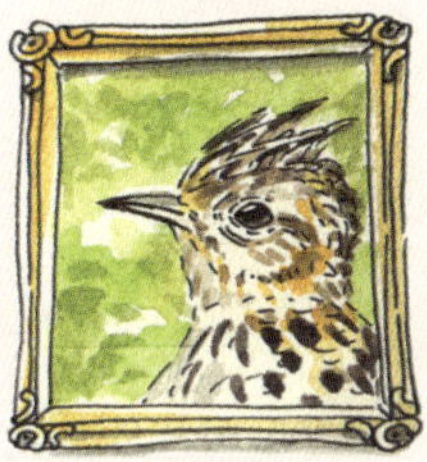

Raso lark

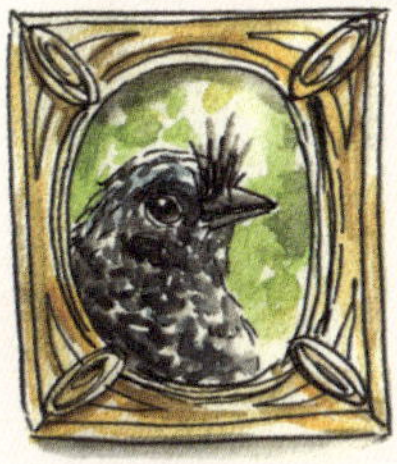

Stresemann's bristlefront

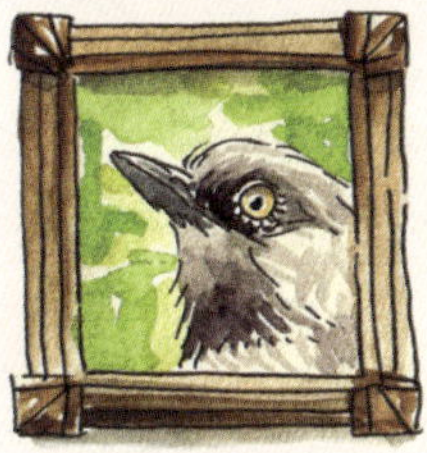

Taita apalis

You could use a more detailed approach, studying each bird in depth. Learn why these birds are becoming extinct. Focus on the bird's distribution range, habitat, number of species, the risks they face and potential conservation efforts.

It's important not only to learn for yourself but also to share this knowledge. Sometimes it feels like we can't make any difference to a bird going extinct, especially if it's somewhere far away. But even small actions – spreading awareness or supporting fundraisers – can create a ripple effect that helps conservation efforts.

This project can be sad at times, but it's meaningful and important. It's a way to combine art, learning and action to support birds that need our attention. Use your art to save these birds.

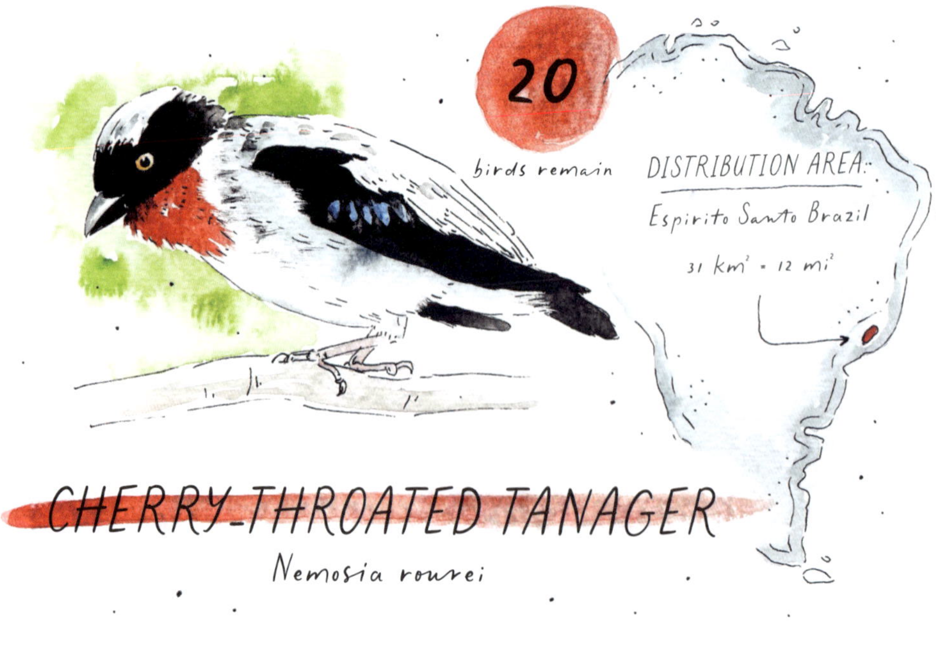

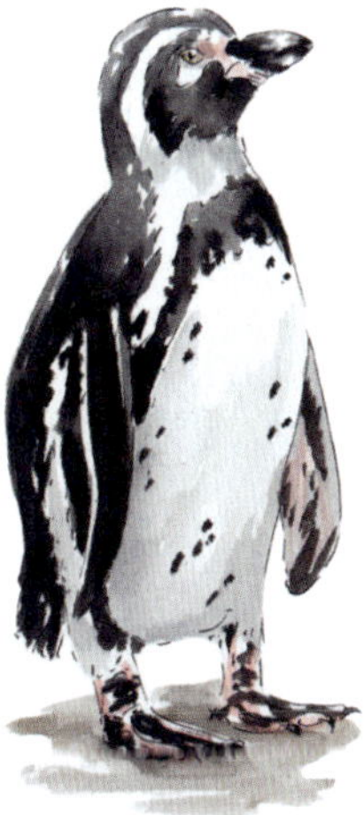

HUMBOLDT PENGUIN
Spheniscus humboldti

VULNERABLE

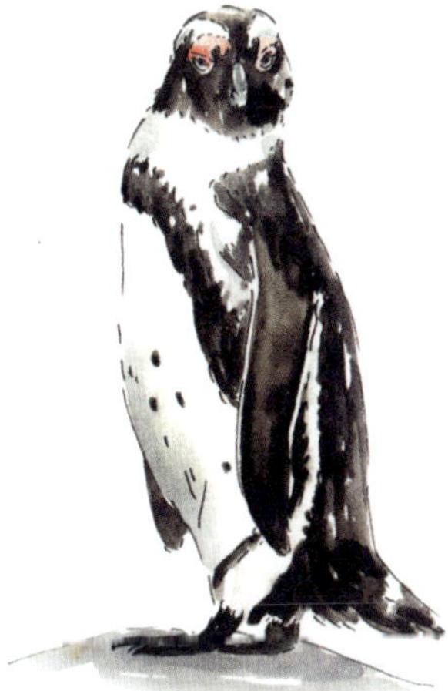

AFRICAN PENGUIN
Spheniscus demersus

CRITICALLY ENDANGERED

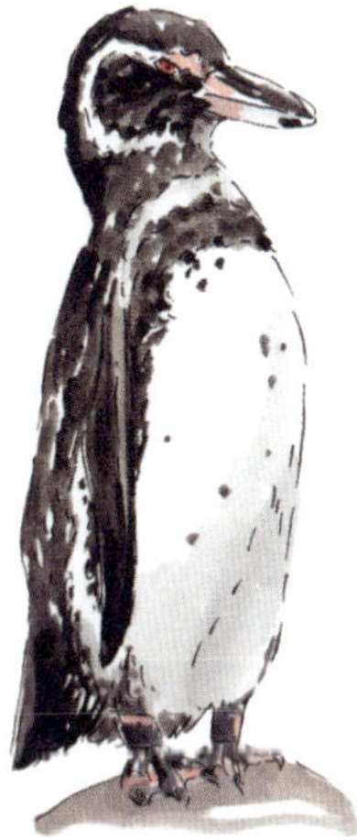

GALAPAGOS PENGUIN
Spheniscus mendiculus

ENDANGERED

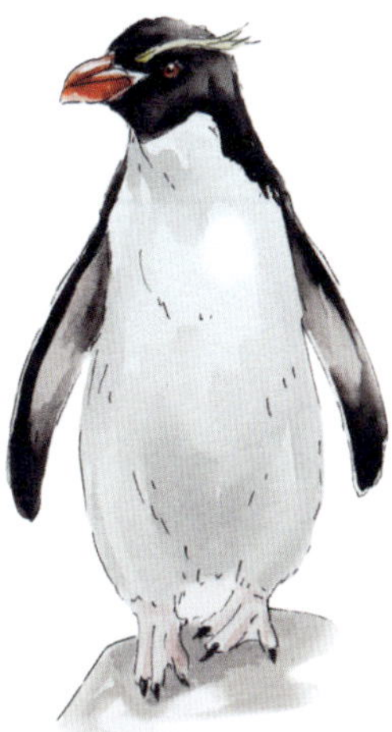

SNARES PENGUIN
Eudyptes robustus

VULNERABLE

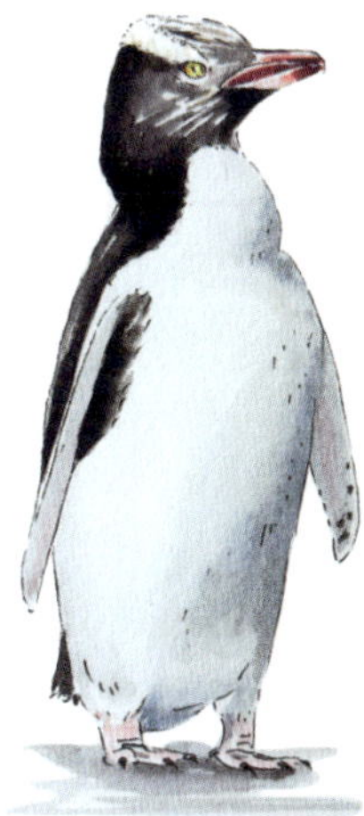

YELLOW-EYED PENGUIN
Megadyptes antipodes

ENDANGERED

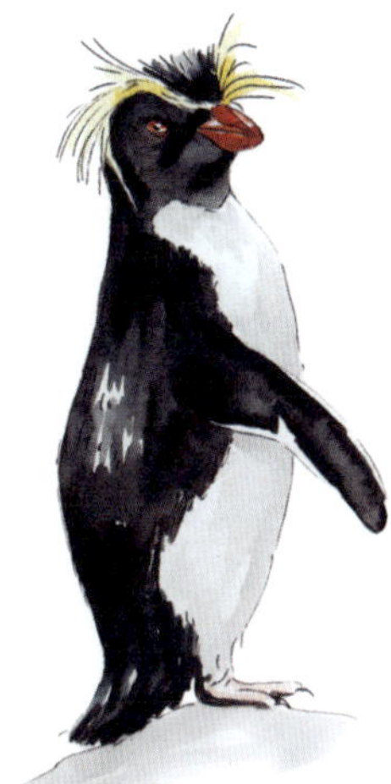

ROCKHOPPER PENGUIN
Eudyptes chrysocome

VULNERABLE

Field sketching

Introduction to nature journalling

Drawing birds in the field from life might seem tricky. I'm still learning myself how to do this properly. But the main rule is: do not expect your field sketches to be as detailed and polished as they are when you make them from static references at home. Even very experienced, talented artists who can produce stunning works and who have years of practice in drawing birds, still have to make some messy sketches first when they are drawing from life.

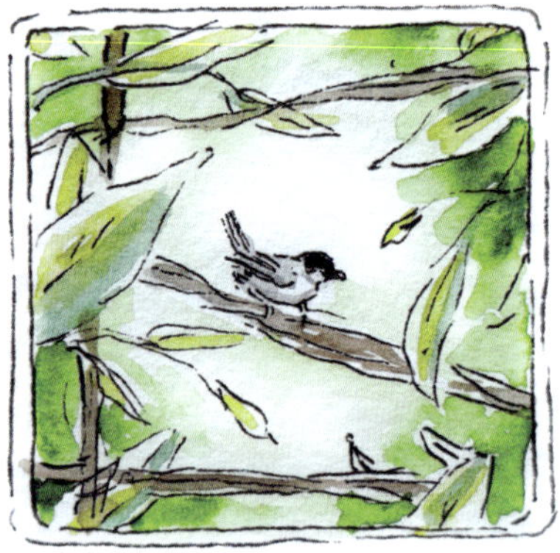

Top tip

Another thing with field sketching is that you have to draw only what you see. Just learn from nature at this moment. If something is blocking the view of the bird, draw only those parts you see. And if the bird is in shadow, just draw it dark and simplified as it looks.

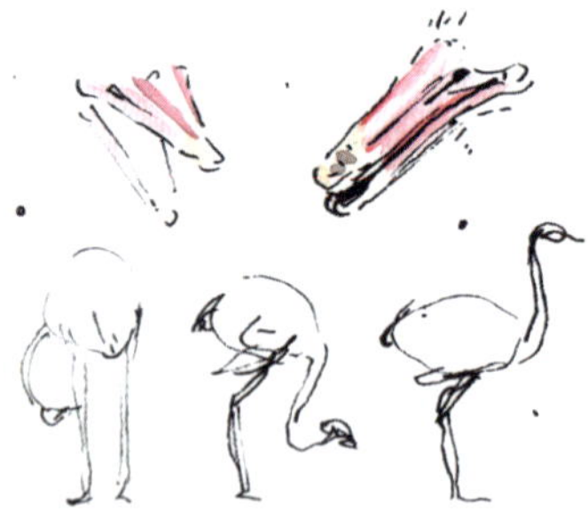

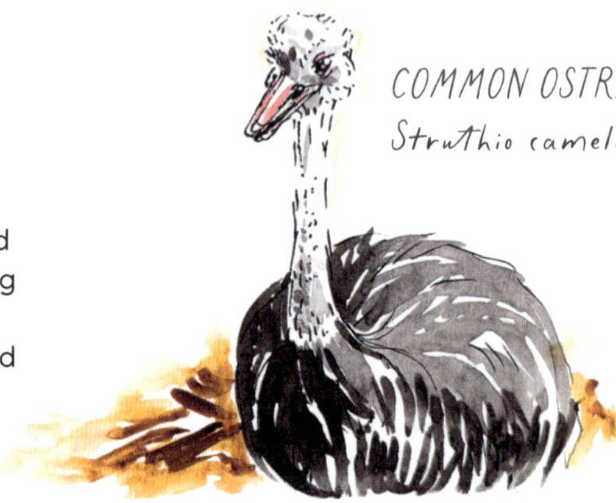

COMMON OSTRICH
Struthio camelus

Use field sketching to understand how colours work depending on the light and shade. This is something you are missing when you watch references online – you don't know how much the light impacted the way the bird looks in the picture. When you see it live, it's clearer what colours the bird has.

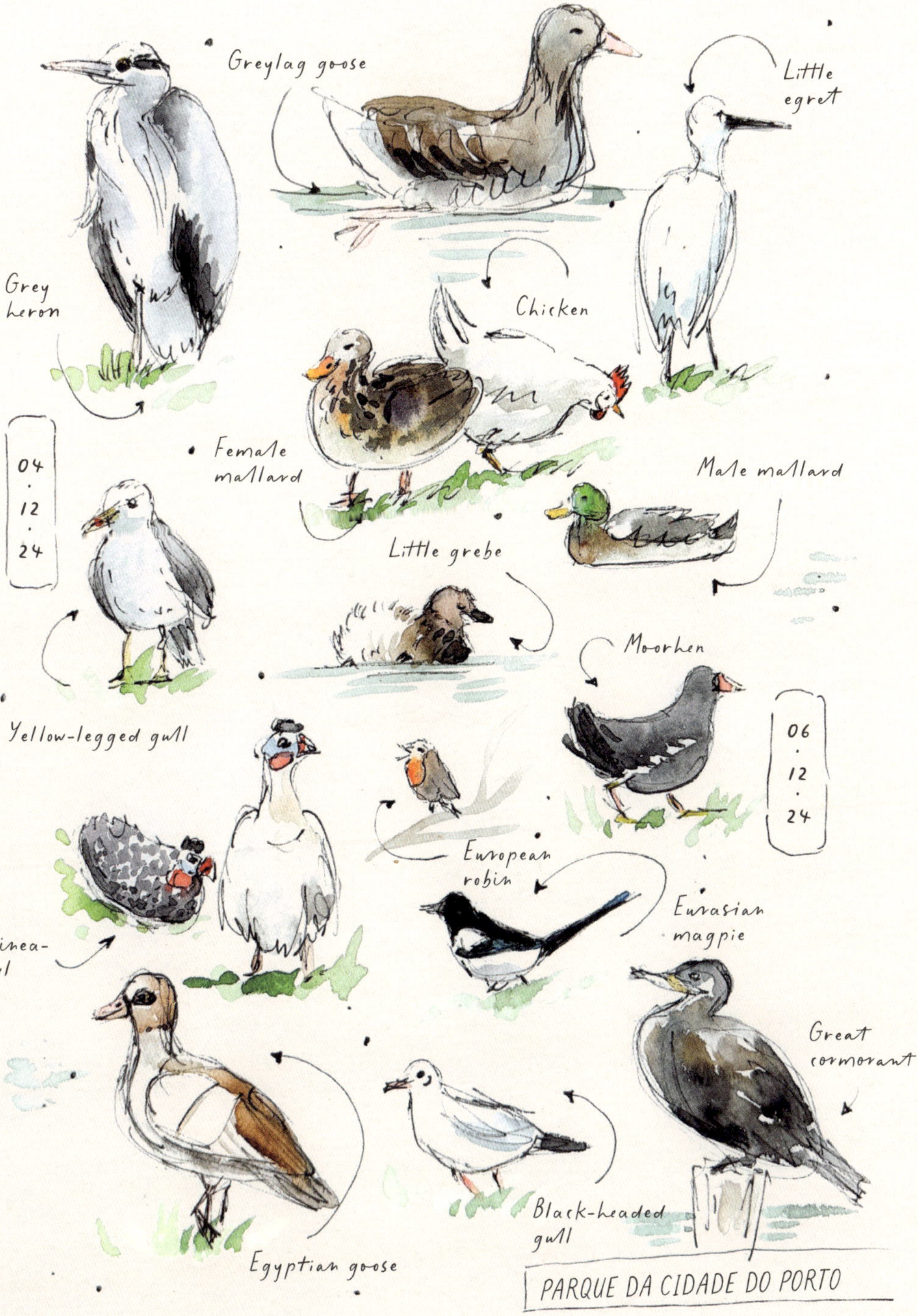
Greylag goose
Little egret
Grey heron
Chicken
04 . 12 . 24
Female mallard
Male mallard
Little grebe
Moorhen
Yellow-legged gull
06 . 12 . 24
European robin
Eurasian magpie
Guinea-fowl
Great cormorant
Black-headed gull
Egyptian goose
PARQUE DA CIDADE DO PORTO

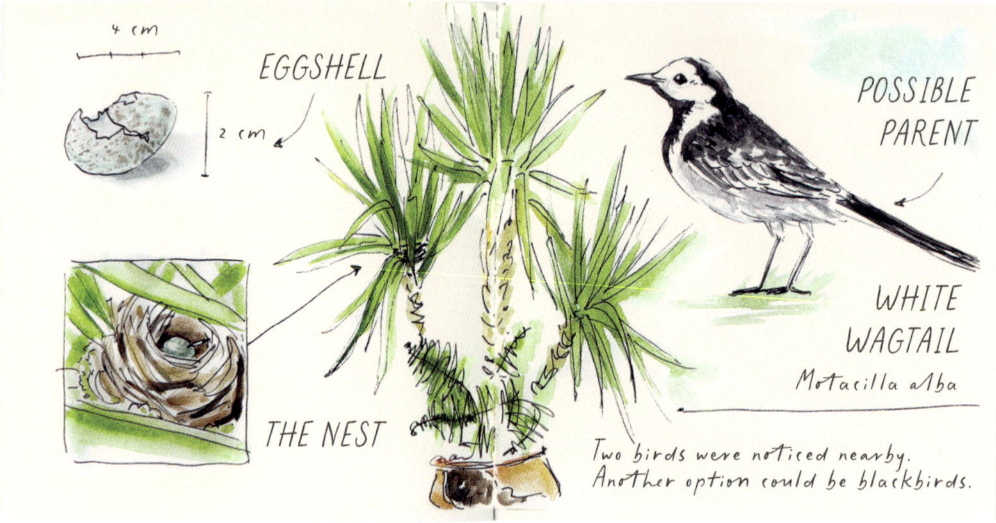

Starting to field sketch

I recommend beginning with big birds. For me, the best first models were gulls. You can also try drawing geese, chickens, peacocks or ducks, depending on what you can find nearby. These birds are used to people and won't go far when you approach them. Pigeons, in particular, are ideal for beginners. They are quite quick, but they don't fly away when they see you. Plus it should be easy to find a pigeon no matter in which part of the world you are.

When you choose a bird to draw, start by making some posture sketches, where you define the proportions of the bird. Understand first the size and position of the main ovals – the body and the head – in different poses. After you outline them, you can start paying attention to other main parts: legs, tail, beak and wings. Continue to more detailed sketches gradually.

You can focus on a specific view and wait for the bird to get back to this pose. When the bird moves, draw from your memory, and then when it returns to the pose – focus again. This approach is natural, but the bird might never resume the pose you began from. You can end up feeling frustrated when trying to finalize this one view of the bird you started drawing at first.

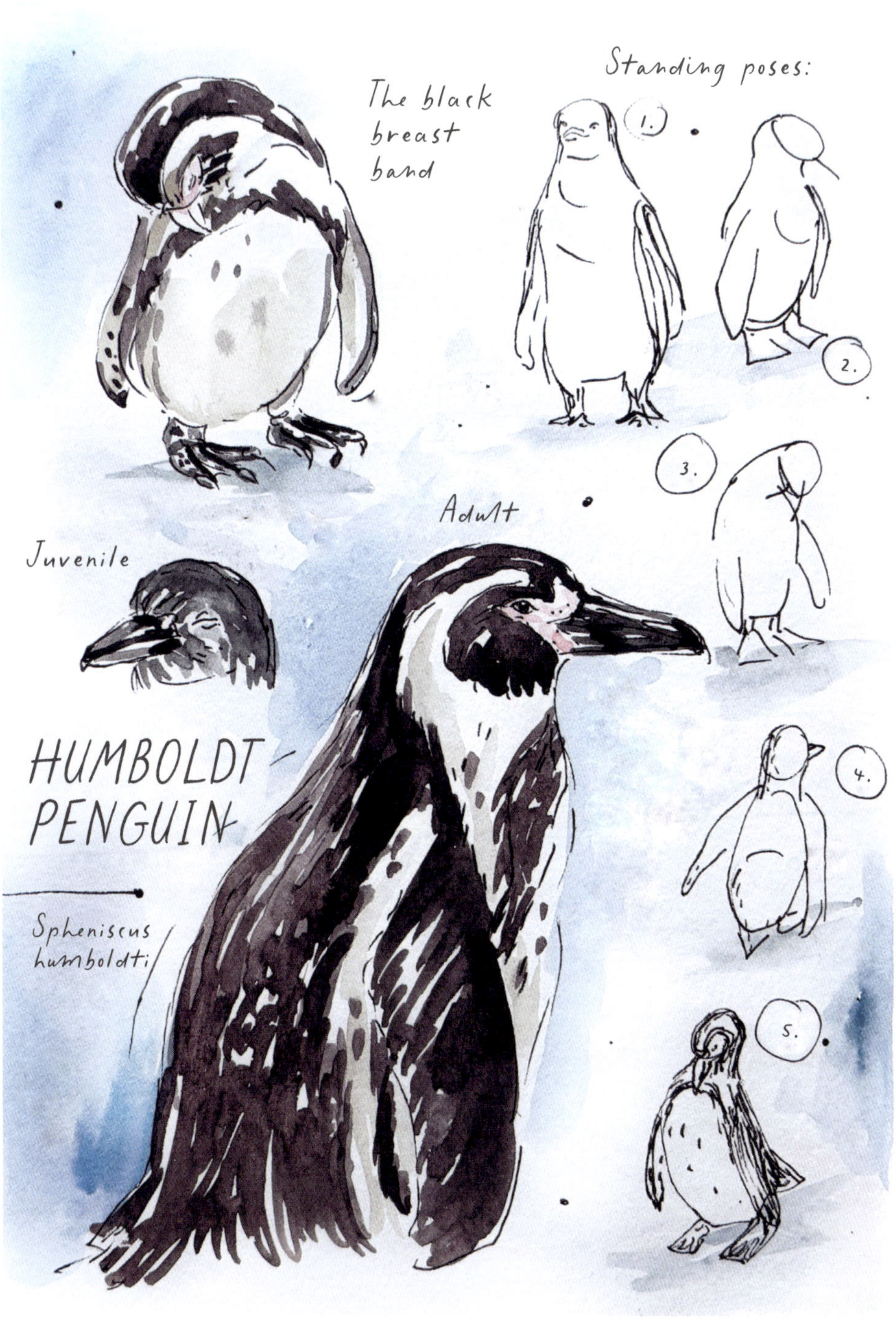
Standing poses:
The black breast band
1.
2.
3.
Adult
Juvenile
HUMBOLDT PENGUIN
Spheniscus humboldti
4.
5.

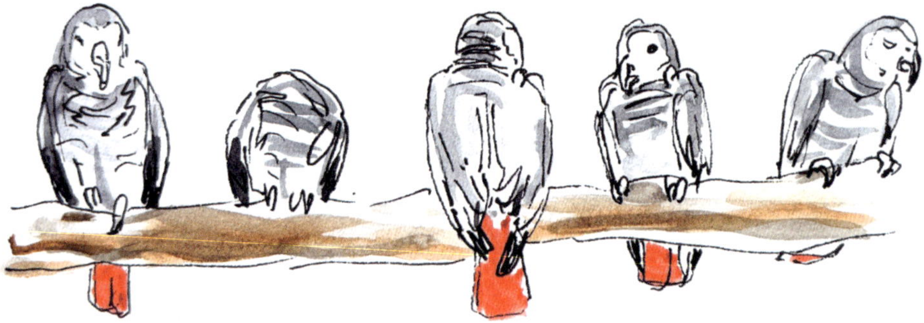

Alternative poses

That's why I suggest you try another way. When the bird moves, just start drawing it in this new pose. If it gets back to the first pose, you can continue working on it. If it doesn't – no worries. Focus on capturing as many poses as possible instead of making one perfect sketch.

A bird might be in a pose that you would never choose as a reference, but don't neglect it – maybe you are the first person alive drawing this bird from such an angle!

Of course, sketching with pencil would make life easier, but here in the field, it's the same as when you are sketching at home – you might start erasing things. There's nothing worse than when the bird flies away while you are focused on removing what you drew so far, leaving you with nothing. Observe and draw – don't waste your time on erasing. Plus, you can always add a lot of things next to your field sketches and turn the page into a nice piece. Simply leave some empty space to add the proper detailed drawing of the bird later at home.

Field sketching is definitely a more advanced way to draw birds. And it's completely different from sketching from steady references. Just let go of your inner perfectionist and treat your messy sketches as a perfect study of the bird and an amazing opportunity to connect with nature.

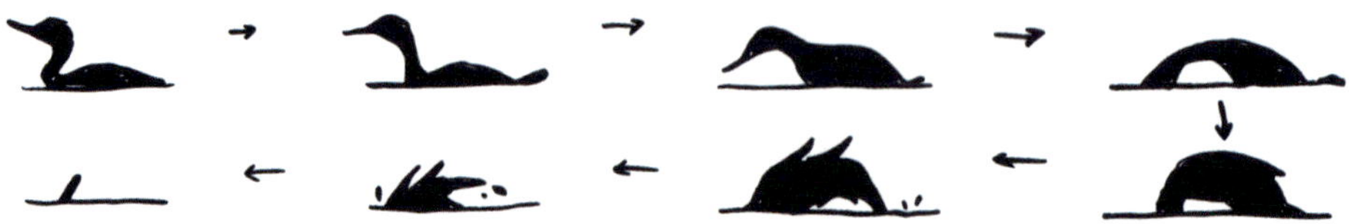

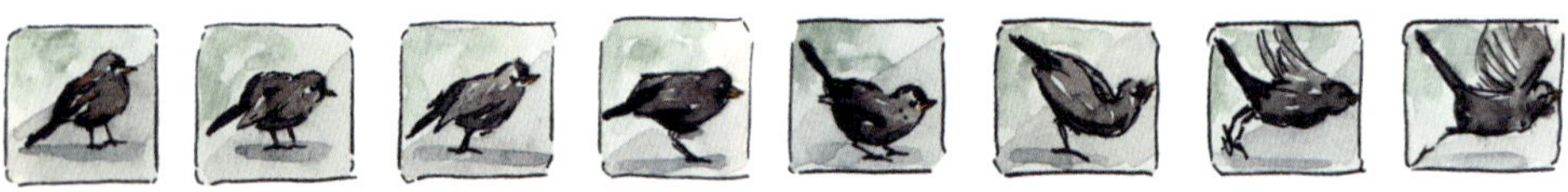

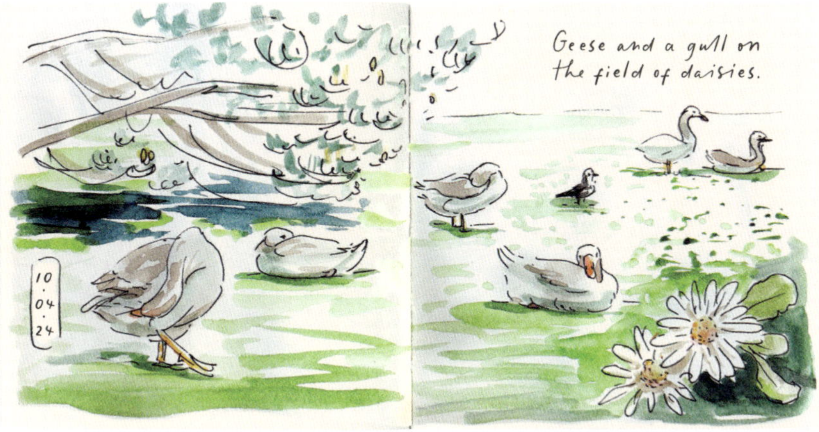
Geese and a gull on the field of daisies.
10.04.24

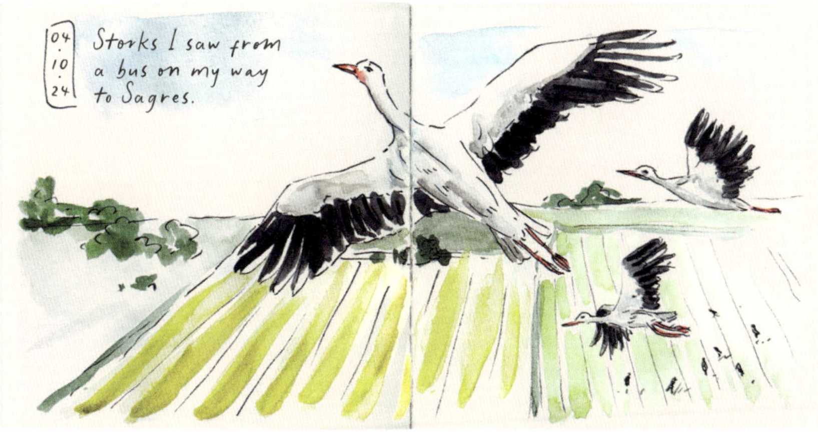
04.10.24
Storks I saw from a bus on my way to Sagres.

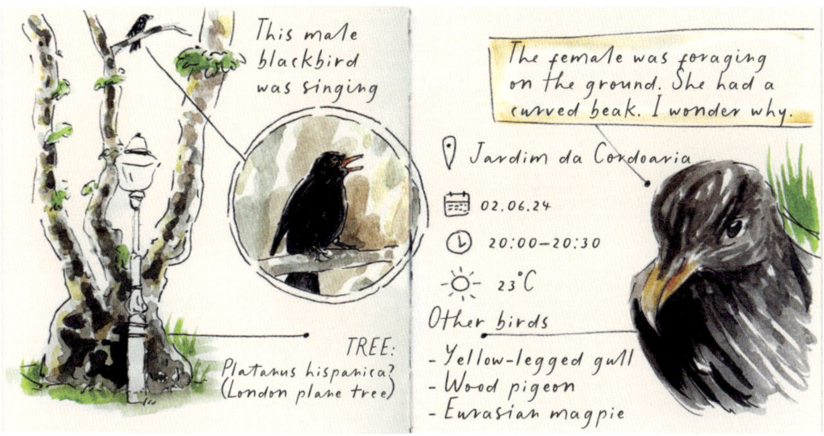
This male blackbird was singing
TREE:
Platanus hispanica?
(London plane tree)
The female was foraging on the ground. She had a curved beak. I wonder why.
Jardim da Cordoaria
02.06.24
20:00–20:30
23°C
Other birds
- Yellow-legged gull
- Wood pigeon
- Eurasian magpie

Conclusion

Now you know enough to start your own journey into the wonderful world of birds. I find a lot of inspiration in the works of nature explorers of the past. You can also consider yourself a scientist making a new discovery. Maybe it's not that insightful for others, but it's new for you! New bird, new interesting fact, new emotions.

Combine the drawing techniques you learned with the ideas for your pages and create projects that are meaningful personally for you. Turn it into a habit, and your life will never feel boring and mundane again.

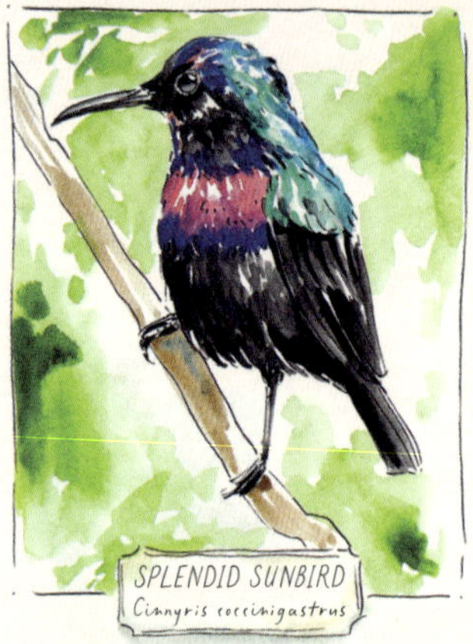

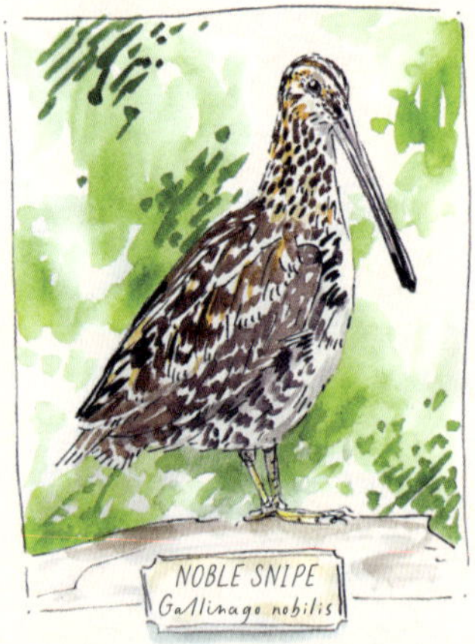

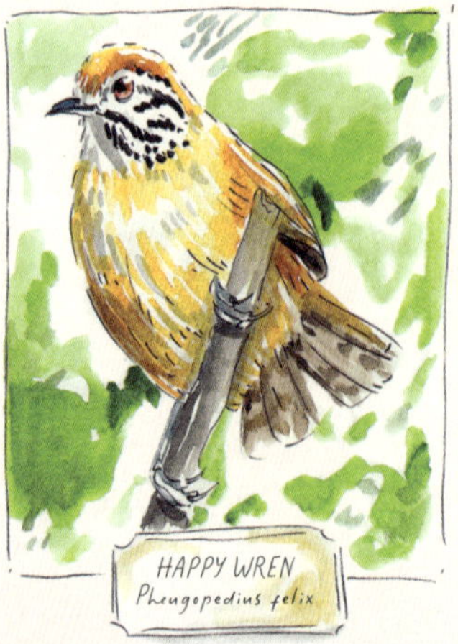

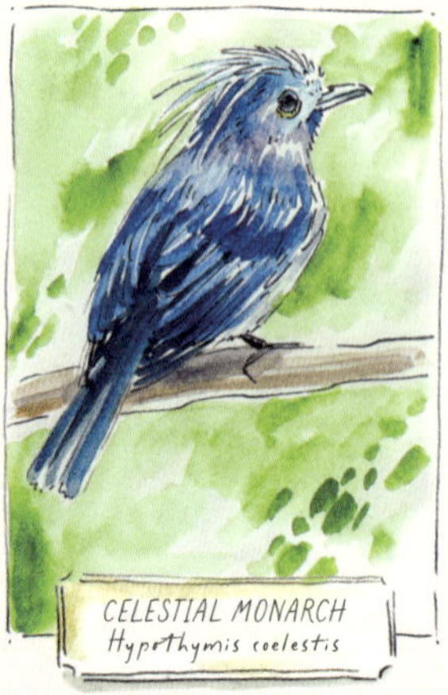

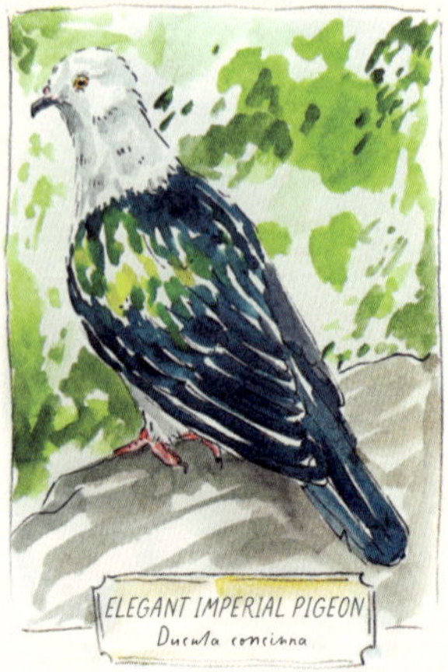

About the author

Sofia Gazarian is a professional graphic designer and illustrator. Completely self-taught, she believes anyone can draw – even if they've never picked up a pen before. Inspired by the vintage journals of early naturalists, she wanted to capture her fascination with birds in the same raw and personal way. In 2024, she challenged herself to draw one bird every day. By the end of the year, she had developed so many ideas and techniques that she created an online course, Watercolour Bird Sketching, which hundreds of people from around the world have taken.

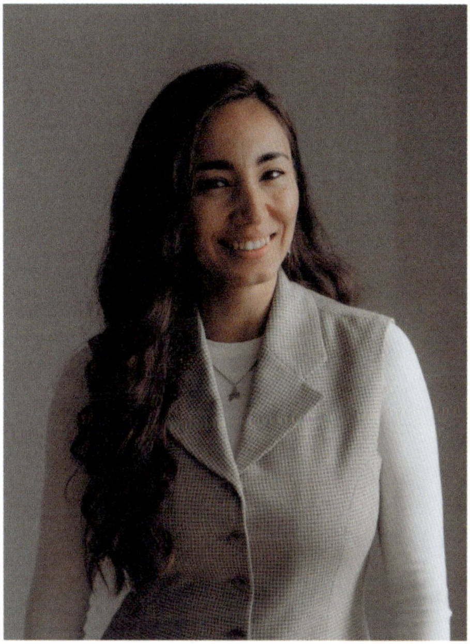

She has built a community of like-minded nature lovers on social media, collaborated with conservation and educational organizations and co-created a video game about birds. Sofia sees drawing birds as a way to stay connected to nature and believes it should be easy and approachable for beginners. She hopes more people can deepen their love for birds through sketching.

sofiagazarian.com

Instagram, TikTok & YouTube:
@printyourbird

Quadrille, Penguin Random House UK,
One Embassy Gardens, 8 Viaduct Gardens,
London SW11 7BW

Quadrille Publishing Limited is part of the Penguin Random House group of companies whose addresses can be found at global.penguinrandomhouse.com

Penguin Random House UK

Published by Quadrille in 2026

www.penguin.co.uk

A CIP catalogue record for this book is available from the British Library

ISBN 978 1 8 3783 681 9
10 9 8 7 6 5 4 3 2 1

Managing Director Sarah Lavelle
Editorial Director Harriet Butt
Editor Sophie Devlin
Copy Editor Marie Clayton
Designer Sarah Fisher
Photographer Evgeniia Arkhipova
Head of Production Stephen Lang
Senior Production Controller Martina Georgieva

Colour reproduction by F1

Printed in China by C&C Offset Printing Co., Ltd.

The authorized representative in the EEA is Penguin Random House Ireland, Morrison Chambers, 32 Nassau Street, Dublin D02 YH68.

FSC www.fsc.org
MIX
Paper
FSC® C018179

Penguin Random House is committed to a sustainable future for our business, our readers and our planet. This book is made from Forest Stewardship Council® certified paper.